Connecticut's Years of Controversy

➤➤-➤➤ ‹‹-‹‹‹

GOVERNOR JONATHAN TRUMBULL
1710-1785
From a portrait by John Trumbull

Connecticut's Years of Controversy

1750-1776

OSCAR ZEICHNER

ARCHON BOOKS
1970

ISBN: 0-208-00988-4
Library of Congress Catalog Card Number: 78-122398
Printed in the United States of America

TO
BOBBIE

PREFACE

THE HISTORY of the origins of the American Revolution has been written largely in terms of the experiences of the larger colonies. That is quite natural, for the issues between the colonies and England loomed greater there, and it was in those provinces that some of the most important steps were first taken in organizing and executing the programs of colonial resistance that culminated in independence. But while the role of the smaller colonies in the drama of the imperial crisis was not so significant as that of their more important neighbors, it certainly was not trivial. It constitutes a story that fully deserves to be told; yet it has not been done. And in the case of Connecticut it has been done only in part. It is true that the Rev. Charles Inglis, the Tory rector of Trinity Church in New York City during the Revolution and later the first bishop of Nova Scotia, once warned another historian of Connecticut that the whole history of the colony made only "a poor figure on Half a Sheet of Paper unless the Margin had been uncommonly wide." But even the Rev. Samuel Peters did not agree with Inglis. It is because there is no single volume that tells the complete story of the last years of Connecticut in the British Empire that this book was written.

The history of those background years of the Revolution in the Puritan self-governing colony of Connecticut was more complex than old traditions have made it out to be. The characterization of the colony as a land of steady habits was probably correct for the greater part of its provincial experience. But the traditional picture is not the entire picture, for the evidence that is presented below indicates that during the several decades before the Revolution the people of Connecticut were bitterly divided. Issues of local origin split this colony as they did others, even before the imperial question became acute. Religious differences, disputes arising out of economic developments, and political conflicts filled those few decades before the Revolution with controversy. And they prepared the way for the Revolution by creating the groups that were to take the Whig and Tory sides in the last quarrels with England. This, in over-simplified summary, is the thesis that is developed in the pages that follow.

The search through the records was facilitated by the many kindnesses shown to me by librarians and their assistants. They helped me find and use the collections from which a large part of the evidence in this book was drawn; and they displayed remarkable patience when I came to them for assistance in checking references at a later stage of the research. It is a pleasure to express my grateful thanks to the courteous and friendly staffs of the following institutions: the New York Public Library, New York Historical Society, Connecticut Historical Society, Connecticut State Library, Yale University Library, and the Library of Congress. The illustrations appear through the cooperation and courtesy of the first three institutions named above and also the Yale University Art Gallery, the Wyoming Historical and Geological Society, and the Historical Society of Pennsylvania. Permission to use and quote from the typescript copy of Consider Tiffany's The American Colonies and the Revolution in the Library of Congress was granted to me by Dr. Clarence E. Carter.

The manuscript was read in various stages of progress by Professors John A. Krout, Allan Nevins, Nelson P. Mead, and Richard B. Morris. I am indebted to these scholars for their helpful suggestions; without the benefit of their advice the book would have included many more faults in style and content than it now has. I should like to express my gratitude to Mr. Julian P. Boyd and Mr. Carl Bridenbaugh for reading the book while it was still in manuscript, to the Institute of Early American History and Culture under whose auspices the book is appearing, and particularly to Mr. Lester J. Cappon, Research Editor of the Institute, for his help in getting the book to press. Responsibility for whatever defects the volume may have must, of course, be acknowledged as my own.

I owe a deep debt of gratitude to my wife. Without the sacrifices that she cheerfully made it would have been impossible to complete my research and to write this book.

OSCAR ZEICHNER

City College, New York
January, 1949

CONTENTS

CONTENTS

· *xiii* ·

Illustrations

Connecticut's Years of Controversy

→»→»«←«←

CHAPTER ONE

The Land of Steady Habits in the Early Eighteenth Century

C ONNECTICUT early acquired the reputation of being a "land of steady habits." Perhaps more than any other colony it had attempted to preserve the ways of life and institutions of its first settlers. Its solemn leaders tenaciously clung to the principles and traditions of their past, especially in matters that touched upon their political and religious institutions, and their success, if not complete, had still been remarkable. Even before the Revolution this steadiness was the subject of proud comment. On the eve of the final break from Great Britain a local contributor to the *Connecticut Courant* claimed that the people of Connecticut were "peculiar for caution, moderation and steadiness in their public affairs." Some skeptics might have questioned this judgment, since the colony's freemen were then involved in a rather turbulent land dispute and election campaign, and were already girding themselves for war. But the consensus in the colony probably would have agreed with it and history has confirmed it.[1]

Connecticut's leaders had good reasons to be wary of changes. As a "satiated" colony Connecticut was content with what it had. Its ministers repeatedly flattered the people by comparing them with the Israelites, the chosen of God.[2] Timothy Cutler maintained in 1717 that Connecticut's privileges were even greater than ancient Jerusalem's. Jared Eliot, minister, physician, and scientific farmer, did not think that "Humane Prudence could contrive" any more abundant advantages than those possessed by the fortunate colony, for were they not already "Extensive to the utmost bounds of a Rational wish"?[3] Indeed, with such great privileges, Isaac Stiles lectured the General Assembly, the people of Connecticut had no reason to envy anyone else under heaven. Thirty years later, on the eve of the Revolution, Judah Champion expressed the same sentiments.[4]

Among the most prized of Connecticut's privileges in the early eighteenth century were its political powers and rights, in part assumed before the charter of 1662, legalized and perpetuated in that document, and then stoutly defended against all attempts to modify or destroy them. The incorrigible Tory, the Rev. Samuel Peters, wrote in one of his frequently sour moods that "properly speaking" Connecticut had no government.[5] By that Peters meant the colony had too much government, at least of the popular kind. What the Tory rector condemned, Connecticut's magistrates and ministers loudly praised and dearly cherished. "This is a beautiful and respectable Government," the Rev. Joseph Fish declared rhapsodically in 1760.[6] And where else, he and his fellow ministers demanded, could one find that happy combination of a good civil constitution and a just administration, where "Liberty stretches forth her Hand without Controul, to give her Suffrages for Men to rule . . . in the Fear of God."[7]

Connecticut was indeed a fortunate colony. It practiced a fuller measure of self-government than did any other British province excepting Rhode Island. Qualified voters ran their own affairs in the practically independent towns and the larger self-governing state.[8] The towns were empowered by the colonial government to make all "Orders, Rules, and Constitutions" affecting the welfare of their communities.[9] Under this broad grant of discretion the miniature republics took "care of their own public concerns,"[10] electing their many officers, ranging from the deputies to the colonial legislature and the selectmen down to the more humble branders, gaugers, packers, haywards, list- and rate-makers and fence-viewers.[11] It was with good cause and with pardonable pride that the Rev. Judah Champion boasted in 1770, "Every town is a corporation, yea, every family is a little kingdom."[12]

The colonial government exercised even more control over provincial affairs than did the town in the smaller community. In fact, Connecticut was almost an independent commonwealth, wielding broad powers derived from its liberal charter and maintaining but slight contacts with the royal authority. The colony's voters elected their own governor and lawmakers. A bicameral legislature, the General Assembly, was the most powerful political body in the colony. Of the two branches, the Council and the Assembly, the latter, sometimes called the House of Representatives, was the more important.[13] The Assembly's jurisdiction was practically unlimited under the charter. It could not be dissolved or prorogued without the approval of its own majority. With the Council it made and repealed laws, granted levies, disposed of lands, and set up and established the powers of courts and offices as it deemed necessary for the good government of the people.[14] The councillors exercised, at various times, executive, judicial, and military functions, but their influence was subordinate to that of the lower house. The governor, who was elected annually in the spring, had great prestige but little power. The colony did not have an independent judiciary. Judges, from the local justices of the peace up to the members of the Superior Court, were appointed by the legislature, and were consequently under its control.[15]

This semi-independent, self-governing province had some of the outward characteristics of a democracy. Not only was it allowed to go its own way, relatively free from the supervision and interference of the Crown, but its elected officers ran the colony's political machinery. Democracy, however, never existed, nor was it ever desired by Connecticut's leaders during the colonial period. It would be a distortion of the historical picture to see democracy in the Connecticut representative system as did the Loyalist minister, Samuel Peters.[16]

Connecticut's founding fathers never proposed to build their political institutions upon the principle of equality.[17] Their conception of human nature made that impossible. Man was evil and corrupt.[18] A government of the "Multitude" was, therefore, the worst tyranny.[19] Only the elect were fit to rule. From the very beginning, distinctions based upon property and religion set off those who had political rights from the rest of the population. Connecticut's Fundamental Orders distinguished between admitted inhabitants, men who had been accepted by the town after meeting religious and economic qualifications, and the freemen who were to be "the trusted pillars of the commonwealth."[20] Admitted inhabitants could participate in the affairs of the town, vote for local officials, and, before 1662, for the deputies to the General Court; but only freemen could be elected deputies, vote for the higher officers or be magistrates.

The differences between the politically privileged and non-privileged were continued throughout the 1600's and into the eighteenth century.[21] In 1702 property qualifications were adopted that were retained through the Revolutionary era. Under this law, to be admitted into a town a man had to be of legal age, possess a freehold estate rated at fifty shillings a year or forty pounds in the common list, be of "Honest Conversation," and be found acceptable by a majority of the town voters or the town authority. It was more difficult to become a freeman, although the age and property qualifications were practically similar to those asked of admitted inhabitants, an age requirement of twenty-one years and a freehold estate of forty shillings per annum or forty pounds personal. For, in addition, one had to be of "Quiet, and Peaceable

Behaviour, and Civil Conversation," be approved by the town selectmen, and finally, accepted at an open meeting of the freemen.[22]

No effort was made to extend the liberal powers of colonial citizenship to all the people. On the contrary, the General Assembly periodically reminded the towns to exclude those who were not suited to join the elect.[23] The local authorities heeded these orders carefully. They maintained a careful watch in their communities to make certain that undesirable newcomers did not settle among them or acquire political rights. As early as 1659 Hartford banned transients unless they were "first Concented to by the orderly voat of the Inhabitanc" in town meeting.[24] In 1678 Norwich hesitated to admit a leather-dresser because it was doubtful of "his comely behaviour." The doubts of the cautious townsmen seem to have been justified, for after trial the candidate was expelled, apparently because he did not carry himself "comely and comfortably."[25] Hartford's town votes indicate that not all who applied for admission were accepted. Other towns were equally suspicious of new settlers and as exclusive in their attitude.[26] The 1750 revision of the colony's statutes retained an early ban on "Persons of Ungoverned Conversation" who attempted to establish themselves in the towns allegedly "by some under-hand Way, as upon pretence of being Hired Servants; or of Hiring Lands, or Houses, or by Purchasing the same."[27]

Only a small minority of the population was fortunate enough to become admitted members of the towns. Some of the residents of Ashford complained in the early 1720's that "if none were allowed to vote but those qualified . . . by law, affairs would be managed by very few hands and be to the discontent of many."[28] This may have been an extreme case. But participation in town affairs was normally the privilege of a few. As late as 1761 only about 20 to 25 per cent of the adult males took part in a New Haven town meeting.[29]

The number of freemen was even smaller. It is estimated

that in 1669 there were 1789 freemen out of a total male population of 3000. This was a good proportion. But in 1740 only four thousand votes were cast when the male population was fifteen thousand.[30] Less than one-half of the adult males in Killingly were freemen in 1728. Between 1709 and 1717 Waterbury added only thirteen freemen to the twenty-seven already in that status in 1702.[31] Connecticut's seventeenth-century Tory, Gershom Bulkeley, charged in 1692 that "The greatest part of this colony (I believe five or six to one,) never were made free of the company."[32] Bulkeley's figures were probably close to the truth. As late as 1766 New Haven's freemen did not include more than one-fourth of the adult males in the town. And in the same year Ezra Stiles placed the total number of freemen at only one-ninth of the colonial population.[33] It is apparent that during the colonial period the limits placed by the provincial government upon the electorate effectively excluded all but a small minority from the privilege of exercising any serious political power.

These differences in political status and rights were attributed to divine will, for it was argued that God had placed men in "their Several Stations and Conditions." The conclusions in this reasoning were remorseless. "Persons of Lower Rank," Puritan divines maintained, "should not Envy those of a more Exalted Station." Nor should they interfere in matters that concerned only those who were fortunate enough to occupy a "higher Sphere." Equality was a degenerative principle because it destroyed the "Motives and Encouragements to Vertue and Restraint from Vice" and thus made government impossible.[34] True liberty, as Connecticut's ministers defined it, was to be found somewhere in "between the two Extreams of Supream power lodg'd in the People, on the one hand, and Despotic Monarchy on the other."[35] It was not to be confused with licentiousness.[36] Twentieth-century conceptions of popular government would have been denounced as levelism; and levelism was not only destructive of real liberty, but "an open Defiiance to God, his Wisdom and Will, as well as the Reason of Mankind."[37]

Political facts tended to conform to the preaching. During the colonial period the elective offices were monopolized by a small number of prominent families. Men were not rotated in office. Once chosen, it was customary for them to be re-elected until death separated them from all worldly honors. There were no real political parties in the colony; neither were there any long-standing issues that might have split the small electorate. Under these conditions provincial and local elections tended to become routine ceremonies of keeping incumbents at their posts.[38]

In the one hundred years between 1689 and 1788 Connecticut chose but eleven governors, thirteen deputy governors, and ninety-seven members for its twelve-man Council. Only two eighteenth-century governors, Roger Wolcott and Thomas Fitch, were turned out of office. George Wyllys was Secretary, first of the colony and then of the State, for an unbroken period of sixty years, from 1735 to 1795.[39] Norwich sent one deputy to the Assembly for thirty-seven sessions, and another for thirty-four.[40] Joshua Hempstead of New London records several instances of "Strife and hot words" in the town's elections.[41] But it was much more common for towns to choose officers "as in the year past."[42] In an apt comment on this aspect of Connecticut's political institutions Professor Andrews once observed that the chief business of the voters "was to vote and to vote, as a rule, to continue in office those who were already there."[43]

Political stability was recommended and blessed in long, dull sermons. Connecticut's Congregational ministers repeatedly exhorted the freemen to "reverence Authority, and honour those that are improv'd in the Administration of Government . . . considering them as God's Vicegerents amongst Men." The dominies held that "Authority is a sacred Thing," and rulers, the "Lord's anointed," were deemed to be "subordinate Gods to Men."[44] In 1775 this made good Tory doctrine, but it was political orthodoxy throughout the colonial period.

The almost unreserved support given to the magistrates by the ministers was fully reciprocated. Connecticut was settled by men who considered true religion more important than any worldly activity.[45] The colony's founding fathers believed that good government could be established only "according to God," and that its chief duty was to "mayntayne and presearve the liberty and purity of the gospell."[46] These words in Connecticut's Fundamental Orders expressed the principle that was to govern the relationship between church and state in the colony. The ruling hierarchy of officers and ministers scrupulously attempted to preserve that relationship throughout the colonial period. The ministers, "the Salt of the Earth," never tired of repeating that the duty of the magistrates was "to take care for the Support and Defence of the Church, in her Interests, Rights and Privileges."[47] The provincial authorities did their best to realize this advice.[48]

They did not have to be reminded that the Fundamental Orders had prescribed for them the responsibility of preserving "the disciplyne of the Churches, wch acccording to the truth of the said gospell is now practised amongst us."[49] Due provision was early made for the support of the church. The code of 1650 directed the "Civill Authority . . . to see the peace, ordinances and rules of Christe bee observed in every Church" according to the "Word" of the minister. Punishments were ordered for those who failed to attend services or who dared to speak contemptuously of ministerial doctrine.[50] Throughout the seventeenth century the colonial legislature continued to add to its laws supporting the Congregational churches.[51]

In 1708 the ministers, at the request of the legislature, drew up a code of ecclesiastical discipline, which was then approved and adopted by the Assembly. Those churches that were "united in doctrine, worship, and discipline" to the code, known as the Saybrook Platform, were declared by the colonial government to be established by law. Dissenting denominations were permitted to worship and govern themselves in their own ways, but their members were required to contribute to the support of the established church in the town of their residence.[52] In addition to restating the Puritan doctrines of the Westminster Confession, the Saybrook Platform set up ecclesiastical bodies, consociations of churches and associations of ministers. These were organized by counties and were supposed to help maintain religious discipline and order among the churches. The primitive Congregationalism of the first settlers thus gave way to a more closely knit form of church organization that resembled the Presbyterian polity.[53]

The Saybrook Platform was Connecticut's religious constitution throughout the remainder of the colonial period. Under its provisions an official church was set up with the sanction of the provincial political authority. Everyone had to contribute to the financial support of the legally established church in his community. The consociations and associations concerned themselves with ecclesiastical and doctrinal matters within their respective counties, while the Assembly kept a close watch over everything that affected the general welfare of the church, and, of course, over the people's morals.

Numerous statutes enforced the Puritan concept of strict Christian behavior. "Prophaneness and Immorality" were duly punished, and regular attendance at church was required. In fact, the colonists were expected to be diligent in the performance of all their religious duties.[54] The educational system was cast in the Puritan mould. It probably was not necessary to require every family to have at least one Bible, and the larger families to own catechisms, but that was the law.[55] Yale was set up to prepare young men "for public employments in church and civil state."[56] Whether the original objective of the college was primarily "to Educate Persons, for the Ministry of the Churches, commonly called Presbyterian or Congregational," as President Clap maintained, is a questionable point.[57] There can be no doubt, however, that the students were instructed "to know God in Jesus Christ and answerably to lead a Godly sober life." [58] By 1745 Yale had graduated 483 young men. Of this number one-half entered the ministry, and 137 became Congregational pastors.[59]

There was obviously substantial cause for Isaac Stiles, father of Yale's Revolutionary president, to exclaim in 1742 that "as to our Religious Privileges and Enjoyments this has been Eminently a Land flowing with Milk and Honey." [60] Yet all was not well with the established church. It found it impossible to preserve unchanged the religious principles of the original settlers and to exclude all other Christian denominations. Even before the seventeenth century had come to an end the religious make-up of the colonists varied from the "strict Congregationall," through "more large Congregationall" and included "some moderate Presbeterians." [61] More disturbing to the old religious order was the appearance of small numbers of Quakers, Baptists and some "Seven-day men," later known as Rogerenes. These dissenters were never more than a few, but they were obdurate and troublesome. The Puritan majority persecuted them, at times harshly, for failure to observe the laws supporting the established churches. Fines, imprisonment, and even floggings were suffered by the dissenters, but they held to their convictions.[62] Their denominations, however, never became important enough in the colonial period to rival the official religious order.

Connecticut's Anglicans proved to be a much more serious problem. Not only did their numbers increase steadily, but their responsibilities to the established colonial church inevitably gave rise to embarrassing difficulties.[63] Anglicans thought it anomalous that their church, the official establishment in the mother country, so august and powerful, could suffer the ignominy of having its members in the little colony of Connecticut subject to the power of a dissenting sect and forced to pay for its upkeep. On the other hand, Connecticut's Puritans feared and opposed the expansion of the English Church.[64] In the words of one Episcopal minister, most of Connecticut's Congregationalists considered the Church of England "Rome's sister," "little better than Papist," its giving the sign of the cross a "mark of the beast" and the devil, and its practices nothing more than "idolatrous worship and superstitious ceremonies."[65]

In 1708 a colonial statute had extended a small measure of relief to a few dissenting sects. The people had not demanded the law. On the contrary, it was passed primarily to appease the mother country, and to abort a possible move of the home authorities against the colony on the ground that its religious constitution was repugnant to English law. Connecticut's act permitted dissenters to take advantage of the English Toleration Act of 1689 by organizing congregations separate from the established church, but before this could be done, the dissenters had to qualify themselves before the county court. To do so they were required to take an oath to the Crown, repudiate the doctrine of transubstantiation, and declare their dissent from the Congregational church. The oath requirements effectively prevented the statute from granting any significant relief to the Rogerenes and Quakers. And, what was more important, the law still required all dissenters to contribute to the Congregational establishment.

Connecticut's Toleration Act was designed to disarm critics of the colony's religious and political constitutions, but it did not propose to decrease the support that the provincial government gave to the Puritan churches.[66] Anglicans continued to complain, even after the colony's Toleration Act had been on the statute books for some time, of persecution more serious than "that of the tongue." Like the Rogerenes they suffered fines and imprisonment.[67] But although, as one of their leaders lamented, they had little or "no expectation from the government and generality of people but to be laughed at and looked awry upon," their faith held out against these trials and their numbers increased.[68] In 1718 there were in the town of Stratford alone thirty-six communicants and a congregation that varied between two and three hundred.[69] Eight years before, the church wardens of this town had asked, in their address to the Bishop of London requesting a minister, "What signifies what becomes of the body, if our precious souls . . . be saved?" [70] It was with the determination that inspired this question that the members of the English communion took the lead in the struggle for a wider religious toleration in Connecticut in the early eighteenth century. In so doing they inevitably concentrated upon themselves the inveterate hostility of the Puritan majority.

All but a few of Connecticut's first settlers had been farmers. Most of their descendants in the third and fourth generations continued to live off the colony's reluctant soil, although some of their children also turned to trade and the sea.[71] The land, "mountainous . . . full of rocks, swamps, hills and vales," was crudely cropped with backward tools. "Hard blows" at first yielded but "smal recompence."[72] But diligent toil and an increasing population inexorably subdued the wilderness; and the colony's farmers gradually forced the stubborn soil to yield moderately large amounts of agricultural products.[73] By the opening of the eighteenth century Connecticut was able to boast of a growing number of well ordered and prosperous communities. Tax lists showed regular increases in the values of estates. Wallingford's list was rated at £2466 in 1680; twenty-five years later it was £6868. Between 1685 and 1710 only twelve persons were added to the tax rolls in Derby, but the list of estates rose from £2041 to £2856. In 1725 the town's list jumped to £5310. The first settlement in what was later Windham County was made in 1686. Forty years later the county had eight growing towns.[74] New London's list in 1699 was only £9196; in 1730 it was £18,985.[75]

Commerce was relatively undeveloped and merchants were few in number. Traders early found it difficult to expand their small enterprises. Connecticut's economy failed to produce any staples comparable to those raised on the southern plantations. The farmer's chief products, in the eighteenth as well as the late seventeenth century, were "provisions,"[76] which were sent to Boston, and later to New York, where they paid for the manufactured goods that were imported from England. Little manufacturing was done in the colony itself. Merchants sent some ships to the West Indies to exchange lumber, provisions, and horses for sugar, rum, and specie,[77] but the lack of capital, the lure of free land, and disadvantages in competition with the ports of Boston and New York, hindered any extensive commercial growth.[78]

In 1680 only twenty-seven ships, mostly small vessels, were owned in Connecticut. At the same time there were only twenty "petty" merchants in the entire colony.[79] The provincial government complained to the Commissioners of Customs in January 1680, that

. . .After forty yeares sweating and toyle in this wilderness . . . we have neither had leisure or ability to lanch out in any considerable trade at sea, haveing onely a fewe small vessells to carry our corne, hoggs, and horses unto our neighbours of Yorke and Boston, to exchange for some cloathes and utensills, wherewithall to worke and subdue this country; likewise some of those comodities are carryed to the Barbadoes and those Islands, to bring in some suger and rumm, to refresh the spirits of such as labour in the extream heat and cold.[80]

After another fifty years of sweating and toil Connecticut's merchants were able to add fifteen vessels to the twenty-seven that they had owned in 1680.[81] But while Connecticut's trade remained small, and was conducted "with much difficulty,"[82] its influence on the colony's life slowly increased, and in later decades of the eighteenth century the merchants were to take an important part in shaping the colony's destiny.

Connecticut's institutions were a blend of both aristocratic and democratic principles; but during the colonial period the former were dominant. Neither state nor church sanctioned any arrangement whereby all the people determined either political or religious policy. The germ of democratic growth was inherent in the colony's representative system of government and its Congregational church polity. But the ministers and magistrates constituted a ruling hierarchy in town and colony, and as the leaders of the elect they strove to preserve the features of the society into which they had been born.[83] As if to recognize the differences that God had created among men, towns ordered their inhabitants to be seated in the churches according to "Dignity of Descent; Place of Public Trust; Pious disposition and behaviour: Estate: Peculiar serviceableness in any kind."[84] Although the Rev. Samuel Stone's definition of Connecticut's ecclesiastical system "as a speaking Aristocracy in the face of a silent Democracy" was not universally accepted by his seventeenth-century contemporaries, it succinctly expresses the general tone of colonial Connecticut's institutions.[85]

The economic basis of an aristocracy, however, did not exist in the small, agrarian, Puritan colony. There were no huge landed estates presided over by lordly imitators of the British aristocracy in the New York or Virginia manner. Nor were there any great merchant princes in the trading towns to flaunt their wealth in the faces of poor artisans. Economic differences were obvious and common enough; and some fortunate freemen had possessions that made them rich in their day. The estate of the Rev. Daniel Wadsworth of Hartford was valued at more than £4000 at his death in 1747.[86] On the other hand, the colony was not so utopian that it had no poor.[87] But Madam Knight found that most of the colonists "lived very well and comfortably in their famelies." And, she observed, "No one that can and will be dilligent in this place need fear poverty nor the want of food and Rayment."[88] The town lists reflect this general and moderate distribution of wealth. Joshua Hempstead, prominent New Londoner, was rated at but £82 in 1720. In the same year the largest return in the East Windsor list was only £198. Greenwich's most valuable estate was rated £165 in 1695, Wallingford's at £168 in 1701, Derby's at £226 in 1718, and Torrington's at £180 in 1732.[89]

Throughout the seventeenth century Connecticut's Puritan magistrates governed their colony as if they were at the head of an independent republic; their ties with the mother country were few and relatively unimportant. The latter fact was just as much a part of Connecticut's way of life as were its great powers and its established Congregational church. Sober-miened colonists might have considered themselves faithful subjects of the King, and their province as much a part of the empire as New York or Virginia. But those officials in England who managed the King's affairs in America generally thought otherwise. On one occasion the Board of Trade protested that most of the time it knew very little about the colony and what it was doing, and that the King derived no revenue from it; and in 1741 the Board accused the charter colonies of not recognizing their dependence upon the Crown and of seldom obeying royal orders.[90]

Connecticut's magistrates sedulously labored to keep the colony free from the growing controls of the empire. Even before they received their extremely liberal charter they had begun to shape their institutions according to their own lights. The great powers the charter conferred upon the colony strengthened this tendency and gave it an extra measure of legal protection. It really was not necessary, therefore, for the ministers to remind the colony's magistrates so insistently that the people of Connecticut were "very tender" of their privileges "and jealous lest by any means they are invaded or taken from us."[91] The objectives of Connecticut's Puritan politicians were clear, but not always easy to reconcile. To preserve the colony's institutions they had to keep the charter privileges intact. At the same time, however, they also had to maintain friendly relations with the imperial authorities who were frequently suspicious of those privileges, if not openly hostile to them.[92] Under these circumstances Connecticut's political leaders quickly learned to become prudent and skilled diplomats.

Despite the competent diplomacy of Connecticut's governors

and agents, however, numerous attempts were made in the late seventeenth and early eighteenth centuries to place the colony under the closer supervision of King and Parliament. But while other provinces had to accept new charters or were brought under a fuller measure of royal control, Connecticut succeeded in avoiding any substantial loss of power to the home government. Its success was not entirely due to its own efforts; but the outcome was none the less satisfactory to its inhabitants.[93] The colony's defensive strategy varied in accordance with the peculiar nature of the emergency, from begging the Crown on bended knees, to dignified but vigorous advocacy of its claims.[94] It submitted when but minor issues were at stake because it was judged expedient.[95] It held firm, however, when vital colonial powers seemed to be in jeopardy. In this way it successfully retained its unusual position as an almost independent state within the empire throughout the colonial period.[96]

Early eighteenth-century Connecticut could have rightfully claimed that it was a "land of steady habits." Its homogeneous population[97] was in almost perfect agreement on major policies and ends. All but a small minority belonged to the Congregational church and accepted the principle of a state-supported religious establishment. The governmental system was set firm on a representative, not democratic, basis, and although it was occasionally disturbed by the expanding jurisdiction of the imperial government, within the colony there was, on the whole, a placid political peace. The colonial economy was simple. Most of the people grew farm products for their own use. The small surplus that they produced was exchanged for English manufactured goods, imported chiefly through Boston, and some raw materials from the West Indies. But as yet the merchant class was small in number and relatively insignificant in influence.

In the early eighteenth century, however, this apparently stable Puritan province was on the verge of experiencing several important religious and economic developments; and these, in turn, were to have serious political repercussions. For try as it did to avoid disturbing changes from the traditions and habits of its early history, the colony was unable to prevent new forces from raising new issues and creating new problems. In the few decades before the Stamp Act these issues and problems split the colonial population into opposing groups. These divisions shattered the unity of the once stable colony and prepared the way for the later political differences of the revolutionary era.

CHAPTER TWO

Some Unsteady Habits, 1730-1765

CONNECTICUT'S ministers frequently struck a pessimistic note in their sermons during the early and middle decades of the eighteenth century. They complained of religious decline, an increasing worldliness, political strife, disrespect for superiors and old traditions, and other unwholesome symptoms of evil. They warned the colony that God was obviously in "Controversie" with the people and the land.[1] They lamented "the times, the times, the badness of the times."[2] And they querulously wondered why Connecticut, so generously blessed with a goodly heritage, should show such a "Spirit of Discontent. . . Murmurings and Complainings, and. . .Desire of Change."[3] But their plaints, prayers, and sermons did not eliminate these evils and bring about the thoroughgoing "Reformation-work" that they all so fervently desired to see. As late as 1761 "A Freeman" sadly deplored the fact "That a contrary Spirit had been too predominant" in Connecticut for some years past.[4]

Both ministers and magistrates were seriously concerned about the appearance of other denominations in the colony and the decay in the religious zeal of the third- and fourth-generation Puritans.

Although the dissenters who had thrust themselves among Connecticut's Saints in the late seventeenth and early eighteenth centuries were few in number, they were regarded as dangerous enemies to the Puritan churches. The colonial authorities severely repressed the Rogerenes, whose more or less violent demonstrations outraged the staid members of the established church. They had to be more discreet towards those religious minorities whose political influence carried weight in the mother country, the Quakers, Baptists, and Anglicans.[5]

Even more serious was the evidence of "the Sad Decays of Religion, the Mighty prevalency of Sin" among the Connecticut Puritans themselves.[6] The General Assembly solemnly warned in May 1714 "that the glory is departed" from the land. Recommendations for "healing and recovery" and a more careful enforcement of the religious laws were suggested, but the remedies did not succeed.[7] To Benjamin Trumbull this period was marked by a decline in religious "purity and zeal" and a "general ease and security in sin."[8] Contemporary ministers mournfully likened the colony to "the degenerate Plant of a strange Vine."[9]

These gloomy observations were climaxed by the outbreak of Connecticut's first Great Awakening. The causes of that movement have been thoroughly discussed elsewhere. Here it is sufficient to note that basically it arose out of dissatisfaction with the Half-Way Covenant, the religious compromise that allowed persons who could not testify to a saving experience to be members of the church, although not in full communion; with the cold formalism that pervaded Connecticut's religious beliefs and practices in the late seventeenth and early eighteenth centuries; and, in general, with the religious settlement embodied in the Saybrook Platform.[10] A slight religious revival had taken place in the town of Windham in 1721,[11] but the first major phase of the Great Awakening did not occur until the early 1730's. At that time at least sixteen towns experienced an unusual religious excitement, which, after subsiding temporarily, reached a new height in the early 1740's, during and after George Whitefield's visit to Connecticut.[12]

The revival blazed through the colony like a wildfire, searing the emotions of the average Puritan and his family. Opponents of the Awakening scornfully derided its followers as a deluded group of *"unlearned, common, labouring men"* and "Apostates" who did not have the slightest "Spark of Grace,"[13] and the General Association also found that the people who were "awakened" were "Chiefly of the lower and younger Sort."[14] Tortured at first by terrible thoughts of being damned, many of these humble folk subsequently claimed a saving religious experience. They became convinced that they had been chosen to be God's elect, and their emotions frequently gave way under the psychological strain.

Meetings are described in contemporary reports as generally attended by large numbers of people "Crying after *Raptures,*" and were commonly highlighted by "screechings, faintings, convulsions [and] visions." Revivalist ministers wandered about from town to town, holding services, preaching the necessity for personal conversion, and denouncing the established church. When James Davenport appeared in New London in July 1741, an Anglican priest, the Rev. Ebenezer Punderson, was present to witness the occasion. Unsympathetically he described Davenport's preaching as "boisterous behavior and vehement crying." But he noted in amazement that many of Davenport's listeners "were *struck,* as the phrase is, and made the most terrible and affecting noise, that was heard a mile from the place."[15]

The religious principles of the Awakening rejected the Half-Way Covenant of the Saybrook Platform. Only those, it was maintained, who could claim the saving miracle of personal conversion were entitled to membership in the true church. Churches that were not convenanted according to God's word were corrupt; and, since it was denied that the Saybrook Platform conformed to that word, the established church of the colony was attacked as a false church.[16] Advocates of these doctrines were known as

New Lights. But the Rev. Isaac Stiles, one of their most violent opponents, denied that their inspiration was a true light. On the contrary, he accused the New Lights of being "easily led aside by the Ignis Fatuus of their own heated Imagination and deluded giddy Fancies." And their zeal, he charged, while furious, was quite blind.[17]

Most of the ministers, "magistrates and principal gentlemen" of the colony bitterly opposed the religious revolution. To Daniel Wadsworth of Hartford these men were naturally "the most Judicious among ministers and people."[18] Some of the Old Lights, as the opponents of the Awakening were called, associated the movement with the insidious work of the devil, and therefore denounced it as destructive of true religion and public welfare. To all Old Lights it was "a time of rebuke and of treading down," of wild enthusiasms, hysteria, and frequent violations "of scripture and Reason." The very pillars of the religious order seemed to be tottering. Old Lights protested that the "Laws of God and the King" were commonly flouted. And their ministers, the "salt of the earth," suffered to see their authority denied in the loud "bawling" of itinerant preachers and their very persons slandered in a "rabble of Invectives."[19]

Connecticut's churches were violently shaken by these irreconcilable differences between their Old and New Light members.[20] Many of the latter refused to remain in the same church with the "unconverted" and split off to form Separatist churches. Where the majority in a congregation became "New Lighted" it generally forced a secession of the Old Light minority. Whichever took place, the result was the same. The unity of the established religious order was rent violently, and the effect seemed to tear the whole fabric of society.[21] The Old Lights deplored the bitter "Strife and faction," and were sorely grieved at the way the "fierce and wrathful people" criticized "their rulers and teachers."[22] All about them they heard "Murmurers and Complainers ... despising Government."[23]

To prevent and heal divisions the Assembly called upon the General Association to meet in November 1741, hoping that it would be able to restore "settling peace, love and charity" to the colony. But the Association condemned the extremism and separatist tendencies of the Awakening and thus fanned the fires of the religious controversy even higher.[24] Peace was not re-established in the colony. Ignoring the call to be loving and charitable, the opposing sides in this religious war continued to attack each other as vehemently as ever.[25] Those who broke away from the established order were convinced that the separations were desirable and necessary. But the conservative believers in the old ways were equally certain that the province had come upon evil days and had fallen into "awful Sins."[26] Bitter disputes continued to rage through the towns, accompanied by the spread of New Light doctrines and the frequent formation of Separatist congregations.[27]

The Standing Order in the state intervened to support its counterpart in the church when it became apparent that the latter could not preserve its unity unaided.[28] Itinerant preaching was banned; New Light extremists were fined and imprisoned on various charges, including alleged subversion of the government and refusal to pay taxes for the maintenance of the regular ministers; students were expelled from Yale; a New Light school at New London was closed by legislative action; and public officials failed to be re-elected or were removed from office because they sympathized with or belonged to New Light congregations.[29] Governor Wolcott must have had his tongue in his cheek, or else construed the word "equality" in a way that would be difficult to agree with to-day, when he maintained in 1752 that in Connecticut all Protestants enjoyed "equal Liberty."[30]

But despite the vigor with which the repressive laws were at first executed, they failed to restore the religious conditions prevailing before the revival. Radical New Light groups continued, during the late forties, the decade of the fifties and into the years immediately preceding the Stamp Act, to separate themselves from the established church and form new congregations, with the towns frequently recording the fact that they were "melancholy divided."[31] Religious controversy intermittently flared up in pamphlet debates, the disputants going at each other, in the phrase of one Old Light minister, "hammer and Tongs."[32] Truly, from the standpoint of the religious conservative, Connecticut was in "unhappy and divided circumstances."[33]

It was impossible to separate religion from politics in colonial Connecticut. Consequently, the religious differences stirred up by the revival quickly assumed a political aspect. And from the combination of religion and politics there emerged two factions roughly identical with the religious alignment caused by the Awakening.

One faction derived its chief support from the more conservative elements in the province, the "wealthier and more aristocratic families;" and its most prominent figures were the magistrates and ministers who had sought to restrain the religious revival. The other faction drew its strength from the New Lights and those freemen who, while they did not sanction indiscriminate separations from the established church and the emotional extremes that accompanied the revival, opposed the restrictive legislation enacted in the 1740's against the religious radicals.[34] These groupings were not fully developed parties in the modern sense, but the differences between them were sufficient to establish a rough political division in the colony.

During the early stages of the Awakening, some officeholders were removed from their jobs or failed to be re-elected because they were considered friendly to the New Lights.[35] In the years that followed, political labeling became more common; and with increasing frequency elections hinged upon the changing strength of the Old and New Light factions.[36] When the struggle began the Old Lights had complete control of the towns and the colonial legislature,[37] but the more radical party gradually increased its influence. President Clap became known as a political New Light in 1754-55, and although the election of Thomas Fitch to the governorship in 1754 was considered a victory for the more conservative party, the number of New Lights in the Assembly grew larger in the later years of that decade.[38] In 1759 a religious dispute in Wallingford gave the New Lights an issue which they exploited in an ambitious attempt to block the re-election of Governor Fitch and several unfriendly Councillors.

Daniel Lyman, a prominent New Haven New Light, and William Williams, who was later to be one of Connecticut's most stalwart patriots, were involved in this plan.[39] Lyman, confident in Williams' "great Esteem of the Calvinistical Interest and the Religious Constitution of this Govt," appealed to him to do everything in his power to help forward the design. It was Lyman's hope that the eastern and western counties would spare "no Pains . . . to put our Publick Affairs, both Civil and Sacred on a more Solid and Safe Foundation, and not forever be obliged to Truckle to a few Designing Men on the other side the Question." To help attain this end, Williams was asked by Lyman to suggest other possible sympathizers in nearby towns whose cooperation might be of advantage.[40]

This interesting effort to bring about "a mighty change in Government" fell through. The plot was "despised . . . by the . . . better part of the People," according to the Old Light view of the matter, but the New Lights were not at all discouraged.[41] The following year Samuel Johnson reported that the New Light party, whose influence, he carefully noted, was increasing in the lower house of the legislature, was still planning "to get out the governor and several of the upper house for not favouring them."[42] Although these plans were again frustrated, the New Light party had succeeded by the early 1760's in becoming "nearly the ruling part of the government." William Samuel Johnson attributed its success to the superior attention that its followers gave "to civil affairs and close union among themselves in politics."[43]

The Old Light element was distressed and frightened. By

1760 the colony had suffered almost twenty years of "Church-rending, Unpeaceable, Party Spirit." Old Light leaders had warned the people to beware of "Secret Plots or Intreagues against the State" which subverted the peace and discipline of government.[44] But the New Lights spurned their advice. To the conservatives it appeared that liberty was being confused with licentiousness. Good magistrates had been the victims of the political plots of "designing Men" who merely sought to "serve a Turn;"[45] and, what was worse, this selfish party spirit seemed to grow rather than diminish. Should that spirit become dominant, the Rev. Joseph Fish pessimistically concluded in 1760, it would convulse the colony and "shake our Noble Frame to Pieces."[46]

The strength of the New Lights centered in the eastern counties of New London and Windham. There, as Ezra Stiles observed, the people were of "mixt and uncertain character as to religion."[47] Although some parts of the southwestern sections of the colony, notably the eastern half of Fairfield County, also fell under New Light influence, they were not as deeply affected by the extremes of the revival as were the towns in New London and Windham Counties.[48]

In no small measure it was the work of the Anglican missionaries that made the southwestern parts of Connecticut steadier and more conservative in their religious principles. In fact, the Church of England generally increased its membership at the expense of the Puritan majority during the bitter disputes brought on by the Awakening. Both town and colonial authorities continued hostile toward the Anglicans; and yet they were unable to check the slow but regular growth of their most serious religious rival. Anglicans were fined and imprisoned for such "crimes" as reading their prayer book and working on public fast days, and failing to contribute to the support of the established ministers, but their congregations increased.[49] Some of the Puritan ministers realized that "the civil wars of the Lord" in which they were engaged weakened their hold upon the people, and a few among them began to fear that they would be "swallowd up by the Episcopal church." They therefore counselled peace and forbearance among themselves. But the reports of the Anglican priests in the 1740's, 1750's, and early 1760's emphasize that their church continued to benefit from the upsetting effects of the Awakening upon the Congregational establishment.[50]

Between 1740 and 1755 the number of Anglican ministers increased from seven to eleven. In 1750 there were twenty-five Episcopal parishes and twenty-four churches in the colony. Ten years later the number of Anglican pastors and churches had grown respectively to fourteen and thirty, with most of their following concentrated in the towns of Fairfield County.[51] Contemporaries, Congregational as well as Episcopalian, agreed that by the early 1760's the Anglicans constituted a significant proportion of the total population in several of the Fairfield County towns.[52]

As in the case of the break between the Old and New Lights, the increasing influence of the Anglican church had important political implications. The treatment that the ruling powers in Connecticut accorded to the members of the English Church did not dispose them to regard the colony's political system with any great favor. The Episcopal clergy quickly developed an emphatic dislike for Connecticut's charter, which they blamed as the cause of their troubles. As early as 1726 the Rev. Samuel Johnson advised the Bishop of London that it would be in the interest of the Church of England to have Connecticut's charter destroyed.[53] Twenty-five years later Johnson was still urging that Connecticut be reduced "to a state of mere dependence on the Crown, by obliging them to accept of a new or explanatory charter."[54] In the eyes of this conservative minister, the leading Anglican in the colony, Connecticut's government was "a meer Democracy . . . hence the prevalency of rigid enthusiasticals and conceited notions and practices in Religion and republican and mobbish principles and practices next-door to anarchy in polity." What was even worse, according to Johnson, was that the people under this government had little or no "notion of any King or the Kingdom to which they are accountable."[55]

In addition to frequently flaying Connecticut's political system in their letters to important clergymen in England, the Anglican ministers in the colony repeatedly requested that a bishop be sent over to care for the church's interests.[56] Although they were unsuccessful in their petitions they kept Connecticut's elders in a constant state of fear.[57] But while the Episcopal clergy failed to have an American bishopric established, they were performing other significant services for the Crown, inculcating a spirit of loyalty and devotion to the King and Empire. Their work was to bear important results during the Revolution. In this respect it is worth quoting part of a letter written on the eve of the Stamp Act crisis by the Rev. Mr. Winslow to the Secretary of the Society for the Propagation of the Gospel in Foreign Parts:

It has not been unnoticed by the Gentlemen, who have had the direction and management of the Publick Transactions . . . here since the War that in the concerns they have occasionally had with the popular Governments, wherever the Ch of England has been propagated among the various Sectaries Its Influence has been Visible, towards increasing and confirming a becoming zeal and attachment to that happy national Constitution.[58]

At the same time that these religious and political developments were dividing the colony into conservative and radical factions, another issue, which was ultimately to have a similar effect, was becoming prominent in Connecticut's public affairs. This issue was bound up with the changing fortunes of the Susquehannah Company.[59]

Several economic trends had culminated in the organization of this land venture. During the early decades of the eighteenth century the population of the colony grew rapidly despite large emigrations and the inter-colonial wars. In 1730 it was 38,000; in

1749 it was 70,000; and by 1756 it had almost doubled again, the total in that year being 130,611.[60] The agricultural resources of the colony, however, did not increase in the same proportion as did the population, nor were they sufficient to satisfy the growing desire for more land. Poor agricultural techniques prompted Connecticut's scientific farmer, the Rev. Jared Eliot, to suggest such improvements as crop rotation, a more intensive use of fertilizers, and the reclamation of marshes and swamp land.[61] But Connecticut's farmers were more interested in new and more fertile lands than in changing habits on their old farms. This attitude was reflected in the speculative fever which seized the colony in the 1730's when three hundred thousand acres of land in the western part of Connecticut were offered for sale.[62] By the 1750's the appropriation of the last of the colony's public lands had been completed. But even before they had all been taken up, much of the uncultivated land was already in the hands of absentee owners who held it primarily for speculative purposes.[63] It was under these circumstances that the General Assembly began to receive petitions in the early 1750's for land, asserting that towns were "Grown full of Inhabitants so that a Great many must unavoidably move to Sum other Place."[64]

Connecticut had not claimed any land west of its New York boundary for over a century, and its reports to the Board of Trade had consistently cited that line as its westernmost limit.[65] Nevertheless, between 1750 and 1755 several petitions were received by the legislature requesting the right to colonize or settle on lands beyond the Hudson.[66]

Of these petitions the most important in the later history of the colony was that of the Susquehannah Company, which was organized in July 1753 in the town of Windham. Among the company's early members were men who were influential in the affairs of town and colony.[67] The company's minutes recorded a judicious combination of motives, imperial, religious, and private; but its history was to indicate that their own temporal interest was undoubtedly the chief objective of its proprietors.[68] In 1754, anticipating opposition from Pennsylvania and Sir William Johnson, the company managed through its Indian agent, John Henry Lydius, to get the signatures of some Indian chiefs to a deed of sale of rather dubious validity. The deed transferred to the company a strip of land within the 42d degree of latitude, some sixty to seventy miles long and extending in width from a line ten miles east of the Susquehanna River to about two degrees of longitude westward.[69] The boundaries of the company's project thus included practically the northern third of Pennsylvania.

The Susquehannah Company quickly pressed its claim. Citing the sea-to-sea clause in Connecticut's charter as the source of the colony's right to the western lands, it requested the General Assembly, May 7, 1755, to approve its plan proposing to establish a new colony on the banks of the Susquehanna River.[70] Although the legislature had formerly opposed similar claims, it provisionally sanctioned the venture, prefacing its consent with the explanation that the settlement would be a boon to the empire, and recommended the company's proprietors "to His Royal favour."[71]

The Susquehannah Company's claim challenged the jurisdiction of the Penns to a huge slice of their domain. This was sufficient cause to arouse the violent antagonism of the proprietary authorities. That hostility was inevitably increased by the fact that the company's project proposed to establish a land system free of quit-rents in an area subject to such fees, thus endangering the entire structure of proprietary privilege. If this were not enough, the officials of the Quaker colony saw in the expansionist scheme of the Connecticut Yankees still another likely irritant in their already unstable relations with the Indians.[72] Those officials, therefore, with the more than moral support of Sir William Johnson, registered strong protests with the Connecticut government against the company.[73]

The mixed reaction of the colony's two leading magistrates, Governor Roger Wolcott and Deputy Governor Thomas Fitch, to these remonstrances foreshadowed the divisive role that the company was destined to play in Connecticut's politics for the next twenty years. Wolcott supported the company, wishing it "Good Success" and hoping that it would "never want Encouragement from the Throne." Fitch, however, informed the angry Pennsylvania officials that he thought the whole project was a wild scheme which would come to nothing.[74] This difference of opinion over the Susquehannah Company did not seem to matter very much in 1754. But in a few years the company was to become a major issue in Connecticut, and the struggles it precipitated were to contribute to the crystallization of colony-wide political sentiment and organization.

The combined opposition of the Indians, Sir William Johnson, and the Penn interests forced the Crown to intervene against the company.[75] Early in 1761 the Susquehannah proprietors had delegated Eliphalet Dyer, one of the colony's rising political figures, to petition the King for the right to establish a new colony on the lands they coveted.[76] This somewhat fanciful request never had much chance of winning the approval of the mother country. Nevertheless, Dyer submitted the petition to the King in Council in the summer of 1764. The request was referred to the Board of Trade, where it was quietly buried.[77]

Even before Dyer presented the company's petition to the Council, the Crown had taken steps to clarify the issue; but these steps were not to the company's advantage. In May 1762 the Susquehannah proprietors had voted to start a settlement.[78] A month later, Fitch, who had become governor in 1754, issued a proclamation warning the company not to do so because "much Disturbance may be apprehended and opposition made to such Settlement, to the Hazard of the Publick Peace; in the Blame whereof, this Government may possibly become involved" and incur royal displeasure. But the company, instead of reversing its intentions, voted to defy the proclamation and increased from one hundred to two hundred the number of settlers it proposed to send out.[79]

Some Unsteady Habits, 1730-1765

The apparent inability of the Connecticut government to restrain the company prompted Sir William Johnson to suggest to the Board of Trade that the Crown intervene in the matter. Johnson also suggested that in the meantime it would be advisable to forbid any additional settlements, in order to placate the Indians.[80] On January 14, 1763, the Board of Trade recommended to the King in Council that immediate measures be taken to ban all settlements, and on the twenty-seventh of the same month the Secretary of State, the Earl of Egremont, wrote to Governor Fitch, advising him that the Crown expected him to do everything possible to prevent any colonization in the disputed territory and to withdraw any Connecticut settlers already in the area "till the State of the Case can be laid before the King."[81]

Although some members of the company continued to favor an immediate colonization, the company did not dare to defy the King's order as it had the governor's proclamation. Its proprietors, therefore, formally voted a "ready submission and acquiescence" to the royal instructions and hoped that the near future would bring a change for the better in their fortunes.[82] But, instead, the massacre of the Wyoming settlers in the fall of 1763 seemed to bear out the fears and predictions of the company's enemies in the colonies and justify the intervention of the imperial authority.

By 1765 the Susquehannah Company was fast becoming a stirring issue in Connecticut. In a short time it had managed to bring into being an imposing group of opponents, including the powerful Penn interests, the Indians, and the Crown's Superintendent of Indian Affairs, the capable Sir William Johnson. Even the British government had become an interested party in the dispute. More significant for the colony's local politics, however, was the fact that this imposing alignment of anti-Susquehannah forces had provoked a growing reaction within Connecticut against the expansionists. But those freemen who were beginning to turn against the company found that it had strong backing.

Shortly after it was organized the company was already reported to be a political power. Its close relationship with several members of the General Assembly was well known both in Pennsylvania and Connecticut.[83] As early as 1763 the Rev. Ezra Stiles claimed that the company "with their connexions are large eno' to influence one Third of the Votes in the Government, and might possibly shake some out of the Council and Assembly."[84] Stiles was also of the opinion that the company was "headed by Men of the first Sense and Character in Connecticut." And the Congregational minister was right, insofar as these qualities were possessed by the colony's political leaders, because a number of the latter already held shares in the company.[85]

But while the Susquehannah Company had powerful backers, by 1763 it was also generating a significant opposition within the colony. That opposition was as yet not well organized, for its members apparently had not been convinced of the rightness of their position until 1763. The events of that year, however, made up their minds. It now seemed to them that the company might have to engage in a long, expensive, and perhaps dangerous controversy that was likely to bring the colony into collision with the Indians, the Penns, and possibly the mother country. In order to avert these dangers, several prominent men began to form the nucleus of an anti-Susquehannah group. Among them were the merchant Joseph Chew; Killingworth's able deputy, Benjamin Gale; Jared Ingersoll, one of Connecticut's leading lawyers and politicians; and probably Governor Thomas Fitch.

As early as 1754 there were conservative-minded men who, upon learning of the Penns' hostile reaction to the company's claim, were not inclined to make an issue of it.[86] And a report to the governor of Pennsylvania made in the same year maintained that "the Generality of the more knowing People despise the [company's] Scheme as wild and preposterous."[87] When Connecticut gave its blessing to the Susquehannah project in 1755, some conservative freemen bought shares in the company, according to an explanation offered later by Benjamin Gale, in order to forestall any "mischievous consequences" to the colonial government.[88] But when the difficulties with the Indians and Pennsylvania brought the controversy to the attention of the mother country, the qualms of these more cautious subjects began to outweigh their other motives. To Joseph Chew "the Displeasure of the great" on both sides of the water was a clear sign that the company had little, and probably no chance of being successful.[89] Jared Ingersoll, New Haven's conservative lawyer, vigorously argued at a company meeting that its cause was hopeless and then sold out his interests in the venture.[90]

On the eve of the Stamp Act crisis there was a definite division within Connecticut between the company's supporters and its more conservative opponents. Ezra Stiles noted that when the letter from the Earl of Egremont prohibiting the colonization of the Wyoming Valley was made public it was "difficult to say whether it threw more Discouragt upon the Affair, or augmented the Eagerness and Resolution of the Company."[91] It did both. And in the critical decade after 1765 the dispute over the western claim was to become even more violent and bitter.

The effects of the religious awakening, the increasing strength of the Anglican church, and the activities of the Susquehannah Company combined to destroy Connecticut's political homogeneity. The colony's commercial development had a somewhat similar result, although it produced none of the obviously hostile reactions within Connecticut that accompanied each of the other movements. That development, however, gave rise to problems that had serious political implications. Not the least of these was the fact that Connecticut's commercial problems affected the province's relations with England on a political as well as on an economic level.

In the early eighteenth century Connecticut's commerce was small, and in the words of one official summary, was "carried on with much difficulty."[92] Agricultural surpluses continued to make up the major items of the colony's exports. Reports describing the colony's products in the 1740's and 1750's do not differ from those made earlier in the century. Lumber and provisions, such as horses, cattle, hogs and grain were consistently recorded as the province's chief commodities. Manufacturing was a minor industry producing small amounts of coarse textiles, and leather and metal goods. The mining of copper and iron was limited. Large supplies of manufactured stuffs, woolens, silks, glass, nails, scythes, pewter, brass, firearms, and cutlery were imported from Great Britain, primarily through Boston and New York. To pay for these, Connecticut sold its agricultural products to merchants in those ports and also expanded its direct trade with the West Indies. From the latter, Connecticut merchants secured badly needed specie and bills of exchange as well as some raw materials that were in demand at home or were profitable in balancing their accounts.[93]

This organization of Connecticut's trade reduced its direct economic contacts with England to a minimum. At the same time it linked the colony's economic welfare to the Boston and New York merchants and to the West Indies.[94] Connecticut's position was similar to that of the other New England colonies in that its products found no market in the mother country; and they all depended on the West Indies to consume their surpluses and to provide sorely-needed exchange. Connecticut, however, differed from its neighbors in that it did not import its manufactured goods directly from England. It relied upon merchants in other colonial ports, notably Boston and New York, for these items; and its farmers and merchants depended upon the traders in the latter ports to dispose of a large proportion of the colony's surpluses. Under this arrangement Connecticut's merchants inevitably became indebted to their Boston and New York connections.[95]

Varied remedies to improve the colony's economic plight were devised and applied, but, on the whole, they were all unsuccessful. As early as 1680 Connecticut futilely suggested to the home government that several towns be made free ports in order to encourage the growth of important commercial centers in the colony.[96] Efforts to stimulate industrial activity such as the manufacture of silk,[97] canvas and fine linen,[98] and the mining of copper brought no significant changes. Benjamin Trumbull thought that New-gate prison, converted from an old copper mine into a jail, was more valuable to Connecticut "than all the copper dug."[99] Some progress was achieved in the manufacture of iron. Eight small mills were producing iron and steel in 1750, but Governor Law reported that they did not make enough to satisfy the colony's needs.[100] For a while some enterprising freemen dreamed that a staple export might be found in the masts cut from the fine trees that lined the upper Connecticut River. But it all came to nothing, finally, when Jared Ingersoll's plan to have a Vice-Admiralty Court established in the province to protect the Connecticut beneficiaries of the project fell through.[101]

Connecticut's report to the Board of Trade in 1756, as in 1730 and 1749, noted that domestic manufactures were inconsiderable. And, significantly enough, it complained that the colony's imports of manufactured British goods yielded large profits to the importers, but that the latter were "principally in neighbouring governments."[102]

These efforts to stimulate local industries were supplemented by attempts to discourage the importation of British manufactures through ports outside the colony, and to encourage the direct sale of Connecticut goods to their ultimate markets. The obvious objective of these measures was the destruction of the hold that the Boston and New York middlemen had upon the colony's commerce.

In 1714 an export duty was levied on barrel, pipe and hogshead staves sold to merchants in New York, New Jersey, and the other New England colonies.[103] Eighteen years later Connecticut explained to the Board of Trade that a recent provincial law placing a twelve-shilling tax on every hundred pound's worth of goods brought in from the neighboring colonies was in line with its effort to promote a direct trade with Great Britain.[104] The export of lumber to Connecticut's neighbors was again condemned in 1747 as destructive of the colony's commercial interests, and another export tax was therefore placed on lumber products sold to merchants in the adjacent colonies.[105]

In the same year an excise bill was passed taxing anyone who brought into Connecticut more than fifteen pound's worth of commodities from any other New England colony, New York, New Jersey, or Pennsylvania, five pounds for every hundred pound's worth of goods so imported. Non-resident importers had to pay an extra duty of 7½ per cent, but local merchants who brought commodities on their "own proper risque and account" from Great Britain or Ireland into Connecticut for sale in the colony were to receive a premium.[106] This ambitious scheme collapsed in less than a year when the demand for goods became too great for Connecticut's merchants to satisfy with the small volume of their direct imports from Great Britain.[107] The colony, however, did not give up. In 1750 it ordered that its reimbursement for expenses incurred in the recent capture of Louisburg was to be retained by its inhabitants in order to encourage trade from Connecticut to Great Britain,[108] but that trade never prospered.

On the eve of the Stamp Act troubles Joseph Trumbull, son and commercial associate of Councillor Jonathan Trumbull, who was then probably Connecticut's wealthiest merchant, was still hopefully outlining a comprehensive plan to destroy the economic dependence of Connecticut upon Boston and New York. At the same time, however, he admitted that "most of our Traders know nothing of Trade in any other way, [but with Boston and New York] and have been so long in it, they are like a Horse in mill, they keep on the same beaten way, without Turning to the Right Hand or the left."[109]

Vexing currency problems aggravated the economic difficulties of the Connecticut merchant. He bought English goods on credit at Boston, Newport, and New York. The debtor interest created by this economic relationship was made more burdensome by the general money shortage in New England, which restricted the opportunities for the accumulation of capital and mercantile expansion. Under these circumstances the Connecticut trader was therefore likely, at times, to advocate a policy of moderate currency inflation. Within the colony, however, the merchant sold his wares to Yankee farmers on credit, "Cash or Country Produce." His creditor interests in this relationship demanded a stable and dear currency.[110] The merchant's attitude toward the paper money question tended to vary, therefore, with his business needs and credit status in and outside the colony. While the complete and complicated history of the paper money issue in Connecticut is not relevant to this study, one major incident in that story is: that concerning the New London Society for Trade and Commerce.[111]

According to Governor Wolcott, Connecticut issued its first bills of credit in 1709.[112] By 1715 £24,875 in this currency was in circulation. The amount was sharply reduced in the following years, only £12,198 remaining out in 1725 and £4,380 in 1730.[113] This acute contraction made money extremely scarce. Merchants planning new business ventures found it impossible to secure needed capital;[114] and, debtors, of course, did not relish the deflation.

In 1726 and in 1728 some sporadic expressions were heard favoring the establishment of a land bank.[115] And in October 1729 a group of business men organized the New London Society for Trade and Commerce and petitioned the legislature for the right to issue bills of currency on the company's credit. This unusual request was refused. Three years later, however, the Society, which now included many influential figures and supposedly had a large political influence, was incorporated by the General Assembly on the petition that its organization proposed to promote the trade with Great Britain and the West Indies and to develop the fishing industry.[116]

The New London Society was not destined to have a long life. Shortly after it was approved by the colonial legislature, the company, under pressure of commercial reverses, began to issue bills of credit based on the real estate mortgages which had been deposited by the members of the Society as security for its capital loans. A few months later the Assembly, called in extra session by Governor Talcott, found that the Society had been printing several thousand pounds similar to the paper money of Connecticut and other New England colonies. Fearing possible repercussions against the colony's precious charter, the legislators promptly prohibited the emission of any bills on the credit of an individual or society intended to pass "for a general currency in lieu of money or a medium of trade," and revoked the company's privileges.[117]

The dissolution of the New London Society created financial problems that took decades to solve and planted a feeling of dissatisfaction that was rooted chiefly in the trading town of New London and among the merchants in neighboring communities in eastern Connecticut.[118] The Society itself was a symptom of Connecticut's commercial growing pains; and its experience emphasized the commercial handicaps resulting from an inadequate money supply and a lack of capital. In the larger perspective of colonial Connecticut's economic history, the downfall of the New London Society represents another example of the colony's failure to develop a commercial center independent of the rival ports of Boston and New York. The paper money remedy to end Connecticut's indebtedness to Boston and other colonial merchants and "to Encourage . . . Trade and merchandize" continued to have its advocates.[119] But although Connecticut issued more paper money after the New London Society fiasco to pay for the growing expenses of the colonial government, it was careful not to permit its currency to be endangered by becoming entangled with private economic schemes.[120]

Despite determined, and at times near-desperate, resorts to varied expedients, Connecticut failed to develop a thriving direct trade with Great Britain. Nor was it able to expand its manufacturing industries sufficiently to sever its reliance upon Boston and

New York for British imports.[121] Its commercial welfare, therefore, continued to depend upon the vitality of its direct and indirect trade with the English and foreign West Indies. As long as Connecticut was able to find a market for its agricultural surpluses in those islands its economic condition was not intolerable.

During the decades of the 1740's and 1750's, when the French and Indian wars stimulated the demand for agricultural products, the colony prospered. Connecticut merchants owned seventy-four ships in 1756 whereas in 1730 they had only forty-two. In 1762 they operated 114 vessels chiefly from the eastern towns.[122] Ezra Stiles estimated that in the same year one-fourth of the tonnage registered in the colony's two ports, New London and New Haven, was engaged primarily in the West Indian trade.[123]

It was inevitable, therefore, that Connecticut's merchants would vehemently object when they were confronted with the British decision to choke off the traffic with the foreign West Indies. The colony's governor protested to its agent, May 25, 1751, that shutting the markets in the foreign islands would be a "mischief."[124] The following fall the General Assembly condemned the proposed restrictions, arguing that "there must be great loss if our trade be crampt, and maney persons put out of theire business."[125]

Ten years later Connecticut's merchants felt the same way about the matter. It is significant that just before the storm over the Stamp Act broke there was among the colony's merchants a strong current of dissatisfaction with England's commercial policy. This discontent is succinctly described in a letter written by Jonathan Trumbull Jr., younger son of the prominent merchant and magistrate who was then deeply involved in the West Indian trade. It is reasonable to suppose that the commercial problems of Trumbull Sr. were no secret to his active sons. In any case the position and grievances of the Connecticut trader are clearly drawn in this letter of Jonathan Jr. to his brother Joseph, partner in the firm of Trumbull, Fitch and Trumbull:

We must contrive some other Business than that to the W Indies—as the Station Ships prevent any Thing in the illicit Way and the Trade to the English Islands is much overdone. Indeed it seems hard that these Colonies should be mined to gratify the Avarice of a few Individuals in England whose Interest lies in the W Indies—But this by the Bie—[126]

In the three to four decades preceding the Stamp Act crisis, Connecticut's traditionally sober Yankees displayed some rather unsteady habits and a robust capacity for acrimonious contention. With varying intensity they had disagreed over religious, economic, and political matters; and their differences had more or less violently split them into hostile groups and factions. Two religious developments had contributed to these differences, the Great Awakening, with its dramatic and bitter conflict between Old and New Lights, and the continued expansion of the Anglican church. And another two were the result of economic pressures arising from the claims of the Susquehannah Company and the mounting tension of the colony's merchants over British commercial policy.

Each of these developments had also tended to divide the colony along rough geographical lines. The New Light revival did not sweep through the western part of the colony as fiercely as it had in the eastern counties. Moreover, it was in Fairfield County that the Anglican church made its greatest gains, building new churches, winning additional converts, and increasing the number of its active ministers. On the other hand, eastern Connecticut, the center of religious extremism, was the same region in which the Susquehannah Company was formed and its leading members resided. This section was also the focus of the paper money troubles in the 1730's and 1740's, and it was in the eastern seacoast towns that Connecticut's commercial problems produced an uneasy merchant class.[127]

Under the impact of British imperial policy in the 1760's and 1770's these divisions within Connecticut became more ominous.

Some Unsteady Habits, 1730-1765

The somewhat nebulous factions took more definite shape in the heated differences with the mother country. It is to these differences that we must now turn to see how the growing split between Connecticut's radical and conservative freemen, created originally by domestic issues, was affected by the colony's reaction to Britain's proposed changes of the imperial administration.

CHAPTER THREE

The Stamp Act and the Election of 1766

-»>->»>->»>->»>->»>->»>->»>->»>->»>->»>->»>-»<-«<-«<-«<-«<-«<-«<-«<-«<-«<-«<-«<-«<-«<-«<-

-»>->»-«<-«<-

*T*HE TIGHTENED imperial system proposed in the 1760's by the home government was not the first threat to Connecticut's privileged colonial status. In the late seventeenth century the colony had weathered several storms which had threatened to overwhelm its charter rights;[1] and in the first half of the eighteenth century it periodically faced new challenges to its relative political independence. These experiences taught the careful Yankees to beware of any measure, inter-colonial or imperial, which seemed even in the slightest way to infringe upon their freedom.

Between 1728 and 1765 several incidents centered the unwelcome attention of the Crown upon the colony. The annulment of Connecticut's intestacy law by the Privy Council in 1728 was one of the most serious dangers that ever confronted the little Puritan colony, for that decision not only jeopardized Connecticut's entire land system, but for a while brought the charter itself into question.[2] But Connecticut's magistrates, bent on preserving the charter, that "choicest part of . . . [their] inheritance," successfully maneuvered the colony through the troubles caused by this trying issue.3 The paper money difficulties between the New England provinces and Great Britain also threatened to involve Connecticut's charter, as did the possibility that the mother country would establish an American bishopric.4 And intermittently throughout the eighteenth century the Mohegan case, a dispute over lands in eastern Connecticut, compelled the colony to defend itself before the Crown.5

Even in its relations with the other colonies Connecticut was reluctant to commit itself to any plan that might have restricted its initiative under the charter. Thus, among the reasons reported by a committee of the General Assembly against the Albany Plan was that in at least one provision, the power to levy taxes, it would be an "innovation or breach of charter privileges."6

When the third Hanoverian king, George III, ascended the English throne, Connecticut, in the fulsome language of the day, pledged him its "Faith and Constant Obedience, with all Hearty and humble Affection."7 Two years later the colony expressed its relief at the final defeat of the French and celebrated the end of another threat to its great "Inheritance."8 And in 1764 the Rev. Noah Welles concluded, after analyzing the contemporary scene, that although there was an "awful prevalence" of sin in the colony, "no people under heaven, have more reason to be satisfied and pleased with their situation" than the inhabitants of Connecticut.9

Not all of the omens, however, were propitious. A month after the Crown had prohibited the Susquehannah Company's settlements in the Wyoming Valley the news was received that Parliament had tightened up the administration of the acts of trade.10 And in 1764 the Sugar Act was passed.

Even before the bill became a law Connecticut's merchants had united to oppose it.11 Boston's merchants appealed to the traders at New London for aid on January 9, 1764, and on January 20 Jared Ingersoll, on behalf of Gurdon Saltonstall and other merchants, petitioned the General Assembly to protest against the bill. Ingersoll warned that the enforcement of the measure would cause "very much Distress." [12] Prominent merchants faced ruin. [13] Samuel Gray reported that Eliphalet Dyer, Councillor from eastern Connecticut and a leading Susquehannah Company proprietor, feared the taxes on trade and thought that now was "the Time for the Colonies to Exert Themselves if Ever or Wee have have [*sic*] Seen our best Days." [14]

The legislature was not unmindful of the danger. It appointed three important New London merchants, Colonel Gurdon Saltonstall, Nathaniel Shaw and Thomas Mumford to draw up Connecticut's argument against the act and send them to the colony's agent. [15] The protest, of course, had no effect. Significantly enough, it was the conservative lawyer, Jared Ingersoll, who felt that the British "have overshot their mark" in the Sugar Act. [16] And in a few months the question of whether independence might not result from America's opposition to the authority at Westminster was to be raised in the Connecticut press. [17]

The dismay with which Connecticut's merchants and farmers anticipated the effects of the reinvigorated enforcement of the acts of trade was heightened by the severe depression that fell upon the colonies after the French and Indian War. The little province of Connecticut was hit hard. During the war it had prospered, selling its surplus agricultural products. The end of hostilities brought in its wake a severe deflation.

Economic adjustments made necessary by the peace were frequently disastrous. As early as 1762 and 1763 it was reported that many were falling into debt and losing their lands. [18] Merchants were unable to convert produce into remittances for their creditors. [19] And to make this bad situation worse for the Connecticut Puritans the British proposed to enforce their obnoxious restrictions upon the colony's most profitable markets in the West Indies. The colonists were pessimistic and bitter. "All our money is gone and going to England to pay our debts," the Hartford newspaper mournfully declared. And it went on, "No money is like to be in the country. Our trade to the *French* and *Spanish* islands, from whence we used to get money is stopped; men of war being placed along our coasts for that purpose. Husbandry is discouraged for there is no vent for that purpose. Merchants and farmers are breaking; and all things going into confusion."[20]

The confusion that the economic collapse caused was indeed serious. Early in 1764 Jonathan Trumbull informed his British creditors that trade was confined, "the Markets in the English Islands extreamly full—their Produce high and Bills that are good difficult to be had there."[21] His anxiety and alarm were more openly expressed in letters to his sons. He was convinced that since the trade of the colonies was largely prevented by the home government America would have to cut down on its purchases and develop its own manufactures.[22] Several months later Trumbull's son and partner, Joseph, who had recently returned from England, was overwhelmed when he saw for himself how completely the colony's trade had broken down. He described it as "embarrassed and Clog'd . . . even beyond what I had imagined. . . . We have nothing but the Name of Money left among us, the Substance is fled nor have we one Source left whence we can draw any." He too complained that the causes of these troubles were the closing of the foreign West Indies, "no Mines of Gold or Silver, no Markets, that are open to us, but are Abundantly Supplied with those Articles we have to dispose of."[23]

Farmers also felt the full effects of the depression. They found it impossible to sell their products profitably; their markets were glutted and prices depressed.[24] Land values, which had begun to fall in the early 1760's with the opening up of new townships in New Hampshire, were pushed down even further.[25] John Ledyard, despondent over the "Strange Scene of Bankruptcy and ruins," estimated that "the valuable Landed Interest of the Colony is Sunk in its Value more than 50 p. Cent."[26] Connecticut's farmers and merchants, who seemed to have a passion for litigation even in normal times, now clogged the courts with suits for debts.[27] Indeed, the heavy burden of indebtedness threatened to become intolerable. Ezra Stiles discovered that the farmers in Stonington and Groton—he included an "etc" for the other towns he did not specifically name—were "in debt all their Stock and half their Land."[28] A flood of petitions for relief on behalf of insolvent estates descended upon the Assembly in the late 1760's,[29] while in the crucial year of 1765 taxpayers were eighty thousand pounds in arrears on their payments due to the colonial government.[30]

It was under these inauspicious circumstances that the mother country decided to impose her new financial levy upon the colonies in the form of the Stamp Act. Had Connecticut been enjoying the benefits of a lush prosperity it would still have been seriously affected by the proposed taxes; a list of the documents and papers subject to the original draft of the tax bill covers more than a page of print.[31] But Connecticut's economy-minded Puritans were in the throes of a severe economic depression and were in no mood to pay more taxes to anyone.

Their tempers rose when they considered how the new measure seemed to menace their constitutional rights under the charter.[32] Joseph Trumbull gloomily anticipated that if the new tax policy were successfully established it would be followed by a government of "Kings, Govrs Councils, without a House of Representatives in all America."[33] His younger brother, Jonathan Jr., was equally dejected about the future and predicted that Britain's policy would inevitably alienate the colonies.[34]

The views of other notable sons of Connecticut more than matched the pessimism of the Trumbulls. Puritan divines like Ezra Stiles and Chauncey Whittelsey condemned the proposed tax as a blow "at the Root of american Liberty and Rights." Stiles even compared the times with the historical nadir of Puritanism, the Stuart era of Charles I and James II.[35] Samuel Gray of Windham was melancholy and alarmed at the news from abroad. It was bad enough, he complained, that "wee the most Dutifull and Loyal Subjects of any in the universe must have a number of men of warr station on our coast, To Rob and pilfer all our Navigation."

But "to Crown our Misery," Gray lamented, Connecticut's "happy Constitution" was now in imminent danger of destruction. And Eliphalet Dyer agreed with all the others that "if Taxes are once begun to be levied . . . our charter goes."[36] These sombre reactions foreboded serious trouble in the self-governing charter colony of Connecticut.

Connecticut's agent had warned the colonial government in March 1764 of the impending tax. Immediately the Assembly set up a committee to assist Governor Fitch in the preparation of the colony's arguments against the bill. The committee's report was approved at the October 1764 session and ordered sent abroad as Connecticut's case against the Stamp Act.[37] The colony's brief rested on two fundamental contentions: one stressed the right of English subjects to be taxed only by laws to which they had given their approval; the other maintained that the Stamp Act violated rights granted to Connecticut by the charter. The tone of the protest was moderate, but there was no doubt as to the colony's intention not to surrender any of its great powers. The protest acknowledged Parliament's supreme position, but in the words of Governor Fitch, it also tried "to Shew that the Exercise of Such Power in that Particular Instance [the Stamp Act] or in like Cases will take away Part of our Antient Priviledges."[38]

America's objections to the stamp tax were unavailing. Connecticut's petition was not even heard in Parliament.[39] Jared Ingersoll, then in England, saw it was futile to fight the new tax and labored with more success to moderate some of its provisions.[40] Trouble was obviously in the offing, and he stressed the need for "wisdom . . . prudence and good Discretion to direct the Councils of America."[41]

Neither the colonial and British leaders nor the people possessed all these virtues. But even if they had it is doubtful whether the exciting events that accompanied the Stamp Act to America could have been prevented. Moreover, there was substantial disagreement between the British and the Americans, and among the Americans themselves, as to what was wise, prudent, and discreet in the matter. In Connecticut, once the stamp tax had been enacted, conservatives who had originally opposed the measure prepared themselves to accept the inevitable.

Governor Fitch admirably described their reasoning. He explained to Richard Jackson that "if . . . the Parliament in their Superior Wisdom Shall Judge it Expedient to and accordingly do pass an Act for laying those Burdens upon us we must Submit. We never pretend in the least to Question whether Acts of Parliament expressly extended to the Plantations are binding but always Submit to them as binding." To Connecticut's governor the English legislature was "Supreme" and criticisms of its powers "bold and impolitic."[42] And Jared Ingersoll, who had spoken and written against the principle of parliamentary taxation of the colonies as "of dangerous Tendency" felt that once the Stamp Act had been passed "the People of America would most probably submit to it."[43] Acting on this assumption and expecting the colonists to prefer a native tax collector to strangers, Ingersoll secured the position of stamp distributor for Connecticut.[44] Others reacted similarly for reasons of principle or profit. Prominent freemen in Hartford, Stratford, Windham, Stonington, Litchfield, Windsor, and Fairfield offered to assist Ingersoll in administering the act.[45]

Large numbers of colonists, however, were of a contrary mind. Throwing discretion to the winds, they identified prudence and wisdom with uncompromising opposition to the Stamp Act. They violently denounced the new tax as brutal slavery, and for those in Connecticut who were willing to distribute the stamps they had nothing but anger and harsh censure. Speaking for these more extreme elements "Tom Touchit" told Ingersoll that he would rather receive the stamps from a "savage Hottentot, or a barbarous American Indian" than from him.[46] That was the way the radicals let it be known that they would not accept the stamps from anybody.

Extremists immediately began to prepare the colony for the

coming battle. They sanctified the people whom they were organizing and were about to lead in noisy demonstrations as the
"Lord's anointed" and "the darlings of Providence," and defended
them against the charges of "the tools of power" who "may affect
to disparage the people and stigmatize them with the opprobious
names of Mob and Rabble." Taking as their political maxim the
proposition that government was set up to secure the people's
happiness, they concluded that whenever it was used for contrary
purposes the people had the right to examine "the conduct of
their superiors" and still another "right to complain whenever
their liberties are invaded."[47] Complain was just what their spokesmen did throughout the summer and fall of 1765. The newspapers
overflowed with violent attacks upon the Stamp Act and reports
of meetings held to give vent to the popular dislike of the new
taxes.[48] Congregational ministers participated heavily in the verbal
bombardment both from the pulpit and in the press.[49]

Aroused by the exhortations of their leaders the people began
to take more direct action. In the last week of August Ingersoll
was hung in effigy in the eastern towns of New London, Norwich,
Lebanon, and Windham.[50] "People of all Professions" attended the
ceremonies in New London, with "even the Children crying—
'There hangs a Traitor, there's an Enemy to his Country.'"[51] A
fiery address helped to celebrate the occasion for the New Lon-
doners.[52] And in Windham the crowd hung the effigy of the
stampmaster between heaven and earth "as an Emblem of his
being fit for neither."[53]

Conservatives morosely wondered what the outcome of all this
"perfect Frenzy" would be. But the radicals, intent on inflaming
the people, had no such qualms about the results of their dramatic
protests.[54] In their own words "the British (no, the American)
Spirit of Liberty was aroused; it catched from Breast to Breast, it
ran; it flew thro' all the Colonies."[55]

In Connecticut this ardent spirit originally caught more people and flew more swiftly through the eastern towns. There dis-

contented elements had been churned up by the religious and economic movements of the previous decades.[56] And it was in these communities that violence against the Stamp Act first broke out, and the Sons of Liberty were initially organized.

Benjamin Gale, Killingworth's impetuous and unpredictable Old Light deputy, traced the evolution of the groups that were absorbed into the Sons of Liberty as follows:

> Several Factions wh. have subsisted in this Colony, originating with the N London Society—thence matamorphisd into the Faction for paper Emissions on Loan, thence into N.Light, into the Susquehannah and Delaware Factions,—into Orthodoxy— now into Stamp Duty.[57]

Each new issue, according to Gale, had swelled the ranks of the radical faction. Now with the Stamp Act as its enemy it had its biggest issue. The leaders of the Sons of Liberty were not humble men. Colonel Israel Putnam of Pomfret, John Durkee of Norwich and Hugh Ledlie of Windham were to direct the people in action. And behind them stood some of the most prominent figures in the colony, ministers, merchants, and magistrates, Stephen Johnson of Lyme, the Huntingtons of Norwich and Windham, Dyer of Windham, Griswold of Lyme, and Trumbull and Williams of Lebanon, all easterners.[58]

In the late summer of 1765 the radicals in the eastern towns marshalled their strength and prepared to make certain that the hated stamps would never be used in Connecticut. In Windham they forced Nathaniel Wales, who had been appointed stamp distributor for the town, to reject the position, which he did in rather unseemly haste.[59] They burned Ingersoll in effigy and made ready to coerce him in the flesh. The stampmaster appealed to the angry townsmen not to condemn him without a hearing, explained his motives in assuming the job, and promised not to exercise the duties of his office if the people, speaking through the voice of the legislature, wanted it that way.[60]

The General Assembly was not scheduled to meet until the

regular October session, but the people were angry and impatient. Jeremiah Miller described them as being "put into . . . a rage against the poor Governr for not calling the Assembly" in extra session.[61] Councillor Jonathan Trumbull, speaking for several towns in eastern Connecticut, pointedly informed Governor Fitch that "the people in this part of the Colony, are very Jealous for their Liberties; and Desire That The most Vigorous Exertions be made for the Repeal of" the Stamp Act. He further advised the governor that it was their wish that a special meeting of the General Assembly be held immediately so that delegates could be appointed to the intercolonial congress scheduled to meet in New York.[62] Newspaper articles also urged the extra meeting.[63] And in a note of expectation one of them predicted the obvious: "A little Time will bring Matters to a Crisis and oblige every Man to take his Side. We shall then see Who is Who."[64] Popular pressure, and not the desire to find out "Who is Who," finally forced Governor Fitch to call the Assembly into special session.[65]

Trouble, however, was on its way from the eastern towns. Extremists were not willing to wait for the slow machinery of protest to start moving; they were determined to give it several strong shoves of their own. To one conservative the radicals seemed to have a "Flashy Zeal that is only attended with Noise and Smoke."[66] But Jared Ingersoll was soon to learn that where there was smoke there was sure to be fire.

On his way to the General Assembly, which was to meet at Hartford on September 19, Ingersoll was stopped by a body of five hundred men who demanded that he immediately resign his position as Connecticut's stamp distributor. Before the incident was over the radicals had doubled their number.[67] Practically all of them had come from towns in Windham and New London Counties. When Ingersoll expostulated that it was not fair "that the counties of Windham and New-London should dictate to all the rest of the colony" the leaders of the crowd brusquely retorted that they had not come "to parly—here is a great many people waiting and you must resign."[68] The stampmaster could do nothing but accede to the wishes of the multitude. After he had given in he joined the jubilant radicals in some cheers for "liberty and Property" and then rode with them to Hartford where he read his resignation out in the open, within hearing distance of the building in which the legislators were meeting.[69]

Most of Connecticut's magistrates probably did not need this object lesson on what their policy toward the Stamp Act should be. And yet it is not likely that the lesson was wasted on them. Ingersoll, in a letter written to the Assembly the day before his collision with the eastern Liberty Boys, had urged the lawmakers "in this Day of Difficulty and Perplexity" not to be influenced by the "Rage of Men, not altogether acquainted perhaps, with the Nature and Extent of the Subject."[70] After the Ingersoll incident the legislators could not help but be influenced. On the same day that Ingersoll resigned the Assembly appointed Connecticut's delegates to the Stamp Act Congress.[71] Two days later the extraordinary session was adjourned.[72]

Only three weeks separated this special session from the regular fall Assembly.[73] Having succeeded in forcing the resignation of the stamp distributor and getting the colony to send representatives to the inter-colonial congress, the extremists made ready to control the regular session. They were not completely satisfied with Ingersoll's resignation, which a New Haven report noted had not been very "hearty and voluntary."[74] The Stamp Act, moreover, was still very much a law and was soon scheduled to go into effect. The radicals, therefore, continued to issue their bitter blasts against the hated act and its supporters.

Some were relatively moderate in their anonymous counsel and urged the people "to avoid violent proceedings if possible."[75] But others did not hesitate to give much more belligerent advice. They stridently called upon the people to rouse themselves and defend their liberties.[76] They even threw predictions of bloody revolution and "the loss of two millions of the best affected subjects" at the British.[77] And they made special and somewhat frantic appeals to the voters to elect only anti-stamp men for their representatives.[78]

Most of the freemen faithfully executed these instructions, for the October Assembly was dominated by anti-stamp men. Ezra Stiles, usually a keen observer, thought that "a considerable Part of both Houses" was moderate enough to prevent the adoption of special anti-Stamp Act resolutions.[79] Jared Ingersoll, however, found the new legislature much more radical than its May predecessor. In letters to Richard Jackson and Thomas Whately he wrote, "Our Assembly of last May, I am told, were moderate" but the recent "Confusions . . . occasioned a choice of new Members," about one-half of the lower house, with the new men being "generally such as were very warm against the Stamp Act."[80] Radical Windham, for example, chose the Rev. Ebenezer Devotion, the patriot pastor of a Congregational church, as its deputy. Stiles admitted this was "a very singular Instance."[81]

The new Assembly's chief business involved a consideration of the report of its delegates to the Stamp Act Congress and the question whether any additional resolutions against the act should be adopted. The radical composition of the legislature assured its approval of the petitions drawn up by the New York Congress to the King, Lords, and Commons. And Connecticut's agent was instructed to support these views with his "utmost influence, skill and ability."[82]

But this was not sufficient, for the Assembly also proceeded to adopt its own resolutions condemning the Stamp Act as a violation of Connecticut's charter and destructive of the colony's "great and inestimable liberties and priviledges."[83] Stiles had predicted that Connecticut's remonstrance would be couched in less violent language than those of some other colonies, "with a little more softness of Expression, with more Respectfulness to the Crown and Parliament."[84] But, although the Yankee lawmakers professed to be loyal, their resolutions and the accompanying letter of instructions to the colony's agent categorically declared that they could never recede from their principles, and would never be induced willingly to part with them. And they warned the mother country of "the fatal consequences, both to Great Britain and her Colonies, which must flow from this exercise of parliamentary power."[85]

Ingersoll probably was not the only one who felt that the British would call such doctrines "notions of independence."[86] In the lower house of the legislature, however, only five deputies refused to support the resolution condemning the Stamp Act while eighty-five voted for it.[87] The Council approved it by a majority of voices.[88]

The Stamp Act became effective on November 1. As that day approached when, according to the lament of a patriot poet, "Liberty was doom'd to brethe her last,"[89] Connecticut's conservative governor, Thomas Fitch, was forced to make the most crucial decision of his life. The Stamp Act required him to take an oath to carry out its provisions. But although under pressure from the radicals he had delayed acting until the very last moment.

Fitch, reputedly Connecticut's most brilliant lawyer, had been the colony's chief magistrate for a decade.[90] He had been called upon in 1764 to help draw up Connecticut's protest against the Stamp Act. In fact, according to Stiles, the governor was the first in the colony to sound the "alarm about the Stamps."[91] He had repeatedly and effectively explained to the colony's agent the reasons for Connecticut's opposition to the act, both before and after the new taxes were passed. Conservative by nature and training, however, he instinctively supported established institutions and shrank from the implications of the radical arguments. He hated strife and disunity. The very same year that he was to commit political suicide by defying the radicals he published a religious pamphlet in which he deplored the "divisions, contentions, uncharitableness, and the necessary concomitants of such evils" which had made "the churches of this colony crumble into parties and become seats of dispute and controversy."[92] Now the colony was being torn by new divisions and contentions, and the governor realized that whichever way he turned he would become the object of an uncharitable criticism.

That criticism was not slow in coming. In September Fitch had antagonized the radicals by condemning their forceful coercion of Ingersoll.[93] And in view of the people's violent attacks, both verbal and otherwise, upon the British authorities, the governor had advised Connecticut's delegates to the Stamp Act Congress to try to emphasize that those "illegal steps" were really nothing more than "the excursions of the Giddy Populace," and that actually, the "Principal Authority" in the colonies disapproved of the people's "wild and unjustifiable Measures."[94] The governor's conservative suggestions were apparently ignored, but they did not add to his popularity. At the October session of the legislature Fitch had irritated the extremists even more by not being "forward in the Resolves." He did just the opposite, for he criticized the people's "public spirit" and, according to Stiles, declared rather rashly that "the Act must go down, that *forty* men regulars could guard the Stamp papers, and that the American conduct would bring violent measures from home, and particularly the loss of Charter."[95]

The governor had been counselled to move with "Caution, Coolness . . . and . . . Vigor."[96] But he must have known that if he took the oath to support the Stamp Act the radicals would never accept that step with similar coolness and moderation.[97] Nevertheless, after attempting to get the advice of others, Fitch made up his mind to uphold the law.[98] Leverett Hubbard described what took place when the governor called the councillors together to administer the oath to him: "A long debate ensued, finally the Gentlemen on the east Side the River refused, and withdrew. Esqr Sheldon twisted and restled about but finally staid in the Council chamber: the Oath was administered by Esqrs Silliman, Hamblin [sic], Chester, and Hall."[99]

Why did the governor and the four councillors choose to conform to the letter of the law when they knew that their decision defied the popular will? Fitch later explained his conduct to the people. His apology reflected the workings of the conservative mind in this crisis.

Fitch agreed with most of the colonists that the Stamp Act was probably an infringement of their "Equal Rights and Equal Priviledges." He persisted in that belief even after he took the oath to uphold the act.[100] But it was a law, and as such it must be obeyed no matter how distasteful and repugnant it was to American sensibilities. According to Fitch the governor and councillors were bound by "Allegiance . . . Office, and . . . Agreement or Contract, by accepting their Offices . . . to yield to the Requirements of the King and Parliament."[101] To defy these authorities, the governor argued, would in the case of Connecticut, where the provincial officials were chosen by the people, have jeopardized the colony's right to govern itself, "and then the whole Charter would be at once struck up."[102] Fitch also pointed out that failure to obey the law would have subjected him to the possible punishment of a thousand-pound fine and removal from office.[103]

The governor's conservative, legalistic approach to the question would probably have embroiled him in more serious difficulties with the radicals had not the Windham and New London extremists forced Ingersoll's resignation. For Fitch seems to have planned a stubborn defense of the stampmaster had Ingersoll decided to distribute the stamps.[104] The governor persistently claimed, however, that what he had done was for Connecticut's best interests. But the latter were not his only interests, for Fitch admitted that he and the councillors who went along with him "were moved from Principles of Loyalty to the King, from a serious and tender Concern for the Privileges of the Colony; a conscientious Regard to the solemn Obligations of their Office-Oaths; and a just Value for their own Interest, Reputation, and Usefulness in Life."[105]

There were some—Ingersoll described them as many—who

agreed with Fitch that the governor and the four councillors deserved "the Applause of all who desire the Safety of the Privileges of the Colony."[106] But even the ex-stampmaster admitted "their Voice is drowned amidst the general Cry." That cry was loudest in the eastern towns where the radicals were "universally displeased," as Dyer mildly put it, by the governor's submission.[107]

The continued economic depression further soured the people's temper. If better times had accompanied the year 1765, the course of events might have been somewhat different. As it was, however, fears over the political and economic consequences of the Stamp Act were aggravated by Connecticut's economic troubles: an extreme shortage of money, trade in the doldrums, and merchants and farmers heavily in debt.

Throughout the spring, summer, and fall months of 1765, when the colony's "darling liberty" was thought to be in greatest danger, loud and numerous complaints about the bad times were heard.[108] In March the *Courant* had reported the situation "melancholly; foreign trade embarrased; our private debts many, and the cries of the needy continually increasing."[109] And in May, Jedidiah Huntington, scanning the economic horizon, saw "little Business —Less Money—" while the Hartford newspaper wailed that the current epidemic complaint was "THERE IS NO MONEY."[110]

The fall and winter months went by with no change in the economic picture. It was in November, a few days after Governor Fitch had taken the oath to obey the Stamp Act, that Ingersoll informed Connecticut's agent that the colonists were eighty thousand pounds in arrears on their taxes.[111] The following month Governor Fitch described Connecticut's commerce "at a very low Ebb through the Poverty of the People the great Scarcity of Money etc." And a week and a half later a prominent merchant was forced to return to his English dealers over three hundred pounds sterling worth of goods because he had found it impossible to dispose of them to the money-starved colonists.[112]

The discouragement and despair induced by these conditions

heightened popular fears and helped whip up mass discontent. Caution probably explained why the *Courant* stopped publication during November, the first month stamps were required under the law. But the opposition of the people to stamps and stamp officers generally was not restrained by any such scruple. Ingersoll reported the colony "in a great ferment," and so it was.[113] The Sons of Liberty were ready and eager to do much more than "mourn, lament and sigh, and hope, and pray."[114] Middletown greeted November 1 with muffled church bells tolling all day, flags at half mast, numerous toasts to "Liberty Property and no Stamps," a mock play, and huge bonfire.[115] In New Haven on the same day "a large number of the lower sort of people" ceremoniously buried a copy of the Stamp Act and raised the King's flag over the grave,[116] and from Hartford came news that an effigy of the governor had accompanied the act to its mock resting place.[117]

Popular hostility to the tax was so great that Ingersoll doubted whether it was possible for it to increase.[118] Yet increase it did. Fearing what the mob might do if it were provoked further, both he and the governor recommended that Connecticut's stamps be held in New York.[119] In New London the "respectable Populace" forced Duncan Stewart, the port collector, to clear ships from the town harbor on unstamped paper. Advised that he might be sued for property damage if he refused, and that he stood little chance of being successful in the local courts, Stewart gave in. He too had carefully learned the lesson on prudence from the "many extraordinary Outrages committed by the populace."[120] Throughout eastern Connecticut the people demanded that the courts and lawyers immediately resume their business and ignore the legal requirements about the use of stamps.[121]

In New Haven County, however, the courts remained closed. Hoping to confine the opposition within legal bounds, the New Haven town authorities refused to do anything requiring the use of stamped paper, despite a victory of the radicals who got an overwhelming majority of the votes at a town meeting, February

3, 1766, for a resolution requesting the officials to carry on as usual.[122]

Although this motive was temporarily realized in New Haven the colony's popular reaction was not characterized by any respect for caution. In the fall and winter months of 1765-66 self-constituted radical groups, ignoring the provincial and town governments, met, drew up lengthy resolutions, and threatened and coerced their enemies, both real and fancied. The regular authorities either aided them or stood by, practically helpless, unable to control the course of events. By the latter months of 1765 the force of the radical movement had gained such momentum that to the conservatives it seemed about to destroy the colony's venerable political institutions.

These fears were not entirely groundless. Connecticut did show some rather unsteady and near-revolutionary symptoms. Stiles reported in October that more than three-fourths of the men were "ready to take up Arms for their Liberties" with the "very Boys as well as the hardy Rustic . . . full of fire and at half a Word ready to fight."[123] The colony's leaders hoped to retain control of the situation by cautiously restraining the extremists. But Stiles' prayer that the legislature would successfully induce the people to show "cooler sentiments" went unanswered.[124] The previous month the mob that had forced Ingersoll to resign had defiantly flouted the authority of those legislators who had attempted to intercede with it on the stampmaster's behalf.[125] Some members of the Assembly had urged that body to intervene, but Ingersoll doubted whether it could have had any effect upon the mob.[126]

The governor was equally helpless. Even before Fitch took the oath to uphold the Stamp Act he had discovered that he was unable to control the radicals. When he intervened at the Ingersoll resignation one of the leaders of the crowd pointedly told him that this was "the cause of the people, and that they did not intend to take directions about it from any body."[127] Immediately after the Ingersoll affair the Assembly, fearing that an unbridled power in the hands of illegal bodies might destroy "all order and government," ordered the governor to issue a proclamation requiring local officers to suppress "riots, tumults and unlawful assemblies."[128] Fitch promptly issued the proclamation.[129] But it had little effect, for the official guardians of public order either were not inclined or were not able to enforce the law. To Ingersoll it seemed that "no one dares and few in power are disposed to punish any violences that are offered to the Authority of the Act; in short all the Springs of Government are broken and nothing but Anarchy and Confusion appear in prospect."[130]

During the late months of 1765 and the first few months of the following year the regular governments in town and colony were practically superseded by a new and unofficial authority. Policies were made at popular meetings organized and run by the Sons of Liberty. At these gatherings persons who normally did not have the right to vote under colonial law probably joined with admitted inhabitants and freemen to approve the plans of their radical leaders. When a decision was to be carried out, the people took matters into their own hands. At such times, when the radicals claimed that they were in the act of preserving their liberties, the conservatives saw nothing more than an irresponsible mob.

On November 11, 1765, representatives from several eastern towns met at Windham. They resolved to oppose the distribution of stamps "by all due and effectual means," and in order to preserve "union and liberty" they recommended that regular meetings be held and that a county organization be set up.[131] Eliphalet Dyer explained that these gatherings enabled the popular "Inspector Generals" to keep a "jealous bright and watchful eye" over the stamps. He was relieved to note that they did not seem to menace property or person.[132]

Only two days after Dyer had expressed these comfortable thoughts another meeting, held at New London, issued a most forceful warning to all and sundry in the colony not to "inculcate the Doctrine of passive Obedience or any other Doctrine tending to quiet the Minds of the People in a tame Submission." Ministers were advised not to hold these views in or out of the pulpit. And public officers were reminded that if they failed to behave properly they could "expect the Resentment of the People," whereas those who acted in accordance with the people's will could "depend on their Protection." [133]

These were no mere idle words. From the "eastern, uneasy part of the Colony" came delegations to "catechize" and threaten members of the Council and the governor himself. [134] Israel Putnam blandly advised Governor Fitch, according to a traditional tale, that if he did not permit his house to be searched for stamps, should these be sent to Connecticut, the building would "be levelled with the dust in five minutes." [135] Wallingford's Sons of Liberty ruled the Stamp Act unconstitutional and promised an all-out opposition "to the last extremity, even to take the field." [136] And Lyme's radicals violently berated those who dared criticize these meetings of the populace and praised the latter as having only "righteous intentions" and producing "salutary effects." [137]

Even the more conservative towns in western Connecticut were organized by the Liberty Boys and began to join their more radical eastern cohorts. In the middle of December Dyer correctly pointed out to William Samuel Johnson that "the fire is broke out in your part of the Country." [138] The "true" Sons of Liberty in Fairfield had hung and burned the usual effigies in November; and two months later they were warning their public officers, both high and low, not to submit in the "least Degree." [139] Stratford's Liberty organization admitted its lateness in joining the parade of protests, but promised that its members would venture their "Lives and Fortunes," even "to the last Extremity," to prevent the hated act from being enforced in Connecticut. [140] The resolutions of the Milford Sons of Liberty were equally patriotic; they castigated those who even insinuated that stamps might be used as "stupid, ignorant Apostates and no Friends to Liberty." [141]

These boastful and threatening resolutions were accompanied

by deeds which in ordinary times would have been quickly suppressed and severely punished by the law-abiding Connecticut Puritans. The Liberty Boys, for example, took it upon themselves to meddle with Ingersoll's mail.[142] Ingersoll surrendered to the wishes of the radicals in public but gave vent to his wrath in private. He exploded:

Were there ever times like these? any man has it in his power at this time by suggesting any ill natured thing about what he may suppose I have wrote . . . to Occasion a Deputation of a Comte from a Body of People consisting of not less than three or four thousd men, to come to me and tell me if I will satisfy 'em in the matter by letting that body of people see the Copies of my Letters it will be well—if I won't they cannot promise in what way they will see Cause to resent it.[143]

Pomfret's Sons of Liberty were more specific about the punishments they were prepared to hand out, predicting that their victims would experience the "Horrors of falling a defenceless Prey into the Hands of a free and enraged Populace."[144] Joseph Chew, under a heavy cloud of suspicion because he corresponded with Ingersoll, was watched closely by the Liberty Boys, which led him to comment sourly, "A fine Country of Liberty we live in."[145] Massachusetts' scholarly and very conservative magistrate, Thomas Hutchinson, was equally disgusted at the news from Connecticut, but he concluded that was what one had to contend with in a degenerate democracy, a "government of the Multitude."[146] When Hutchinson learned that Ingersoll's mail was being tampered with he remarked acidly, "The Guardians of Liberty have erected an Inquisition."[147] Even Samuel Gray, one of Windham's most respectable Whigs, became somewhat apprehensive at the possible consequences of such events. He admitted to William Samuel Johnson that he had planned to write something on the Stamp Act. "But the times are so high," Gray complained, "that I scarce dare think."[148]

The times were not appropriate for thinking. In Milford and New London angry radicals seized and burned some stamped paper that had come into the towns.[149] Flushed with their success, New London's Sons of Liberty turned their resentment against the Rogerenes, who had long been a painful thorn in the side of the Saints.[150] And in New Haven a mob, led by Benedict Arnold, seized an informer who had tattled about Arnold's smuggling activities, gave him a severe whipping, and ran him out of town.[151] New Haven's moderate citizens shuddered at all these signs of "Vice and Disorders" and wondered what would come next.[152] Even Joseph Trumbull confided to his father as the critical year of 1765 drew to a close, "It is dangerous to Write, or even Speak with Coolness now a days—whose Private Papers will next be demanded We can't Tell—hope these things may soon Subside—and that Order and regularity may Succeed the present Confusion."[153] In a prayerful amen to this sentiment the pastor of New Haven's First Society Church, the Rev. Chauncey Whittelsey, looked forward to the time when the "Rage of the Mobility" would be ended.[154]

These extraordinary and violent proceedings were not universally approved in Connecticut. Although the colony's opposition to the Stamp Act had a much broader popular basis than merely "the lower and more ignorant of the People,"[155] there were some among the "better people" who took a more restrained position.[156] According to Ingersoll these moderate and conservative subjects were "generally the same people who . . . were pretty much against all Acts of Force and Violence, and disposed to pay rather more Deference to Parliament than some others in the general Matter of the Stamp Act."[157]

Ingersoll did not mean to imply, however, that they wanted the tax. Very few, if any, in Connecticut ever considered the Stamp Act a desirable financial measure. It is true that in February 1766 Jonathan Mansfield of New Haven, who described himself "a Frend and Lover of Peas and good Order," openly praised the Stamp Act as harmless to the "Husbanman and Comon People."[158] But that was after the mobs and rioters had complicated the issue by upsetting domestic order as well as defying Parliamentary law. While the Stamp Act was still being considered in Parliament, conservatives as well as radicals had rallied against the proposed tax, seeing in it not only a heavy and undesirable economic levy but a blow to the colony's political privileges. Conservatives, such as Governor Fitch and Jared Ingersoll, had protested learnedly and forcefully against its adoption. When they failed, however, they thought it best to submit rather than "risque the Consequences of a non-Submission."[159]

Connecticut's Standing Order had always been a bulwark against social disorder, but now it seemed to be breaking before the storm of radical protests. The very year before the tumults and riots of 1765 and 1766 a Connecticut divine, speaking before the assembled magistrates and ministers on election day, had sharply distinguished between true patriotism and the false variety which he associated with too much zeal and enthusiasm. His audience had probably been in complete agreement with him when he had declared that

There are hypocrites and imposters, wild enthusiasts and frantic zealots in patriotism and politics, as well as in religion. Too often the restless spirit of disaffection and discontent,—the wild zeal of ambition and faction, or the ungovernable fury of sedition, treason and rebellion, assume the mask of patriotism, artfully mimic the air of public-spirit, and endeavour to obtrude themselves upon a world for a disinterested regard for the common happiness ... True public spirit ... is a prudent zeal for the public, chastized by reflection, calm steady and dispassionate in its operation.[160]

A year later, when the nature of true patriotism had become a more debatable subject, Connecticut's conservative freemen reiterated these principles; and in the turbulent months of 1765 and 1766 they were certain that they were witnessing living proofs of the good minister's homily. Those who were against the Stamp Act at any and all costs, "even unto blood," deprecated the use of violence, but at the same time condoned it as necessary for self defense.[161] Conservatives, however, were disgusted at the frequent show of force and were frightened by the seeming collapse of the colonial government. To them it was obvious that the mob and their leaders were false patriots.

Pleading for the re-establishment of public order, moderates and conservatives reminded their more hot-headed neighbors that Parliament was an august institution and would not act "idly and Wantonly merely to exercise Power." They deplored the popular pastime of calling the British ministers "Tyrants and Oppressors;" attacked what they called the lunatic expressions of "Sivil Inthusiasm;" and warned the colony that bonfires, mobbings and other frenzied manifestations of popular resentments were rash and impudent and might even invite military retaliation.[162] Quite obviously, these subjects feared the "brand of disloyalty and distraction." And because they valued their membership in the empire they were determined "to cast no contempt on its authority."[163]

Ezra Stiles was one of those who did not completely support the radicals at this time. Yale's future president had quickly seen the dangers inherent in the Stamp Act and had originally condemned the tax.[164] But he could not sanction the use of violence to oppose the law. His conservative comments about the radicals and their methods take a political slant that is surprising in view of his later fervent Whiggism.

Stiles confided to that high Tory, Lieutenant Governor Hutchinson of Massachusetts, that "In all parliamentary Resolutions respecting the colonies (except on Religion), so long as the Alternatives are *Submission* or *Civil War,* I shall not hesitate to chuse and declare for the *first,* till the consequences of the *latter* are less far less tremendous than the Effects of Oppression." He firmly asserted his pride in being an American, devoted to the liberties of the colony, but he promised he would "never be disloyal to my King, nor by violence oppose any public Ordinance in which the King has an Act."[165] Stiles further declared that he would remain a loyal subject even though Parliament should destroy the charter governments.[166]

The Puritan pastor did not relish the Connecticut radicals' ready resort to violence. As early as July Stiles had attempted to dissuade a visitor from his native province from "certain forceable Measures which he told me were meditated then."[167] He condemned the coercion of Ingersoll, and in October expressed the hope that Connecticut's Assembly would be able to moderate the people's eagerness to resist the Stamp Act "by force and violence," for he felt that these methods would "prove the Ruin of us, if the parlt are resolute."[168] Stiles categorically denied in a letter to Franklin that he had advocated or approved of the violence of Rhode Island's radicals, and claimed that he had acted soberly as befitted "a Minister of Christ, and as an obedient and loyal Subject."[169] Any story to the contrary the Puritan minister attributed to Anglican malice against the Presbyterians.[170]

Other moderate Whigs also refused to "run the extravagant Length of a giddy and distracted mob."[171] Joseph Trumbull professed to be able to understand how the pulling down of houses might be explained away as the result of "Sudden Passion, Liquor etc," but he could not comprehend how private property could be attacked and "Rested from a Man in Cool Blood." "Good Heavens," he nervously exclaimed, "where will these things End?"[172] Roger Sherman was as distressed as young Trumbull by what seemed to be a threatened dissolution of orderly government.[173] And Samuel Gray, upset about the trend toward mob rule, promised to see that the "authoritative part" in Windham would exert itself to preserve public order.[174] All these hostile reactions to popular violence were neatly summarized by Seth Pomeroy Jr., who declared that the leadership of the legislature ought not to be surrendered to mobs.[175]

Concern over the state of public disorder was the subject of some warning comments in the election sermon of 1766, the theme of worried articles in the press, and was even echoed in the sober resolutions of town meetings. Although the minister who preached the sermon asserted that Connecticut would never submit to slavery, he also reminded his listeners that it was necessary to obey authority "so long as the design of government is inviolate," and to maintain "the honour and authority of the King, Lords and Commons . . . by all lawful means."[176] Conservative spokesmen even dragged in Cicero to help prove the proposition that a degenerate popular government was equivalent to tyranny.[177] And the revolution that would usher in that tyranny was inevitable, still another conservative warned, unless the methods of the radicals were quickly dropped.[178] Evidently fearing such a revolution, the local authorities and prominent gentlemen in several conservative towns denounced the "Riotous Assemblys" of the people, the "routs and tumults," the threats to colonial officials, and the "growing Disorders, Violences, and Breaches of Law."[179]

The Anglican ministers in the colony and most of their parishioners loyally supported the mother country in the Stamp Act crisis.[180] The position taken by the Episcopal church undoubtedly tended to confirm the Congregational pastors in their belief that the Anglicans were not only attempting "to import episcopal tyranny and such superstition"[181] but were also plotting the colony's political downfall. On the other hand, Connecticut's venerable Anglican leader, the Rev. Samuel Johnson, thought it desirable to have the home authorities informed of the Anglicans' loyalty and political steadiness. His more cautious son did not agree with him, but practically all the Episcopal pastors in the colony did.[182]

Missionaries in Norwalk and Newtown advised the Secretary of the S.P.G. that where the Episcopal church was influential "rebellious outrages" were few or non-existent. But where the church was absent or its influence weak, the people were constantly "cabaling" and rather than submit to Parliament were ready to "spill the last drop of blood."[183] Five Anglican ministers warned their congregations "of the unreasonableness and wickedness of their taking the least part in any tumult or opposition to his Majesty's acts."[184] The Rev. Mr. Davies described his parishioners at New Milford as "peaceable and loyal" although great excitement raged all around. This he attributed to his constantly emphasizing in "public and private . . . the various obligations we are under of subjection and obedience to our rightful and gracious Sovereign."[185] To that high Tory, the Rev. Samuel Peters, the times seemed as full of anarchy and confusion as the terrible year 1648 had been, with "their high mightinesses," the people, running everything and threatening everybody who was not fully as hostile to the Stamp Act as they were.[186] Other ministers were not as vehement as Peters but they had the same thing to say. Connecticut's Anglicans were regularly described as faithful to the mother country, with the missionaries carrying on their political as well as their religious work despite "calumny and insults" and threats that their houses would be torn down over their heads.[187]

These differences, ranging from extreme radicalism through various forms of moderate opinion to the extreme conservative, were further crystallized in the election of 1766. The radicals proposed to purge the colonial government of every official who had been lukewarm in the battle against the Stamp Act or who had antagonized the extremists by his reluctance to follow the leadership of the Sons of Liberty. They were opposed by a coalition of moderates and conservatives. The latter sought to retain in office those few men who, in their view of things, had represented the forces of law and order and had upheld the unity of the empire against the menace of revolution.

The spearhead of the radicals' attack was directed against Governor Fitch, who had taken the oath to enforce the Stamp Act, and the four councillors who had administered the oath to the governor. The submission of these magistrates created an issue upon which all who sincerely feared for Connecticut's religious and political privileges were able to stand. However, within the large group of freemen that took this position on the imperial

question were factions that had originally come into being in disputes over local issues, the political New Lights and the backers of
the Susquehannah project. These factions had been grinding their
axes for some time. The election and its patriotic issue gave them
the opportunity to cut off the political heads of some of their old
opponents.

It was no accident that the radicals identified the Old Lights
with those who allegedly supported the Stamp Act. The charge
was by no means completely true, but it made good propaganda.
John Hubbard angrily complained that "among other fine Devices
to set People together by the ears a Man's religious Principles are
made the Test or shall I say rather badge of his political creed. An
Arminian and a Favourer of the Stamp Act signify the same
Man."[188] The proprietors of the Susquehannah Company had little
cause to support Fitch. They were therefore able to merge their
economic interests with their patriotism in the single project of
removing the incumbent governor for another who was likely to
be less of an obstacle to the company's venture than Fitch had
been.[189]

As early as the summer and fall of 1765 the radicals had threatened to end the political career of any colonial official who dared
to defy the people's will. Deputies knew that if they did not vote
properly they were likely to be declared enemies to their country,
be burned in effigy, and their political futures "stowed away with
the Stamp Officers."[190] And after Fitch took the Stamp Act oath
it was common knowledge that the extremists proposed a speedy
political death for all supporters of the act.[191] Two months later
the people's gloom had become so deep and their temper so "sow-
ered" that they were ready to condemn everyone who did not go
along with them "as Enemies to their Country and Betrayers of its
Liberties."[192]

It was to no avail that some moderates cautiously pointed out
the dangers of partisan political strife and identified those who
sought to prevent it with the really "intelligent, rational and deter-

mined Lovers of Liberty."[193] One conservative writer argued more bluntly. He too warned the colony about the upsetting effects of "Tumults" upon its political constitution and the harm that was caused when "self-designing Men, and Men of a hot enthusiastical Turn of Mind, are at the Head of Public Commotions." "Be Prudent," he pleaded, "Don't let blind Enthusiasm, or a low, mean, party-Spirit . . . sweep all before it." For, he reminded the colonists, nothing was more likely to destroy "the Well-being of Society, than Divisions, and create Jealousies, than Parties of Men combining, and forming Schemes of Oeconomy distinct from the settled Constitutions of the Country."[194]

This advice had little effect upon the radicals who had already decided to execute the sentence of political death upon Fitch and the four councillors.[195] In 1755 Benjamin Gale had predicted that eastern Connecticut would in time seize control of the governorship and Council.[196] Ten years later the eastern radicals tried hard to realize this prophecy, which made the choleric doctor more than unusually angry.

The radicals started to hatch their plot before the old year was out. The moderate William Samuel Johnson noted at the end of December that although the people in western Connecticut were against the governor and the four councillors they did not seem to have a plan to replace them. He was certain, however, and so told Eliphalet Dyer, that in the eastern counties where "you are more used to Politicks and more consistent in your Views" some more substantial scheme was taking shape. Johnson readily offered to cooperate with the radical easterners if "it be an eligible Plan."[197]

But the radicals had not yet completed all their preparations. Two weeks after Johnson wrote this letter, on January 13, 1766, representatives of the "respectable Populace" of New London County met in the town of Lyme. One of the radical leaders, Major Durkee, was appointed to correspond with the Sons of Liberty in the other colonies, and the delegates let it be known that they wanted the affairs of state and commerce resumed without the use of stamps.[198] Their business did not end here. According to Gale the more important purpose of the meeting was the selection of candidates "who they conceive will serve their Turn." Gale thought that the final choices were not made at this meeting, but that did not deter him from denouncing its attempt as the spawn of "Rage and Folly."[199] Rumors that the Sons of Liberty were plotting wholesale changes in the government rapidly spread through the colony. In the face of these persistent reports, the Litchfield County Sons of Liberty denied, in February 1766, that they planned to alter the composition of the Assembly.[200]

If the Litchfield Sons then had no such intentions, they, and their associates in the other parts of the colony, soon changed their minds. On March 25 the Sons of Liberty held a colony-wide meeting in Hartford. Delegates "from a great Majority of Towns" were present. They elected William Pitkin Jr., son of the deputy-governor, clerk of the meeting. Formal expressions of loyalty to the King and esteem and respect for the British constitution were adopted, after which the delegates quickly approved Connecticut's resolutions of October 1765 against the Stamp Act, applauded the spirit of liberty in the other provinces, and indicated their desire to establish a regular correspondence with the Sons of Liberty in those provinces. To this end they set up a committee of correspondence for the Connecticut Liberty organization. This concluded the more formal items on the agenda.

When the more important business on hand came up, the spectators were asked to leave. Someone thereupon inquired as to the real purpose of the meeting. It was then made clear that the engineers of the convention intended to change some of the colony's magistrates. To guarantee that this would be done properly they proposed to give the freemen "a Lead" as to how they were to vote at the coming election. Some delegates balked at these doings. They maintained that the meeting had not originally been called for this purpose, that they were uninstructed on the matter, that such interference in the colonial elections would constitute an evil precedent, create factions, and in any case was illegal. Their protests were futile.

On the following day the convention was reorganized on a county basis and the desired candidates for governor and deputy-governor were agreed upon. Again there was some opposition to the procedure, this time from the Litchfield and Hartford County representatives. The reluctance of these delegates to accept the entire radical program resulted in the convention agreeing that it would not be "prudent to make too great an Alteration in the Body Politick at once." [201]

Despite this last disclaimer it became known that the Sons of Liberty had completed their plans to bring about a "great change in the Civil ministry of this Colony." [202] Even among the Liberty Boys some hesitated to be pulled along by the unbridled leadership of the eastern radicals. But the delegates from Windham and New London Counties who, it was noted, "more generally attended [the convention] than any other Part of the Government," dominated the proceedings at Hartford. [203] Abel Stiles, who was aware of the plot but who was "not one of the Schemers," looked to time to "show either the Bene or the male" of the plan. [204] The radicals, however, had no doubts about the wisdom of their work.

The minister who preached the election sermon in 1766 urged that no change mar the religious *status quo,* but emphasized the need for "peculiar care . . . in the appointment of executive authority." He prayed that the successful candidates for governor and Council would "be cordial friends to *Christ and his Church, and patriots to the republick."* [205] Most of the freemen evidently did not consider Fitch and Councillors Silliman, Chester, Hall and Hamlin sufficiently strong "patriots to the republick," for they elected Deputy-Governor William Pitkin to the chief magistracy in the place of Fitch, ousted the four councillors from their offices, and picked Jonathan Trumbull, merchant and Susquehannah Company proprietor, for their new deputy-governor. [206] One of the more surprising results of the election was the elevation of William

Samuel Johnson to the Council. Johnson had apparently been satisfied by the plan of the eastern radicals and had cooperated with them. And, in due course, Eliphalet Dyer's prediction, made as early as December 8, 1765, that Johnson would become a councillor was fulfilled.[207] Johnson, a cautious, moderate Whig became the first Anglican to sit in the Council.[208]

Pitkin, of course, got the votes of the more radical freemen in the eastern counties while in the western towns his totals were increased by the "New Light Interest."[209] The political rebuke administered to Fitch and the four councillors was not sanctioned by a great part of the colony,[210] but that part was now only a minority. Fitch's supporters, residing chiefly in the towns of western Connecticut, were the moderates and conservatives who had rejected mobbism and violence as methods of opposing the Stamp Act. In addition, he probably had the backing of many of the Anglicans who acknowledged a more uncompromising allegiance to the doctrine of Parliamentary supremacy.[211] Fitch's defeat distressed these conservative freemen who regarded themselves as the more "Steady thinking Sort."[212] The radicals, however, boasted of their "Spirit" in removing the conservative governor and his Assistants.[213]

On May 12, 1766, after twelve years of service as Connecticut's chief magistrate, Fitch said his good-byes and prepared to return to his native Norwalk. He was fully aware of the causes that had brought about his political setback. Yet, even after his defeat, he asserted that he had always been most "concerned for the Security of the Privileges of the Colony."[214] A voluntary escort of "gentlemen," including some deputies, accompanied Fitch on his departure. And a newspaper item went on to say, "All appeared deeply sensible of the inexpressible Loss the Colony hath sustained in the Removal of so wise and able a Pilot from the Helm, in so dark and difficult a Day, and at such a critical Conjuncture."[215]

Much of the sadness that Connecticut's moderates and conservatives felt at the political success of the radicals was probably dissipated by the general thrill of joy that ran through the colony

when it became known that the Stamp Act had been repealed.[216]
The legislature set aside a special day for public thanksgiving and
rejoicing.[217] Throughout the colony the people celebrated the good
news by ringing church bells and shooting off small arms and
cannon. In the evenings they made merry with displays of fire-
works, bonfires, and dancing.[218] Ministers congratulated themselves "upon the most eminent Deliverance ever granted to
America," [219] and towns vied with one another in expressing their
revived loyalty to the mother country.[220]

More sober thoughts, however, probably tempered the joy of
Connecticut's conservative freemen. For over twenty-five years
their once stable colony had been torn by bitter religious quarrels
which had been carried over into politics. And for a decade speculative land companies had been scheming to gain the support of
the provincial government for their ambitious projects, only to
drag the colony into what seemed a dangerous conflict with powerful colonial and imperial interests. The dreary gloom into which
these developments threw the conservatives must have been deepened by the knowledge that even before the Stamp Act Britain's
commercial policy was fast producing a rising resentment and
aversion among their neighbors.[221]

The Stamp Act had climaxed these dismal signs of colonial
and imperial disunity. Practically everyone in the colony had
agreed that the law was bad, a menace to Connecticut's political
and religious privileges.[222] But the explosive vehemence with
which the supposedly steady colonists had reacted to the measure
startled and frightened Connecticut's more moderate freemen.

They had witnessed turmoils such as had not occurred even
in the days of Governor Andros, mob violence, illegal political
meetings, and a reckless defiance of the legislature and governor.[223]
They had read newspapers and pamphlets and had listened to
orators boldly prophesy the possible dissolution of the empire and
civil war.[224] And finally, they had seen the governor, a conservative
and tried magistrate, and his equally conservative councillors fail

to be re-elected, an extremely unusual incident in itself in Connecticut, and replaced by officials of more radical tendencies.

Shortly after the exciting events of 1765 and 1766 one of these more conservative freemen predicted that "The Stamp Act has laid the foundations for America being an Independent State," and, he grimly added, the years to follow would be "a Period of Slaughter and Blood."[225] History proved Benjamin Gale a good prophet.

CHAPTER FOUR

Taxes and Trade

->>>->>>->>>->>>->>>->>>->>>->>>->>>->>>->>>-><-<<<-<<<-<<<-<<<-<<<-<<<-<<<-<<<-<<<-<<<-<<<-

->>>->>>-<<<-<<<-

*T*HE REPEAL of the Stamp Act and the political victory of the radicals in the election of 1766 did not inaugurate the return to a lasting peace either within the colony or in its relations with Great Britain. Deep differences separated Connecticut's radical and conservative factions. And the effect of new imperial policies and legislation in the next several years tended to perpetuate and harden those differences.

It was not easy for some of Connecticut's Yankees to return to peaceful ways after the violent demonstrations of 1765 and 1766. In June 1766 debtor farmers in Wallingford threateningly informed the County Court that they were opposed to summer sessions, and brazenly told the judges that it was not safe for them to carry their "Breath in the Nostrils of the People." Conservative Whigs who first denounced the boldness as the work of "some selfish Sons of Slavery" subsequently admitted it to be the product of their own extremists. They entreated their more radical associates to note the "Difference between Liberty and Licentiousness." But when that failed some of the Wallingford farmers were brought to trial.[1]

A similar radical spirit permeated the resolutions of the Windham town meeting, September 9, 1766, which drew up instructions for the town's representatives in the General Assembly. The people advised their deputies that they favored a relaxation of the debt laws, were opposed to the monopolizing of public offices, wanted the debates in the colonial legislature to be open and public as they were in Commons, and were concerned about the preservation of their liberties.[2]

Connecticut's liberties were the concern of all the eastern radicals and of the officials whom they had helped to put into office. The General Assembly and Governor Pitkin submitted formal addresses of loyalty to the King and his ministers in the summer of 1766, in which they described Connecticut's connection with the empire as the cause of "the Safety and Hapiness of this Country," and spoke grandly of the "indissoluble Union . . . between Great Britain and her Colonies."[3] Behind this loyal exterior, however, there was a noticeable feeling of unrest about Connecticut's future relations with the mother country. The Sons of Liberty did not forget the events of the previous year.[4] Nor was every Yankee willing to admit that Parliament had a sovereign right over the colonies.[5] As the year 1766 came to an end, an observant Anglican minister warned that while the people's turbulent spirit seemed to be abating, it was "only under cover for the present."[6]

News from England did not help to quiet the restiveness of the radicals. In the summer of 1766 an Order in Council revived an appeal of the Mohegan Indians against the holders of lands in the eastern towns of New London, Lyme, Colchester, and Hebron. The legislature immediately appointed a special agent, the politically moderate and very able lawyer William Samuel Johnson, to defend Connecticut's interests, but it could not prevent a new gloom from spreading over the colony.[7]

The gloom was deepened by the rumors of English policy and impending legislation affecting America. Richard Jackson, Connecticut's regular agent, repeatedly warned the Yankee magistrates of the ill-will and hostility against the chartered provinces which he said existed both in England and America.[8] The danger that Jackson wrote about seemed to come closer when General Gage asked the colony to arrange for the quartering of some of his troops. A special session of the General Assembly, January 1767, however, agreed to make provisions to billet the soldiers. This provoked at least one Congregational pastor to predict worriedly that now "The Wedge has entered . . . Glut upon Glut" might be expected.[9]

The anticipated calamity did not follow immediately. In fact, Connecticut's special agent, William Samuel Johnson, at first found no particular animosity against the colony in England. But he concurred with Jackson that Connecticut's privileges were menaced by proposed British measures affecting "the universal liberties of America." Johnson, however, soon began to report more ominous incidents. And in one of these the Secretary of State for the Colonies, Lord Hillsborough, made it clear that he had little affection for Connecticut's traditional powers of self-government.[10]

Johnson was not in England long before he realized that Parliament was determined to assert its supremacy. This boded ill for a colony that had "so many and so valuable privileges to lose," and he therefore conservatively recommended that Connecticut be especially prudent and cautious.[11]

But would it always be possible to confine the colony's course within these discreet limits? Governor Pitkin probably expressed the views of many Connecticut minds on this question in a letter acknowledging the receipt of some gloomy and discouraging tidings from England. "The Americans," Pitkin wrote to Johnson, "have been firmly attached to Great Britain; nothing, I trust, but severity will Dissolve the Union."[12] Colonial prudence and caution, then, might not always be adequate; even at this time, Connecticut's chief magistrate did not exclude revolution as a possible result of America's reaction to the British imperial program.

The Yankee farmers and merchants found the economic aspects of that program almost as distasteful as the Stamp Act had been. For although the financial condition of the colonial government was generally good, thanks to British aid, and much better than its magistrates pretended it to be,[13] Connecticut's taxpayers were unwilling and unable to assume any additional economic burdens imposed upon them by Parliament.[14]

Connecticut's fiscal condition may have been fundamentally sound, but the same was not true of the finances of many of its inhabitants. Numerous merchants and farmers would have disagreed with the Rev. John Devotion's critical comment that commonly heard complaints of "Poverty and bad Times" were due only to "Luxury and Pride."[15] Governor Pitkin claimed early in 1767 that land values had depreciated almost 50 per cent since the last war. And the general cry from the merchants echoed the strain of the past few years: "Little Trade and less money."[16] In Stratford even the well-to-do Samuel Johnson found it extremely difficult "to get in money." Others, he reported, were "much drove in these hard times."[17]

Debts weighed heavily on many business men, both prominent and obscure.[18] Deputy Governor Jonathan Trumbull found that burden so difficult to carry that he suggested the desirability of having a colonial paper currency "under due restraints." This, he believed, would relieve the hard pressed Connecticut merchant who found it impossible to meet his bills because of the "great Scarcity of Money or Bills and the want of a Circulating Medium."[19] Apologetically, Trumbull explained to his own creditors that he was unable to meet his obligations, partly because cash was "very scarce," so much so "that it is almost impossible to collect it for outstanding debts, or by sale of lands."[20] Reports of bankruptcies regularly appeared in the press in 1767.[21] And a year later a London merchant was advised against doing business with the colony after his informant had learned that the merchants in Connecticut's two most important ports, New London and New Haven, were "mortgaged to the full to the Bostonians and New Yorkers."[22]

Connecticut's generally poor industrial and commercial position aggravated the difficulties arising from the shortage of money. Only small amounts of manufactured goods were produced for sale.[23] A few mills turned out some iron and steel, but there did not seem to be much possibility of further expansion. And it is significant that even the anti-radical politician Benjamin Gale, who operated a steel furnace among his many other activities, feared the destructive effects of Parliamentary restrictions upon the industry.[24]

Nor had the peculiarly unfavorable organization of the colony's trade been altered for the better. Projects for establishing a thriving direct commerce between England and Connecticut never got far beyond the talking stage.[25] In his letters to the British authorities Governor Pitkin repeatedly stressed the importance of the trade with the foreign West Indies for Connecticut's prosperity. Relief along these lines, he promised, would "establish the Union and Interests of Great Britian and America upon a Basis that can never be shaken."[26] But while he urged that the bans on the commerce with the foreign islands be relaxed, the British planned a tighter enforcement of the existing laws.

Connecticut's merchants showed no greater regard for the restrictions established by the Molasses Act than did other New England traders. Between 1733 and 1750 no income under that measure was derived from the colony's trade with the foreign West Indies beyond prize money of ninety-nine pounds.[27] Smuggling had obviously become common and easy. When the British resolved to crush the practice they were met by the equal determination of the Connecticut merchants to continue their illicit trade.

Between 1766 and 1770 the customs officers found it difficult, if not practically impossible, to prevent the running of smuggled goods into the Puritan colony. They suspected that many of Connecticut's merchants, especially in the leading ports of New London and New Haven, actively opposed their work and were probably instrumental in organizing popular demonstrations against them.[28] It was only infrequently, however, that they were able to accumulate adequate legal evidence against the smugglers. They could not prove, for example, that New London's most prominent merchant, Nathaniel Shaw Jr., shipped smuggled sugar to New York under flaxseed labels.[29] But they were convinced, and so they wrote in their reports, that a great many goods were being run.[30]

The efforts of the customs officers to search for these goods were severely limited by their inability to secure writs of assistance from the colonial authorities.[31] When the Collector did manage to seize some smuggled goods he was likely to complain, as Duncan Stewart did in 1769, that "the Stores are broke open, the Goods taken away, and Wo to him that would make a Discovery."[32] The same popular elements who so efficiently sabotaged the work of the customs service also disciplined informers who dared to aid the British authorities. Instances of mob violence occurred in New London and New Haven. In the former town the tide-surveyor "thought it best to retire" after experiencing a sample of the mob's vengeance.[33] And when Nathan Smith tattled to a custom house agent on one of New Haven's prominent merchants he was given a generous dose of tar and feathers, the newspaper account noting, perhaps in justification of the treatment, that the whole affair was "conducted by the principal Merchants."[34]

It was the issue of taxation, raised by the Townshend duties, that prompted the colony to take its strongest stand against the mother country since the Stamp Act controversy. To the King's ministers the idea of producing a revenue by taxing certain provincial imports from England seemed to avoid the constitutional scruples of the colonists against internal taxes. But in Connecticut that same idea was regarded in another light.

The "Snare" in the new taxes was not too difficult to discover.[35] Even Benjamin Gale succinctly pointed out that it would be extremely unwise for Connecticut to buy British manufactures when in addition to the profits made by the English "Manufacturer and Merchant there will be added a Revenue to the Crown."[36] That this revenue would be established without colonial assent and would be used, as Jonathan Trumbull feared, for the

> Support of Tax gatherers and Their Numerous Train, for rendering Governors and Judges independent of the people for their Support, and for the Maintenance of Troops in the Colonies, to Overawe them to Compliance with things grievous and hard to be born

made it specially unpalatable to Connecticut's political taste.[37]

The colony, however, reacted somewhat slowly to the new danger.[38] The provincial government did not take any official action against the Townshend duties until the late spring of 1768.[39] But on June 10 of that year it vigorously petitioned the King for relief against the new taxes, which it attacked as violating the colony's charter-given privileges and reducing its people to free subjects only in name.[40]

Similar sentiments were expressed by the governor and deputy governor and other prominent citizens, all of whom would have concurred with the belief expressed by the Rev. William Hart that Connecticut "had too much to loose [sic] and too just a sense of its value to surrender all at the first demand."[41] Their opinions ominously hinted at the future disruption of the empire. Governor Pitkin's protest to Hillsborough denied that the people of Connecticut had any desire to be independent. But in another communication sent to Johnson the governor rather bluntly declared that "oppressive measures will break the coalition."[42] In a long letter to Connecticut's regular agent, Pitkin elaborately described the economic and political reasons for the colony's opposition to the Townshend duties. He asked Jackson, apropos of the effects the duties would have in the colony, "Is not mistrust and disaffection the natural result of restraint and oppression?"[43] To Johnson the governor made it clear that the only way Britain could preserve the empire was to see that "the colonies are treated friendly and indulged their freedom." And again there was the warning, "Bare naked power is an awful thing and very unamiable to a people that have been used to be free."[44]

Roger Sherman, Jonathan Trumbull and William Williams argued in the same vein.[45] They denied that Connecticut was disloyal or revolutionary. But as Williams put it, where its privileges were involved Connecticut would stand fast forever. And should the British force the issue, he asserted defiantly, "our Blood is more at their service than our Liberties."[46]

There was more than rhetoric in these protests. Although the colony did not organize its opposition to the Townshend acts rapidly enough to please the eastern radicals, it did not remain content with mere "Vapouring."[47] While its more zealous patriots exhorted the people to stop importing and consuming British goods and to make their own manufactured products they were also setting up a machinery of protest.[48]

Eastern towns led by New London, Norwich and Windham were again the first to act. Others shortly followed their example.[49] In May 1768 the Assembly indirectly supported the movement by levying a special 5 per cent duty upon goods brought into the colony by non-resident merchants.[50] By the fall of 1769 Connecticut's merchants had subscribed to the non-importation agreements of the New York, Philadelphia and Boston traders. And in October of the same year the lower house of the legislature applauded the merchants of Massachusetts, New York, Pennsylvania and Connecticut who, in the words of the deputies, were so nobly "sacrificing their private fortunes to the cause of liberty."[51] At the suggestion of the merchants of Hartford and some neighboring towns a meeting of the colony's trading interests was held in Middletown in February, 1770. This interesting gathering drew up a general non-importation program and organized a society to promote the "Arts, Agriculture, Manufactures, Trade and Commerce."[52]

Most of the colonists were as determined as the merchants "to be frugal and industrious."[53] In Stratford it was reported that the "People are getting more and more into manafacturing and bying Less and Less every Day n[or?] will they by aney that is imported at this time." Yale's seniors resolved to be graduated "wholly dressed in the Manufactures of our own Country," and William Williams happily testified to the prevailing competition as to "who shall run fastest into home manufactures."[54] Governor Pitkin noted that industry, frugality, and the domestic manufacturing of linens and woolens were on the increase; and less than a year later the new governor, Jonathan Trumbull, boasted that the Connecticut-made paper he wrote on was "better than British gilt."[55] A great economic reformation seemed to be in the making.

Connecticut's few Yankees who did not immediately take to the idea that their economic habits should be so "mightily reformed" received the special attention of popular committees of inspection.[56] On the whole these semi-inquisitional bodies did their job thoroughly and efficiently. Merchants who broke the non-importation agreements were penalized by having their names and "crimes" publicized in the press, were denounced in town meetings, and threatened with boycotts.[57] George Chapman's fears were probably somewhat exaggerated when he claimed that "the temper of the times" was such that "if a Purcill of Good was Sent to me from England I deare not Recive them for my house and them would certainly be Burnt Down."[58] But the people and their committees were not lightly defied. A rumor that Hezekiah Huntington had imported British goods was sufficient to harm him a good deal politically. William Williams thought that if the story had been true and had been more widely known "it would without doubt have proved fatal to his Station."[59]

Connecticut's radicals were bent on preserving their agreements not to take British goods, even after the non-importation movement in the major ports had begun to collapse with the partial repeal of the Townshend duties and the revival of normal inter-colonial competition.[60] William Williams was for "the People (the last and only Sure Recourse) to stand up and unite as one man" should the merchants desert the fight.[61] For a time this was not necessary, since Connecticut's merchants, upon learning of the New Yorkers' change of heart, vigorously denounced the defection, threatened the Yorkers with the loss of their Connecticut trade, and resolved in numerous meetings held during the summer of 1770 to refuse to import British goods until the tax on tea was repealed or the merchants throughout America generally agreed to resume their trade with England.[62] A short-lived but fervid newspaper appeal, directed at Connecticut's farmers, exhorted the people to hold out with the merchants in their determination not to import. But it failed when the less resolute traders began to trickle into the importing towns to buy the newly-received English wares.[63]

The trickle quickly became a flood as Connecticut's merchants sought to replenish their low stocks. Richard Law despondently noted how they were "flocking down" to New York. "It looks," he wrote to Johnson, "as tho the Country would again be filled with Goods and Deludged in Debt. Thus has the boasted Patriotism of our Merchts ben conquered by all powerfull Interest!" The radical politician Eliphalet Dyer also informed Johnson that the non-importation resolutions "after so much Noise are Vanished in Air and smoke" with "Vast Quantitys of goods Importing etc into every Colony."[64] And it amused George Chapman to find that the very merchants who a few short months back had violently scolded the New Yorkers for deserting the non-importation agreements were among the first to rush to New York for the now precious imports.[65]

The breakdown of the non-importation movement in the colony, with the people buying the once "forbidden fruit . . . greedily at almost any lay,"[66] coincided with the announcement

in October 1770 that the effort to stimulate the whale fisheries
had temporarily failed. And several months before, in May, British
pressure had forced the Assembly to repeal its 5 per cent tariff
on goods brought into the colony by non-resident merchants.[67]
Thus another attempt to reform Connecticut's economy ended
in dismal failure.

Despite loud complaints Connecticut quickly slipped back
into its former commercial habits. But the political lessons of the
past few years were not lost upon the province's ruling elders.
Both conservatives and radicals realized that continued differences
between Britain and her colonies were leading straight to a revolutionary civil war.

Speaking for the more radical leaders of the colonial aristocracy, Jonathan Trumbull, who was elected to the governorship
in the fall of 1769, reiterated what Pitkin and others had frequently maintained. "Mutual Interest alone can bind the Colonies
to the Mother Country," he wrote on one occasion. But "When
those interests are separated," he predicted, "each Side must
assuredly pursue their [*sic*] own." He bitterly denounced the
British officials whose job it was to enforce the acts of trade as
"dependent wretched sychophants and their detestable tools."
Changes in the old relationship between the colonies and England,
he bluntly warned, could not be made without the utmost danger.
The governor admitted it would be difficult "to break connections
with our Mother Country." But, he grimly added, "when she
strives to enslave us and turn all our labors basely to her own
emoluments without considering us as her own sons and free
born fellow subjects, the strictest union must be dissolved."[68]

Benjamin Gale, the eccentric conservative, had reached practically the same conclusion two years earlier. And the Rev. William
Hart, the Old Light minister at Saybrook, had confided to Stiles
in the summer of 1768, "We are in a strange, dangerous, unsettled
disposition meditating great changes in all respects, in America
and in Brittain. I suspect things are ripening for some great revo-

lution."[69] Four days after the shooting in Boston, March 5, 1770, Stiles predicted "that a general civil War will take place in the Colonies before two Generations are passed."[70]

Discerning and thoughtful men agreed that a continuation of the differences between the provinces and the mother country could end only in revolution. But they did not regard the political trend with the same emotions. Jonathan Trumbull was right when he denied "that the Oposition to Ministerial Measures is owing to a few hot headed Faction men."[71] In protesting against the Townshend measures the colony displayed greater harmony than it had shown in the bitter debate over the Stamp Act. Fitch and the four councillors who had supported him had antagonized the radicals. But Pitkin and Trumbull generally expressed their political and economic philosophy. Conservative and radical merchants also joined, at least temporarily, in united protest against the Townshend taxes and the acts of trade.[72] Nevertheless, the implications in Trumbull's assertion that there was complete agreement among the colony's inhabitants was more of a hope than a reality.

The fact that Connecticut initially reacted somewhat slowly to the Townshend measures might be attributed, in part, to its commercial backwardness and its customary prudence.[73] And that the non-importation agreements ultimately broke down was inevitable, according to one contemporary rationalization, because every merchant could not be expected to be sufficiently patriotic to bankrupt himself for a political principle.[74] More than opportunist considerations, however, are needed to explain the position of Connecticut's conservative minority during these years.

This minority had no special affection for the new economic restrictions; but it was not prepared to follow the colony's radical leaders in their opposition to Parliament. Perhaps the more conservative freemen did not talk about liberty as much as the extremists did, but they claimed to prize it as dearly. They were not always certain, however, that the people properly understood the nature of the liberty they were striving to preserve.[75]

Connecticut's conservatives shuddered when they heard angry radicals argue in the spring of 1768 that the British Parliament had as little jurisdiction over the colonies as the Parlement of Paris.[76] They could not see how the provincial cause was being the better preserved by such rash challenges to the authority of the mother country. And upon hearing some similarly defiant comments several months later, the ex-councillor, Ebenezer Silliman, morosely observed that "Some among us seem to be afraid of the Consequences, but others seem to be carried above fear."[77]

Those whom Silliman had implied were becoming irresponsible undoubtedly agreed with William Williams that the mother country was the only one basically at fault;[78] but the conservatives would have divided the blame. Although they concurred with the radicals in condemning the new taxes and the more stringent enforcement of the acts of trade they were also worried about some of the measures that the "maddened" colonists were bringing to bear against those laws. It was in that spirit that Joseph Chew criticized both the British and colonial extremists. He favored "a steady, manly behavior and Constant and Decent Representation to the Crown and parliment." He recoiled at the prospect of seeing "the Nation . . . go to Destruction" and hoped, therefore, that the British would adopt "Conciliatory measures." But, according to Chew, the colonists also had responsibilities for preserving the empire, and these were not compatible with belligerent resolutions or violence.[79]

The Rev. John Devotion and John Hubbard, Ezra Stiles' father-in-law and a leading New Haven freeman, also thought that too much loose talk was likely to provoke retaliation from abroad.[80] Hubbard went further. He felt that there was a "proper Decorum due to Superiors" and that it was not "canceled by their ill Behaviour or even Malice." To the Yankee extremists who would have dissented rather strongly from this doctrine Hubbard would have preached, *It is not meet to say to Princes ye are wicked.*"[81] And though it appeared to Benjamin Gale, that doughty enemy of the Sons of Liberty, that "the desolution of our Charter privilidges" was not far off, he promised that he would not "spill one single drop of Blood in this Controversy with the Parent State."[82]

The political catechism of the established church between 1767 and 1770 was naturally Whiggish, but it was not strikingly revolutionary. The Rev. Edward Eells' election sermon in 1767 was almost exclusively devoted to the religious theme implicit in its title.[83] His successors gave greater attention to the political questions of the day, emphasizing in the Puritan tradition the rights of the people and the duties of rulers.[84] But what they said could not always have encouraged the extreme radicals.

Although the ministers invariably invoked the sanction of natural rights some of them also accepted the Hobbesian concept of human nature and with it the political implication of strong government.[85] In what probably was a reference to both provincial and imperial political developments, one pastor denounced those who were constantly murmuring and complaining, the "*factious* and *contentious disobedient* and *rebellious*." He urged, instead, that "all study to be thankful and quiet, *mind our own business, and follow the things that make for peace; rendering honor to whom honor, and tribute to whom tribute is due.*"[86] The ministers also praised the British constitution and protested Connecticut's loyalty to it. And they hoped and prayed that the blessings that the colony had derived from the good administration of that constitution, especially since the Glorious Revolution, would be continued.[87]

Connecticut's Anglicans were deeply skeptical of the sincerity of these protestations of loyalty. While the Episcopal rectors continued to report that they were successfully inculcating upon their congregations "the great duty of obedience and subjection to the Government,"[88] they had less complimentary things to say about Connecticut's Puritans.

From Newtown in western Connecticut the Rev. Mr. Beach

happily informed the S.P.G. that "the Church People in these parts are the best affected towards the Government of Great Britain and the more zealous Churchmen they are by so much the stronger affection they discover for King and Parliament."[89] But the only interest that the Rev. Samuel Peters was able to find in and around Hebron in 1768 was "the Glorious idea of an Oliverian Revolution or something nigh as bad." And two years later the erratic Anglican minister hoped he might escape from the land of the Sons of Liberty "who imagine his Sacred Majesty is capable of rebellion against his Supreme subjects in America."[90] Godfrey Malbone, a wealthy churchman who had recently moved to eastern Connecticut, also advised the home authorities that Connecticut's Puritans would, despite "their much vaunted loyalty very gladly exchange monarchy for a republic, so very compatible with their religious system."[91]

William Samuel Johnson probably best expressed the cautious philosophy of Connecticut's moderates.[92] As a liberal conservative, or a conservative Whig, his political position was to the left of most of his Anglican co-religionists in the colony. But Johnson also stood somewhat to the right of the radical Whigs with whom his political fortunes were then linked.

Between 1767 and 1771 Johnson represented his native colony in England. There he ably defended Connecticut's interests to the general satisfaction of radicals and conservatives alike.[93] American rights, especially those of Connecticut, were as important to the learned Anglican lawyer from Stratford as they were to the eastern firebrands.[94] Indeed, his efforts on Connecticut's behalf were so vigorous that he became suspect in the eyes of administration supporters in England who thought he leaned more towards "the popular democratic scale than that of government."[95] Johnson's father, however, defended his son's viewpoint as "truly English," and denied that it was in any way similar to the "principles and practices" of the Sons of Liberty.[96]

Johnson's political philosophy lies somewhere in between these last statements. He was too good a lawyer not to recognize the logical necessity of a supreme political power, presumably to be lodged in Parliament. But Johnson believed that a mechanical application of the principle of parliamentary sovereignty could result in the annihilation of American rights. He refused, therefore, to accept the doctrine of an absolute supreme power because he thought it would destroy "Liberty and Property ... the ultimate Objects of all social Convention."[97] He condemned the Townshend acts as just such a violation of the colonists' privileges.[98]

The differences between the colonies and the mother country had even more serious implications for Johnson. He clearly saw that the issue arising from the conflicting claims of parliamentary supremacy and colonial rights portended disaster for both the mother country and America. He was therefore dismayed and frightened when the dispute between them was revived. He hoped and prayed that prudence, good faith, and the will to compromise of moderate men on both sides of the Atlantic would successfully put an end to the irritating and dangerous debates between colonial radicals and the King's stubborn ministers.[99] And he persisted in these beliefs even when later events seemed to destroy the possibility of any reconciliation.[100]

Johnson's special advice to Connecticut was the product of the same conservative philosophy. He repeated time and again that it was the essence of wisdom on the part of the colony to be cautious.[101] He sanctioned the quiet refusal to import English goods and the discreet encouragement of domestic manufactures. Union among the colonies was eminently desirable.[102] But he strongly disapproved of "noise or tumult" and "ostentation of what we do." The counsel of English friends of America might very well be appropriated as his own: "Do the thing ... but make no Bustle about it." Connecticut radicals like Israel Putnam, Samuel Holden Parsons, and Eliphalet Dyer lightly excused Boston's violent reactions to British policy. Johnson, however, was upset and worried over the possible effects that a lot of "noise and stir" would have upon the other provinces, particularly his own.[103] He warned everybody he could in Connecticut that the colony was watched "with a very jealous eye" and that "the least handle would be gladly Seised to deprive us of our Charter."[104] Under these circumstances it was not only wise to be cautious; it would be foolhardy to act otherwise.

But what if colonial prudence and English wisdom proved to be inadequate to compromise the differences? This question frightened Johnson as more and more Americans stirred uneasily lest they lose their great "priviledges, so long enjoyed and highly prized."[105] To Robert Temple, who asked him a similar question, Johnson answered, "The Rights of the people are not inconsistent with those of Great Britain. Those who separate them are enemies and traitors to both." But Johnson went on, "if (which God forbid) they must be considered as in opposition to each other, I adhere to my country and will stand or fall with it. I will have no hand in enslaving the Colonies—may those perish who would— nor on the other will I join those who would turn liberty into licentiousness—they are both extremes in conduct equally to be avoided." He said the same to Nathaniel Rogers. He was supporting the "popular party" and would continue to do so "by Principle and Conscience. Yet I would support Goverment as essential to the felicity of the People."[106] Revolution would be a "shocking . . . catastrophe."[107]

But should it come Johnson's course of conduct was inexorably marked out for him by his philosophy of moderate conservatism. "I must live in peace," he confessed to Nathaniel Rogers, "or I cannot live at all." And he admitted in another letter to the same correspondent that if he had to choose between the people and the empire he would be painfully stuck on the horns of an insoluble dilemma. For, in Johnson's own words, "I would not serve the people against the Crown nor can I [serve] the Crown agt the People."[108]

Between 1766 and 1770 the differences that separated Connecticut's conservatives and radicals were perpetuated, and in some respects sharpened, as the colony maneuvered to avoid the menace of an expanding imperial jurisdiction. Radical spokesmen, including some of the province's chief magistrates, did not hesitate to challenge that authority. And, as in the Stamp Act controversy, they hinted at the possibility that the colonies would ultimately break off from the empire.

Connecticut's more conservative freemen, however, were loath to antagonize the home authorities. Most of them had no desire to see the colony lose its privileges. But they felt that such a calamity could be brought about by colonial rashness as well as by severity on the part of Parliament and the King's ministers. Excitable political tempers were not assets, they thought, either in London, Hartford, or New Haven; and wise public policies required much more prudence than Connecticut's Whigs were then willing to use. Although the conservatives who reasoned this way no longer controlled the provincial government they still represented an influential minority.

It is significant that in the midst of these disputes, which in the words of Jonathan Trumbull seemed "to thicken up and Blacken upon" America, Connecticut's radicals had already branded this minority "Grumbletonians" and "Tories." [109]

CHAPTER FIVE

Religion and Land

→>>->>>->>>->>>->>>->>>->>>->>>->>>->>>->>>->>>-><-⟨⟨⟨-⟨⟨⟨-⟨⟨⟨-⟨⟨⟨-⟨⟨⟨-⟨⟨⟨-⟨⟨⟨-⟨⟨⟨-⟨⟨⟨-⟨⟨⟨-⟨⟨⟨-⟨⟨⟨

→>>->>>⟨⟨⟨-⟨⟨⟨

*T*HE unrest and the occasional turbulence that Connecticut's
Yankees exhibited after the Stamp Act were caused by more
than obnoxious British policies. For other issues, more peculiarly
local in nature, also provoked excited controversy and strained
what was already a heavy tension. And, significantly enough,
these issues tended to divide the colony in the very same way that
the spectacular disputes with the mother country did.

Connecticut's Puritan ministers, "the salt of the earth," were
uneasy. They were as much concerned as the secular half of the
Standing Order over the menace to the colony's political privileges
implicit in all the recent policies of the mother country. But as
the special vessels of the Lord they were worried about something
even more important, the supposed dangers to their religious
establishment. They saw a "dark and threatening aspect . . . upon
our nation and land, in regard to our civil liberties and public
interests," and they were sorely troubled.[1]

The fears of the Puritan ministers for their religious interests were heightened by the realization that the Anglican communion in Connecticut continued to grow, slowly perhaps, but

perceptibly, during these critical years. In 1767 Ezra Stiles estimated the number of Anglican families in the colony at one out of every thirty.[2] And the same year an Anglican missionary boasted that his parishioners made up a majority of the voters in the west Connecticut community of Newtown in Fairfield County.[3] What pleased the Rev. Mr. Beach about this news only soured the Congregational divines, one of whom bitterly mourned that the expansion of the Episcopal church was taking place while "We are breaking to pieces . . . very fast in Connecticut."[4]

The traditional prejudice of the Yankee Puritans toward the Church of England was aggravated by their displeasure at the fact that their Anglican neighbors had almost universally supported the mother country during the controversy over the Stamp Act. The Simsbury priest, the Rev. Mr. Viets, complained that in return for what the Anglicans deemed their "decent and loyal conduct" at that time they were "treated with unusual cruelty." Indeed, he lamented in 1766, they were "constantly pointed out as the worst of traitors to our country and betrayers of her most essential interest and liberties." And when they were not being called these names, he wrote two years later, they were criticized for being "too much connected with Europe."[5] Samuel Johnson, Connecticut's leading Anglican, praised that connection when he pointedly reminded the Archbishop of Canterbury that the Anglicans were the King's "best friends" in Connecticut.[6] But the Congregational majority in the colony derived little satisfaction from it.

Most of the Episcopal ministers reciprocated, at the least, this dislike for their church. The Rev. Samuel Peters, of course, had little respect for any of Connecticut's institutions. He scathingly described the colony as "the very bowels of contention, where faction is state policy, and envy religion."[7] William Samuel Johnson's son-in-law, the Rev. Mr. Kneeland, did not have much more esteem for Connecticut's political rulers than did his colleague at Hebron. At one time all that Kneeland was able to say about the colony's most prominent political figures was that they were men of great cunning. And he seemed to have thought even less of the people, for he sympathized with those who happened to be their political favorites as being "severely cursed." [8]

Connecticut's Congregational ministers were not aware of these privately expressed opinions about their colony. But they did not need this information to agree with Ezra Stiles that the *"Stamp Act, Episcopal Hierarchy,* and military Government were all branches of the same Policy or Grenvillian System of Plantation Colony Dominion." [9] Indeed, Stiles and other Puritan worthies were already convinced that the Anglicans had become the inveterate enemies of Connecticut's political and religious institutions. [10] Listing what seemed to be the many "Trials and Difficulties" confronting the colonies, Stiles wrote in a despondent moment, "So many Enemies, especially Chhmen and Tories." [11] Yale's future president compared the religious crisis with the "first hundred years of the Reformation"; and he prayed that the Puritans would be as vigilant and tenacious in the defense of their church as the first Protestants. [12]

Between 1766 and 1770 the fears of Connecticut's pastors were intensified by the rumors that an episcopate would be established in America. The Anglican ministers eagerly and repeatedly requested that a bishop be sent over. They more than hinted that the political loyalty of their parishioners deserved an appropriate reward of this kind; and again and again they stressed the beneficent effects that an American bishop would have upon the church in Connecticut. [13] But more than that, the ministers claimed that the establishment of a bishopric would strengthen the Crown's authority as well as serve the religious interests of churchmen. It was an obvious necessity to foster the church's welfare, the Rev. Mr. Leaming argued, "both in a civil and Religious view." [14]

What Connecticut's Anglicans eagerly anticipated, however, horrified the Standing Order in the colony. Governor Pitkin painted a dismal picture of the supposed effects that an American episcopate would have in Connecticut. It "will tend to heighten our difficulties," he solemnly advised Richard Jackson, "throw us into a very disagreeable situation, and have the most fatal tendency to complete our misery."[15] Councillor Roger Sherman and Pitkin's successor in the governorship, Jonathan Trumbull, repeated this dreary thesis in their own words. Both denied that Connecticut was intolerant, but for them its tolerance stopped short of approving a colonial episcopate. And they made it very clear that their religious privileges being "much more precious to us than those of a civil Nature," would never be easily surrendered.[16]

To the embittered Episcopal ministers, however, and probably to most of their parishioners, all this was pure intolerance with an added dash of hypocrisy. That is what the Rev. Mr. Graves must have thought when he angrily reported that Connecticut's Puritans were ransacking hell "for Infidelity and perverseness," and were resorting to all devices "to oppose Authority and prevent Episcopacy from residing among us."[17] Samuel Johnson, despondent over the virulent opposition that the proposal for a bishop had aroused in New England, confided to his son, "Thus the violent asserters of civil liberty for themselves, as violently plead the cause of tyranny against ecclesiastical liberty to others."[18] Indeed, some Anglican ministers were already becoming apprehensive about their possible fate in an independent America. "God have Mercy upon us," the Rev. Mr. Dibblee exclaimed, "if the Provinces here should throw off their connection, dependance and subjection to the Mother Country."[19]

Anglicans were not alone in their quarrels with the Standing Order. New London's chronic dissenters, the Rogerenes, occasionally were the cause of local disturbances;[20] but the Rogerenes were only a handful and they did not constitute a colony-wide problem. The radical New Light Separatists, however, were much more numerous, Stiles estimating in 1767 that there were about as many of them as there were Anglicans.[21] Bitter memories of the Awakening aggravated the doctrinal differences that separated these religious radicals from the regular churches. And the persistent demands of the Separatists for the right to be released from the compulsory upkeep of the official establishment, a privilege which other "sober dissenters" had long since won, agitated the entire colony.[22]

Although the religious strife was not as violent as it had been during the Awakening, it continued to split churches, inspire bitter pamphlet debates, and gravely concern the General Assembly.[23] John Devotion mournfully observed that Connecticut's churches were still being broken up, not only by the growth of Anglicanism but by the disputes between "N.Light" and "Orthodoxy."[24] The Anglican minister, the Rev. Mr. Dibblee, also reported, but probably with much less regret than his Congregational colleague, that Connecticut's churches were "breaking and crumbling into parties and factions." And, he added, "religious liberty is as warmly contended for as civil."[25]

This struggle for religious liberty intermittently flared up between 1767 and 1770 as the privileges of the established church were vehemently attacked and stubbornly defended in pamphlets and newspapers. The Separatists, or the Strict Congregationalists as they were also known, were quick to emphasize the inconsistency in Connecticut's religious policy about which Samuel Johnson had complained. They vigorously maintained that there was as much justice in their demand for religious liberty as there had been in the colony's fight for political liberty in the Stamp Act affair.[26] One partisan of the Separate cause even compared the compulsory taxation of the radical New Lights with the unjust taxes laid upon America by the British.[27] Other Separatist appeals drew upon scripture, history and expediency to supplement the sanction of logic.

But the defenders of the established churches lightly brushed these pleas aside. One religious conservative denounced the criticism of the colony's ecclesiastical constitution as "impertinent." To him it was obvious that the people of Connecticut enjoyed "the greatest Freedom and Liberty that can consist with Government." It was therefore absurd to ask for more liberty.[28] But the Separatists, enemies to "bigotted clergy," continued to flay the established church-state relationship and demanded the right, long before won by Anglicans, Baptists and Quakers, to be released from the compulsory support of the majority churches.[29]

Their campaign achieved some success in 1770. Religious reasons were probably not alone in making that success possible. For the colonial goverment, convinced that the province was menaced from abroad, was preparing to meet the danger by setting its domestic affairs in order. It therefore granted a few concessions to the Separatists. The latter were still requested to pay taxes for the maintenance of the official church. But as Protestants "who soberly and conscientiously" dissented from the colonial establishment and "attended publick worship by themselves," they were no longer subjected to the penalties they formerly suffered for not worshipping according to law.[30]

Thus on the eve of the Revolution the stringent laws against the religious extremists were partly relaxed. Seven years later, one year after the Declaration of Independence, the Separatists were completely freed from the obligation to support the established church.[31] Ever since the Awakening they had fought for a larger measure of religious liberty. The Anglicans had also sought to achieve this objective; and their combined efforts had helped to undermine the foundations of the established church.

This similarity, however, went no further. The Anglicans hoped that the political and ecclesiastical power of the mother country over the colonies would increase. But the "Strict Congregationalists" were political as well as religious radicals. Anglican leaders sought relief for their church in the ecclesiastical authority of a bishop and the curbing of Connecticut's self-government by a strong royal jurisdiction. The Separatists, however, were not only democratic in their ecclesiastical polity, but their political theory also tended to advocate a fuller measure of democracy.[32] These differences explain why, when the Revolution broke out, Connecticut's two major religious minorities were not on the same side of the political fence.

Among the participants in the religious debate was a member of a new sect that had acquired a small following in a few western towns. This correspondent had attacked the mandatory support of religion as impious and a practice of popery. He had boldly defied Connecticut's mores in maintaining that it was "debasing the religion of Christ to the lowest degree, to call in the aid of human force to support it." True worship could not be compulsory, he argued. It must "be carried on by a willing people" and "solely by the authority of Christ."[33]

The basic teaching of this unusual sect, which was known in Scotland as the Glasites and in Connecticut as the Sandemanians, assured salvation to all who had complete and unquestioning faith. To doubt was a damning sin in which, they held, all the Christian world but their own followers was involved. They condemned a paid ministry. Sandemanian doctrines were obviously not of the sort to allay the suspicions or soften the antagonism of their Puritan neighbors.[34]

The Sandemanians made the already troubled religious waters even more turbulent. Although their influence was limited to but a few towns in western Connecticut the more orthodox ministers in that part of the colony were not inclined to ignore them. On the contrary, they quickly joined in consociation and association to denounce the new movement, and disciplined two pastors who were supposedly tainted by its teachings.[35] But Sandemanianism was not rooted out of the colony. Sandeman himself preached in western Connecticut in 1766. And Newtown's Anglican minister testified that "Many of the Independents in these parts, both ministers and people, appear to be strongly captivated" by his doctrines.[36] The Assembly had recommended in May 1765 that the people of Danbury temper their religious differences with "forbearance, condescention and charity."[37] But Sandemanian influence remained strong in the town and gradually increased in neighboring Newtown.[38] In a few short years the Sandemanians were again to find themselves in severe disagreement with the Puritan majority. In this clash their doctrines made them heretics in politics as well as in religion.

Connecticut's magistrates had plenty to contend with in their disputes with Parliament and the religious minorities in the colony, but their responsibilities became even more complex when the case of the Susquehannah Company was revived in the late 1760's. For the major issue that the company created also revived the serious inter-colonial differences with Pennsylvania, aroused further fears over the relations of the colony with the Crown, and divided the Yankee freemen into bitterly hostile factions.

The company's project had been stalled since 1763.[39] Although the Susquehannah proprietors had not regarded the events of that year as an irrevocable setback, the ban upon Connecticut emigration to the rich lands of the Wyoming Valley had probably contributed to the unrest and agitation that preceded and accompanied the troubles over the Stamp Act in the colony.[40] On the other hand, even before 1765 conservative freemen had begun to differ with the company's supporters and to criticize its claims.[41] These differences now became sharper as the company's proprietors strove to realize their speculative ambitions.

At the end of December 1768, the proprietors thought that the way was again clear for them to resume colonizing activities. Claiming that the Fort Stanwix treaty of the previous October obviated the danger of Indian trouble, the ostensible cause of the Crown's interference in 1763, they voted to establish a settlement as soon as possible.[42] Early in January 1769, they petitioned the Assembly for a deed of "Lease and release" to the disputed land. This request was approved in the Council but it was defeated in the lower house. The company and its supporters in the Council stubbornly persisted. The upper house again gave its consent in May to another petition for a "Grant or release" of the colony's supposed right to the lands. But the lower house as stubbornly voted not to commit the colony to back the company's claim. Still another effort in October 1769 brought the same negative result despite strenuous lobbying on the part of some of the company's agents.[43]

The company's pressure, however, was not completely unproductive. Its petitions failed to induce the colony to assert its alleged authority, under the charter, over the western lands. But it succeeded in having the legislature establish a committee to search for all deeds relating to land titles granted by the Crown to Connecticut, "and in general all other Grants that can Affect us." The committee, which included Jonathan Trumbull, a member of the company since 1761 and one of its chief figures, was directed to report back to the Assembly as soon as possible.[44]

Emigrants sent out by the company had in the meantime planted a settlement on the green and fertile land that bordered the Susquehanna River. There the first permanent colonizing work of the company took root despite conflicts with the proprietary officials of Pennsylvania, who arrested the intruding Yankees on charges of rioting and breaking the peace. Refusing to be frightened by these tactics the company defiantly voted not to recall any of its settlers. Nor was force any more successful in intimidating the pioneers, for in August 1769 they petitioned the General Assembly to create a new county in the territory claimed by the company.[45] Interest in the settlements spread quickly. Attracted by the possibilities of owning lands unencumbered by quit-rents, inhabitants of New York, New Jersey, and even of Pennsylvania began to ask the colony for western grants supposedly within the jurisdiction of Connecticut's charter.[46] And in Pennsylvania the company got the support of the "Paxton Boys," the rowdy frontiersmen who had long fought the Penn interests.[47]

In Connecticut the stage was set for a warm public debate

which was destined to become more heated and acrimonious as the Revolution approached. The arguments were violent in the papers and pamphlets. And the probabilities are that they were even more so in the local taverns where the men commonly mixed grog with their politics.

Benjamin Gale, stubborn Old Light and implacable enemy of the Sons of Liberty, was the most vocal critic of the Susquehannah Company. His bitter attacks upon it were a powerful blend of personal and political motives. To a fellow conservative, the former stamp distributor, Jared Ingersoll, he explained that the Susquehannah affair had been "Coll Dyers Hobby Horse by which he has rose [sic] and as he has been unmercifull to Govr Fitch and Yourself I never design to Give him rest untill I make his Hobby Horse throw him into the Dirt."[48] The vigorous doctor tried to accomplish this objective by letting loose several verbal blasts at the hobby horse and its rider in 1769 and 1770. Dyer's reaction was immediate and equally violent.[49] Others quickly joined the fray, taking sides for and against the company.

Essentially, the argument of the opposition to the Susquehannah Company was a conservative's argument. It played upon the fears of stable and substantial citizens who would never deign to be associated with the "dregs" of society—the company's settlers were accused of being the "dregs of Connecticut"—and who would consider it a disgrace that the company's "miscreants" had accepted Pennsylvania's "Paxton Boys" as allies. Spokesmen for the company heatedly denied these accusations. They glorified its settlers as "gentlemen of education and fortune" and labelled as a lie the charge that it had admitted the "Paxton Boys." But this did not stop the company's enemies from maintaining that the supporters of the western project were either "deluded or riotous."[50]

The anti-Susquehannah brief further argued that it was doubtful whether the colony had any legal rights to the lands in question and that, consequently, a grant to the company would throw the province into a potentially dangerous controversy. Such a grant would certainly be expensive, probably more so than the Mohegan case, a touchy point in view of the tortuous and costly litigation which that land dispute had long caused.[51] Other doleful predictions drew a dismal picture of an inevitable economic catastrophe, which, it was warned, would come in the form of depreciated land values and swollen taxes, both certain products of an "enthusiasm of colonization."[52] Gale scoffed at the pious claim that the company had an evangelical mission to the Indians.[53] And finally, the company was accused of stooping to the disreputable tactics of dictating the votes of its friends in the legislature and of making a political football of its speculation.[54]

In other words, the Susquehannah project was indefensible "by reason and argument," was already a cause of faction and political immorality, and, if supported by the colony, would lead straight to political and economic disaster.[55] Pleas of this sort were designed to arouse a sympathetic audience among the colony's more conservative freemen, men who naturally shied away from new and dangerous schemes, or who, because they already held substantial amounts of land in the province, would fear economic losses from a large-scale emigration.

Partisans of the Susquehannah Company played another theme. They had no qualms about urging the colony to claim the disputed western lands, for they confidently held that legal title rightfully belonged to Connecticut. Only enemies of the colony's interests could think otherwise.[56] Moreover, the company's supporters saw no significant obstacle in the fact that Connecticut did not have actual possession of the lands; and they repeatedly denied that the taking over of Indian territory would provoke a frontier massacre.

Nor did the possibility of an economic collapse, should there be an extensive migration to the western lands, frighten Eliphalet Dyer, the Susquehannah Company's chief protagonist.[57] Attacks upon the company appealed to the conservatives' fear of change.

But Dyer's defense of the western project exploited the fears of land-hungry and speculative farmers as to what might happen should there be no change. In a lurid passage Dyer predicted that if new lands did not drain off Connecticut's surplus population the colony could in time expect to see the

wealthiest farmers engrossing all the lands, the poor lying in the streets, starving for want of employment, lordships, tenants, and slaves . . . one house . . . erected upon the tops of another, and all filled with inhabitants, till the upper lofts tumble down, and dash them in pieces, and the lower buried in the ruins! [58]

These heated charges and counter-charges were more than the products of a local land squabble. Had they been merely that, the issues provoked by the Susquehannah Company's claims could scarcely be considered important. Those issues, however, were more than minor, for they were linked to larger political questions affecting both Connecticut's ties to the mother country and its internal politics.

The first of these cropped up several times during the debate over the Townshend duties and provoked William Williams, ardent patriot and a member of the Susquehannah Company, to some acid comments. Williams did not think that the company's claims, then under attack in England by the Penn interests, properly concerned the royal authority, for he held that the disputed lands "are doubtless granted and gone from the Crown." Moreover, he argued, Connecticut could more quickly populate those lands than any other colony, and this was to England's advantage.

But as the Lebanon radical angrily denounced the recent measures of the mother country pertaining to western land, commerce, and politics he clearly indicated that he was not primarily interested in questions of English welfare. Instead of the Americans sharing "in the Honors of conquest," Williams declared, a privilege they more than deserved in view of their efforts against the French, "Great Britain possesses the whole advantage, and not an American entitled to an inch of the Lands." And while this policy deprived the colonies of the valuable Indian trade "the late extraordinary Regulations" of the British were wresting "from us the power and profits of every other." Williams bitterly concluded this was "A Policy vast and profound;" and, significantly enough, he did not think that it was calculated to have the colonies regard Britain as a parent state much longer.[59]

These radical sentiments would have evoked the hearty assent of the Rev. Jacob Johnson, one of Groton's New Light ministers and a missionary to the Indians.[60] Johnson had been present at the treaty making negotiations at Fort Stanwix in October 1768. He had then expressed the belief that should the British "superseed and proceed contrary to charter rights and privileges, and Govern us with a Rod of Iron, and the mouth of Cannons . . . I should think it my indispensable Duty to seek a retreat elsewhere, or joyn with my Countrymen in Forming a New Empire in America, distinct from and independent of the British Empire."[61] The radical New Light minister was confident that every true Son of Liberty would join him in this worthy project.

Johnson's radical neighbors in Norwich, a center of unrest in eastern Connecticut, may not have been ready to go so far. But it is noteworthy that in their uneasiness they combined an eager desire for western land with the more commonly heard objections to Britain's political and commercial legislation. At a meeting held September 12, 1769 to instruct the town's representatives in the Assembly, the townsmen advised their deputies to "exercise an unremitting Care and Attention to our Constitutional Rights," to encourage inter-colonial "Harmony and Unanimity," and to stimulate the development of "useful and necessary Manufactures." Capping these instructions was the admonition to see

That speedy and effectual care be taken of the Western, unimproved, and as yet ungranted Lands within the Colony [sic] by granting Townships, or otherwise to encourage the settling the same, that said Lands be not lost through Neglect; the Right of which is undoubtedly in the Colony by Charter.[62]

Opponents of the company also invoked the charter and introduced the imperial question into the debate, but only to warn that if the colony became embroiled in a dispute over the Wyoming lands the charter itself would be jeopardized in the process. Gale tirelessly reminded the colonists of the Mohegan case and underscored the trouble it had made and was still making. And he predicted that Connecticut could anticipate "a controversy of a more dangerous tendency" if it identified itself with the Susquehannah speculation.[63] Joseph Chew, the conservative merchant, did not at all concur with Governor Trumbull that the colony's claim was unassailable. On the contrary, this former member of the company now condemned its project as "Very Romantick," and an affair which "the Colony or assembly . . . had best have nothing to do with."[64]

Connecticut's agents in England, William Samuel Johnson and Richard Jackson, repeatedly and earnestly counselled the colony not to become involved with the company. Ever cautious, Johnson reminded Connecticut's magistrates that the colony's enemies would quickly take advantage of any convenient opportunity to assault the charter. Again invoking "Wisdom and Prudence," therefore, he urged the provincial government not to assume the burden of carrying the Susquehannah Company's speculation.[65] Johnson's radical eastern friends were exasperated at his fears and wondered how they would ever succeed as long as he dissuaded and terrified "the Colony against making any Claim or Exercising their Jurisdiction over that Country."[66] But Johnson's warning was supported by Connecticut's old friend and regular English agent, Richard Jackson, who explicitly advised Governor Trumbull that he thought the Wyoming claim was "more likely to be a burthen and expence than to add any Happiness security or substantial Benefit to the Colony in its Political Capacity, whatever advantage it might be of to individuals."[67]

The freemen who directed the affairs of the Susquehannah Company thought otherwise. Their strenuous and determined efforts to swing the provincial government's full support behind the company had failed. But as later events were to prove, this was only a temporary setback. Even in defeat, however, their influence was strong and on the increase.

In October 1769 the company counted among its members 24 out of the 135 deputies in the Assembly, while another nine representatives were closely associated with its work. More illustrative of the company's influence was the fact that in one of the ballots on its petitions in 1769 the total in its favor was only two or three votes less than the majority was able to muster against it. Active lobbyists aggressively pushed the interests of the company in the very halls of the Assembly. The company did not need them in the Council, for there its influence was already dominant. And Jonathan Trumbull, who was elected governor upon the death of Pitkin in the fall of 1769, had long been a member of the company and did not think it improper to continue his vigorous efforts in its behalf when he became the colony's chief magistrate.[68] It was obvious, as Johnson put it, that "many who have a principal share in the Managemt of the Colony Affairs are zealously"—and Johnson also thought—"whimsically engaged in it."[69]

The political strength of the "very many" who, according to Johnson, had opposed the company in 1767 had dwindled to a tenuous majority in the lower house of the legislature in 1769.[70] Benjamin Gale, Killingworth's Old Light deputy and zealous foe of the Sons of Liberty, was their most active and vocal agent both in and outside the chambers of the Assembly. In the colony's politics they represented the more conservative freemen, while the supporters of the pro-Susquehannah faction were identified with the radicals.

It was no mere coincidence that Joseph Chew lumped together the "land schemers [and] Colonizers" with the Sons of Liberty.[71] From the viewpoint of one of Connecticut's most steadfast patriots, however, the anti-Susquehannah elements were nothing more than the "timid," the "disaffected," or the "covetous."[72] Conservatives and radicals alike agreed that it was the party that supported Governor Fitch, "those who are here Called the Old Administration," that blocked the company's way in 1769.[73] Dyer explained that "the principal opposition arises from the old party."[74] On another occasion he described the political opposition to the company as "the old Stamp party," while Johnson tried to make it clear to Richard Jackson in 1770 that the dispute over the company was "a party affair" in the colony.[75]

All the important and stirring issues of the day thus converged into the mainstream of the colony's politics. Policies that originated in Westminster tended to produce the same political alignments within Connecticut that developed over provincial questions. The colony's conservative and radical political parties consistently differed over these policies and questions in the decade that preceded the outbreak of the Revolution. Their differences are clearly mirrored in Connecticut's political campaigns and elections between 1767 and 1770.

CHAPTER SIX

The Political Struggle, 1767-1770

≫≫≫≫≫≫≫≫≫≫≫≫≫≫≫≫≫≫≻✕≺≪≪≪≪≪≪≪≪≪≪≪≪≪≪≪≪≪

≫≫≫≪≪≪

*T*HE successful campaign of the radicals in 1766 against Governor Fitch and Councillors Chester, Hamlin, Silliman and Hall was the first of a series of violent political battles the like of which had never before been seen in the colony. In the years immediately following their defeat in 1766, the conservatives consistently sought to restore Fitch and the ex-councillors to their former offices. The radical party, now in the saddle, as strenuously fought to hold on to the political reins. The resulting struggle was unprecedentedly drawn-out and bitter.

In 1769, two campaign pieces, both written in sailor's jargon, reviewed the political events of the past few years. "Tom Lanyard," the author of one, was apparently a keen observer and a moderate in his politics. According to his narrative, the Connecticut ship of state had been "capcised" in 1766. Officers had been thrown out and many had been hoisted "a peg higher or lower." Fitch had been replaced in the "great Cabin" because some thought he was "too apt to *Scud* away upon every gust."[1] The other contemporary tale agreed with "Lanyard" that Fitch had been a good captain. But a "mutiny," "Fomented by Chaplain and Gunner," that is some Congregational ministers and the Sons of Liberty, had driven Fitch "from the quarter deck." To the "old decrepid Seaman" who told the story, that was a near disaster. Connecticut's new captain, "Our old friend Will" Pitkin, a good enough leader when the going was calm, was more popular with his crew whom he was careful to please with "friendly art." [2]

Not all the "seamen," however, were happy about the change in their officers. Those who cared little for the popular ways of their new leaders were distressed at the "Ship's misfortune" in losing its former officers and planned to reinstate them in the "great Cabin." They quietly bore their political defeat until the winter of 1766-67. [3] Then, several months before the spring elections, they opened the attack. The radicals quickly counter-attacked and the battle was joined.

A newspaper article by "Plaind Facts"—who was probably Benjamin Gale, Killingworth's most famous opponent of the political New Lights, the Susquehannah Company and the Sons of Liberty—started the controversy. The author of this piece did not directly call for an overthrow of the dominant political party. He probably considered that strategy too crude; but he spoke plainly enough for all to understand.

In a lengthy analysis he charged that the eastern counties controlled the posts of governor, deputy governor, the Council and the Superior Court. He further alleged that western Connecticut, much richer than the eastern counties according to the tax lists, was under-represented in the public offices. [4] These accusations had obvious implications. What "Plaind Facts" wanted the freemen to do was to turn out the easterners, who represented the more radical political party in the colony, and to restore Fitch, a resident of the western town of Norwalk, and the ex-councillors to their old positions. [5]

The radicals were not slow to recognize the nature of the attack upon them. They immediately denounced "Plaind Facts" as an "Incendiary . . . tending to inflame Men's Minds, and stir up

Feuds and Factions, Mutinies and Seditions." Borrowing a leaf from the traditional election sermons, they warned the freemen against indiscriminately altering the composition of the government and exhorted the voters, somewhat unrealistically, "to suffer no Tool of Party or Spirit of Dissatisfaction to corrupt their Disinterestedness." 6

Now that they were in power the radicals condemned party strife as most objectionable and fraught with all sorts of horrible dangers to the colony. "Shufflings, Party Rage, Animosity, and Confusion for Days to come" would be inevitable. Even the charter would be imperiled.7 One radical had a choice piece of advice for his opponents. He recommended that the political supremacy of the east be accepted in a spirit akin to Calvinistic resignation. For if that part of the colony was now blessed by Providence in possessing "the best men" there was not very much that ordinary mortals could do about it. Perhaps in the future western Connecticut would be similarly favored. But until "such an event takes place," this writer suggested, "we think that every one should be easy with their present rulers." 8

This medley of counsel and harangue did anything but mollify the conservatives. They denied responsibility for stirring up political factionalism and threw the blame for this evil on the eastern radicals. The supposed concern of the easterners about the dangers of party spirit, they remarked in sharp criticism, would have been much more appropriate in 1766 when a "Rump Assembly" of Liberty Boys helped to choose a new governor and oust Fitch's supporters in the Council. "It is easy to raise a spirit in a people," they pointedly reminded the radicals, "but to set proper bounds is extremely difficult." 9

The conservatives believed that those bounds could be restored by returning the ex-governor and his assistants to their old positions. In this way the harm done the previous year would be undone. And the radicals, caustically described by one staid writer as "the Regiment for *pulling down Houses,*" who had led the freemen under "pretended Principles of Liberty" to defeat those magistrates, would thus receive a just retribution.

Furthermore, the conservatives argued, there was no good reason why the former officials should not be elected. Most of the "more judicious Freemen" supposedly now recognized the foolishness of having succumbed to the wiles of the eastern schemers in 1766. Voters who were still unconvinced of that fact were offered attractive explanations of Fitch's conduct in the Stamp Act affair.[10] And a special bit of political propaganda charged that the eastern towns were centers of turmoil because "many Gentlemen" there secretly backed the Mason claims against the colony in the Mohegan case.[11] If this argument did not sufficiently impugn the patriotism of the radicals others were ready at hand, such as the cry that fraud and intimidation had been used in at least one town in 1766 to prevent the freemen from voting for Fitch and the four ex-assistants.[12]

Conservative spokesmen supplemented this propaganda with specific instructions telling the freemen how to vote in the coming elections. In issuing such advice the conservatives acknowledged their indebtedness to the tactics that the radicals had used so successfully the previous year. First, they told the voters to admit as many new freemen as were eligible. Then they urged them to give their votes to "the four Gentlemen last Year drop'd, and two or three others, and . . . no more." Easterners, of course, were not to be supported. This strategy, it was hoped, would concentrate the political strength of the western towns upon Fitch and the four ex-councillors, and thus ensure their election. The freemen were also asked to choose deputies whose views coincided with those held by the former magistrates. "Play the Man for your city, and hold fast your Privileges," they were told. To permit the party now in control of the government to remain in power under the pretense that it was for liberty was nothing short of delusion. For the "factious Men" of the east would in time involve "the State . . . in eminent danger" and "enslave the colony." But those upright men in the eastern towns who had not "lowered the Knee to Baal" were invited to join the west in reversing the political decision of 1766.[13]

The "paper war" of the 1767 campaign was perhaps the bitterest in the Yankee province's political experience.[14] The Rev. John Devotion was unpleasantly surprised to find that "Plaind Facts" was called an "Incendiary." From his conservative point of view it was indeed "strange! that the Narration of plain Facts in a free State should be so criminal."[15] And another freeman glumly noted that it was apparently easy for the supposedly sober colony of Connecticut to outdo its less stable neighbors "in point of parties Devisions and Lybels in the Newspapers."[16]

Moderates appealed for unity and harmony and an end to "Party-spirit, that Bane of Society." But the pleas that the literary "Swords may be beat into Ploughshares" were ignored.[17] New Haven's *Connecticut Gazette,* which in September 1766 had boldly announced in a new masthead that "Those who would give up ESSENTIAL LIBERTY, to purchase a little TEMPORARY SAFETY, deserve neither LIBERTY nor SAFETY," appropriately added a new line in March 1767 which read "Be you to Others kind and true As you'd have Others be to you."[18] This charitable maxim, however, failed to abate the violence of the campaign.

The outcome of the election was uncertain until the very end. Some conservatives optimistically anticipated that their "great struggle for the old governor" and his assistants would be successful.[19] But Samuel Johnson was doubtful "as the East side and their Sons of Liberty are indefatigable."[20] The Rev. John Devotion was similarly skeptical about the likelihood of Fitch defeating Pitkin. He reported, however, that at least two of the juring councillors, Silliman and Hamlin, had good chances to experience "A Resurrection." Only those whose political faith was very deep could have had any hopes that a similar miracle would befall the other two ex-magistrates. Even the conservative party's most stalwart partisan, Benjamin Gale, was inclined to agree with Samuel Johnson that the "paper War, Squibs, Curses, Rhimes" would not be sufficient to carry the election.[21]

The pessimism in these forecasts was fully justified, for although early returns gave Fitch a large majority in the western towns,[22] his party failed to capture any of the high offices for which it had campaigned. Pitkin's popular majority was approximately 1300 votes. And yet, it is worthy to note that only one year after Fitch had been defeated for his stand on the Stamp Act he was able to attract three-fourths of the popular vote that Pitkin got, since 4777 freemen cast their ballots for the incumbent chief magistrate and 3484 for the former governor. Equally significant was the fact that one of the ex-assistants, Ebenezer Silliman, was kept out of the Council by less than a hundred votes.[23] Gale claimed with some satisfaction that both the former governor and "the Excluded Councillors, have gained greatly in their Votes."[24]

As Stiles explained the results, the western, conservative towns gave their votes to Fitch while the more radical eastern counties and the western New Lights supported Pitkin. According to Stiles, the only freemen in the eastern towns who backed the conservative ex-councillors were the Anglicans.[25] William Samuel Johnson, however, the moderate Episcopalian, was still in the good graces of the radicals and was therefore re-elected. Jared Ingersoll explained to Johnson that the radicals had decided to allow him to "Come *in* Just now and for a little while, but that it would not do to let you be *in* long." Johnson frankly admitted that he would "never so much wonder at their leaving me out as I did at their putting me in."[26] At New Haven the results were in closer conformity with the general outcome. There the radical party defeated the conservative candidate for deputy, John Hubbard, by two votes and elected Daniel Lyman, the New Light who had been in the thick of the "plot" against Fitch in 1759. News of this naturally led Gale to blame "N Light, St . . . Act, & Satan."[27]

Though Gale's commission as a justice of the peace was held up by the Assembly on suspicion that he was the author of "Plaind Facts,"[28] Killingworth's peppery character took heart at the gain made by the conservative party. "The Honest party," he assured Johnson, "have not lost Spirit."[29] He also took comfort in the fact that Governor Pitkin was very old, and Gale added in the vindictive spirit of party, "as age is Honorable I wish he was as old again as he now is."[30]

But the results of the campaign were more depressing to other conservatives than they were to Gale. John Hubbard was convinced that there was something peculiar, if not fraudulent, about the election, since seven thousand votes were cast for governor while only four thousand ballots were received by any one candidate for councillor. "We improve apace," he sadly concluded, "in all the Refinements of a corrupt Policy."[31] John Devotion was equally mournful. He bemoaned the failure of the Old Lights to awaken to their political needs. "Multitudes will not leave their Plow," he complained, "to have a Govr to their Taste." Devotion was also worried over the growing political factionalism in the colony and dolefully predicted that it never "will be Laid among us . . . till we have a Kings Govt nay till we have a King in Person, and are like Other People."[32]

William Samuel Johnson received happier reports from Jabez Huntington, who belonged to the more radical party and was therefore quite content about the outcome of the election.[33] But the Stratford lawyer could not help fretting over the political trends in the colony. When news of the bitter political struggle reached him, he warned that party strife could lead the province astray, in which case there was the dangerous possibility of it "receiving a Box in the Ear" from the mother country.[34]

Two of the most interesting and important analyses of the 1767 election are to be found in the correspondence of Benjamin Gale with Ezra Stiles. The Puritan pastor, thoroughly frightened by the steady expansion of the Anglican church, had by this time practically swung around to the pole of radical Whiggism. Stiles now dreaded the possibility of a political alliance between Connecticut's two conservative factions, the Old Lights and the Anglicans. "Which would a Colony of Dissenters chuse," he asked an unknown correspondent, "that the Supreme Dominion should be in the hands of Foreigners and Episcopalians who thoroly hate us?—or in Hands of New Lights (if that be the Alternative) who are fellow Dissenters, and whose Posterity will naturally become Old Lights?"[35] Stiles regarded the political struggle in the colony with dismay, for it seemed that the Episcopalians were taking advantage of it to play the old game of divide and rule. And their goal, he felt, was nothing less than the destruction of the colony's religious and political liberties.

Stiles attributed to the Anglicans a campaign to besmirch "the Appellation 'Sons of Liberty' by constantly holding up the Excesses and New Lightism of the Eastern Sons." Instead of succumbing to this insidious propaganda, Stiles prayed that Connecticut's Old Lights would join with the New Lights and glory in a strengthened and united Sons of Liberty. He acknowledged that the latter had been guilty of excesses of "Enthusiasm" in 1765 and 1766. But he now justified these popular outbreaks since they were committed in a good cause. The Reformation had also produced some "Excesses"; but, Stiles asked, had it not also "emancipated Britain from the papal tyranny?"[36] Some conservatives thought that Connecticut's charter was menaced by the political changes which had turned Fitch out of the governorship and put the more radical party in power. Stiles, however, belittled this fear. He saw no threat to the charter in the dominant position of the New Light party. The danger was elsewhere. That was why Stiles, though promising never to be a New Light, declared he hoped he would never "be brot to make a Transition from Hatred of New Light to wish the Loss of Charters."[37]

To Gale, however, it was a fundamental axiom that the political supremacy of the radical eastern New Light party was Connecticut's greatest evil. "We all ride our Hobby Horses," he bluntly told Stiles, "an Episcopalian is yours a Political N Light is Mine."[38] And Gale was determined to ride his hobby horse as hard as Stiles drove his. He rejected Stiles' warning about the urgency of the Old and New Lights burying their differences in face of the supposed danger of the Episcopal church to both Puritan groups. Stiles had asked Gale which he would prefer, a colonial governor, deputy governor, and Council controlled by the Anglicans and

an awd lower house; with £15 or £20,000 ster Tax for Support of Govt, wc sd Govt etc hate Dissenters more than New Lights can —or—New Light Administration with the Retention of Charter Lib and Rel and only 3 or £4000 ster Expences of Govt?[39]

Gale unequivocally and heatedly replied that he knew the differences between these figures, but that he had not yet determined

the exact Proportion of Cubic Inches of fraud, deceit, Juggle, low cunning, wicked Tricks, Judging Parties and not the cause, Imperiousness when in power, malevolence, and right down damnable wickedness subsisting in the Heart of a thorough [?] *Political N Light*, gilded over with a Specious Shew of Religion without the least Appearance of solid and Substantial Virtue, and real Goodness.[40]

Gale, indeed, rode his hobby horses hard.

Killingworth's conservative deputy had no monopoly of this brand of bitter political partisanship. The campaigns of 1766 and 1767 had pulled party alignments taut and had inflamed the entire colony. Throughout the next few years political passions remained close to the boiling point, and at election time they practically always ran over.

Ancient differences between Old and New Lights were recalled to justify a miniature "purge" carried through by the dominant radical party in the spring of 1767.[41] And several months later Fairfield's radicals wreaked a further revenge upon the former councillor, Ebenezer Silliman, by keeping him out of the

Assembly because he had fought the appointment of a Son of Liberty to some office.[42]

This "High Discipline" must have troubled every conservative Yankee as sorely as it did the Rev. John Devotion; and yet, the events of the next two years tended to draw that discipline even tighter. In 1768 radicals found it easy to accuse the more conservative towns in western Connecticut of shameful apathy towards the Townshend acts.[43] They found it just as simple to identify the most stalwart defenders of the colony's privileges with the Liberty Boys and the sponsors of American commerce and industry.[44] But when the expansionists revived the Susquehannah project the following year, the conservative party retaliated with a series of attacks, some veiled, others open and incisive, against the speculative land scheme.[45]

Connecticut's parties regularly lined up against each other at the actual elections.[46] The conservatives consistently backed the former governor, Thomas Fitch; with equal determination the radicals supported Pitkin, and after his death, Jonathan Trumbull. After their candidate had been defeated for governor in the 1768 campaign the conservative deputies in the Assembly almost succeeded in electing Fitch Chief Judge of the Superior Court. But the radicals parried the thrust and chose Deputy Governor Trumbull to the seat.[47] Undaunted by these setbacks, the conservatives stubbornly supported Fitch for governor in 1769. Again the freemen rebuffed them and re-elected Pitkin.[48] But when Jonathan Trumbull failed to get a majority of the votes for deputy governor the conservatives in the Assembly tried to capture the office for Fitch. And when that failed they again sought to elect Fitch Chief Judge, but with no success.[49]

Providence gave the conservatives still another opportunity later in the year, when Pitkin died. With party lines as severely drawn as they ever were, the special election in the Assembly was sharp and bitter.[50] The more radical deputies united behind Trumbull for governor; the conservatives voted for Fitch as usual.

Again Trumbull won.[51] But when the first ballot for deputy governor was taken Fitch came out substantially ahead of his closest rival, Matthew Griswold. Since neither had a majority, however, their backers engaged in a brisk competition to capture the votes of the other major candidate, Hezekiah Huntington. On the third ballot Fitch and Griswold were tied with fifty-four votes each; and it was not until the next ballot that the contest was finally decided with Griswold emerging as the colony's new deputy governor.[52] Hoping for a miracle, the conservatives tirelessly supported Fitch for Chief Judge, but they were badly defeated.[53]

The unyielding persistence of the conservative party, despite regular defeats, surprised and annoyed the radicals.[54] But the conservatives suffered more than vexation. They were horrified by the virulence of the polemical wars in which they were already being described as traitors and "branded with every mark of infamy."[55] And some of them were becoming desperate by their inability to check the radicals.

As early as 1766 Benjamin Gale, despairing of the waning influence of the conservatives, privately suggested that the best way to block the radical eastern faction would be to re-interpret the charter so as to deprive the freemen of the power to elect the governor, deputy governor, and assistants. He proposed instead that the colony's chief magistrates be chosen by the Assembly.[56] But Gale's plan to sacrifice the most democratic feature of Connecticut's representative government for partisan political purposes got meager support. Stiles bluntly told Gale in 1766 that he thought very little of it.[57] And when it was offered to the public in 1769 it was practically ignored.[58] But Gale was a stubborn antagonist and he promised "to dye in Armour" battling the radicals to the bitter end.[59]

Many other conservatives proposed to do the same; and in their resolute determination to score an upset they made the campaign of 1770 Connecticut's most stirring and acrimonious political struggle since 1767. Their determination worried William

Williams enough to make him predict in the summer of 1769 that a political "change may take place another Year."[60] Six months later the portents of the coming battle had become so clear that radical and conservative alike freely prophesied a great clash.[61]

The sentiments of the conservatives were vividly expressed in an anti-Trumbull ballad that was sung during the campaign. To the tune of "The Vicar of Bray" the conservatives chanted:

> Now Will is dead and his Purser broke[62]
> I know not who'll come next, Sir;
> The Seamen call for old Pitch again,—
> Affairs are sore perplexed, Sir.
>
> But the Gunners and some midshippers
> Are making an insurrection,
> And would rather the ship should founder quite
> Than be saved by Pitch's inspection.

To which the chorus responded:

> But this is what I will maintain,
> In spite of Gunners and all, Sir,—
> If Pitch can save the Ship once more,
> 'Tis best he overhaul her![63]

The radicals strained every effort to prevent the former governor from getting a chance to overhaul the ship of state. They warned the freemen that an insidious political plot was on foot to restore a "discarded Statesman" to office. And should it succeed, the radicals went on, the colony would lose its patriotic magistrates and find itself headed by "compliant managable Gentlemen." To defeat these "wild Projects" they exhorted everyone to follow the leadership of the Sons of Liberty.[64]

The most forthright radical plea came from the pen of "Unanimous" who claimed to write for "The Friends of the Constitution and Liberties of this Colony, in New-London and Windham Counties," and for the most resolute enemies to "Stamp Acts, Revenue Taxes and Officers." Repeating the warnings of his radical associates, he notified the colony that the friends of liberty in the eastern towns were determined to keep out of public office "all those who have appeared unfavourable to their interests in the time of the stamp-act, who have not openly and avowedly disapproved their conduct in that affair." And he let it be known that the eastern Sons of Liberty expected the aid of their allies in all the other counties to prevent the government from being seized by persons "whom by far the greater part of the colony esteem as favourable to *parliamentary encroachments*."[65]

The conservatives vigorously lashed back at their political enemies. "A Westward Unanimous" excoriated the eastern radicals for having caused unrest and commotion in the colony "with respect to the choice of our rulers" for the past fifty years.[66] And another conservative slashed at the piece written by the alleged spokesman for New London and Windham Counties as nothing more than an "open high handed Attempt to violate and destroy the equality, the independency, the liberty of the subject." His parting advice implored the freemen to be on guard against those men "who with liberty on the lips, harbour the most tyrannical designs in heart."[67] "Pacificus" offered the same counsel: beware of the propaganda from the eastern towns, for "under the mask and vizzard of patronizing the cause of liberty," it was nothing more than "an attempt to stir up faction, [and] scatter the seeds of discord."[68]

When the campaign was over and the votes were counted it was found that the conservative party had come closer to returning Fitch to the governorship than in any year since he had first been defeated. Trumbull received 4700 votes; Fitch was the choice of 4266 freemen. Since 805 votes were scattered among other candidates Trumbull failed to win a majority of the ballots. This sent the election to the legislature where Trumbull finally triumphed.[69] Unfortunately, there is no evidence to indicate what the exact division was within the Assembly.

The battles that Connecticut's parties waged between 1766 and 1770 not only crystallized their differences over both local and imperial issues, but hardened those differences along geographical lines. How sharply sectionalized the colony's political factionalism had become may be seen in a breakdown of the returns of the fall, 1770, nominations. According to this source, Trumbull received a total of 2930 ballots; 899 votes, or about 31 per cent of the governor's total, were cast in Hartford County; 499 freemen, 17 per cent of Trumbull's supporters, backed him in New London County; and 618 freemen, 21 per cent of Trumbull's total, followed suit in Windham County. But in conservative Fairfield County the governor was unable to get the approval of more than 140 freemen, a scant 5 per cent of his total. Dyer, Windham's prominent radical leader, received but 246 ballots in Fairfield County, 7 per cent of his total of 3301 votes. He got almost four times that amount, 829 ballots, 25 per cent of all his votes, in Hartford County; and more than twice Fairfield's returns, 534 votes, 16 per cent of his total, in New London County. In his own county of Windham the Whig lawyer-politician got the support of 681 freemen, 21 per cent of his total votes.

Equally revealing is the fact that out of the total of 1979 votes given to Fitch only 85, 4 per cent of his entire backing, were cast in New London County and a paltry 11, .6 per cent of all his votes, in Windham. The ex-governor's strength was concentrated in the western counties and in the towns along the Connecticut River. The four ex-councillors were similarly rejected in the eastern part of the colony. In the same nominations Ebenezer Silliman had only 3 votes in Windham and 80 in New London County; his total for the colony was 1721. John Chester had but 5 in the former county and 64 in the latter, while Benjamin Hall failed to get a single nominating vote in either of the two radical eastern counties.

A final interesting contrast in the nominating lists may be found in the geographical distribution of the popular support given to the New Haven conservative and ex-stampmaster, Jared Ingersoll, and the radical Lebanon patriot, William Williams. Of the 308 votes that the former received, 218 were cast in his native county in New Haven. Both Hartford and Fairfield Counties gave him 43 votes, but not one freeman nominated him in all the towns of New London or Windham Counties. On the other hand, out of the 470 votes that Williams gathered only five came from the conservative stronghold, the western county of Fairfield.[70]

Ten years separated the defeat of the conservatives in the election of 1766 from the time when America was to become an independent nation. During the first four years of that decade neither the mother country nor the colonies indicated that they were capable of permanently resolving the differences that were splitting the empire. Similar signs of an impending revolutionary break were evident within the colony of Connecticut.

In this so-called "land of steady habits" the freemen were sharply divided into conservative and radical parties—contemporary partisans called them "factions"—that regularly clashed in bitter political struggles. Moderates repeatedly warned that "Faction and Party [were] fatal to all free Constitutions,"[71] but their advice was spurned. In every election between 1766, when the conservatives first lost their hold on the governorship and four seats in the Council, and 1770, the two parties spiritedly battled over both provincial and imperial issues. Conservative candidates were consistently nominated for the highest magistracies, and twice, in 1767 and 1770, they came close to winning some of these political prizes. But they failed in the last resort to convince enough freemen that it was desirable to eject the radical party from power.

Rebuffed by the "unthinking Many," at least two of the conservative leaders, ex-councillor Ebenezer Silliman and the former governor himself, had begun to look to the home government for adequate rewards to soften the "sufferings" they had experienced in their endeavors "to support Government."[72] They thus foreshadowed the reaction of the loyal remnant of their party when, a few short years later, the colonies were to be involved in the final crisis of the empire. For that remnant, in then turning to the mother country, turned against the dominant Whigs in the colony. In so doing it was destined to be branded and outlawed as Connecticut's Tory party.

CHAPTER SEVEN

The Lull Before the Storm

THE AMERICAN colonies did not move in a straight course towards the Revolution. For several years after the repeal of the Townshend acts and the collapse of the colonial program of economic resistance an uneasy calm settled over the land. Worried radicals labored incessantly to preserve inter-colonial unity and to keep the memories of the recent struggles fresh in the popular mind. But most Americans did not object to the unusual experience of enjoying a political peace. They did not know that it was to be very short-lived.

Connecticut was no different in these respects from the other colonies, for there too there were signs of peace. Indeed, it was possible for some observers to feel that despite the rather tumultuous events of the past five years the colony might yet end its internal factionalism and, together with the other provinces, restore a fuller measure of harmony in its relationship with the mother country.

More auspicious religious and economic developments encouraged this optimism. A few Anglican ministers testified that the Puritan pastors were somewhat more cordial;[1] and the resumption of imports in 1771 created an atmosphere of prosperity, even though it was built upon the shaky foundation of credit. All sorts of manufactures deluged the colony, prompting one Yankee to remark in the spring of 1772 that "we flow in goods."[2] And the fiscal condition of the provincial government probably inspired an extra degree of optimism, for the colony announced in October 1772 that it would be able to retire all the outstanding bills of credit whenever they fell due.[3]

Political signs also seemed to be more encouraging to the moderates who constantly prayed for the return of peace. While ex-governor Fitch continued to seek a political reward from the mother country that would appropriately recognize his "faithful Service to the Government at Home and here for which . . . [he] Suffered a Political Martyrdom,"[4] the number of the juring ex-councillors was cut down by the deaths of John Chester and Benjamin Hall.

Conservatives were undoubtedly grieved at the loss of two of their stalwart friends, magistrates who had fought for "Order and Peace," and who, "unbias'd either by popular Applause, or Disapprobation," had refused to act contrary to their political principles.[5] But the distress of the conservatives was probably eased by the comparative quiet in the colony. In the middle of May 1771 a contributor to the *Courant* remarked with little regret that the season must be considered "backward" since there had been only one political piece in the newspapers, and that was only a "small diminutive sprout."[6]

What probably gratified Connecticut's moderates and conservatives even more was the fact that for the first time in several years there was no major dispute to strain America's ties to the empire. The repeal of the Townshend duties seemed to herald the establishment of a more harmonious relationship between the colonies and the mother country. Governor Trumbull's fears and apprehensions loomed large early in 1771,[7] but they were dissipated in the later months of the same year. And William Samuel Johnson, who was about to return to his native land after an absence of four years, reassured the provincial authorities that the colony had "nothing particular to fear." Later in the same year Johnson, now again at Stratford, happily informed his English friends that the "People appear to be weary of their Altercations with the Mother Country and disposed to return to their former quiet and good humour." In 1772 Johnson found the state of affairs "very quiet," and on another occasion he contentedly termed it a "perfect political peace."[8] That peace enabled Governor Trumbull to report to the Assembly in October 1772 that there was nothing to divert it "from a close attention to those things that relate to our internal police."[9] Saybrook's Old Light minister, the Rev. Joseph Fish, was so impressed by the general tranquillity that he wryly commented "we have nothing more to fear than a Sinfull, wretched, dangerous *Security,* in a Graceless Condition."[10]

But the calm was deceptive in Connecticut as it was throughout the American colonies. Provincials who hoped that the imperial fire had been put out for all time were soon to discover that it had been merely smoldering. And if they had been close enough observers of the scene in Connecticut they might also have seen ominous wisps of smoke from factional fires even while the political skies were supposed to be clear and serene.

There was no real religious peace in the colony, for Baptists and Anglicans continued to wrangle more or less acrimoniously with their Puritan neighbors;[11] and although the number of open conflicts between the Anglicans and the Congregational establishment declined, there was no indication that the province's two major denominations were permanently destroying the religious and political fears and antipathies that they aroused in one another.

Connecticut's Puritans could never be at ease so long as there was the possibility that an Anglican episcopate might be set up in America, and the Episcopal clergy in the colony were untiring in their efforts to get a bishop.[12] In 1772 they finally secured the assistance of the province's most prominent Anglican layman,

William Samuel Johnson. From that time, until the war ended his efforts, Johnson pushed the project among his influential English friends, and in so doing he ultimately stressed the point his father had made decades before, that an American episcopate was "both in a political as well as religious light an object of the highest Importance."[13]

But Connecticut's Congregational pastors, of course, did not think so. The Rev. Ezra Stiles, whose writings constitute a veritable barometer to the reactions of the Independent clergy, fretted more and more about the progress of the English church. He regularly recorded its expansion in his diary; and, although he reassured himself in 1773 that the Anglican churches were but a small minority in comparison with the Congregational establishment, he admitted that the former were steadily gaining.[14] His famous colleague, the Rev. Charles Chauncy of Boston, was more pessimistic, and predicted to Stiles that Connecticut would be the first New England colony to have a bishop.[15] Chauncy was not alone in dreading the fulfilment of his prophecy. Connecticut's religious affairs quite obviously did not produce perfect contentment.

Nor were economic conditions so uniformly promising as they seemed to be. The very trends that pleased some colonists gravely alarmed others and helped to stir up unrest, especially among the merchants.[16] A shortage of grain in the eastern counties forced the colonial government to embargo the export of grain products in the spring of 1772.[17] This, however, was only a temporary emergency. Much more serious was the inability of the colony's merchants to extricate themselves from their dependence upon Boston and New York. The society that had been set up in accordance with the decisions reached at the merchants' meeting at Middletown in 1770 weakly attempted to encourage the expansion of commerce, agriculture, and manufacturing; but by 1772 its failure was plainly and painfully evident.[18] While Richard Jackson and Governor Trumbull still exchanged hopeful letters about the prospects of a thriving direct commerce between Britain and the colony,[19] Connecticut continued to ship most of its exports to the neighboring colonies and the West Indies and to receive its finished goods through Boston and New York importers.[20]

On the eve of the Revolution Connecticut had no vital, direct economic tie with the mother country. And its trade continued to be saddled with the profits made by New York and Boston merchants on the transactions whereby rural Connecticut exchanged its surplus agricultural products for needed British manufactures. The evils of this condition were severely aggravated when the colony's merchants, eager to participate in the commercial revival after the Townshend duties were repealed, quickly bought up large amounts of manufactured goods on credit, only to find themselves soon thereafter unable to meet their commitments. Many merchants sank so deeply into debt that they were forced into bankruptcy and out of business. After 1771 and up to the very outbreak of hostilities insolvent traders flooded the legislature with pleas for relief and stays on debts.[21] And in 1774 New London's merchants found that the returns from their coastal and foreign trade were insufficient to balance the cost of the manufactured products that they received from New York. The gloomy result, according to an official report, was that many of them "have failed, and the New Yorkers have taken their landed interest in this Colony in payments to a very considerable amount."[22]

The peculiar commercial problems that involved so many of Connecticut's merchants in debt also forced some of them to seek relief by stubbornly evading the British acts of trade. The West Indian traffic remained the most important branch of the colony's commerce,[23] but it would have been even more important had the restrictive British laws not narrowed and practically prohibited some phases of the trade with the foreign islands. That was why Nathaniel Shaw Jr., a leading patriot and New London's most prominent merchant, evaded these restrictions, smuggled goods into the colony, and justified his participation in the illicit traffic.[24] He probably was not the only one to do so. Port officers at both New London and New Haven thought that their measures against smuggling were "very effectual."[25] But they apparently were not effective enough to eliminate the practice.

It was not easy for the customs officials to enforce the laws against smuggling in the traditionally law-abiding colony of "steady habits." Neither the people nor the colonial government were very cooperative. Several incidents that occured early in 1773 expose the predicament of the King's customs officers in his province of Connecticut.

In December 1772 some smuggled goods were seized by the British ship *Swan*. These were delivered to the Collector and Comptroller at New London and put away for safekeeping. One night early in February the store in which the confiscated wares were being kept was broken into and part of the contraband was removed. Several nights later the robbery was daringly duplicated and the remainder of the coveted goods was stolen.

The Collector and Comptroller appealed to Governor Trumbull to issue a proclamation offering a reward for the apprehension of the culprits. But the governor at first refused the request on the ground that such a proclamation would be useless and, instead, suggested that the customs officers seek the assistance of the local civil authority. Three days later, however, Trumbull changed his mind, explaining to the Collector that the repeated use of violence had altered the situation. He therefore issued a proclamation offering a reward of one hundred pounds for a solution of the crime and called upon all the law-enforcement officers in the colony to assist in solving the mystery. Despite the offer of an additional fifty pounds reward by Collector Stewart and Comptroller Moffat, however, there is no evidence that the guilty parties were ever caught or the goods recovered.[26]

While these interesting events were taking place the customs officers again asked the Superior Court for writs of assistance. The request inevitably provoked a flurry of excited and angry comment. Throughout February and early March, 1773, newspaper articles savagely attacked the writs as illegal and unjust. And with equal feeling they bluntly warned the judges not to grant the general search warrants upon pain of falling a prey to popular revenge at the coming elections.[27] Confronted by the dilemma, as William Samuel Johnson sympathetically described it, of "disobeying an Act of Parl and thereby exposing the Colony to the resentment of the Governmt at home, or of incurring the Indignation of the People and exposing themselves to insult and abuse" and suffering political destruction in the colony, obviously "a very disagreeable Alternative," the judges put off making their decision respecting the "dreaded" writs until the fall.[28]

Shortly after this discreet decision was made the readers of the *Courant* were treated to a vivid and elaborate account of how arbitrary and brutal the customs service could be. The lesson that was drawn from this narrative was ominous, coming so close as it did to the final crisis of the empire. "Thus," were the colonists told, "is thy parent Britain, with the Expence of Millions now shewing to you her Splendour and Affection."[29] In view of their experiences, however, the King's customs officers might very well have retorted that there seemed to be even less affection for his authority among the subjects of his colony of Connecticut.

Connecticut's political parties never forgot their differences during the supposedly quiet years of 1771 to 1773. Although their bitterly fought struggles subsided somewhat after the violent 1770 campaign, they did not cease entirely. The "old party" regularly continued to support former governor Fitch at the annual elections, but the majority of the freemen as consistently rejected the conservative candidate.[30] In so doing they uniformly followed the advice of their radical political mentors. Thus on the eve of the 1771 election the same "Unanimous" whose article had created such a stir the year before issued another bulletin "From the Chambers of the East." Again he reminded the freemen that he spoke for the Sons of Liberty in New London and Windham Counties. And again his message exhorted them to beware of the "malicious and wicked endeavours of a small discontented party."[31] Most of the voters faithfully heeded his counsel.[32]

Disagreements over imperial politics also underscored the deep differences that separated Connecticut's radical and conservative freemen. The Whig whose exercise in logic sought to prove that "Every fool is not a Tory, but every Tory is a fool," and "The man who maintains the 'divine right of kings to govern wrong' is a fool, and also a genuine Tory," inspired a brusque retort from a conservative opponent.[33] The latter's political syllogism was as bluntly argued as that of his Whig antagonist. It ran, "Every persecutor is not a whig but every whig is a persecutor— but the man who believes 'the divine right of mobs to govern wrong' is a persecutor, a tyrant, and a modest whig."[34]

Other conservatives announced their political sympathies in various ways, but those sympathies were always for the King and the empire. One Yankee royalist accused the colonial government of no longer ordering its traditional fasts in the King's name. Professing great surprise, he wondered whether the province was still "a part of his Majesty's territory," and rather innocently asked the Whigs what the monarch had done to "lose his honor in the colony of Connecticut."[35] And another local gentleman enthusiastically praised Tryon's suppression of the Carolina Regulators, for he saw in the discontent of the southern frontiersmen nothing more than a horrid "Scheme of all the Sons of Faction" to destroy "Government in North America."[36]

"Honestus" was more particularly worried about what the local "Sons" were doing to his liberties in Connecticut. In what was soon to become a typical Tory lament, this conservative freeman contended that the dominant Whigs were fast throttling real liberty. For, he complained,

Bad as our present Ministers are universally represented to be by the News Papers, they still allow us some degree of Freedom;

they suffer us to think, talk, and write as we please, but the Patriots allow us no indulgence: Unless we think, talk, and write as they would have us, we are Traitors to the State, we are infamous Hirelings to the Government.

To the author of this piece "popular prostitution" was as infamous, if not more so, than "ministerial prostitution," and the demagogue at least as despicable as the placeman.[37]

To still another conservative it was perfectly clear that Connecticut's rabble-rousing leaders were not espousing Whiggism, but of all things, the principles of Toryism. Real Whigs, he argued, sought to preserve the imperial constitution; opposed the monopolization of political powers by any one part of the government; gratefully acknowledged King William's deliverance of the nation from "popery and tryanny"; happily accepted the Brunswick dynasty and the rule of the first two Georges; considered themselves fortunate subjects of George III; and prayed "that his life and reign may continue as long as any of his predecessors." But Connecticut's so-called Whigs, he charged, neither believed nor acted upon these principles. Instead,

They strive with all their might to overthrow the constitution, pretending that it is incompatible with their natural rights. . . . They struggle to place all power in one branch [of the government] to the exclusion of the other two. . . . They are traitors to George the third. . . . They call the father of his people, and a sovereign who is most tender of the rights of his subjects, a tryant and an opposer, and threaten a revolt and rebellion. . . . They mask themselves with the name of Whigs, but espouse the principles of Tories—I hate the principles as well as the name. But if they will be called Whigs, let it be New Whigs—I love the principles and I desire the name of an 'Old Whig.'[38]

It is quite unlikely that any radical was convinced by this lesson in political terminology. In the eyes of Connecticut's Whigs the writer had probably convicted himself of being a worse Tory than before.

It is apparent that Connecticut remained divided and uneasy

even during the relatively tranquil years that preceded the crises of 1773 and 1774.[39] Continued disunity over local matters paralleled the differences between the colony's radicals and conservatives over imperial politics. The double responsibility which the Rev. Mark Leavenworth referred to in his 1772 election sermon of being "true and faithful to his majesty" and at the same time safeguarding "the interests of this dear colony as established by charter," seemed to be too heavy a burden for some Whigs to carry.[40] If pressed, they threatened to lighten their load at the expense of the former obligation. Confident of their growing strength, they were prepared to rebuff any and all "attempts to infringe upon their liberties."[41]

Connecticut's conservatives, however, persisted in carefully distinguishing between what they habitually called "lawful and licentious liberty."[42] While professing to be as determined as the radicals to preserve the former liberty, they could not countenance the latter. In that spirit William Samuel Johnson insisted that he was a firm and devoted friend to the cause of American liberty;[43] but he also believed that "the closest connexion" with Britain was indispensable for the colony's happiness.[44] Indicative of the conservative's scale of political values was his assigning to "Old England" the tribute of being the best country on earth. It must be said, however, that Johnson accorded to New England and the neighboring provinces the honor of being second best.[45] Connecticut's radicals, of course, would have reversed this order.

The critical year 1773 began quietly enough. To John Trumbull "the ferment of politics" seemed to be "pretty much subsided"; and he believed there were fair prospects that the colony would be free for a while "from the struggles of patriotism and self-interest, from noise and confusion, *Wilkes and Liberty.*"[46] But radicals bewailed this decline from the patriotic fervor of the non-importation movement. No more, one of them lamented, was anything heard "about Liberty."[47] Even the outburst against the writs of assistance early in the year was deemed insufficient evidence of a vital "Public Spirit."[48]

These plaints of Connecticut's radicals about the province's political lethargy were soon to disappear, for signs of a growing crisis were becoming noticeable throughout America. Repercussions of the *Gaspee* affair aroused uneasy feelings among conservatives and radicals alike. William Samuel Johnson condemned the destruction of the King's ship; but he believed, as did most Americans, that the ship's officers were partly to blame. Much more serious was the British proposal to try the case in England. In the self-governing colony of Connecticut this was a dangerous precedent, even to conservatives.

Equally distressing to Johnson, if not more so, was the nature of the discussion that the *Gaspee* incident provoked, especially in Massachusetts. Principles of colonial right and Parliamentary power were "nice political Questions" that Johnson thought "had better never be meddled with." He anticipated that these matters, "like some intricate perplex'd Points in Divinity" would result in little good and "much Mischief." And he clearly perceived that "While they serve to whet the Wits of Men they more surely sharpen their Tempers . . . and are equally fatal in the one case to virtuous practice and in the other to obedience to governt and in both to the peace of society." With apprehension he traced the rapid growth in America of those "Bold Doctrines" that denied the ability of Parliament to bind the colonies. This argument, Johnson feared, was "big with important consequences."[49] It was obvious to him, as it must have been to many others, that should it prevail a violent collision between the colonies and the mother country could not be long postponed.

While some Connecticut radicals also anticipated an impending conflict, their fears were exclusively for the colony's privileges. The Rev. Ezra Stiles looked forward to the "final prevalence" of American liberty, but he admitted that only God knew "by what means and in what ways" that would be accomplished.[50] Stiles confided the same views in his diary. He was certain that the British in their fear of New England's "religious and political principles" were determined to "alter Times, Customs, Names, and all usages having Liberty and Charter powers connected with them." He sorrowfully expected, therefore, that the assault on America's liberties and the Congregational churches would continue to be pushed "with great Vigor." Stiles even prophesied that "many Branches of the Tree of Liberty will be lopt off [and] many Puritans will desert the Cause and bow the knee to Baal." But despite these gloomy predictions the Puritan pastor remained staunchly confident in the ultimate victory of the colonies and his cherished church.[51]

The almost impassable gulf that separated Connecticut's radicals and conservatives made it inevitable that such a victory would have to be bought at the expense of a civil war. For while the conservatives, scornfully labelled by Yale's future president as "the Prerogative people," linked the "Ideas of the Patriots" with "Anarchy and Confusion," and seemed "to bid Defiance to all Principles of Right and Liberty," Connecticut's radical Whigs perceptibly moved to take up a revolutionary position. A more "absolute Government" became the hope of the conservatives.[52] The radicals, however, were already perfecting their plans to organize an aggressive, popular, patriotic movement for the ultimate emergency.

As early as March 1773, Samuel Holden Parsons, Lyme's radical deputy, expressed some "broken Thots" on these matters to Samuel Adams, Massachusetts' master Whig propagandist. Parsons applauded Boston's radicals for leading the opposition to the British "Invasion of their Charter Privileges," and suggested that in view of "the present critical Situation of the Colonies" an inter-colonial assembly be immediately convened "to Consult on their general Welfare." He bluntly admitted that he could not accept "The Idea of unalienable Allegiance to any Prince or State." Adams must have happily nodded in agreement when he read Parsons' opinion that the first settlers "were as independant of the Crown or King of Great Britain as if they had never been his Subjects." The only way the King had secured "Rightful Authority" over the colonists, Parsons argued, was through the latter assigning him the right to govern them.[53] The Lockeian implication in this was clear: what the people once had given it was in their power to take away.

Benjamin Trumbull, moderate New Light, patriot, and later historian of Connecticut, was as confident in the powers of the people as Parsons was; and as critical of the home government. The theme of Trumbull's sermon preached to an anniversary meeting of the New Haven freemen, April 12, 1773, was the meaningful verse from Exodus: "Now there arose up a new King over Egypt which knew not Joseph."[54] Much of his lengthy discourse was a long paean of praise on self-government and the marvel of its achievement in Connecticut.[55] The Congregational pastor admonished New Haven's citizens never to forget the principle that rulers should be kept "as much as possible dependent on the people whom they govern and intimately connected with them." For whenever rulers escape this dependence, Trumbull warned, the welfare of the community was menaced, and life and property, and all the laws of nature, reason, and religion were likely to be subverted.[56]

It was in this highly charged atmosphere that a radical Whig thought it appropriate to revive the memories of the Stamp Act crisis and to exult in the happy results that had come from the people's "bold exertions" at that time. He half-heartedly acknowledged that "Mobs are always hurtful to the community in their immediate actions." But he went on to say in a tone that boded no good to the colony's conservatives, those very same mobs "are sometimes very advantageous in their consequences."[57]

Connecticut's radicals, however, did not yet think it necessary to organize the people again in order to secure additional consequences of the same sort; they still found it adequate to move through the channels of the official colonial government. Thus, at the spring session, the Assembly approved the "weighty and important" Virginia resolutions, and created a standing "Committee of Correspondence and Enquiry." As might be expected, the majority of the committee consisted of outstanding leaders of the radical party including William Williams and Samuel Holden Parsons.[58] Less than a month later this new committee was already in action ferreting out suspected enemies of colonial liberties in Connecticut.[59]

Popular feeling against Connecticut's more conservative freemen, already considered traitors, was rising threateningly fast. An ancient tale about a prominent Wallingford Tory tells us that upon his death in July 1773, the local Whigs refused to permit his remains to be buried in the town cemetery.[60] It was in October of the same year that a radical Whig, probably Samuel Parsons, openly called upon the colonies to set up an intercolonial congress.

In itself this proposal was not very startling. But if the other points in this radical's program had been realized, America might have achieved independence several years sooner. For he advocated that the intercolonial congress should meet annually, "draw up a BILL OF RIGHTS," dispatch an ambassador to the British court "to act for the united colonies," and consider the desirability of taking every necessary step to safeguard American rights. In special deference to Connecticut's economy-minded farmers the author of this grand scheme denied that the congress would be expensive. Nor did he admit that it would be essentially anti-British. On the contrary, he protested with appropriate ambiguity that it was likely to bring about "a right understanding" with the mother country. But conservatives who read his article in the *Courant* must have been legitimately skeptical about the nature of such an understanding. For in another place the article defiantly promised that the Americans would never surrender their privileges, "but rather, as they find their power perpetually increasing, look for greater perfection in just liberty and government than other nations, or even Britain ever enjoyed."[61] This was not the language of compromise.

At this very point, however, the confusion resulting from the final great explosion of the Susquehannah issue seemingly diverted the search of Connecticut's radicals for a fuller measure of liberty. For coincident with the climax of the colonial resistance to the new tax on tea the colony's parties entered upon their last struggle over the Susquehannah Company's western claims. Late in 1773 and in the early months of 1774 this conflict overshadowed everything else in Connecticut. Even the crisis precipitated by the tea party was temporarily subordinated to it. But the diversion was more apparent than real, since the political consequences of the debate only served to sharpen the split between the radical and conservative parties within the province. Regarded in this light, the battle over the Susquehannah Company's western speculation must be considered as the immediate prelude to the revolutionary contest in Connecticut.

CHAPTER EIGHT

The Susquehannah Issue and the Election of 1774

SLOWLY but perceptibly the Susquehannah controversy had been rising to the boiling point. Failure to induce the colonial government openly to assume their claims in 1769 had not discouraged the company's proprietors. On the contrary, they had persistently pressed their project despite continued opposition to it within the colony and violent skirmishes between their colonists and Pennsylvania's agents at the actual settlements.[1] After October, 1769, they had the competent assistance of the colonial governor, Jonathan Trumbull, who had long been a member of the company and who now devoted much of his energy and skill to the task of furthering the company's interests.[2]

The speculative motives of the company's prominent proprietors were not the only forces that pushed the Susquehannah issue to its dramatic climax. Many of Connecticut's farmers suffered from a deep land hunger that was made more acute by a static, if not declining, agricultural economy and a rapidly increasing population. Crevecoeur, who was perhaps the keenest foreign commentator on American life in his day, later learned from the Wyoming settlers that the Connecticut farms they had given up had been fast losing their fertility. Incessant cropping and deplorably backward agricultural methods had already exhausted the soil in some places.[3] Not that all the good farm lands had been taken up and worn out; there was still plenty of desirable land in the colony. But the evil in the situation from the standpoint of the small farmer was that these lands were owned by absentee proprietors who either held on to them for speculative purposes or who were willing only to rent them out to tenants.[4]

Neither of these possibilities appealed to Connecticut's farmers. They found the prices of Connecticut farms too high in comparison with the relative cheapness of undeveloped areas such as the New Hampshire lands, and most of them were too independent to be willing to rent farms from others. William Samuel Johnson explained to Richard Jackson, who owned a large farm in the colony, that it was extremely difficult to induce respectable farmers to become tenants. They preferred to emigrate, Johnson wrote, so that "none but the most worthless of Mankind will stay below and labour upon the Lands of others."[5]

Johnson's conclusion is easily buttressed by statistical evidence. A very high birth rate increased the population by more than fifty thousand between 1762 and 1774, and made Connecticut the second most densely populated colony in New England on the eve of the Revolution.[6] At the same time thousands of its inhabitants moved out of the colony at a phenomenal pace in the hope of finding more and better land in other provinces. Benjamin Trumbull placed the total emigration in the twelve-to-fourteen-year period before 1774 at "not less than *thirty thousand Souls.*"[7] Silas Deane's figures were even higher; he estimated the annual emigration at about one thousand families, ar at least four thousand people.[8]

Connecticut's self-reliant farmers were confronted by obviously unequal alternatives. They might remain in the colony and cultivate "in Poverty twenty poor acres of their own," if they had them, or rent "farms [Johnson claimed these were "extensive"] ... belonging to others," or quit Connecticut for cheaper and more fertile western lands. It is not surprising that under the circumstances so many chose the latter way out.[9] To a large number of sturdy but poor farm families the territory claimed by the Susquehannah Company seemed to be the ready solution of their economic problems.[10]

Rooted in the aspirations of these people and nourished by the ambitions of its politically powerful proprietors, the company's influence steadily grew on the eve of the Revolution. In 1770 the Board of Trade had refused to intervene in the dispute between the company and Pennsylvania on the ground that the conflict was not properly an inter-colonial question;[11] and a year later a committee of the Privy Council had reported a similar decision.[12] But in the very same month that this report was made the colony moved to assume the company's claims as its own responsibility, the Assembly voting in May 1771 that the disputed lands were "well" within the boundaries of Connecticut's charter. The legislature thereupon set up a committee to collect proofs of the legality of the claim and to transmit such evidence to the colony's English agent. The latter, in turn, was asked to secure the opinion of several learned English lawyers on the matter.[13]

Early in 1772 Connecticut's case for the western lands was in the hands of its English agent.[14] But the company was restlessly impatient. Without waiting for a reply from abroad it petitioned the Assembly to extend the colony's authority over the company's settlers in the Susquehanna country.[15] The legislators were reluctant, however, to take such "a very extraordinary step . . . before they . . . had an answer from England," and therefore refused the request.[16] Special newspaper articles that elaborately described the attractive features of the western claim and exhorted the Assembly to "Rouse up, our fathers, rouse, and take care of your children's inheritance," failed to remove the legislators' caution.[17]

The Susquehannah Company had much more success in 1773. In the middle of that year the colony finally received an opinion from abroad that did not oppose Connecticut's title. Almost immediately the company's advocates moved to have the colonial government throw its full support behind the claim.[18]

Governor Trumbull devoted part of a speech delivered before the October Assembly to the subject of the western lands. He frankly espoused the expansionist cause and openly appealed to the legislature to take a similar stand. Trumbull saw the American colonies "hastening with an accelerated progress to such a powerful state as may introduce new and important changes." And he wanted to make certain that in that not too ambiguous future there would be a larger and stronger Connecticut. That was why he urged the Assembly to do all it could to bring the present colonies "near an equality."[19]

Most of the deputies concurred in the governor's reasoning and announced their determination to claim the lands west of New York which were supposedly within the charter's limits.[20] The Assembly appointed a committee to try to reach a last-minute agreement with Pennsylvania, but the committee's mission was a complete failure.[21] Thereupon, the legislature, in special session in January 1774, extended its jurisdiction to the Susquehanna settlements and erected the latter into a new township, named appropriately enough, Westmoreland.[22] The Assembly also created a committee to assist the governor to take all necessary steps to "pursue and prosecute" Connecticut's title to the lands west of the Delaware River, and to see that the colony's case was properly advanced in the mother country.[23] And finally, in order to implement its official assumption of authority in the Wyoming territory, the legislature ordered Governor Trumbull to issue a proclamation prohibiting all settlements within Westmoreland unless permission was first secured from the Connecticut Assembly. On January 27, 1774, such a proclamation was duly issued.[24]

These measures stirred up a violent political storm. The company's proprietors were overjoyed at the great victory they had finally won, a victory that shot the value of one Susquehannah Company share up to one hundred pounds in Connecticut currency.[25] But Pennsylvania and Connecticut's conservative anti-

Susequehannah party prepared for an ultimate showdown with the Whig expansionists who had finally led the colonial government to underwrite their program of westward expansion.

Assisted by Connecticut's eminent conservative, Jared Ingersoll, who had been residing in Philadelphia since 1771 as a judge of one of the four newly created Courts of Vice-Admiralty, Provost William Smith prepared and anonymously published a cogently argued pamphlet in January 1774 denying Connecticut's right to the Susquehanna territory.[26] Smith, who had more than an academic interest in the disputed lands, privately warned William Samuel Johnson that "no giving way is now to be expected from us." And, he predicted threateningly, the Crown would certainly oppose Connecticut's "intrusions." America was big enough for everyone, Smith told Johnson, so that if the Connecticut "hive must swarm," let it leave Pennsylvania alone and breed elsewhere.[27] Johnson, however, was not a Susquehannah enthusiast whose ardor on behalf of the company had to be restrained. When the colony voted to support the company's claims in 1773 he had pessimistically anticipated nothing more than "tedious controversy." And, while wishing that "the event may prove happy," his better sense made him fear the reverse.[28]

Johnson's reactions were typical of many moderate and conservative men in the colony. But Silas Deane, though a personal friend of Johnson, had little respect for the foes of the western claim or for their opinions. A zealous expansionist, he saw nothing praiseworthy in opposing the Susquehannah Company's speculation.[29] "The late Resolutions of our Assembly," he wrote Johnson, "will . . . give motion to every principle in the Colony, in one direction or another." But Deane was able to speak only in scornful anger of those who refused to follow the company's direction. In his own words, the opponents of the company were:

The Fearful timorous [who] are told of certain inestimable privileges, and truly invaluable, which if they thus attempt to exercise freely they will certainly Loose. *The Enemies* to Susquehannah and to the Leading Members in in [*sic*] Company. The Jealous of every order which are generally the ignorant, and Sluggish—Those dissatisfied with a former sudden revolution in the Colony made as they conceive partly by the influence and in favor of those, now promoting the present Measures—The restless, busy, and factious, will I expect all be in motion, and join in one direction [against the] patronizers of a Western Claim.[30]

Deane's comments are very important, for they clarify and underscore the two most important reasons, other than personal ones, for the opposition to the company within the colony: first, the fear of many conservatives that the western claim would jeopardize the charter; and second, their identification of the radicals who had engineered the political "revolution" in 1766 with the company's backers. For these reasons the conservatives were prepared to fight it out with the company and the radical political party until the bitter end. Deane made no mistake when he predicted that everyone would be in motion over the colony's western claims, but it is quite improbable that Deane or anyone else realized just how bitter the political battle over those claims would be. Benjamin Trumbull, who actively participated in the struggle, was guilty of understatement when he later described the conflict as a "considerable tumult and faction."[31]

The arguments of the conservative opponents of the company were not new, most of them having originated in the campaigns of 1769 and 1770. But time had not dulled their pertinence; nor had they lost any of their sharpness. Legislators who held stock in the company were accused of gross political immorality in considering and voting on "Matters in which they are immediately concern'd." Other word-barrages were aimed at the heavy financial costs that the colony would probably have to bear in prosecuting the claim; the supposed dangers to the charter of a lengthy litigation similar to the Mohegan case; the disreputable motives of the wealthy proprietors who allegedly proposed, if the colony's claim was successful, "to make tenants of the middling sort of people in this colony," while "they and their families live in affluence"; and the equally reprehensible motives of the bankrupts "and men of desperate fortunes" who planned to get land for nothing in the west since "they have no estates here to pay rates for."[32]

Jared Ingersoll, who privately expressed the opinion that the establishment of the town of Westmoreland was an act of "imprudence little short of madness" and likely to produce menacing results from abroad,[33] publicly attacked the company and the expansionists in the newspapers. The radicals had accused the old stampmaster of being "inimical to this Colony" for opposing the western project.[34] But Ingersoll's stinging retort claimed that the "conduct of the principal leaders and managers" of the Susquehannah Company for the past twenty years had been anything but praiseworthy. More specifically, he sharply accused the company's partisans of being so rabid in their cause that they would not hesitate to crush all criticism. He affirmed his right to speak up, and did so unequivocally by warning the colony that if it persisted in claiming the western lands it must expect absolute ruin.[35]

To prevent this catastrophe the anti-expansionist, conservative party called upon its followers to act. As early as December 1773, one of its sympathizers had urged the towns to instruct their deputies not to support the western project,[36] but his plea had failed to halt the rush of legislation in January on behalf of the expansionists. Obviously unable to control the legislature, the conservatives now proposed to resort to another kind of political action. In February one of their number, under the pseudonym of "Many," issued a call for a convention of delegates to be elected by the towns to meet at Middletown on the last Wednesday in March.[37] Ostensibly, the purpose of the convention would be to consider the emergency arising from the Assembly's assumption of the Susquehannah Company's claims.

The call for a convention joined the issue and intensified the struggle between the two parties. The Whigs were not slow in replying. Prominent patriots, including Benjamin Trumbull, Ezra Stiles, and Roger Sherman ably and vigorously defended the action of the legislature in taking over the company's project.[38] And, together with other Whigs who preferred anonymity, they continued to exploit the land hunger of the colonists with attractive accounts of the vast fertile west merely waiting their plows.[39]

The Rev. Benjamin Trumbull emphasized the numerous private and public benefits that would flow from the colony's "possession of a large tract of the finest land in the world." Carried away by his own enthusiasm, he ventured to predict that the sale of the land would yield the government an income "sufficient annually to pay all our public expenses to the end of time."[40] Then why should anyone oppose the claim? Sherman had a ready answer: its enemies were grasping land monopolists, selfish men "who love . . . wealth and power" and who preferred to have the "common people" for their tenants instead of allowing them to enjoy "fee-simple estates."[41] And the fears over the supposed danger to the charter? These were nothing more than "senseless bugbears hatched by an ungenerous, narrow contracted spirit."[42] For how, Trumbull asked in derision, could the acquisition of good farm lands "undo" an agricultural people?[43]

As the expansionists saw it the issue was clear enough: would Connecticut

endeavour to obtain a tract of land . . . five times the extent of the present settlements in the Colony, and of equal goodness, procured for, and left us by our worthy predecessors?

Or would it succumb to deceitful lies of timid men whose real design was "to serve party purposes and to stir up a spirit of discord"?[44]

This political objective, the expansionists charged, was nothing less than another attempt of the conservative, pro-British, "old party" to capture control of the colonial government. "Verax," a pro-Susquehannah partisan, accused "Many" of being a spokesman for the enemies of the provincial administration and berated the minority party for again fishing in troubled waters.[45] Another advocate of the western claim repeated the radicals' old boast that Connecticut's victory in the Stamp Act affair had been due to "the vigorous intrepid exertions of *the wise men of the east.*" He caustically compared this achievement with "the mean, mercenary conduct of a number of courtiers, that appear'd ready and willing to resign all our natural rights and charter privileges, under the vain and groundless pretence of saving our charter." And now, he went on, "the same men and their tools [are] as willing to give away part of our colony . . . as they were all our rights and privileges then."[46]

What especially frightened the radicals were the possibilities of the proposed Middletown convention. Concentrating their wrath against it, they violently attacked the convention as an insidious trick that threatened the "Dissolution of Government." And this would be a calamity, they cried, that would make "Philistia rejoice, the *Pennamites* glory, and the Tories triumph."[47] Equally dire warnings were sounded in "The Alarm's" bitter denunciation of the anti-Susquehannah party as would-be pensioners and placemen who were determined to destroy Connecticut's precious constitution. Their plan, he fumed "is not meerly to oppose the Susquehannah proprietors. . . but it is to make a revolution in the government." For good measure, the same writer threw in the charge that the opposition also proposed to tear down the colony's religious establishment and to set up "episcopal tyranny."[48] Every major difference between Connecticut's two parties was thus dragged into the debate over the western lands.

The acrid controversy between the conservative and radical parties over the issue of western expansion threw the colony "into a great ferment." Exploiting the Susquehannah issue to the fullest, the conservative party attempted to engineer a political upset that would throw the leading radical, expansionist Whigs out of office.[49] But despite the strenuous resistance of the Whigs who nervously attacked the Middletown meeting as an illegal and "new kind of legislature," and even hoped that mobs might forcefully break it up,[50] the conservatives successfully completed their plans for the convention. A strong current of fear flowing from the imagined threat of the Susquehannah claims to the charter ran through many towns, especially in western Connecticut. The conservative leaders proposed to dam up this current at the Middletown meeting and then let it loose on the radical party. Thus they hoped to flood that party out of power at the elections.

Throughout March numerous towns met to consider the "very alarming Condition this Colony is involved by laying Claim to the Susquehannah Lands," and the desirability of sending delegates to the Middletown convention. Fairfield's meeting was one of the "fullest that hath been almost ever known in this Town on any Occasion." In Stratford the inhabitants expressed their grave concern over the effects that the claim would have on the colony's "invaluable Charter Privileges."[51] And at New Haven over two hundred men petitioned the selectmen to call a special town meeting. The number of interested citizens who wanted to participate in the proceedings was so large that it was impossible for all of them to get into the State House. They therefore crowded into the Meeting House where they announced by "a very great Majority" that the western claim "will be tedious expensive, and of dangerous Tendency," and then chose delegates to represent them at the Middletown convention.[52]

Many other towns, especially in Fairfield County, were also reported to be "in Motion" as a result of the people's fears for "their present dangerous Situation."[53] Silas Deane worriedly informed Governor Trumbull that "the Towns Westward are getting into a Flame." Several weeks later he changed his simile and called the anti-expansionist movement a "hurricane."[54] He had still another simile for Joseph Trumbull to whom he agitatedly described the attack upon the land scheme as a "Torrent of abuse from the Westward."[55] But whatever it was, it gave Deane a thorough fright, enough to make him feel that popular government, though "agreeable on many Accounts, is perhaps the very worst in the World, when the steadiness, and Virtue, or firmness of the People is lost." The numerous anti-expansionist town meetings were "striking symptoms" to Deane that these virtues had already been lost.[56]

Representatives from twenty-three towns, claiming to possess two-fifths of the wealth of the colony, finally met in Middletown on March 30.[57] The delegates drew up a petition to the Assembly and a remonstrance which was to be circulated among the towns for their approval. The substance of the protest repeated the allegations of the anti-Susquehannah party about the dangers of the western claims to the colony. Connecticut's assumption of these claims was described as "pregnant with the greatest mischief to them and their posterity, and highly derogatory to the honour and interest, and destructive of the peace of the colony, and a great grievance." And those deputies who were members of the company were censured for participating in the debate on the issue in the Assembly and voting on matters in which they were directly interested as proprietors of the company.

Significantly enough, the remonstrance pointed out that it was "especially impolitic, when debates run high between the parent state and her colonies," for Connecticut to extend a dubious claim to the western lands and thus expose its invaluable charter to the threat of destruction. The convention therefore petitioned the next Assembly to exclude the company's proprietors from a voice on the question and to reconsider its pro-Susquehannah decisions of October, 1773, and January, 1774. And in so doing it is most important to note that the petitioners invoked their rights as *"British subjects . . . with the freedom of Englishmen and the duty of subjects."*[58]

The convention did more than protest. For, once the remonstrance was drawn up, some of the delegates prepared a list of candidates "from the west" for governor, deputy governor, and the Council. They probably supplemented this list, which was practically an extra-legal nomination, with plans for electing their anti-expansionist, anti-Whig slate.[59]

The radical who exposed this political "plot" excitedly denounced the convention and its work, demanded that the public officials who had participated in the meeting be stripped of their authority, and called upon the next Assembly to ban all such gatherings in the future.[60] Despite this alarmed appeal, however, most of the towns that had been represented at the convention proceeded to approve its remonstrance.[61] Redding, a conservative stronghold, ratified the protest and remonstrance without a dissenting vote and specifically instructed its deputies to support the petition at the coming meeting of the legislature.[62] Other towns, notably in Fairfield County, did the same.[63] At New Haven there was an extremely close and exciting contest with "much altercation" between the conservative and radical parties. At the April 11 town meeting the radicals put up a strong fight to defeat the protest. But despite the able arguments of several Congregational ministers, especially Professor Daggett and Benjamin Trumbull, the anti-Susquehannah petition was approved by the narrow margin of three votes, 102 to 99.[64]

Tension mounted rapidly as the campaign continued to rage up to the very eve of the elections. Charges and counter-charges filled the air and the newspapers. Spokesmen for the conservative party frantically appealed to the freemen in the western towns to unite and throw the incumbent administration out of office. In last solemn pleas they warned the colony not to take rash steps that would jeopardize the charter, not to sacrifice its rich privileges "for the uncertain rights of the western lands."[65] But Benjamin Trumbull, speaking for the other side, pointedly reminded the voters that the company had "thousands of friends in the colony, great numbers of them men of fortune, figure, and influence." And he promised there would be no "peace in the government" until the matter was finally settled.[66]

The good minister was right. There was no peace in Connecticut on the eve of the 1774 elections. Passions had been whipped up to fever heat by the party differences over the Susquehannah issue and the more serious dispute with the mother country raging at the same time. The harsh intolerance that always accompanies civil wars began to appear in the colony.

Ebenezer Watson, publisher of the *Connecticut Courant,* had the misfortune of feeling it, as a consequence of his printing an article critical of the western claim. Immediately the Susquehannah Company denounced this attack upon it as "false and scandalous," presumptuously demanded that Watson reveal the author's name, and empowered the standing committee of the company to take all necessary measures against the publisher in order to safeguard the company's interests.[67] For a while some of the Whig leaders, including Silas Deane, Eliphalet Dyer, and Joseph Trumbull, contemplated setting up a rival printer in Hartford in order to punish Watson, whom Deane considered as generally "indifferent, never friendly to the public." But through the intervention of Timothy Greene of New Haven Watson was brought "to a Sense of his Errors" without the necessity of establishing another Hartford newspaper.[68] William Samuel Johnson did not exaggerate when he told Provost Smith of Philadelphia that the controversy over the western project was being "much more warmly Agitated between our different Parties at home and with much more animosity than it ever has been or hope it will be between" Pennsylvania and Connecticut.[69]

The climax of the campaign had been reached. All the arguments for and against expansion had been stated and stated again. Now both parties awaited the outcome "with anxious suspence." Would the conservative, anti-Susquehannah party be able "to displace some of the Leading Men in office?"[70] Or would the Whig expansionists succeed in staying in power?

A last-minute detailed narrative of the Middletown "plot" and its dangerous implications reflected the fear of at least one radical freeman that his party might be defeated. According to this partial source, three different lists of nominations had been drawn up. One of these had Fitch for the governorship; the other two had Matthew Griswold for the office with a generally conservative slate that included Fitch for the Council. Obviously, the conservatives hoped to divide the voters and thus increase their chances for success. These extra-legal nominations, it was charged, were being offered "with great address and art" to sympathetic freemen. But now that "such licentiousness" had been exposed it must be crushed. Otherwise this wicked plot, "one of the lowest pieces of artifice and fraud," would subvert the authority of the Assembly, "our liberty," and the "very shadow of government." [71]

The election returns showed that most of the freemen concurred in this reasoning, for they completely rejected the nominations of the conservatives and re-elected the radical, pro-expansionist, Whig administration.[72] The eastern towns, of course, almost solidly backed the Whig party. Dyer reported that those towns were even "fuller than Common" and "very full" for Governor Trumbull. Ashfield, Mansfield, and Coventry, for example, were all strong for Trumbull and his party. Windham, Dyer's own town, faithfully gave the incumbent governor all but one vote.[73] In Lyme Trumbull received 137 votes; Fitch got one.[74] And the new town of Westmoreland voted as it was expected to do, unanimously for the pro-Susquehannah party's candidates.[75]

Complete harmony, however, did not prevail even in the eastern towns. Dyer was opposed in Windham; and in Lebanon, where the meeting was most full, seven ballots had to be taken before the town's second deputy was finally elected.[76]

Party divisions within the towns along the Connecticut River were much more serious. Silas Deane heard that Trumbull carried Wethersfield by a two-thirds majority. But in Glastonbury, although the governor won easily, the anti-expansionist party temporarily forced the election of three deputies to the Assembly. East Windsor, which had sent representatives to the Middletown convention, repudiated the remonstrance and with "usual steadiness," according to the Whig point of view, backed Trumbull by a great majority. Enfield also returned a majority for the governor; but Suffield, Deane declared, was "divided and uncertain." And in Windsor the differences were so great that it took nineteen ballots to elect one deputy.[77] Hartford was also "greatly divided." In April the conservative party had succeeded in getting the town to approve the Middletown remonstrance. But a month later another meeting reversed this decision, denounced the remon-

THE DISPUTED WESTERN LAND CLAIMS

Reproduced from a copy in *The Susquehannah Company Papers*; original in the Historical Society
of Pennsylvania

strance, and condemned the extra-legal nominations that the conservatives had drawn up as dangerous and subversive.[78]

Hartford's opinion was also the general verdict of the colony's freemen. Unfortunately it is not known how many voters supported Fitch for governor; but fragmentary evidence indicates that only 2655 freemen gave him their votes for the Council. Fitch's total was almost nine hundred less than the smallest number received by the least successful candidate who was elected to the upper house of the legislature.[79] To the conservative who glumly criticized his own party for being "strangely careless and indifferent considering the Importance of the Affair" just concluded, the results of the election were ominous. The colony, he dolefully predicted, might now expect the loss of its charter.[80]

But the fears of this conservative freeman did not dissuade the radical Whigs, now guaranteed control of the colonial government for the critical year ahead, from proceeding with their plans. They immediately acted to request the Privy Council to settle the boundaries between Connecticut's claims and Pennsylvania.[81] There was not much opportunity, however, for the home government to intervene further in the dispute.[82] Its authority was under attack throughout all America. And the radical party in Connecticut, fresh from its success in the elections, had already begun to subordinate the issue of western expansion to the more pressing matter of the colony's relationship with the mother country.[83]

To the conservatives, defeat in the 1774 elections was to mean more than popular approval of the colony's western claim. For that defeat ensured Whig control of the provincial government during the grave months when the colonies were to be engaged in their last controversy with Britain. Although the conservatives must have realized that they were but a hopeless minority, numerous die-hards chose to stand by the mother country. Within one year events were to transform this Tory position into treason against the colonial cause.

CHAPTER NINE

The Last Debate

➤➤➤➤➤➤➤➤➤➤➤➤➤➤➤➤➤➤➤➤➤✳↞↞↞↞↞↞↞↞↞↞↞↞↞↞↞↞↞↞↞↞

➤➤➤➤➤➤::↞↞↞↞

C ONNECTICUT'S parties were preparing for their struggle over the western lands when a new tea act clouded the
political horizon. The old threepence tea tax which had remained
in effect when the other Townshend duties were repealed in 1770
had not seriously disturbed the relations between the colonies and
England. Boston's radicals, of course, had not liked it. But most
of the merchants had either evaded the duty by smuggling or had
succeeded in adjusting themselves to it. Few, if any, colonists
troubled to change their drinking habits because of the tax. But
when, in 1773, Parliament permitted the East India Company to
ship its tea to America without paying the customary duties in
England, a new and dangerous issue was born.

Merchants were naturally the first to recognize the danger.
Both legitimate importers of tea and smugglers anticipated ruin as
a result of the monopoly of the colonial market that Parliament
had in effect granted to the East India Company. Other elements
in the province also saw the implications of the new tea issue,
but their interests and energies were almost completely absorbed
in the debate over the Susquehannah Company. As early as Oc-

tober 22, 1773, Nathaniel Shaw Jr. observed that the people were determined not to buy any tea. Two weeks later, however, William Samuel Johnson reported that excepting the "Mercantile" interests in Boston, New York, and Philadelphia "we are tolerable quiet in peace."[1] Newspapers appreciated the importance of the tea issue sufficiently to reprint articles that the obnoxious herb had provoked in other provinces.[2] But as late as November and December, 1773, there was more excitement in the colony over the Susquehannah Company's claims than there was over the monopoly that Parliament had granted to the more important East India Company.

Radicals were upset at this relative lack of interest in the tea question. One of them suggested that immediate meetings be held in order "to adopt Measures similar to those of our Sister Colonies respecting the baneful Article of TEA."[3] But the suggestion went unheeded. Other efforts to galvanize the people into action quickly followed. Several days after Boston celebrated its tea party a Connecticut radical expounded upon the necessity of the colonies preserving their property and rights, according to the laws of the land if possible, but, if necessary, by the "perpetual and universally binding law of self defence."[4] And, inspired by the poetic muse, still another extremist exhorted his Boston colleagues with a few crude rhymes:

> Parliament an Act has made
> That will distress and ruin trade,
> To raise a Tax as we are told,
> That will enslave both young and old;
> Look out poor Boston, make a stand,
> Don't suffer any Tea to land.[5]

This advice came somewhat late. Boston's radicals had already dumped three shiploads of tea into the town harbor. News of this daring destruction of private property and defiance of Parliament frightened conservatives all over America. William Samuel Johnson voiced the sentiments of Connecticut's "sober

People" who condemned "the steps taken at Boston as highly reprehensible and are apprehensive of their Consequences." Johnson was distraught. He lamented the failure of the colonies and Britain to reach "a right understanding about the great or at least curious Questions of Right of Parlemny Power and provincial Liberty." It would have been best had these "deep and difficult objects" been avoided. Stratford's leading lawyer-politician prayed that a violent collision over these questions might still be averted, but he feared the worst.[6] So did Suffield's New Light minister, the Rev. Israel Holly. In a sermon preached in the town on the twenty-seventh of December Holly declared that the colonies were "in a sad and woful plunge let them turn which way they will, either submit to or resist these parliament acts."[7]

Most of Connecticut's radicals probably did not agree with the Suffield pastor. Woeful consequences, they were certain, would come only from submission, not resistance. And in the opening months of 1774—the year that, John Hempstead later noted in his father's diary, brought "civil war" to the colonies[8]—they exploited the tea issue as thoroughly as they possibly could in view of the colony's preoccupation with the land question and the approaching elections.

They exhorted the people to preserve their rights, criticized their "supiness" and "total silence at this important crisis," and urged them to act although no tea had been sent into Connecticut.[9] "What think ye of the Times," one radical brusquely demanded of his neighbors, "or are ye ignorant of the Effort of America to disembogue the Vermin that are feeding on its Entrails?" He pleaded with them to show as much zeal in the cause of liberty as they had in the past.[10] And in the same breath that another Whig denied any desire to see the empire broken, he called for the immediate meeting of an intercolonial congress.[11] "For the love of your country, the love of justice, and for God's sake," an unknown patriot frantically appealed to Elizur Talcott, "take all possible care that your town don't submit."[12] Acting in this spirit of violent resistance, Lyme's Sons of Liberty presented the colony with a "laudable example" of patriotic non-submission when they promptly burned some tea that an unsuspecting peddler had brought into the town.[13]

The Rev. Samuel Lockwood, who preached the election sermon in 1774, apparently tried to balance his discourse between the conservatism traditional to the occasion and a becoming patriotism. As the theme of his lecture he took the old maxim that "Civil Rulers [are] an Ordinance of God, for Good to Mankind." He praised the British constitution as "preferable to any other we have the knowledge of," and prayed that it "may long continue." But that constitution, he unequivocally declared, required that "the just claims" of the subject as well as the Crown be "acknowledged, and fully enjoyed."[14] Lockwood admitted what the Puritans had always maintained, that rebellion against "just authority, properly exercised" was a breach of God's will. But he emphasized even more the fundamental doctrines that rulers were "made for the people," and governments must therefore be conducted for the people's good.[15] Pleading for an end to factionalism, then reaching a climax in the colony, the Congregational pastor called upon his listeners to "Fear God, honour the king, and pray for all in authority over us; that we may lead a quiet and peaceable life, in all godliness and honesty."[16]

By the spring of 1774, however, it is doubtful whether all the people of Connecticut were willing to honor the King. And recent events, some radicals probably reasoned, had made a quiet and peaceful life somewhat impractical, at least if they were to preserve their liberties. Their emotions had already been inflamed by the battle over the Susquehannah Company's western project; and the stirring election campaign had acutely sharpened their differences with the conservative party. The political kettle was thus at the boiling point when the Coercive Acts, intended both to punish Boston and to vindicate Parliament's authority, were imposed upon the Bay colony.

LEADERS IN CHURCH AND POLITICS

Upper left, the Reverend Benjamin Trumbull, from a portrait in the Yale University Art Gallery; *upper right,* the Reverend Ezra Stiles, from an engraving in the New York Historical Society; *lower left,* Joseph Trumbull, from an engraving in the New York Public Library; *lower right,* Eliphalet Dyer, from a painting in the Connecticut Historical Society

ARDENT WHIGS

WILLIAM WILLIAMS
From an engraving in the
New York Public Library

ROGER SHERMAN
From an engraving in the
New York Public Library

The Coercive Acts aroused all America, and especially the self-governing province of Connecticut. Dependent for its great privileges upon its old charter, the Puritan colony shuddered as the charter government of its neighbor was practically destroyed by a mere parliamentary statute. If Parliament could by a simple legislative decision modify royal charters out of existence, the future seemed to hold little security for Connecticut. At the same time that one of William Samuel Johnson's friends was enviously praising the Yankee colony "where the Libertys of Mankind are better understood and enjoyed than in any other Spot on earth,"[17] Connecticut's Whigs were worrying lest they would soon be deprived of those very liberties.[18]

As early as April many towns were already taking steps to defend their privileges. Silas Deane found that the practice of calling special town meetings was "growing fast into fashion in the colony." In his own town of Wethersfield the sheriff, driven by a "boiling zeal," dropped his regular duties. About all that he did was to preach; and he did that with so much fervor that he lost his voice while the townsmen were preached "almost to death."[19]

Fiery articles, dashed off by patriots whose very pseudonyms shouted resistance—"Join or Die," "An Unconquered American," "A Friend to American Liberties," and "Americanus"[20]—further fed the people's anger. These appeals conjured up all sorts of horrible taxes and miseries that the British were supposedly preparing for the colony. Connecticut's Yankees were asked by "An Unconquered American" to

Conceive of a Land Tax grappled upon your Estates, and imagine your Wheat, your Corn, your Beef, your Pork, your Butter and Cheese, and your Teams, all tax'd to maintain Pensioners and Placemen, and support the Extravagancies of a Bankrupt Nation ... The Bishops they say, are linked in this diabolical Scheme, and is it not probable they will soon take Tythes of all our Children ...?

This propaganda helped to swell the people's patriotic enthusiasm. Boston's radicals had urged the other colonies to come to their support by immediately stopping all trade with Great Britain, Ireland, and the West Indies.[21] But Connecticut's Committee of Correspondence, speaking through Silas Deane, favored a plan of action based upon the decisions of a general inter-colonial congress. Local programs of non-importation, Deane claimed, were praiseworthy but likely to be partial, productive of suspicion, and, in general, ineffective.[22] Some of Connecticut's towns did not think so; and most of them, especially those in the eastern counties, were not backward in expressing their opinions on the subject—and on other pertinent matters as well.

Throughout the spring and summer, worried Yankee farmers and merchants gathered at town meetings, drew up lengthy resolutions supporting Boston, called for an inter-colonial assembly, condemned the Coercive Acts, declared their willingness to support non-importation and exportation programs, and set up committees of correspondence. They feared the dangers threatening their privileges under the charter, that palladium of their liberties, which in the words of the townsmen of Killingly, "we once Doted upon as unalterable as the Laws of the Mead and persians"; and their fears made them belligerent. Preston, in New London County, menacingly reminded the British that the charters were the only sacred bonds tying the colonies to England. And Norwich spoke for every radical Whig in the colony when it vowed to defend Connecticut's charter liberties to the utmost of its abilities.[23]

In some towns deeds matched the violence of the words. The people of Farmington, one of the first communities to act, voted ringing resolutions on behalf of colonial rights, set up a liberty pole, elaborately tarred and feathered and then burned an effigy of Massachusetts' Tory governor and a copy of the Boston port bill, and finally cursed away the King's ministers as "pimps and parasites."[24]

Minister and law-maker were as seriously alarmed as the people at large. The General Association of the Congregational ministry deeply sympathized with Boston's plight and vigorously applauded its struggle for civil liberty.[25] Numerous deputies were eager to do more than applaud; and at the spring session of the Assembly, which Stiles found "full of Concern about Boston,"[26] the lower house adopted a long series of resolutions reaffirming the rights of the people of Connecticut as "Freeborn Englishmen," guaranteed by the laws of nature and the charter. While formally acknowledging their loyalty to the Crown, the deputies elaborated upon the powers of the colony to govern and tax itself; condemned at equal length the British violations of colonial rights, particularly Connecticut's; and warningly reminded the imperial authorities that they were determined "to maintain, defend, and preserve . . . our rights and liberties, and to transmit them entire and inviolate to the latest generations."[27]

The lower house favored entering these resolutions on the records immediately, but the Council, in a more cautious mood, postponed that action for several months.[28] This, however, did not stop Connecticut's rapid march toward revolution.

In June the Assembly empowered the colony's Committee of Correspondence to appoint Connecticut's representatives to the first Continental Congress, an unusual delegation of legislative prerogative in view of the Assembly's customary jealous attitude towards its powers. The committee met on July 13, at which time it selected Eliphalet Dyer, William Samuel Johnson, Erastus Wolcott, Silas Deane, and Richard Law, or any three of them, to represent the colony. When Johnson, Wolcott, and Law declined, the committee nominated two firm Whigs, Roger Sherman and Joseph Trumbull, one of whom was empowered to attend the Congress.[29] Before this was done, however, an attempt was made to balance the colony's representation between the eastern and western counties in order, as Silas Deane recorded the argument, "to quiet the Minds of the People by an equall location."[30] But the move was blocked and Connecticut finally sent as its delegates three staunch Whigs, Roger Sherman, Dyer, and Deane.[31]

Wolcott and Law had refused to attend the Congress on

grounds of ill health; Johnson ostensibly for business reasons. Actually, however, Johnson had declined because his conservative philosophy prevented him from assuming an obligation that might have ended in his becoming a revolutionary.

Once before Johnson had expressed the necessity of his living in peace or not being able to live at all.[32] Now he explained to intimate British friends that he had not thought "it advisable either on my acct or, on acct of the Colony, to make one of that Assembly."[33] And to Benjamin Latrobe he admitted that his refusal was the result of his belief that "being present at it, [the Congress] especially as a Measure so hostile towards Great Britain would . . . in the present state of things but tend to widen the Breach already much too great." The crisis demanded "Plans of Reconciliation" and "cool and wise" delegates. Instead, the prospects for peace were most gloomy with everything and everybody "in Motion and the Minds of the People . . . greatly Alarm'd and highly inflamed."[34]

But Johnson was not entirely without hope, and promised that he would try to prevent the people from "running into Mobs and Outrages" despite the fact that he knew that his efforts would be condemned. "A moderate man," he sadly confessed to Richard Jackson, "is a very unpopular character."[35] Johnson was correct, for while his refusal evoked the applause of the Rev. Mr. Beach, Newtown's Tory rector, and the sympathetic but gullible confidence of Silas Deane, it antagonized the radicals of eastern Connecticut.[36]

Connecticut's minority of moderate and conservative freemen agreed with Johnson that the emergency demanded more than turbulent meetings and defiant resolutions. And as time fast ran out on them they desperately pleaded and argued for moderation in the hope that they might yet stop the colony's headlong plunge into revolution.[37] They criticized bold threats and deeds, such as burning tea, as "wild or childish licentiousness." Some of them defended the powers and authority of Parliament. And all of them implored their neighbors not to be hasty or reckless, to use "Reason, not wild Passion." It was impossible to "act with too much caution in our disputes," one of them wrote, for "anger produces anger and differences that might be accomodated by kind and respectful behavior, may, by imprudence be enlarged to incurable rage."[38]

Similarly moderate and conservative sentiments might also have been heard at some town meetings. Such expressions were almost completely drowned out in the eastern towns, which were thoroughly dominated by the radical Whigs. That is why, although the latter communities generally denied any desire to see America independent and formally affirmed their loyalty to King and empire, their resolutions breathed an unmistakenly defiant spirit of resistance.[39] But not all towns were this extreme in their views.

While their resolutions also backed America's opposition to the Coercive Acts, they were more carefully worded and sometimes recommended, as East Windsor's did, a more "becoming conduct and expression of loyalty and respect" to the King and Parliament.[40] Traditionally conservative New Haven quickly voted to support Boston; but at the same time it resolved to use "judicious and constitutional measures" to safeguard the colony's rights and to maintain peace and union.[41] The committee of correspondence that was set up to attain these cautious objectives included Joshua Chandler, one of the town's leading conservatives and later a Loyalist.[42] It may have been these incidents that provoked a local radical to declare ruefully that while "the People in general are very spirited" there were still "a Few Anti-Libertines among us."[43] Chandler, however, retained the confidence of the town voters sufficiently to be elected to the Assembly in the fall.[44] Middletown chose the moderate Whig, Titus Hosmer, to its committee of correspondence, while in Glastonbury, which had resolved to oppose all threats to the colony's liberties "in every lawful Way," the Tory Dr. Isaac Mosely "was active to get Loyalists elected as Assembly Men."[45] And though a Wallingford Whig was thankful for the majority of *"true sons of constitutional liberty"* in the town, he was disgusted because there were "too many among us of *tory* principles."[46]

Moderate and Tory principles were more common in western Connecticut than in any other part of the colony. For years the differences between radical and conservative had coincided with rough sectional lines. Conservative strength had become polarized in the western counties, and radicalism in the towns east of the Connecticut River. It was almost inevitable, therefore, that the political differences in this last and most serious of the colony's crises would also follow those lines. An extremely interesting and important letter written by Theophilus Morgan of Killingworth, Benjamin Gale's town, confirms this fact.

The governor's eldest son had informed Killingworth, on behalf of the Norwich committee of correspondence, that a meeting of town delegates from New London County would be held in Norwich on September 8. Among the objectives of the meeting were the establishment of a general non-consumption agreement and "the Removal or Prosecution of Mr. [Jared] Ingersoll as an Enemy of the State." Because Morgan's reply probably spoke for many moderates west of the Connecticut River it deserves to be quoted at length.[47]

Morgan asserted:

that altho' we in the main concur in Sentiments with the eastern part of this Colony and the other Colonies on this Continent, respecting our Rights, Liberties and Privileges as Englishmen, yet you must be sensible the Western Part of this Colony never have concurred in Sentiments with regard to the best method to preserve them.

Consequently, the Killingworth moderate went on to say, "Upon these principles most of the towns on this Side Connecticut River, have no Committee of Correspondence, there has been none appointed in this Town or one Town Meeting on the Occasion." Trumbull's letter, Morgan informed the Lebanon radical, had been turned over to the Killingworth selectmen for their consideration, but he doubted whether a town meeting could be called and a delegation chosen in time for it to attend the county convention. And bluntly adding his own opinion, Morgan declared that it was entirely unnecessary for the towns to do anything about non-importation programs while the inter-colonial Congress was still in session.

His views on the Ingersoll matter were even stronger. To use force against Ingersoll would be dangerous. Such action would probably widen the breach between the eastern and western towns, rally Ingersoll's friends to his defense, and might even cause bloodshed. The Killingworth moderate recalled the numerous and bitter political battles in which the western towns had struggled to restore Fitch to the governorship. Now that Fitch had died he assumed that "all Matters respecting the Eastern or Western Interest in this Colony will naturally subside."[48] But, he reminded Trumbull, this happy state would be possible only if "no new matters are excited afresh."

Connecticut's radicals were not willing to buy the good-will of their conservative foes at this price, but they hoped it might yet be possible to convince the moderates and fence-sitters. Throughout the summer and early fall they cajoled the timid and appealed to the patriotic good sense of the "prudent."[49] And in the conservative stronghold of Fairfield County Congregational ministers devoted themselves to a special mission of political conversion.

In long sermons and hurriedly prepared pamphlets they labored to awaken their more conservative neighbors to the meaning of the crisis. Their message was simple. Never before were the people of Connecticut confronted by such peril, the loss of their charter and "birthright privileges." The alternatives were clear: the western towns must rouse themselves and show their "hearty concurrence" with the rest of America or they would but help prepare the colony and all America for a terrible fate, bondage under a "most cruel, arbitrary, and tyrannical kind of government," and, of course, "ecclesiastical tyranny."[50]

The ministers wrought well, but little time was left for debate. In the space of a few months the colonies had moved to the very brink of revolution, and in another few months they were to be engaged in real fighting. If Connecticut's moderates and Tories were to show their "concurrence" with the Whig majority they would have to do so very soon, for some radicals had already begun to use more than rhetoric to convert their conservative foes.

CHAPTER TEN

On the Eve of Lexington

-»»-»»-»»-»»-»»-»»-»»-»»-»»-»»-»»-»»-✻-«««-«««-«««-«««-«««-«««-«««-«««-«««-«««-«««-

-»»-»»«««-«««-

WHILE Whigs alternately pleaded with and raged against their more timid and pro-British neighbors, a few towns had officially begun to move against the Tories. None of them as yet openly favored violence as a remedy. Instead, they generally suggested the use of various social pressures such as declarations of public contempt and social and economic boycotts. But there could be no doubt that the colony was on the way toward fulfilling the hope of the New Haven Whig who wanted to see America "soon . . . made too hot for every one that is not a Friend of Liberty."[1]

Eastern towns again led the way. Windham and Preston expressed their "Utmost Abhorrence and Detestation" of the Massachusetts Tories who had addressed Governor Hutchinson, while Preston's Whigs closed the town to the addressers until they entertained "Sentiments more kind to their Countrymen."[2]

Other communities adopted similar sanctions against their own Tories. Pomfret resolved not to buy any British manufactures and voted to consider anyone who did so an enemy to his country. "Contempt and a total Neglect" was the formula that Coventry proposed to use against its Tories.[3] Both East Windsor and New Hartford frowned upon the use of violence. But the latter town recommended that the Tory be shown "all the Neglect, Disesteem and Contempt which his Character deserves," while East Windsor thought that he should be deprived of "the Sweets of Society, the Benefits of Commerce, and the common Advantages of the Civil Life."[4] The people of Willington approved similar principles and, in addition, promised to keep the Tories under "a vigilant Eye." And their neighbors in Mansfield promised not to attack Tories or their property "Unless the same be necessary in the Common Cause and can be vindicated by undoubted Reason."[5]

Some radicals, including a few in Mansfield itself, had already reached the conclusion that there was good reason and sufficient need to apply something more than rhetoric and boycotts against the Tories. Like Captain John Wilson, leader of the Harwinton Sons of Liberty, they were "dreadful full o' zeal."[6] Cautionary words had little effect in preventing that zeal from exploding in more or less violent assaults upon Tory supporters of the mother country.

During the summer and fall of 1774 the supposedly sober people of Connecticut took matters into their own hands with increasing frequency. Radicals in Mansfield and Ashford cooperated to induce a resident of the latter town to confess that he had been grievously wrong to speak against the "charter-rights of the American colonies." And to complete his conversion they somehow made him promise to be a good Son of Liberty for the rest of his life.[7] Similarly dramatic incidents took place in other towns. Zealous Whigs compelled Tories to suffer penance for such political crimes as not attending liberty-pole celebrations and dropping uncomplimentary remarks about the American cause.[8] Captain Hezekiah Whittelesey, one of Saybrook's deputies, was one of those whose opinions were considered highly obnoxious. A large number of Liberty Boys duly visited him early in September and convinced him of the serious errors he had committed when he had praised Parliament, denounced Boston for its rebellious attitude, and warned that those who went to the town's aid would probably be hanged.[9]

It was almost inevitable that Jared Ingersoll would fall a victim to the rising patriotic fervor. Some eastern Whigs, including the governor's eldest son Joseph Trumbull, tried to intimidate New Haven's old conservative into leaving the colony and warned him that unless he did so in ten days the "Enraged Inhabitants" would remove him "to a place fitted for your reception where all Such Villains and Traitors ought to be." But Ingersoll, hardened by previous experiences with radical mobs, refused to be frightened, even by the "Voice of Multitudes." He forwarded what he angrily described as this "high handed threat and breach of the peace towards me" to the governor and defiantly remained in his native colony without being molested.[10]

Francis Green, a Boston Tory who had signed the address of loyalty to Governor Hutchinson, was not as fortunate as Ingersoll in escaping the consequences of the people's rage. His visit to Whiggish Windham early in July was suddenly cut short when the local radicals summarily advised him to leave. The following morning the people prepared to execute their warning by hauling a cannon to the door of the tavern in which Green had passed the night. This convinced the Massachusetts Tory of the desirability of hurriedly quitting the town. He found no relief in Norwich, for when he arrived in that predominantly Whig community he got an equally warm and unfriendly reception.[11]

Such violent handling of a loyal subject prompted General Gage to demand that Governor Trumbull see to the prosecution of those who had participated in these lawless and tumultuous acts.[12] But when the leaders of the Windham radicals got wind of Gage's letter they boldly advised their governor not to interfere. "We doubt not," they confidently wrote, "but your Honor will treat the Matter with the greatest Prudence and Propriety."[13] And so he did, from their point of view. But to General Gage the governor's reaction was not at all proper, for Trumbull did nothing to further the prosecution of the men who had been responsible for the unruly demonstrations. His reply to Gage pointed out that there was another side to the story. And he therefore recommended with dry humor that if the victim still thought that he had a grievance he might turn to the county law enforcement officers for relief.[14] Significantly enough, Windham's radicals had offered the same suggestion in their letter to the governor.

The short tempers of the radical Whigs matched their boldness; and they felt that if they could intimidate the governor they might do much more to their Tory foes. Colonel Eleazer Fitch, one of Windham's most prominent citizens and one of its few Tories, brought down the people's wrath upon himself for publicly opposing aid to Boston, condemning the violent treatment of Green, and declaring that his own brother Samuel, a Boston Tory, would be welcome at his home. The local radicals promptly retaliated by voting to boycott the recalcitrant conservative and promised to tar and feather anyone who was foolish or reckless enough to break the boycott.[15] And when a Pomfret "gentleman" accused of giving comfort to Green warned that the current tendency to suspect everyone could produce "the most virulent Feuds and heart-burning Animosities between Towns, Societies and Neighbours, so much to be feared in this Day of Distress,"[16] he was fortunate to escape the tar barrel. So incensed were the extremists at an article in the New London paper criticizing the Green incident that the printer discreetly hastened to explain that he had accepted the Tory article solely to expose the errors of the "Pests of Society."[17]

Clerical supporters of the mother country were not treated more considerately than any other kind of Tory "Pests." Radicals roundly scored New Britain's Congregational pastor, the Rev. John Smalley, for having described Boston's behavior as "rebellion," advising the people not to resist the home government, and criticizing the popular pastime of mobbing.[18] A few Anglican clergymen received harsher treatment than verbal scoldings. About two hundred Farmington Whigs waited on the Rev. James Nichols upon learning that he "had advanced sentiments and principles contrary to the current opinion of British Americans," and after "some considerable conversation" they forced him to .confess and recant his political heresy.[19]

Much more dramatic and violent was the collision between Connecticut's patriots and the notorious Samuel Peters. During the summer the Tory priest had endeavored to dampen the fire of the radical spirit in his own town of Hebron.[20] These efforts earned him the inveterate hostility of the local Whigs and of the patriots in neighboring communities. In August Peters received a visit from a crowd of "Sons of Liberty Friends to America" who proceeded to search his house,[21] and the following month over three hundred patriots, led by radicals from several eastern towns, forced the Tory rector "to make a humble Confession." But before he consented to do so "a violent Affray" took place, during which the mob, becoming "warm and high" at Peters' stubbornness, rushed its victim from his home and forced him to mount a horse and ride some distance to the meeting house green. There Peters finally put his signature to the confession. After applying to the public authorities, including Governor Trumbull, Peters became convinced that it was not safe to remain in the town. Soon after he fled to Boston and the protection of the King's troops.[22] But the wrath of the eastern radicals pursued the Anglican rector even in his flight.[23] Writing from Norwich, the Rev. John Tyler warned Peters that the latter's house was under constant watch "to notify a Mob from Farmington who are redy to visit you on your expected Return."[24] But Peters never returned.

And although Tyler himself had not been molested by the local radicals all but one or two of his parishioners were already "branded with the odious Name of Tory." This gave the Episcopal priest "much concern for mine and their safety should Matters become desperate, as several Individuals here have been threatened, that at the first onset at Boston, of *Blood,* the Tories here will all be put to Death." Tyler, who had three young children, was terrified and implored Peters to burn his letter immediately after reading it.[25] Several weeks later Peters' brother Jonathan also had the shocking experience of sampling the radical temper at first hand. As the climax of a most turbulent visit Hartford's Whigs rode him on a rail, while they shouted "a Tory, a Tory, a cursed Damd Churchman."[26]

Even traditionally staid communities such as Fairfield, Newtown and New Haven witnessed rather stormy scenes. Mobs and rioting rudely shattered the peace in the first two towns, and in New Haven the radical Whigs organized an aggressive "Committee of the Friends of Constitutional Liberty." Soon after it was set up, the committee was defending itself against charges of sponsoring "mobs, riots, and unjustifiable outrages." But although it vehemently denied that it was exercising "unlawful authority to the disturbance of the peace of this town and great terror of his majesty's peaceable subjects" the local Tories were not reassured.[27] Even in Philadelphia Jared Ingersoll knew that this "Patriotick Club" had been formed "to take care of the N.Haven Tories."[28]

Governor Trumbull, Deputy Governor Griswold and other prominent officials condemned these violent outbursts, but it was beyond their power to control them. As magistrates they could not condone the usurpation of their functions by popular committees and mobs. Nor could they justify what they called popular license because it was committed in the act of preserving liberty.[29] Moderate Whigs, including Samuel B. Webb, Titus Hosmer, and Simon Deane also shuddered at "so much petty mobbings and disorders."[30]

But, as Councillor Joseph Spencer had occasion to point out, the people's zeal "for what is Cald Lyberty" ran too high to be repressed; and in the name of that liberty radicals freely assaulted hapless Tories and took pleasure in applying the "New fashion dress of Tarr and feathers" to their unlucky victims. These "Ruff Measures" were contrary to Councillor Spencer's mind, but he ruefully admitted he was "not able to prevent it."[31] New Milford's citizens were so appalled at what was happening that they gathered in town meeting to condemn "all riots, Tumultuous and unwarrantable Meetings Mobs and Combinations." And even Saybrook's Sons of Liberty deemed it necessary to censure the more hot-headed Yankees and to recommend orderly procedures.[32]

The plight of Connecticut's Tories and moderates was becoming desperate, harassed as they were by mobs, and bereft, at least temporarily, of official protection. But while they fumed in impotent rage among themselves they continued to plead for moderation in the public press. In the sanctuary of his Boston refuge the Rev. Samuel Peters, who had an unrivaled vocabulary for invective, savagely denounced the "drunken barbarous People" and raged even more bitterly against "the wretched Empty hypocritical Governor and his Seditious . . . pulpit impostors" who, the Tory rector claimed, had harangued the people to do their work.[33] In the land he had fled, fellow conservatives, carefully shielded by pseudonyms, excoriated the eastern "Scoundrels and Cowards" for their riotous and outrageous behavior, appealed for an end to the licentious rebellion against the "higher powers," and demanded that the authorities repress the shameful disorders.[34]

Enthusiastic defenders of the people's high spirits promptly shouted down the pleas of the conservatives.[35] Radicals denied that patriotic assemblies were mobs. By the same token they maintained that popular proceedings were not "violent outrages," but rather nothing more serious than "cool remonstrances."[36] William Williams openly justified the treatment that the Rev. Samuel Peters had received. And he asserted, moreover, that while he personally opposed mobs, no government could ever be completely free of them; and that in any case Connecticut had fewer than most other provinces.[37]

But other radicals were less squeamish than Williams and did not shrink from frankly urging violence against their traitorous enemies.[38] "Cassius" bluntly called for a policy of terror. "Let us then my countrymen," he cried, "force these . . . more than traitors —these parricides, to hide their heads in silence and darkness . . . or extirpate them from the face of the earth."[39] And, with biblical solemnity, "America's Friend" predicted that the Tories, having stigmatized themselves by their opposition to the colonial cause, would become "fugitives and vagabonds in the earth" carrying their marks to their deaths, and their children after them.[40]

These violent physical and verbal outbursts were the work of Connecticut's extreme radicals. But the political sentiments of the average Whig probably were not very much more moderate. A nervous tension seemed to grip the entire colony. Numerous Yankees were busy with meetings; others drew up plans for resistance and concerned themselves with military preparations. And all sorts of rumors filled the air, setting them on edge for any eventuality.

William Williams prayed that the Continental Congress would recommend an immediate commercial break with Britain and the West Indies. If it did not have sufficient patriotism to do so, he did not think that America would have enough virtue "to take up arms and shed rivers of Blood in defence of our almost infinitely important Cause." Significantly enough, Williams predicted that the salvation of the colonies "is not probably to be expected but from the one or the other of these measures."[41] Christopher Leffingwell of Norwich agreed "that the Controversy will not be decided without the Loss of Blood."[42] In the meantime, he reported, most towns enthusiastically favored non-importation. To his distress, Titus Hosmer discovered that the people of Wethersfield were so "warm" for this economic weapon that "they can't hear the least argument on the other side."[43] Stiles found "Great Tumults about Liberty" in New Haven, while similar exhibitions of an aroused and aggressive patriotism were displayed in the neighboring town of Wallingford.[44]

CONSERVATIVE
WHIG

WILLIAM SAMUEL
JOHNSON

From an engraving in the
New York Historical Society

MODERATE TORY

JARED INGERSOLL

From a portrait reproduced
in *The Susquehannah Society
Papers*, Wyoming Historical
and Geological Society

THE TORY SQUIRE, M'FINGAL

From an engraving by Elkanah Tisdale used as an illustration for
the 1820 edition of John Trumbull's *M'Fingal*, Canto III. Copy in the
New York Public Library

From Boston General Gage apprehensively studied the rapid rise of Connecticut's revolutionary fever and regularly relayed news about it to the home government.[45] Early in September he informed Lord Dartmouth that Connecticut was "as furious as they are" in Massachusetts.[46] A few days after this alarming report was written, representatives from towns in New London and Windham Counties met in Norwich under the leadership of the eastern radicals to recommend, among other things, that both the towns and the provincial government take immediate steps to meet any military emergency. Anticipating that they might soon "be under the disagreeable necessity of defending our Sacred and Invaluable Rights, sword in hand," the delegates, who included some of the most prominent figures in eastern Connecticut, urged that each town properly supply itself with ammunition, and suggested to the General Assembly that the provincial militia be strengthened by the raising of at least five thousand soldiers.[47]

Probably even before Gage learned of this meeting he warned Dartmouth that Connecticut's farmers were "exercising in Arms."[48] A rumor that violence had erupted at Boston was sufficient to end these practice sessions and send what Gage described as "numerous Bodies" of Connecticut's patriots on the march to what they thought was real war.[49] Upset at all these signs of an imminent outbreak of hostilities, the moderate Whig, Titus Hosmer, exclaimed nervously, "Great Heaven, where will these unhappy, truly melancholy affairs end."[50]

Many of Connecticut's leading Whigs had already come to the conclusion that the outcome would be war and had begun preparations for the expected conflict. At the same time that the Continental Congress was meeting to frame policies which William Williams hoped would "be big with Events, great as the happiness of almost countless Millions and lasting as time, and even through Eternity,"[51] Connecticut's patriots eagerly anticipated those policies and were getting ready to execute them.

They made certain that the colony's representatives to the Congress were informed of the proceedings and recommendations that the eastern towns had adopted at Norwich.[52] And in order to establish a more general machinery of economic resistance throughout the province, Hartford's committee of correspondence issued a call for a meeting that was held in the town on September 15. Delegates from towns in the counties of Hartford, New London, Windham, and part of Litchfield duly gathered on that date to announce their belief in the "absolute necessity of a non-consumption agreement." Should the Congress fail to go beyond approving a non-importation program they promised that they would on their own part neither buy nor consume any of the banned goods.[53] Exactly one week later a radical patriot criticized the fact that public assemblies still commonly expressed their allegiance to the King. This Yankee was convinced that most Americans were no longer willing "to be dependant upon and connected with the Mother Country."[54]

All this must have made the Tories shudder. They had little cause to expect the provincial authorities to slow down the rush of the radicals towards independence. Indeed, Governor Trumbull's address to the Assembly on October 13, 1774, must have confirmed the Tories' worst fears for he grimly predicted more trying days ahead. It seemed to Trumbull that the clouds that hung over the colonies were never darker: the colony had better prepare for the storm. Solemnly he reminded the Assembly that it had a great responsibility "to preserve . . . the invaluable blessings of Freedom contained and secured in and by our Civil Constitution wisely laid and perfected by the laborious Virtues, toils, and perils of our Predecessors."[55]

The deputies took this counsel seriously, for the first statute that they placed upon the records of the fall session provided for the encouragement of military skill and defense. At least twelve half-days of training were ordered for the colonial militia between the time the act was passed and the following May, and officers were required to make certain that all weapons were ready for immediate use.[56] Other military measures were added to these. One doubled the amount of powder, ball and flints in the town stocks. Another stipulated that proper carriages for the cannon at New London were to be secured and mounted, that the arms stored in that town be made ready for service, and that a sufficient supply of powder and cannon balls be speedily provided.[57] It did not require much foresight to predict, as Samuel B. Webb did, that "On the first hostility . . . this Colony will most undoubtedly be immediately under arms and march for Boston."[58]

The violence that the Tories dreaded and for which the radicals were hastily preparing became more imminent when the Congress at Philadelphia rejected Galloway's compromises. By denying Parliament's right to tax the colonies and recommending the establishment of a continental machinery of resistance, the Congress took steps that were little short of open rebellion. Connecticut's radicals, however, quickly acted upon its recomendations. Silas Deane promised Samuel Adams that Connecticut would "pay the most sacred regard to the resolutions of the Congress."[59] And so the greater part of the colony did.

Throughout the late months of fall and early winter 1774-75 Connecticut's towns met to ratify the proceedings of the Congress and to set up the committees that the Congress had recommended to enforce the Continental Association.[60] To supplement these local actions the radicals organized county conventions during the first two months of 1775. In several such meetings, held in the counties of Hartford, New London, New Haven, Windham, and Litchfield, the radical Whigs drew up detailed procedures for enforcing the Association, voted resolutions berating those in and outside the colony who had not yet joined their cause, and generally encouraged a vigorous patriotic spirit.[61]

The meaning of these events was not lost on the Tory supporters of the mother country. A turning point in their relationship with the Whigs had been reached in the decisions of the Philadelphia Congress. Connecticut's Tories might still plead for caution and moderation. But the time had come when they had to declare themselves either for or against the colonial position. The decisions of the Philadelphia Congress had made that inevitable. Under these circumstances towns in which Tory influence was still strong began to take their stand.

Most of Connecticut's towns had announced their patriotic position during the spring and summer months of 1774. But it was not until the latter part of that year that some of the western towns began to declare themselves. Stamford, meeting on October 7, considered it expedient to explain to "the people of this extensive Continent, that notwithstanding our long silence, we are by no means unwilling to join with our sister towns to assert our just rights."[62] Other western localities including Greenwich, Stratford, Norwalk, Redding, Fairfield and Danbury similarly announced their intention to support the American cause.[63] It is significant, however, that while Danbury's freemen also apologized for the lateness of their action, they were skeptical about the Whiggism of other communities in their county.[64]

These signs of an awakened patriotism in Fairfield County kindled the hope in some Whigs that at last the long-standing differences between the radical eastern and conservative western towns would be submerged in a common stand against the mother country. After passing through several towns in Fairfield County Samuel B. Webb happily reported in October that "the Spirit of Liberty which has so long been buried in silence seems now to rear its head." And exactly three months later William Williams told Samuel Adams that he was convinced of Connecticut's patriotic unity. What better evidence of this could there be, Williams wrote with obvious satisfaction, than that "the Scales seem to fall from the Eyes of our western Brethren."[65]

But these exaggerated hopes were quickly dispelled, for the transformation of the conservative strongholds in the western towns had been more apparent than real. Connecticut's Whigs should have been much more cautious, especially in view of the comparative apathy of those towns towards the false news that fighting had broken out in Massachusetts.[66] But in any case, the Whigs who had thought that the political conversion of western Connecticut had already been completed were rudely jolted out of their optimism. For, at the end of January and early in February 1775, the Tory sentiment that had been coerced into temporary quiet loudly exploded in several western localities.

More than two hundred voters attended a crowded meeting in the small town of Ridgefield on the thirtieth of January in order to repudiate the Continental Congress, affirm their allegiance to the King "our Rightful Sovereign," and to pledge unyielding support of "his throne and Dignity against every Combination in the Universe." [67] There was but one supreme and constitutional power "over the whole and Every part of the British Empire," they maintained, that of the King, Lords and Commons. Connecticut's governor and General Assembly were admitted to possess a "restricted" right of legislation within the colony. But the local Tories made it clear that because of this right there was no need for any "other political Guides or Guardians than sd Assembly and the Officers Constitutionally appointed by them to keep the Peace and order of the Colony." Ridgefield's Tories thus paid their due compliments to the Whig committees, conventions, and congresses that had been plaguing them for many months. They had even less respect for the Continental Congress, for in scathing terms they denounced its work as "Unconstitutional . . . Subversive of our Real Liberties and as countinancing Licentiousness." [68]

This was only the beginning. During the next four weeks several hundred Fairfield and Litchfield County Tories boldly met to challenge the Whigs and to promise their uncompromising loyalty to the sovereignty of King and Parliament. Patriotic conventions in both counties tried to cope with the situation, but their wordy—and, in the case of the Litchfield gathering, indignant—resolutions had little effect upon the Tory protests.[69] In Newtown one of the selectmen entertained an unusually well-attended meeting by selling a copy of the articles of the Continental Association for a pint of "flip" and burning other papers sacred to the Whigs. In every meeting the Tories promised that they would never be "bound by any unconstitutional assemblies of men," and many of them defiantly announced that, if necessary, they were ready to risk their very lives and property to remain British subjects and to protect the Crown.[70]

Connecticut's local committees of inspection and observation, however, were not as impotent as the Litchfield and Fairfield County conventions. Ignoring the Tory accusations concerning their legality, they were already in action, wielding the powers that their respective towns had conferred upon them to enforce the Association and to coerce inimical characters into showing a more becoming appreciation of the virtues of the colonial struggle. Breaches of the Association, ranging from minor infractions such as engaging in horse racing and the drinking of tea to the more serious political crime of criticizing and opposing the Congress, quickly brought unlucky Tories into trouble. Unless they confessed and publicly apologized for their waywardness they found themselves condemned, branded as scoundrels and dangerous enemies to their country, and cut off from all economic and social contacts with their neighbors.[71]

On several occasions Tories were threatened with or actually suffered more violent punishment. A mob of "King-killing republicans" intimidated a "loyal Constitutionalist" in New Haven.[72] And on March 1 the town government placed an official boycott on the inhabitants of Ridgefield and Newtown which caused Jared Ingersoll to doubt whether his native town would "be a proper asylum next summer for a Tory."[73] Two Ridgefield conservatives who had the temerity to justify their town's Tory resolutions in a Wethersfield tavern discovered that Wethersfield was equally inhospitable to Tory sympathizers. Immediately upon learning that the two men had criticized the Continental Congress and favored passive obedience, the local Whigs went into action. They escorted the brash Tories out of town towards Farmington, which was warned in advance of the newcomers' obnoxious political sentiments. The departure of the Tories was featured by the "Hisses, Groans etc. of a respectable Concourse of People . . . the Populace following them out of Town beating a dead march etc." From Farmington the unlucky Tories were left "to their further Transportation, as is usual, and as by Law is provided in Cases of stroling Ideots, Lunatics etc." [74]

These incidents dramatically warned Connecticut's Tories of the fate that awaited them once war broke out. But they did not transform Tories into convinced Whigs. Individual supporters of the mother country were forced, at least temporarily, to assume neutral and even patriotic roles. But most Tories were not troubled by the semi-inquisitorial Whig committees except to recognize the prudence of more carefully guarding their political opinions, and many of them continued to defy the patriots.

By the end of March 1775 neither Newtown nor Ridgefield had repudiated its Tory resolves. When some fifty Whigs in the latter town voted at that time to adopt the Association, they explained that their efforts would probably be limited and exposed to "peculiar difficulties," because "the Town as a body" would not be the enforcing agency.[75] This was made doubly clear at the April 10 meeting of the town, for the Tory majority then categorically refused to explain or modify its resolutions of January 30.[76]

As the crisis deepened in the early months of 1775, Connecticut's patriots got ready to apply the weight of the colonial government against their political foes. Nathaniel Wales grimly observed that the "Torys" still acquiesced in the apparent intention of the mother country to destroy the Americans' "Lives Liberty and property." But the patriots, Wales promised, would never submit, "no not if the furnice should be heat Seven times hotter than it has yet been heat." [77] Connecticut's "prudent Inhabitants" knew that this determination meant civil war.[78] Its patriots, however, went ahead with their plans to prepare the colony for the "last Extremity."[79] Under their influence a special meeting of the legislature was called for the second of March. That Assembly took the first official action of the provincial government against the partisans of the mother country.[80]

Before the lawmakers began their deliberations they listened to an address by Governor Trumbull. The Whig governor explained that he had called the session with "great concern and Sollicitude," for the situation that confronted the colonies was extremely grave. Increasingly menacing policies from across the sea had caused the people of Connecticut "Distress, dangers, fears, and dismal Apprehensions." And now America's internal enemies were making those dangers even more serious. His anger mounting, Trumbull poured scorn upon the Tories, whom he accused of working "with a depraved Malignant, aviricious and haughty mind" to destroy "the happy Constitution and Liberty of these English Colonies." Conciliation and compromise seemed to be impossible. With "our Freedom and all our Liberties . . . at Stake," the governor therefore exclaimed the time had come for "manly" action "against those who by Force and Violence seek your ruin and Destruction."[81]

The Assembly was not slow to heed the governor's advice. It ordered investigations of several militia officers who had been accused of Toryism and of obstructing the colony's military preparations,[82] and it established a committee to look into the affairs of Tory Newtown and Ridgefield.[83]

In the spring of 1774 Connecticut's conservative party was beaten at the polls in its last great political contest with the Whigs. A year later the Tory remnant of that party was about to be coerced in another way. During the intervening months many of its spokesmen had vainly pleaded for moderation. Even before several hundred Tories defiantly announced their allegiance to their King and empire early in 1775, several of their number had felt the wrath of patriot committees and mobs. As the second week of April 1775 opened, the wealthy New London patriot merchant, Nathaniel Shaw Jr., somberly predicted that soon "the longest sword must decide the controversy."[84] When that time came, less than two weeks later, some of the more radical Whigs were already prepared to use their weapons against the Tories as well as against the King's troops.

CHAPTER ELEVEN

The Beginning of Hostilities

*C*ONNECTICUT was practically in a state of war in the
first months of 1775, even before the skirmishes at Lexington
and Concord plunged America into full-scale hostilities with
England. The colony had rejected Parliament's authority in matters of taxation and was preparing to contest its sovereignty, if
necessary, on the field of battle.[1] Tory partisans of the mother
country were being hounded by patriot committees for their
rigid loyalty to the Crown. And the provincial government itself
had taken its first official steps to curb the stubborn Tories. All
that was lacking to complete this grim picture was a formal declaration of war.

Even in the last critical days of the empire, however, Connecticut's rulers did not discard the traditional caution that had
always characterized their dealings with England; and on the
very eve of Lexington they still affirmed the colony's loyalty to
the empire. The Assembly explained Connecticut's constitutional
position at the special March session in a letter that it ordered
Governor Trumbull to send to the Earl of Dartmouth. This document made it clear that the people of Connecticut could never

assent to Parliament's notions about taxation, since these would destroy their rights as "men and Englishmen." The legislature also denounced the Coercive Acts and complained that the cumulative effect of Parliament's recent measures had practically driven the colony "to the borders of despair."

Yet the Assembly was not without hope that a solution based on constitutional grounds might eliminate these "unhappy dissensions," for it did not believe that the principles of British supremacy and American liberty were mutually antagonistic. On the contrary, it claimed that "the interests of the two countries are inseparable"; that the very idea of disunion was shocking; and that Connecticut, despite the assaults upon its privileges, was still "unfeignedly loyal and firmly attached to his Majesty's person, family and government." Indeed, only the reestablishment of harmony between the colonies and the mother country, the Assembly protested, "can render us truly happy."[2]

These proceedings encouraged a Tory to comment that the more "respectable Members" of the legislature had won a victory over the "firebrands" and "Cromwellites" who were striving for nothing less than complete independence.[3] But William Williams countered this Tory thrust and denied that the Assembly was divided, or that any group in it had opposed the monarchy or favored independence. He did admit that there was a slight difference of political sentiment within the Assembly. But he minimized its importance, since, he claimed, it concerned only the "timeing of measures (one or two children of passive obedience, void of influence, excepted.)"[4]

Whatever moderate sentiment still remained in the colony in March 1775 was blasted one month later by the explosions at Lexington and Concord. The shots that reverberated around the world on Wednesday, April 19, were quickly heard in nearby Connecticut. Fast-riding messengers brought the first accounts to Norwich by four o'clock Thursday afternoon. New London got the news three hours later. Early the following morning it reached the neighboring towns along the Sound. Branford learned of the clash at noon the same day and by Saturday, the twenty-second, the alarm had been carried to Fairfield.[5]

Connecticut's radicals were galvanized into action. The story of the fighting arrived at Glastonbury and Enfield during the Sunday services. The patriotic minister in the former town immediately dismissed the congregation and a company of men formed to march off to Boston. Enfield's more conservative pastor, however, continued the religious services as if nothing had happened. But although a few of the "leading parishioners were measurably influenced" by him, "the *people* were not thus to be put off." They hurriedly gathered outside the meeting house, and then to the accompaniment of drum and fife noisily marched around the building until the minister was forced to dismiss the remainder of the congregation. The "animated" people then organized a company for the relief of Boston.[6]

The radicals won a similar victory in New Haven, which Stiles found "unhappily divided on politics."[7] Five days after the news from Massachusetts reached the town a meeting was held to consider the new emergency. The more conservative freemen stiffly held out against immediately taking up arms. They sought to elect a moderator from among their ranks and came close to doing so, losing by only one vote. But Benedict Arnold, at the head of a volunteer company of impetuous Whigs, was not impressed by the lingering political strength of his conservative neighbors. When his initial request for ammunition from the town's stores was refused he promptly threatened to get what he wanted by force. This induced the authorities discreetly to surrender the keys to the powderhouse.[8]

A feverish excitement ran through the entire colony. On the very day that the news of the fighting got to New Haven, William Williams, writing for the Connecticut Committee of Correspondence, assured John Hancock that "every preparation is making to support your Province." So high was the people's ardor, Williams happily reported, "that they can't be kept back."[9] The printer of the *Courant* agreed with Williams and decided to stop using the tolerant masthead which had formerly opened the newspaper's columns to all parties.[10] The time for tolerance was indeed fast coming to an end. Nathaniel Shaw Jr. was convinced that the shedding of blood made it "high time that all the Tory Party should be made to be Silent."[11]

A special meeting of the Assembly was hurriedly called for the twenty-sixth of April.[12] Again Connecticut's old but capable Whig governor gravely addressed the opening session. He stressed the inevitability of the choice that recent events had thrust upon the colony. Now the only alternative to successful resistance was "Subjugation and Slavery."[13] After pledging itself to a "Solemn Injunction of Secrecy,"[14] the legislature quickly took further steps to implement that resistance.

Although the non-exportation provision of the Continental Association was not scheduled to become effective until September, the lawmakers clamped an immediate embargo upon the export of the colony's chief food products. They ordered one-fourth of the militia out for service, and made provisions for the procuring of munitions, including three thousand stands of arms and other materiel of war.[15] To finance the heavy costs of current and anticipated military operations the Assembly resorted to the money-making powers of the printing press. In May 1773 it had ordered the emission of twelve thousand pounds in bills of credit, and in October 1774 another issue of fifteen thousand; at the special session called after Lexington it approved a fifty thousand pound issue.[16] Indeed, so serious did the legislature consider the crisis that it decided to stop imprisoning hapless farmers and merchants for debt, at least temporarily.[17]

Before adjourning, the Assembly called upon the ministers and their congregations to "cry mightily to God" for divine aid in the colony's struggle to preserve its "great and important rights and privileges."[18] But at the same time it continued to treat the

Tories on the principle that those were best helped who helped themselves. For on complaint that the major part of the west military company in Waterbury was "inimical" and was officered by "wholly disaffected" men, the legislature appointed a committee to investigate the matter and ordered it to report back at the next session.[19]

One action of this special April Assembly merits more particular consideration. This was the mission that it voted to send to General Gage. During the month of April Governor Trumbull and Connecticut's Committee of Correspondence had been in regular contact with Massachusetts. Joseph Warren had written to Trumbull on April 22, 23, and again on April 26, describing what had happened at Lexington and Concord, and requesting Connecticut's immediate assistance.[20] On the twenty-eighth, however, Governor Trumbull wrote a letter to General Gage, which the Assembly directed William Samuel Johnson and Colonel Erastus Wolcott to carry to the British officer and to get his answer.[21]

Trumbull's letter minced no words in describing Connecticut's alarm at the trend of events that had been climaxed by the recent fighting. It bluntly warned Gage that the people of Connecticut could not be merely unconcerned spectators. As much as they abhorred war, and although they dreaded "nothing so much as the horrors of a civil war," Trumbull advised Gage that they were ready "to defend their rights and privileges to the last extremity."

But the communication was not entirely belligerent. It admitted, surprisingly enough, that "we are not sure of every part of our information," and requested the British general to explain his intentions. What is more surprising is that the letter hoped that a last-minute compromise might yet succeed in staving off the impending war. And since, it continued, further military measures on the part of the British forces would not be conducive to this desirable end, it suggested that Gage should "suspend the operations of war." This would enable Connecticut "to quiet the

minds of the people, at least till the result of some further deliberations may be known."[22]

Trumbull's letter and the mission that carried it to Boston
produced mixed reactions, which was quite natural in view of
the different motives that probably inspired them. Many good
Whigs, as cautious diplomats as their forefathers, probably thought
the maneuver desirable in order to clarify for the record the responsibility for the war's first battle.[23] Others deemed it a strategic
expedient to gain time for further military preparation. That was
the way the deputies later excused their unusual embassy;[24] and
Jonathan Trumbull Jr. allayed his brother's fears with the same
explanation. According to the younger Jonathan, the Assembly
planned to "make some Categorical Demand upon Gage to his
Intentions and Designs and att the same Time be arming ourselves
and treat with him Sword in Hand."[25] He denied that the letter
and the mission were products of a divided legislature. On the
contrary, the Assembly was united, "perhaps never more so," and
"almost to a Man warmly animated and engaged for the common Cause."[26] Significantly enough, Trumbull could not say
that there was perfect harmony in the Assembly.

For Connecticut's legislature still included a few Tories and
probably a larger number of moderates.[27] These men undoubtedly
welcomed the mission to Boston for other reasons. An article
that the *Norwich Packet* printed just one day after the session had
convened aptly expressed the fears and hopes of some of these
more conservative freemen. It warned the colony that if the British
were so inclined they could "reduce us to such extremities as
would make us the most miserable of dependent beings." That was
at least one of the reasons why the author of this piece fervently
prayed that the wisdom of the wisest and coolest men might yet
succeed in effecting "a happy reestablishment of the harmony
between the two countries, which is confessedly allowed to be the
only means of supporting their political existencies."[28]

Neither of the two men whom the Assembly picked for the

embassy to Gage was a radical Whig. Johnson, who was regarded in England as pro-British,[29] looked upon the mission as a means of invoking "the temperate Wisdom of the Empire," to the end that peace might be restored and "all Parts of the Empire may enjoy their particular Rights Honours and Immunities."[30] That it failed to do so sorely grieved Stratford's eminent conservative. For a short while, however, the mission seriously embarrassed Connecticut's Whigs who had gone to the aid of Boston and caused Massachusetts' radical leaders a thorough fright.[31] But Governor Trumbull, hoping that "no ill consequences will attend our embassy," reassured the Whigs in the Bay colony that Connecticut would "act in unison and concert with our sister Colonies."[32] And so it did. Even before Johnson and Wolcott returned with Gage's reply the Assembly had adjourned.[33]

Six days later, on May 11, the regular spring meeting of the Assembly opened. No stirring political campaign such as had high-lighted the 1774 elections had preceded it. At least one Whig had considered it desirable to remind the freemen not to choose Tories for their magistrates.[34] But he had little cause to be worried, for the backbone of the conservatives' political resistance had been broken in the election of 1774 and its aftermath.

Ex-Governor Fitch had died in July 1774 and no conservative freeman possessed enough prestige and influence to take his place as the leader of the anti-radical party. Other factors had helped to hasten the political disintegration of that party. Later in 1774 and during the early months of 1775 patriot committees and mobs had compelled some Tories to keep reluctant step with their march towards revolution. By February 1775 even Benjamin Gale, who had led many of the "old party's" battles, professed to be "attach'd to the cause of Liberty." His past differences with the radicals, he now explained, had only concerned "the mode of opposition" to the British measures.[35] More stubborn conservatives in the towns of Fairfield County had openly defied the Whigs, but many of them discreetly preferred to be silent at the elections.

With the political opposition of the conservative party practically destroyed, it should not have been too surprising to Samuel Gray to find the election results of 1775 so "very agreeable."[36] Governor Trumbull reported that the elections had placed new deputies in the Assembly; probably all of these men were Whigs, for the governor noted that the legislature was as firm and resolute as ever in its "Support of the Grand American Cause."[37] The political fortunes of one of the old members of the Council, William Samuel Johnson, reflected the hopeless position of the conservatives. For almost ten years Johnson had more or less managed to hold on to the confidence of the radical Whigs. Now, though re-elected, he no longer had their backing. They probably agreed with William Williams that Johnson was too "fearful of the Almighty Power of Britain."[38] Johnson lost 50 percent of his former followers in the radical town of Lyme. Even in moderate Killingworth where he had generally won about 87 per cent of the votes, Johnson was supported by only one-third of the electorate.[39] According to Thomas Mumford, Johnson's total of 2582 votes was barely sufficient to get the conservative lawyer elected to the Council.[40]

When Governor Trumbull was sworn in he still took the oath required by English law. And in his speech of thanks to the legislature Trumbull promised to use his powers, among other things, "for his Majesty's Service."[41] But these formal nods to the authorities across the sea were more than balanced by other sentiments that the governor expressed. He commended the deputies for their patriotic defense of the colony's privileges "in this day of Darkness and Distress." Indeed, so laudable was their zeal, Trumbull declared, that it was really unnecessary for him "to recommend firmness, Steadiness, Deliberation and Unanimity in the Cause of our Liberty."[42]

Connecticut's liberty was also the subject of the most fiery passages in the Rev. Joseph Perry's election sermon. The Puritan pastor excoriated the mother country for aiming at nothing less than *"absolute despotism . . . cruel tyranny . . . the total slavery* of all America," and, of course, the destruction of the Protestant churches. There was no reason, therefore, he assured the Assembly, "to be afraid to espouse and maintain our just rights." Governments must secure the people's happiness. "When this end is counteracted, Rulers pervert their authority." And in that case, the good minister asserted, both the first law of nature as well as divine revelation justified "opposition to the oppressor." America's cause was thus eminently good. "It is the cause of *religion,* of *liberty,* of our country, and consequently the cause of God!"[43]

Thus sanctified by magistrate and minister, the General Assembly resumed the task of preparing Connecticut for war. It extended the embargo on provisions until the first of August; adopted the same articles of war for Connecticut's troops that had been drawn up by Massachusetts' Provincial Congress; authorized the emission of more paper money to finance the "incident charges of Government," now chiefly of a military nature; and passed a law encouraging the manufacture of "Fire-Arms and Military Stores."[44] And, to assist the governor in defending the colony when the Assembly was not in session, it created a Council of Safety.[45]

It also received and acted upon the reports of two committees that had been set up in March and April to investigate charges of Toryism against several militia officers. One report found Abraham Blakesly of New Haven, captain of a company in the second regiment, guilty of "disaffection to this government and privileges thereof as established by charter." The Assembly therefore "broke and cashiered" him from office.[46] The second committee, which had looked into the affairs of the society of Northbury, in Waterbury, also discovered evidence to substantiate the original complaint. As a result, the Assembly "cashiered and dismissed" the captain and ensign of the west company from their military posts.[47]

These legislative achievements evoked Governor Trumbull's commendation. He was especially pleased that the Assembly's work had been featured by "great Harmony and Concord."[48] But conservative William Samuel Johnson was unable to approve the colony's preparations for war and left the Council one week after the election.[49] East Windsor's deputy, Colonel Erastus Wolcott, who had gone with Johnson to Boston, remained to participate in the affairs of the Assembly. According to Jonathan Trumbull Jr., however, Wolcott's attempts at moderation made no impression upon his fellow deputies.[50]

Even before the May Assembly had completed its deliberations General Gage considered Connecticut to be in open Rebellion.[51] Of course, it had been so for some time, as was all America. During the next two months, and especially after Bunker Hill, Connecticut's revolutionary activities were greatly accelerated.[52] By the end of July Benjamin Church described the colony as "Raving in the cause of Liberty."[53] And to Ezra Stiles it seemed that America had already become a republic, in fact if not in name.[54]

CHAPTER TWELVE

Toryism Becomes Treason

->>>->>>->>>->>>->>>->>>->>>->>>->>>->>>->>>->>>-><-<<<-<<<-<<<-<<<-<<<-<<<-<<<-<<<-<<<-<<<-<<<-<<<-

->>>->>>-<<<-<<<-

*U*NFORTUNATELY, the American people were not in perfect agreement when they established their new republic. Perhaps as many as one-third of the total population were indifferent to the patriot cause; and the Tories, amounting to perhaps another third of the population, were quite content to remain subjects of the British King. In varying proportions, these sentiments were to be found in every colony from New Hampshire to Georgia, including Connecticut. And everywhere, even in the traditional "land of steady habits," the loyalty of the Tories to the empire complicated the patriot struggle and ultimately turned it into a civil war.[1]

It was not easy, however, for every Connecticut Yankee to declare open war upon his Tory foes. Patriot committees had roughly handled a few of the more outspoken supporters of the empire, but as late as the spring of 1775 most of the British partisans in the colony had not been seriously molested. The provincial government had merely begun to put the Tories under a closer scrutiny. And although by May 1775 a formal state of war existed, the Tories were still free to move around, and to speak their minds, if they dared. They might even carry their firearms. The Assembly had ordered a few investigations and had cashiered several militia officers for "inimical" deeds and statements. But few radicals would have agreed that these penalties were sufficiently severe to cope with what they deemed a grave menace.[2]

Anticipating this judgment, the Rev. Joseph Perry had devoted part of his election sermon to a discussion of the most appropriate methods of dealing with the Tory question. As a good Whig he could not unequivocally condemn the violence that patriot mobs had been wreaking on some sorry conservatives during the past year. In fact, he excused the mistakes made by over-enthusiastic Whigs and those instances where "matters may have been carried too far. . . . And no wonder," he exclaimed, "for *if oppression will make a wise man mad,* it may be expected it will make the inconsiderate and less judicious, absolutely frantic."[3]

But it was not desirable, the patriot parson cautioned, to let this frenzied ardor run riot.[4] A prudent zeal guided by suitable men was much better than "rash attempts and spirited tumults." Specifically, that meant the Tories ought not to be assaulted in "persons or property" or referred to "with indecent language." A "deserved contempt and total neglect" would be more becoming. Perry thought this policy was "so proper in itself, and so agreeable to what is recommended by the wisest among us, we hope and wish the same may be duly attended to, in our own case." But he discreetly reserved a convenient loophole for radical Whigs who had to resort to more forceful measures: this moderate policy, the minister concluded, was to be followed only in "*so far as may consist with* absolute safety."[5]

By this time it was becoming increasingly evident to a growing number of patriots that moderation was no longer compatible with such safety. Whigs who were not content with merely repudiating England as their mother country, but who must speak of her only as "a vile imposter . . . an old abandoned prostitute

. . . a robber, a murderer . . . crimsoned o'er with every abominable crime, shocking to humanity!"[6] probably thought even less of the Tory supporters of that country. Scorn and hatred dripped from the article of the "Son of Liberty" which described the Tories as "subtle and malicious beyond Measure . . . a sort of amphibious Beast that can practise his Monkey tricks either by Land or Water."[7] Radical patriots demanded that such "Monsters" be more vigilantly controlled. And until the General Assembly was ready for extreme measures their committees of inspection and correspondence made certain that Connecticut's Tories did not get out of hand.

Although these committees did not literally follow the counsel of the "Son of Liberty" who urged them to give the Tories "no Quarter" and whose slogan was "convince, convert or confound them,"[8] they were quite successful in realizing his desire to force British partisans "to bow . . . and lick the Dust." Numerous Tories suffered this humiliating experience, and considered themselves fortunate that "Trumbull's Mobbs"—Samuel Peters' phrase—did not take their lives.[9] Their fears on this account were unduly exaggerated but not entirely groundless,[10] for it seemed that the "Sons of Oliver . . . trumpeters of rebellion" were really sounding the doom of the King's faithful subjects in Connecticut.[11] By prudently keeping quiet, the way one Middletown Tory temporarily did, they might avoid the "patriotic and searching espionage" of the Whig committees.[12] But while many did preserve a discreet silence, enough Tories refused to trim their political convictions to keep the patriots busy.[13]

All sorts of political misdemeanors quickly stirred the vigilant committees into action. Buying and drinking tea were considered hostile acts, and were duly punished.[14] Even failure to observe the continental fast was deemed a political offense for which the sinners, supposedly Tories, had to confess and repent before they were forgiven.[15] Words as well as acts were judged. Tories who admitted their loyalty to the King or had the temerity to criticize the patriots immediately fell foul of the people's sentinels.[16] To express one's doubts about the political trend of the day was considered as "inimical" as cheering Lord North in Windham's meeting house. New Haven's committee of inspection decided that "reproachful Speeches" were a breach of the Continental Association, and publicly warned all and sundry against making any "contemptible" remarks about the Congress.[17] Even before the committee announced this policy it had compelled Tories to admit their waywardness in having ridiculed the Congress, the committees of inspection, and the colony's preparations for war, including its newly-issued paper money.[18]

Similar confessions were wrung from Tories in Harwinton, Killingworth, Simsbury, and Groton.[19] Soldiers marching through New Milford and Litchfield incidentally forced their Tory victims to eat "Humble Pye," in one case garnished with an external dose of tar and feathers.[20] The more customary treatment, however, was not so violent; generally the local committees merely investigated suspects and ordered the guilty to be "*universally neglected and treated, as incorrigible ENEMIES.*"[21] In Waterbury, where at one time it was rumored that three hundred Anglican Tories were in "Insurrection," British sympathizers actually discovered that they could not even damn the patriots with impunity.[22] This was equally true in the nearby towns of Derby, Woodbury, and Wallingford.[23] Wallingford's Anglican missionary and rector of St. Paul's Church, the Rev. Samuel Andrews, quite naturally became suspect for taking as the text of his sermon, delivered on the day of the continental fast, the following lines from Amos V, "I hate, I despise your feast days, and I will not smell in your solemn assemblies."[24] And Benjamin Hall, also of Wallingford, discovered to his dismay that he had become an enemy to the cause of American liberty because he had hired as a tutor a person reputed to be a confirmed Tory.[25]

This virulent patriotic fever raged throughout the colony in the late months of 1775 and early the following year.[26] And what was even more significant, it spread to the conservative western towns where the local Whigs had not been too successful in curbing their own Tory dissenters. Early in January 1776, after he had been forced to flee to Long Island for safety, the Rev. Richard Mansfield sadly informed Samuel Peters of the changes that had occurred in some of those towns. In Mansfield's own words the

violent Spirit in the Whigs of harassing and oppressing the loyal Tories which then prevailed most in the Eastern Parts of Connecticut spread itself by Degrees into the Western Parts, where during the last Summer and Autumn it raged with as much and I believe more unbridled Fury than ever it had done at the Eastward.[27]

Derby's Anglican rector may have exaggerated the story, which is quite understandable considering the rather trying experiences he had just suffered;[28] but he was not mistaken about the accelerated tempo and the increased efficiency with which the patriots in the western towns were disciplining their political enemies. Sylvanus Whitney learned that to traffic in tea was as dangerous in Stamford as it was in New London. After forcing Whitney to confess his "crime," the local committee of inspection turned over some confiscated tea to the town's radicals, who burned it with great ceremony.[29] Stamford's committee also arrested some Norwalk and Stamford Tories who had joined forces to beat up a Stamford Whig, made them confess, and extracted the promise from them that they would hereafter devote themselves to the colonial cause.[30] Other local Tories were duly punished for "speaking disrespectfully" about that cause and "acting inimically" against it.[31]

What happened in Stamford was duplicated elsewhere in Fairfield County. Stratford's committee thought that to dispute "sometimes . . . one way, and sometimes the other," was a political offense, and convicted several inhabitants of being Tories on that charge.[32] And at the suggestion of their committee of inspection,

Fairfield's Whigs, "choosing rather to die freemen than live in a state of servile subjection to any man or body of people on the face of the earth," organized a patriotic association of 855 men. Some seventy local dissenters who refused to join promptly found themselves condemned as enemies to American liberty.33 By September, Fairfield's patriots had taken it upon themselves to disarm several Tories in North Fairfield and Ridgefield.34 In the same month Norwalk prohibited Tories from coming into the town on the ground that their presence would "disturb the peace . . . and obstruct our endeavours in defence of our liberties,"35 and early in November Danbury's committee recommended that the selectmen approve a similar ban.36

This steadily rising patriot tide threatened to engulf the Tory minority. Every day the conviction that tolerance was weakness became more widespread. One month after Ticonderoga and Crown Point had been taken, Thomas Mumford believed that it was "time to speak out our full sentiments: those that are not for us *now,* surely must be against us. It will be time soon to distinguish the true patriots from the Junto of Ministerial Slavery, and put a mark on the latter, that they may be treated, *if possible,* equal to their deserts."37 By August a radical "Son of Liberty," having lost all patience with judicial procedures, angrily demanded the application of summary measures against the Tory "transgressors."38

Formal town resolutions echoed this caustic appeal for greater severity. On September 19 the once moderate community of New Haven unanimously ordered its deputies to press for the establishment of a colony-wide association and the enactment of a comprehensive anti-Tory law.39 Two weeks later the town of Mansfield hinted that lands owned by Tories could be put to better use by patriots. Another fortnight later Middletown seconded New Haven's recommendations with similar instructions to its own deputies.40

But New Haven's Whigs were impatient and did not wait for

the Assembly to act upon these suggestions. Early in November the local government took the first step to purge the town of its Tories.⁴¹ On the same day this decision was reached, New Haven's most prominent Whig, Roger Sherman, advised a correspondent that it was not wise to have any further dealings with "a Traitor." ⁴²

Despite this rising pressure from Connecticut's most fervent patriots, the General Assembly still hesitated to outlaw its Tory population. During the summer and fall months of 1775 the energies of the colonial government were almost wholly devoted to the "subject matter of the unnatural civil war."⁴³ And yet, although the Council of Safety anticipated that the colony's jails would soon be crowded with prisoners of war and British partisans,⁴⁴ the provincial government was reluctant to direct all its guns against the Tories.

Governor Trumbull pointed out to the new October session of the Assembly that "dark and tempestuous Clouds hang over us," and referred to the fact that "The Sword of Civil War by our Brethren from the other side of the Atlantic is drawn upon us." But he did not request any special legislation against the Tory brethren on this side of the ocean.⁴⁵ The Assembly displayed similar caution. Some deputies submitted a test bill that would have required a pledge of support to the provincial government and a promise not to aid the British in any way, but final action on the measure was put off to the following session.⁴⁶ By comparison, the towns and even the Continental Congress were more aggressive than Connecticut's legislature. As early as April, Norwich's uneasy radicals had demanded that Boston's Tories, even their womenfolk and children, be banned from the town; a month later the Whigs had succeeded in getting the local government to exclude all "Inimical Persons."⁴⁷ And on October 6 the Continental Congress had recommended the arrest of anyone "whose going at large may . . . endanger the safety of the colony or the liberties of America." But, despite these local and intercolonial precedents, Connecticut's October General Assembly failed to take final action on a bill that would have confined suspected Tories.[48] The legislature obviously found it difficult to break traditional habits of caution even when fighting a revolutionary civil war.

Not that it was entirely passive on the Tory question. Upon satisfying itself that there was a dangerous sympathy for the British in Waterbury's west military company the Assembly had the trainband dissolved.[49] And it ordered two Woodbury Tories, one of whom was the Anglican missionary, the Rev. John R. Marshall, to appear at the following session to answer charges that they had spoken "in derision and contempt" of the American cause. But the procedure that the legislature prescribed was soberly judicious.[50] The moderate Whig who felt it necessary to warn the people against the pitfalls of "great warmth and ungovern'd zeal," and who was worried lest intolerance and bigotry poison the colony's public affairs had little cause, as yet, to be concerned about his lawmakers on these accounts.[51]

But while their deputies preferred to be cautious, many patriots refused to be inhibited by similar compunctions. This was especially true of those colonials who had already shouldered muskets against the redcoats. The better part of a year had passed since the Tories in the western towns had defied the Continental Congress and the provincial government. During this time British and American forces had fought several bloody engagements. While Connecticut's Tories had not as yet done anything in an organized military fashion to implement their threats to stand by the throne, there was no telling what they might do in the future, and as long as they had their guns they were potentially dangerous.

Ugly rumors began to float around. In Newtown the Tories dominated the community. Two local Whigs asserted in a lengthy complaint that the Tory authorities refused to give any part of the town stock to the patriots but generously distributed it to the "Malignants." Some Whigs feared that their enemies were planning to "extripate" them, and appealed to the neighboring towns for aid. So serious did the patriots in the latter communities consider the situation that they decided to disarm the Tories, not only in Newtown, but in other near-by towns where the Tories were numerous. Towards the latter part of November Colonel Ichabod Lewis, Stratford's patriot deputy, led an expedition of several hundred men to execute this self-imposed task.[52]

Two days were required to complete the job in Newtown. A Whig's version of the disarming claimed that it was done "in a quiet Manner with many Gentlemen of the first Character in the County" participating in the effort.[53] But Derby's Tory rector, the Rev. Mr. Mansfield, who attributed the belligerent project to some militia officers just returned from Boston, told another story.

According to his unsympathetic narrative, soldiers and minute men were recruited from several towns "for the declared purpose of distressing and subduing the Tories." When the small Whig "army" got to Newtown, they immediately placed its Tory rector, the Rev. Mr. Beach, the selectmen, and several prominent residents under guard, and demanded that they all sign the Continental Association. At first the prisoners refused to bow to superior force. But they were finally compelled to post bonds to guarantee that they would neither take up arms against the colonies nor encourage others to do so. The patriots also got them to promise "not to speak disrespectfully of the Congress." In the meantime they had disarmed all the Tory suspects. But Mansfield charged this was not done without their destroying "a great deal of private property."

Upon completing their mission in Newtown, the patriots repeated their work in Redding, Danbury, Ridgefield, and Woodbury.[54] Isaac Sears assisted in Redding, a town that was scornfully described by a Whig as being "famous for harbouring a Swarm of those detestable Animals called Tories."[55] Some Woodbury Tories who refused to surrender their firearms were immediately arrested by the Liberty Boys and marched off to the Litchfield jail.[56] In Ridgefield the disarming of the Tory majority so heartened the local Whigs that they made another effort to seize control of the town government. On December 7, 1775, they finally succeeded in doing so, whereupon the town officially approved the Continental Congress and its measures "for Securing and Defending the Rights and Liberties of the united American Colonies" and set up a committee of inspection. Inspired by these examples, Derby's patriots, acting through their committee of inspection, disarmed the local Tories during the first week of December.[57]

Derby's Tory rector claimed that not even these violent incidents were able to shake the Tories' loyalty to their King and the empire.[58] In December the truthfulness of this boast was in effect admitted by the provincial government. For the December session of the General Assembly, the last colonial legislature to acknowledge the regnal year, finally approved Connecticut's first anti-Tory law.[59]

Several weeks before, Washington had recommended the seizure of active Tories and those who "are known will be active against us."[60] Governor Trumbull also reached the conclusion that some punitive action was necessary, and in a speech delivered before the Assembly on December 14, asked the deputies to draw up "Rules and Regulations . . . to prevent the Operation of the evil practices and designs of persons inimical to the rights and Liberties of the Colonies."[61] One week later the governor predicted that the Assembly would pass a "sufficiently spirited" act against the Tories.[62] And so it did, according to Trumbull, with "Great harmony and unanimity."[63]

Connecticut's first law against its Tories was severe, but it was not harsh or unjust. Its lengthy provisions outlawed the following activities: the direct or indirect supplying of the "ministerial" forces with food, military or naval stores, and information; enlisting or inducing others to enlist in those forces; taking up arms against the Americans; piloting ships of the "ministerial" navy; or aiding or assisting the British "in any other ways." Tories convicted of any of these offenses before the Superior Court were to forfeit all their estate. Jail sentences up to three years could also be meted out at the court's discretion.[64]

Connecticut's patriotic lawmakers were not content with levying these heavy penalties against the more serious types of possible overt aid to the British military. They were also determined to silence Tory tongues and to still the scratching of their pens. It was therefore made illegal to "libel or defame" by the written or spoken word, as well as by "any overt act," any resolution of the Continental Congress or the "acts and proceedings" of Connecticut's General Assembly. Tories whom the Superior Court found guilty of committing such crimes were made ineligible for all civil or military offices. The statute also authorized the court to impose additional punishment in the form of fines, imprisonment, and disfranchisement, or to require that sufficent bond be posted to guarantee the convicted Tory's continued "peace and good behaviour."[65]

Still another section of the law empowered town officers and their committees of inspection to investigate and disarm Tory suspects, not only within their own localities, but in any "adjoining town in the same county" where committees of inspection had not been set up. Thus what patriot committees and mobs had been doing for some time with more enthusiasm than legal right was now sanctioned by law.[66]

Theoretically, Connecticut was still a British colony, but by this statute it made it a crime to be loyal to the empire in either word or deed. In taking this position, however, the Assembly more than anticipated the recommendations adopted by the Continental Congress on January 2 and March 14, 1776.[67] Moreover, in doing so it was undoubtedly keeping step with the march of Whig sentiment outside Connecticut as well as in the colony. Washington and General Philip Schuyler of New York heartily applauded the measure.[68] Connecticut's first anti-Tory law was both an understandable product, and a necessary preparation for the times, which, in the apt words of Nathaniel Shaw Jr., were to be marked by "Warr, Ravaging Villages, Burning of Towns etc."[69]

The new law did not wait long to be enforced. Andrew Adams, who, ironically enough, still prosecuted cases as the "Attorney of our Lord the King" in Litchfield County, had filed a complaint against Benjamin Kilborn, a lieutenant in Litchfield's first military company, accusing him of having violently condemned the Americans, and having promised that he would soon take up arms against them. The Assembly promptly cashiered their refractory officer and ordered the attorney to prosecute him "in law for said offenses."[70]

Tories were arrested and tried with increasing frequency in the first six months of 1776; and when the Superior Court moved to Fairfield in the spring it found a large number of indicted suspects awaiting trial. Alleged Tories in Ridgefield, Redding, Greenwich, New Fairfield, Norwalk, and even a Yorker from Cortland Manor were arraigned before the Yankee judges.[71] By August, Newtown's grand jurors, now entirely Whig, had begun judicial proceedings to deprive eighty-three men, who had apparently been the leaders of the local Tories, of their privileges as freemen.[72]

If this were not enough to complete their misery, Connecticut's Tories discovered that they had not been released from the probing jurisdiction of the committees of inspection. For while cases against Tory suspects piled up in the court dockets, Whig committees continued to dispose of the British partisans in their own way; and most of the farmers on the committees of inspection did not worry, as the delegates to the Fairfield County convention did, about whether they were treating the Tories "with good order and decency."[73] Good measures were effective ones. The committees followed the procedures of the Continental Association when they were thought adequate. But numerous Tories were commonly subjected to more than public scorn and boycotts.[74]

As a result of being disarmed and jailed, twenty-five New Milford Tories "had much opportunity for information and reflection"; when they were released they had acquired new political convictions.[75] Patriot mobs showed very little order and as little decency when they rode unlucky Tories on rails and forced them to flee their homes in very fear of their lives.[76] By May and June it was again admitted that in some towns the people's "growing zeal" was getting out of control. As one neo-classicist put it, that zeal was about to split on "Scilla in the Attempt to avoid Carribdes."[77]

It was inevitable that this popular ferment would further sour the next Assembly towards the Tories. The regular spring General Assembly opened on May 9. Practically all of the legislators were firm Whigs,[78] so that the many warnings that had come in the press and from the pulpit against the election of Tories and turncoats had either been universally heeded, or perhaps, had not really been necessary.[79] And despite an attempt to clear William Samuel Johnson of the widely-held suspicion that the conservative councillor was pro-British, the freemen refused to re-elect him.[80] On the other hand, with the political opposition of the "old party" virtually destroyed, Governor Trumbull's votes were "almost Universal."[81]

The Whiggism of the Assembly and the governor was fully matched by the aggressive patriotism that glowed in the Rev. Judah Champion's traditional election sermon. Litchfield's Congregational pastor extolled the extraordinary virtues of Connecticut's form of government. Where else in a popular state, he asked, could one find "so little of riotous and factious behaviour." And "if a perfect civil constitution cannot be found existing," he proudly boasted, "yet our own we esteem, by far, the most eligible." That was why it was imperative to preserve that constitution. With great passion, Champion exhorted the deputies

For Heaven's sake and for our own . . . act up to the dignity of our character as free-born Americans . . . Now by the love of God to perishing sinners—by all that Christ hath done and suffered to purchase our privileges and eternal salvation—by the worth of your own precious and immortal souls—by all that is dear and sacred—by all your regard to the sacred Trinity, to yourselves, to posterity, and to your country, we beseech and adjure you to *Stand fast in the Liberty wherewith Christ hath made us free.*[82]

Almost immediately the Assembly approved additional measures to preserve that liberty. It appointed a committee to consider the desirability of revising the oaths of loyalty required by existing statutes. Little time was consumed by the committee to find that it was no longer consistent with "Truth and a good Conscience to make Use of Such Oaths as Impose either allegiance or Fidelity to his Brittanick Majesties person Laws or Government." The Assembly therefore removed the inconsistencies by deleting all references in those statutes to the royal government and the regnal year. Its new test oath demanded allegiance only to the "Colony and Government . . . as Established by Charter."[83]

These were not the only changes. Fast-moving events had already made it anomalous to retain the old treason law which imposed the "Pains of Death" for waging war against the King. The Assembly therefore repealed it.[84] In any case, most of the people of Connecticut would have brusquely denied that they were rebels. In the words of their governor, "the Rebellion is on the part of our Enemies."[85] The implications in this was clear. A new kind of treason law for Connecticut's real rebels, the Tories, would soon have to be drawn up. In the meantime, some deputies were already demanding that Tories accused of committing certain crimes be denied the right of bail. Most deputies, however, were not yet willing to go this far and rejected the bill of their more radical colleagues.[86]

Notwithstanding all these danger signals, Tories continued to be active, especially in western Connecticut. Disturbing news inflated by rumors reached the provincial government from that part of the colony. The authorities were shocked to learn that two Woodbury Tories, one of whom had already been forced to post bond "for his notorious and malicious Language and avowed Conduct," still carried on a profitable business with the commissary department. They immediately sent Jeremiah Wadsworth to investigate and clear up the matter.[87] Much more serious was a report that the Tories in and around Newtown were plotting to "overthrow . . . at Least this part of the Country." Captain Seth Harding relayed the same gloomy tidings to the governor: "the unnatural Combination betwixt the the [*sic*] Tories Dayly grows more and more open."[88]

Governor Trumbull was alarmed at these developments which tended to confirm his pessimistic Calvinistic belief in "the deep degeneracy and Wickedness of which Mankind is capable." He immediately laid the matter before his Council, which speedily prepared necessary precautions to dissolve the danger.[89] Another patriot, much more frightened, frantically called upon the people to crush these "hellish schemes" of the Tories. If this were successfully done, he assured them, "the power of hell and Britain will never prevail against us."[90] But the Assembly was by no means as confident about the ease of the struggle that it had just taken on with the might of the empire. Emphasizing the military danger, it exhorted all able-bodied men not already in the services to prepare to resist the British forces now attempting to execute a "causeless vengeance on these devoted Colonies."[91]

This was one of Connecticut's last references to its colonial status.[92] The regular spring Assembly adjourned on the eighth of June. Six days later it was called back to an extraordinary meeting to begin the legal process of changing that status to independence, and in the forenoon of June 15 the Council approved a resolution, previously passed by the lower house, authorizing Connecticut's delegates to the Congress "to declare the United American Colonies Free and Independent States."[93]

Again this meant that the Tories would suffer. Later in the week-long extra session the Assembly threatened them with the loss of their moveable property as well as their real estate.[94] And when, on June twenty-fifth, John Hancock transmitted to Governor Trumbull several resolutions of the Congress, one of which had to do with the prevention of "insurrections," Trumbull was able to reply that Connecticut already had legislation to obviate just such "mischief and danger from persons inimical."[95]

But those laws were not sufficient; and Connecticut's assumption of the powers of an independent state made it inevitable that its dissident minority would soon be subjected to further penalties. Throughout the new nation the Declaration of Independence tended to eliminate the "tories-timid-moderate and double minded men from the counsels of America" and left the new states with "ten times the Vigor and Strength they had formerly."[96] In Connecticut the effect of the Declaration was less extreme, for even before independence the colony had been purging its political dissenters from the public offices that they filled. But independence radically altered the legal relationship between the Tory fraction of the population and the new state. Aiding the enemies of a state at war was treason. It was time, the patriots felt, to punish the Tories for this most heinous of political crimes.

As early as April Governor Trumbull had urged the seizure of the Tory "Malignants in every Colony." This measure was desirable for military reasons, the governor explained, and, in addition, would shout America's determination "to enjoy Liberty and Freedom while we live."[97] But even before the Council of Safety received the Declaration of Independence on July 11, other patriots were impatiently clamoring for more extreme measures against those whom their governor had called the "Hypocritical Friends who seek our Ruin."[98]

Ominous rumors of Tory plots in the western towns reinforced these demands, while over-inflated suspicions made everyone tense. One nervous account told how a Fairfield County Tory had murdered his Whig employee.[99] A single doubtful expression in a conversation was sufficient to have the wary Hartford Whigs haul a suspect before the local committee of inspection.[100] "Public

Compassion" showed little mercy to the Tories. Lenient measures, he bluntly declared, had outlived their effectiveness, and further efforts to convince the Tories would be worse than useless. Nor would the continued advertising of their names and misdeeds in the newspapers do much good. Putting traitors in jail was expensive and allowing them to remain free was dangerous. The hour had struck when "the utmost rigour of the law of retaliation" must be applied. Those who refused to take an oath of fidelity should be enslaved. "Then our gaols may be uncumbered from the horrid lumber of torryism, and our bosom freed from the adder."[101] David Trumbull also thought that it was "high time to do some thing more with the Tories than just to Confine them."[102]

But although the new state government tightened its controls over the Tories, it was not yet prepared to execute these extreme demands. When Simsbury's committee of inspection complained that Tory prisoners in the Newgate jail were causing the people "great uneasiness," and that the keeper himself was "uneasie with his situation," the Council of Safety authorized the establishment of a special night guard to help quell any outbreak.[103] Most of the "Malignants," however, were not in Newgate or in any other prison. They were still free to move around; and in doing so it was possible for them to be useful to the British in many ways.

To prevent the dangers arising from this condition, the town of Milford voted on July 8 that no one was to be allowed to enter and reside within its limits unless he could fully satisfy the local committee of his patriotism.[104] A week before, the Governor and Council of Safety had been advised to issue an order regulating the movement of persons within the state.[105] The Council accepted the recommendation, and on July 18 ruled that in the future all who were not generally "well known and friendly" would be prohibited from moving from one town to another until they could produce written evidence from some lawful civil or military authority certifying to the legitimacy of their travel and their patriotism.[106]

But the radicals still were not satisfied that these efforts were adequate. Their fears were heightened by Howe's successful campaign against Washington around New York. With that city in British hands it was possible for the numerous Tories in the western towns near the New York border to become an immediate military menace.

"Lenity" voiced these apprehensions in a violent diatribe that belied his pseudonym. Let "the Vengeance of America . . . awake and consume" the Tories, he cried. They were of absolutely no use as citizens. Indeed, they were a mere "deadweight to the Community. . . . They have outstaid the Day of Trial," and certainly they can no longer be convinced of their error. " 'Tis Time to cut them off." This patriot's remedy was by no means lenient, for he would have as soon suffered "a Witch, as a Tory to live." [107] Seconding this demand for extreme punishment, another radical advised the publisher of the *Courant* that it was a pity to pollute the paper by printing the names "of this stinking Race." Such publicity was no longer successful. It might have been useful at an earlier time "to reclaim such as were honestly under a Delusion. But the Tories at this Day require other Means of Conviction, or rather, they Sin with their Eyes open, and don't mean to be convinced." Only one really effective remedy remained— "the Halter and the Gibbet." Tories who did not merit this punishment, "if there be any such," might be put into Newgate "under proper Regulations." Watson agreed with his reader's advice, at least in part, for he immediately promised to stop printing the names of the Tories.[108]

The demand for summary measures reached a climax in September and October. A worried appeal of a group of New Haven Whigs to the Governor and Council of Safety expressed great "fears and apprehensions" about the continued residence of some Tories in the town, and requested that the suspects be removed.[109] Other developments caused the patriots much deeper concern. On October 14 Ezra Stiles recorded in his diary the news that the

Fairfield County Tories seemed to be conspiring and preparing "for Insurrection." This moved the Puritan pastor to the significant comment: "The Patriots and Friends of Liberty dont Love to take violent Courses with them, but begin to think they must."[110]

Stiles was right. The October Assembly, the first to appear in the official records under the new name of *General Assembly of the Governor and Company of the State of Connecticut in New England in America,* was finally prepared to apply much sterner measures against its Tory population.[111] Newtown, which seems to have been unrepresented in the May Assembly, sent two deputies to the October session.[112] But the House of Representatives refused to permit one of the deputies to take his seat after finding him "inimical to the American States." The other deputy relinquished his claim.[113] The presumably all-Whig legislature then approved the Declaration of Independence, absolved Connecticut's inhabitants from "all allegiance to the British Crown," and declared that henceforth "all political connections between them and the King of Great Britain is, and ought to be, totally dissolved."[114] The Assembly was careful to state, however, that the form of government established by the old royal charter would otherwise continue unchanged, since there was nothing in it that was inconsistent with Connecticut's "absolute independence." Most existing statutes were also declared to be in force.[115]

The few changes that were made, however, were extremely significant. All references to the King in the new state's writs and processes were, of course, eliminated;[116] and a new test oath demanded the sworn allegiance of every freeman and candidate for public office.[117] Towns were permitted to confine "inimical and dangerous" persons to restricted areas, or to remove them to places where they would be less dangerous.[118] And finally, to the radicals' undoubted satisfaction, "High Treason and other atrocious Crimes" against the State of Connecticut were made punishable by death.[119]

The Assembly gave its special attention to the western towns. In appointing a committee and investing it with extraordinary powers, the deputies accused those towns of harboring many hostile Tories who had been "forming dangerous insurrections," and relaying information "to comfort, aid and assist the enemies of these united States and to distress the inhabitants of said towns to bring on a general anarchy and confusion among them." Since these dangers threatened Connecticut at a most "critical and convulsed" time "when the ordinary mode of prosecution will not be adequate to the mischief apprehended," the Assembly ordered its committee to disregard the procedures established by previous legislation and to examine, remove, and, if necessary, confine dangerous suspects under proper guard. Such confinement was to continue until the Governor and the Council of Safety thought it no longer necessary for the public security.[120]

The meaning of this last measure was clear. The emergency was deemed too great and the Tory malcontents in the western towns too numerous for the government to rely upon the slow processes of ordinary civil justice against its internal enemies. At least temporarily, therefore, the new State of Connecticut deprived its Tories of the protection afforded by those processes. In Connecticut the revolutionary struggle for independence had finally taken on the full character of a civil war.

The events of 1775 and 1776 marked the passing of an era in the history of Connecticut. To the Yankee patriots and the magistrates who had led them through the critical decade before 1776 and into the Revolution to independence, those events constituted the first chapter of an even greater and more glorious history than Connecticut ever had as a colony.[121] But the Tory minority read the record of the past decade in another light; their future appeared even gloomier.

That dismal future had, in fact, already engulfed them. Familiar worlds of old and cherished loyalties had slowly been destroyed before their eyes. Gradually, with typical Connecticut caution, but inexorably, the dominant patriot party had shattered the last ties between the colony and the Crown and empire. The King's sovereignty, which Connecticut's seventeenth-century Tory, Gershom Bulkeley, had once described as a "sceptre of gold," had been thrown off. Their new sovereign, the Tories found, were the freemen of the State of Connecticut; and every step that these freemen had taken towards independence had been accompanied by progressively sterner laws against those who had preferred to stick to their old allegiance.

By the latter part of 1776 that loyalty had been outlawed as treason to the new sovereign and punishable by death. With some cause the Tories might have echoed the plaint of their seventeenth-century predecessor, that sovereignty "in the hands of a subject" was "a rod of iron."[122] And they might have repeated his lament, which had turned out to be a prophecy: "We are traduc'd and reviled as enemies to God, our country, and to wholesome laws and good government, an ungoverned crew, sons of Belial rebels etc., because we will not rebel, but persist in our allegiance."[123] It was only in the fire of war that the stubborn allegiance of Connecticut's Tories to the British Empire was finally destroyed.

CHAPTER THIRTEEN

A Summary View

CONNECTICUT appeared to take the last steps from a
self-governing province of the British Empire to an independent commonwealth with relative ease. A few simple acts and resolutions had been sufficient to effect the revolutionary transition to
statehood. The existing form of government based upon the more
than century-old royal charter was carried over intact. In other
provinces independence was accompanied by varying demands
for more democratic revisions of the new state governments, but
Connecticut's separation from the empire was not seriously complicated by such discontent.[1] Most of the magistrates in the last
days of the colony were patriots and remained to head the new
state. Only the people's allegiance and the sovereignty to which
they had been subject were changed. Even as Connecticut began
its revolutionary struggle for independence its traditionally "steady
habits" seemed to prevail.[2]

If the preliminaries of the Revolution in Connecticut could
be properly limited to the events of 1775 and 1776 this judgment
would, on the whole, be sound. But even then it would not be
completely satisfactory, since it ignores the dissident Tories who

very much objected to taking up arms against the mother country and finding themselves citizens of a new republic. It must be completely rejected, however, when viewed in the perspective of the long and bitterly fought factional and party conflicts that preceded and led up to Connecticut's final revolutionary stand. A Fairfield County Tory was much closer to the truth when he declared, in the very same month that the colonies announced their independence, that Connecticut had been "greatly convulsed and many of the good people thereof perplexed, confused and distracted to know their duty in the great controversy."[3]

Some embittered Tories subsequently explained Connecticut's participation in the Revolution as a natural outcome of its perverse colonial history. It was almost inevitable, according to these Tory accounts, that Connecticut, founded by Puritan "Rebells" and nourished on seditious "republican Principles," would ultimately renounce not only bishops, whom they had never accepted, but "Lords and Kings."[4] The colony had indeed been established by men who desired to worship God in their own way and who found that it was good to govern themselves with a minimum of imperial interference. Quite naturally, therefore, as Governor Trumbull admirably explained on one occasion during the war, the descendants of those founders, having long "tasted of freedom and . . . personal rights," could never "easily . . . bear with encroachments on either."[5] Always suspicious of British designs on their political and religious liberty, Connecticut's Yankees were inevitable Whigs in the last crisis with the mother country.

Contrary to what vindictive Tories thought, however, early eighteenth-century Connecticut was not a breeding ground for revolution. The colony's ruling aristocracy of magistrates and ministers cherished and carefully sought to preserve their political privileges and religious establishment. But the ministers always inculcated, and the magistrates always demanded, respect and proper subordination to duly constituted authority. Twenty years before he became one of the colony's revolutionary leaders and signed the Declaration of Independence, Roger Sherman described the seditious "as the worst enemies of the state."[6] And although the souls of the elect might be equal in the eyes of God, their bodies in Connecticut were consistently ranked and rewarded on the basis of such selective criteria as family background, wealth, religious affiliation, and apparent godliness. The "democratical" elements in Connecticut's eighteenth-century religious and political institutions were more than neutralized by their aristocratic features. Immediately after the Revolution Yale's learned President, the Rev. Ezra Stiles, voiced the fond hope that the new nation would follow in Connecticut's footsteps and adopt that best of all governments, "a well ordered Democratical Aristocracy."[7]

The well-ordered province of Connecticut had enjoyed relative peace and harmony in the late seventeenth and early eighteenth centuries. Periodic storms from abroad had menaced its charter, but all of them were successfully weathered, and within the colony most of the freemen had generally been in fundamental agreement on religious, economic and political matters.

But during the three decades before the Stamp Act this unity was more or less rudely shattered. Bitter religious conflicts, ruefully described by one pastor as the "civil wars of the Lord," accompanied and followed the Great Awakening. While these religious wars divided the established Congregational church into conservative Old Light and radical New Light factions, the Anglican church slowly but steadily grew in numbers and influence. Much less dramatic, but equally significant, was the gradual transformation of the colony's simple agrarianism and the consequent development of new economic forces. Symptomatic of these changes were the mounting unrest of a relatively small but vocal merchant class, and the organization of speculative land companies which began to stake out vast claims to the unsettled West. Even before the Stamp Act convulsed the colony its freemen had already been split into religious factions, and were beginning to form opposing groups on the issue of western expansion.

The crises that the policies of the home government precipitated within Connecticut during the 1760's re-oriented the colony's factions around the larger imperial question and fused them into two hostile political parties. Most of the Old Light and Anglican freemen, who were numerically strongest in the towns west of the Connecticut River, and especially strong in Fairfield County, probably constituted the bulk of the colony's conservative party.[8]

Although not homogeneous religiously or politically, the ranks of that party more or less held together until after the elections of 1774. Some of the freemen who consistently supported the conservative party's candidates in the annual elections were cautious moderates in politics as well as religion. They were not happy about the extension of Parliamentary power over America, but they feared and resolutely opposed the violent forces that Connecticut's more radical freemen had organized and unleashed against that power. Other conservatives, mostly Anglicans in the western towns, were much less concerned about the colony's traditional religious or political privileges, and much more uncompromising in their devotion to the mother country. It was this political combination of varied conservatives, dubbed by the radicals the "old party," that tenaciously fought the promoters of the Susquehannah Company's project.

Arrayed against the conservative party were Connecticut's more radical freemen. Although the latter were to be found in every town in the colony, they dominated, and were best organized, in the uneasy communities of New London and Windham Counties.[9] Their leaders confessed that they were not always pleased at the violent methods of the Whig mobs, but they always considered the policies of the mother country much more dangerous to their political liberties under the charter, to their economic interests, and to the established Congregational church.

Most of the leaders of the more radical party were New London and Windham County merchants, lawyers, and Puritan, especially New Light, divines.[10] And many of the very same men, notably among the merchants and lawyers, assumed the major roles in the affairs of the Susquehannah Company. This tie-up is most striking in the cases of such stalwart patriots as Eliphalet Dyer, Governor Trumbull, Samuel Gray and William Williams, to name but a few. But the overlapping interests and affiliations of less-known Whigs are equally revealing. Perhaps most interesting is the case of Colonel John Durkee of Norwich, one of Connecticut's "forgotten Sons of Liberty." It was Durkee who headed the mob of Liberty Boys from the eastern towns against Ingersoll in September 1765, and it was the same man, a bankrupt merchant, who led the Susquehannah Company's settlers in the coveted Wyoming lands of northern Pennsylvania.[11]

A decade of bitter political conflict climaxed the difference between Connecticut's parties. In 1766 the radicals exploited the Stamp Act issue to achieve an extraordinary political upset. Meeting in what was practically an extra-legal nominating convention, they decided to oust conservative Governor Fitch and four of his equally conservative assistants. This political plot was successfully executed.

But in every succeeding election through 1774 the conservatives campaigned more or less strenuously to restore their candidates, especially the ex-governor, to their former posts. Issues over which conservative and radical partisans spilled much ink in the newspapers covered both local and imperial questions. When the proprietors of the Susquehannah Company decided to push their project to a final decision, the conservative party concentrated all its guns on the company and its western claims. But underlying every issue that arose between the two parties was their basic inability to agree on what the colony's position should be towards the imperial crisis. In two most bitterly fought contests the conservatives came close to returning Fitch to the governor's chair. Their major effort in 1770 fell short by only a few hundred popular votes.

But they were unable to break the hold of the radical party on the colonial government. Furthermore, Dyer's prediction that the results of the 1770 election "will be lasting for some time" was remarkably prophetic.[12] For although the conservative party stubbornly conducted another stirring campaign in 1774, it was badly beaten. The triumphant patriot party entered the final crisis in full control of the provincial government.

After the Whig victory in 1774 the political opposition of the conservatives began to dissolve. That disintegration proceeded rapidly throughout the next two years. The death in July 1774 of ex-Governor Fitch, the "old party's" perennial candidate for chief magistrate, removed its most important political figure and left it leaderless, and the vigorous organization of Connecticut's patriotic resistance to the Coercive Acts virtually completed its destruction. For out of that organization came the machinery of committees and congresses that was easily and frequently used against those who distinguished themselves by their lukewarmness or outright hostility to the colonial cause.

Moderates in the "old party," convinced perhaps of the futility of continuing their struggle, or agreeing finally that the greater danger to the colony really did come from abroad, began to join their former political foes in a common stand against the mother country. By February 1775, Benjamin Gale, the erstwhile avowedly irreconcilable enemy of the Sons of Liberty, protested that his past differences with the radical party had concerned only "methods not objectives." Explaining his amazing conversion, if conversion it was, Gale maintained that now "different sentiments of the *mode* of opposition must not divide us in making opposition."[13] Conservatives who were less certain of this need for unity against Britain were forcefully convinced by ardent patriotic committees and mobs into maintaining, at the least, a discreet silence on political matters.

With the political opposition of the conservative party practically destroyed, the Whigs encountered little difficulty in the
election of 1775. One of Windham's most prominent patriots happily observed that the outcome was "a very agreeable one." The
results were even more agreeable a year later, for Trumbull, the
patriot party's candidate for governor, was now re-elected by
"almost the universal voice" of the colony.[14] By 1776 all that remained of the conservative "old party" was its politically impotent
Tory fraction.

Connecticut's patriots, in common with most American
Whigs, heartily detested those of their neighbors who for one
reason or another remained loyal to their King and a united empire. In this respect the Revolution produced somewhat the same
symptoms among the sober people of Connecticut as it did elsewhere in America: suspicion, intolerance, and rather violent
hatreds. No less prominent a Whig than Jeremiah Wadsworth
observed that early in the war the suspicions of "unreasonably
jealous" patriots ran "so high as to involve some very good men
in great difficulties."[15]

Persons whose politics were not quite so good undoubtedly
experienced even greater difficulties. And "the tongue of Jealousy,"
to use an excellent Tory phrase, probably confused many a private
disagreement with more serious political differences.[16] No one
will ever know how many charges of Toryism were based on
nothing more substantial than personal grudges. But there must
have been numerous incidents similar to the one in which a Connecticut patriot supposedly admitted that he had "no little Prejudices . . . but a Great one" against the unfortunate person whom
he had accused of being unfriendly.[17] As late as 1779 Governor
Trumbull himself confessed that it was not uncommon for inno-
cent men to find themselves unjustly suspected or accused of
disloyalty.[18]

But although patriots sometimes disagreed as to whether
they should pin the Tory label on some suspicious character, most

of them, especially the radicals, were in very close agreement in their views towards the Tories as a class. Their feelings were succinctly expressed in William Williams' scornful reference to the Loyalists as the "enemies of God and man." [19] Equally popular must have been the half-humorous, half-serious opinion that "A Tory is a thing whose head is in England and its body in America and whose neck ought to be stretched." [20]

Not all of Connecticut's "Malignants," as Governor Trumbull often called the Tories, were quite so evil. Nor was their stand in the Revolution as incomprehensible or as utterly malicious as some contemporary Whigs made it out to be. Virtues and defects common to the human character were probably distributed as generously among the King's supporters as they were among the patriots, even though the latter found it difficult to see any virtues in a Tory. Within the Loyalist camp were many men of strong principle who had defied the dominant Whig party before the Revolution and defied it again during the war and remained true to their convictions. [21] More than a decade of bitter party conflict had steeled their animosity towards the Whigs and deepened those convictions.

Such Tories were, of course, extremely conservative. Most of them were thorough royalists. They never hesitated between what seemed to them the only alternatives of "peace, order and government," or rebellion. [22] Like their seventeenth-century predecessor, Gershom Bulkeley, they believed that kings were not ordinary men who could be trifled with. [23] Born and reared as subjects of the Crown they had been taught to "fear the Lord and the King," and they persistently refused to acknowledge that the people of Connecticut had cause to behave or even to think otherwise.

As they saw the conflict between the colonies and the mother country, there was little "Propriety or Justice" in the revolution. [24] Indeed, one Tory claimed, Connecticut had no substantial grievance whatever. For over a hundred years the colony's interests, together with those of all America, had been the object of lenient and solicitous "British Princes, and Their Ministry."[25] No revolution could ever secure for Connecticut "a more mild and moderate Government" than the one it had been privileged to possess as a part of the empire.[26]

Shocked and terrified by the "unhappy Struggle between prince and people," these Tories did not have a single sympathetic word for their revolutionary foes. They abhorred the Whigs' republican principles, scorned the patriots as a "Factious Multitude," and bitterly complained of the "Infamous" persecution that loyal subjects suffered at the hands of aroused mobs and vigilant committees.[27] "Wo unto you," one Tory cursed his tormentors, "for you make it your dayly Practis to distress and Parsicute those who are conscientious in being Lige Subjects."[28] The revolutionaries, raged the Tory rector, the Rev. Samuel Peters, with his usual venom, say they "hate Tyranny, but . . . their meaning is they hate Tyranny when themselves are not the Tyrants."[29]

These extreme views were held and expressed by men who preferred to live under the orderly rule of what they fondly regarded as English "legal Liberty." But in Connecticut it seemed to them that the revolutionary leaders and their followers, "the Beasts of the People," had inaugurated a reign of anarchy, dominated by the "Sons of Darkness," "The Vulgars," and "Ungovernable, Rioteous, and high-handed moberenes."[30] It is not surprising to learn that Connecticut Tories who felt this way about the Revolution were willing to "Kill more Damnd Rebells than the Best Brittain."[31]

Not every Tory was this bloodthirsty. Nor were they all equally stirred by such deeply held, conservative political convictions. Pardon acts passed by the legislature later in the Revolution were specially designed to appeal to those Tories whose devotion to the monarchy and the idea of a united empire evaporated as the war dragged on. In these cases various personal factors rather than solid political principle explain why some men temporarily espoused the Loyalist cause.[32]

Among such factors were quite common human frailties; fear, selfishness, and plain ignorance. Early in 1775 a Whig described some Tories as "the fearful and unbelieving brood" who were convinced that colonial resistance would be easily crushed by the British armies.[33] And later in the conflict large numbers of penitent Tories petitioned the General Assembly for clemency, confessing that their political heresy had been motivated by a great fear "that the country would be conquered."[34] While these "very gloomy apprehensions for the fate of [their] Native Country" depressed some colonists into becoming Tories, others admittedly cast their lot with the British for more mercenary reasons, such as hoped-for rewards of "Considerable Privileges," good-sized farms, and, of course, the more common instinct to save what was already owned.[35] One Tory petitioner claimed that he had repressed his own Whig sympathies in order to continue working the land that he hoped some day to inherit from his Tory father-in-law.[36]

Surprisingly large numbers of self-described ex-Tories sought to restore themselves to good standing later in the Revolution by throwing the blame for their political mistakes upon close relatives, friends, and religious mentors. Usually such petitioners attempted to clear themselves by protesting that they had originally been completely ignorant of the real issues at stake. Thus, according to their apologies, they had either been "seduced," "deceived," "beguiled," or "perswaded" into opposing the patriots.[37] Somewhat typical of these laments was the admission of one repentant royalist that he had been "entirely unacquainted with Politics, did as almost every ignorant man generally does, swim with the Tide or current near him—and was a Stupid ignorant Tory."[38]

Another group of Tories must be distinguished from the royalists by principle or expediency. Between these extremes were conservatives whose preference for the *status quo* under the charter had led them not to a revolutionary position but to moderate Toryism. In the decade before 1776 these moderates had condemned reckless and violent protests against the mother country, and when the final crisis engulfed them they dreaded the inevitable war.39 The differences between such Tories and the more moderate patriots were almost imperceptible. In the last resort, however, the former hesitated and then refused to participate in a revolutionary war for independence. But, on the other hand, they were equally reluctant to aid the mother country's forceful suppression of the colonies.40

In this dilemma they prayed for peace and hoped to the bitter end that a compromise might yet be worked out.41 Most of them tried to be neutral until independence made that impossible.42 Some, such as Jared Ingersoll; the Secretary of the colony, George Wyllys; Thomas Darling of New Haven; the Revs. Benjamin Woodbridge and Nehemiah Strong, and the conservative Anglican, William Samuel Johnson, ultimately succeeded in reconciling themselves to the idea of an independent America.43 But as late as 1780 Redding's Tory deputy, William Heron, who effectively combined his legislative work with spying for the British, claimed that most of Connecticut's Loyalists still were "for preserving the charter" government within the empire. And, according to Heron, many had originally become Loyalists "because they conceived that the Independent Party, exposed it [the charter] to Dissolution by their intemperate measures."44

Most of Connecticut's Tories were Anglicans. This should have been somewhat of a disappointment to the Rev. Samuel Sherwood, Fairfield's Congregational pastor, who had publicly affirmed his belief in 1774 that there were good patriots in every Christian denomination.45 But the fact is quite understandable, and at the time was fully known to Connecticut's Whigs.

Relations between the Anglican minority and the dominant Congregationalists had never been satisfactory to either group. Long-standing and occasionally very bitter quarrels had hardened their antipathies toward one another. During the Great Awakening the members of the Anglican communion had been a conservative bulwark against the religious extremism that subsequently developed into political radicalism. Connecticut's Anglicans took the same conservative role in the Stamp Act crisis and in every other conflict that arose between the colony and the mother country on the eve of the Revolution. Their clergy had always had something less than admiration for Connecticut's powers of self-government under the charter, for those powers were the means by which the special privileges of the Puritan churches were preserved. And while the established Congregational church dreaded the extension of imperial controls over the colony and the creation of an American episcopate, Connecticut's Anglican ministers eagerly looked forward to both of these developments in the hope that they might thus be released from the evils of a Puritan state and church.[46]

As the Revolution approached, the colony's Congregational pastors commonly blended their preaching with Whig politics.[47] And despite their protestations of neutrality most of the Episcopal ministers spiced their own sermons with another kind of politics, "inculcating upon their Hearers the Duties of Peaceableness and quiet Subjection to the Parent State."[48] These lessons were not lost upon their respective congregations. When the final break from the mother country was made, the Episcopal church, laity and clergy, was thoroughly loyalist.[49]

So were the relatively few members of that peculiar religious sect, the Sandemanians, who had once before found doctrines in the Scriptures that had shocked their Puritan neighbors. For even as Connecticut's Yankees were waging war, the Sandemanians, again claiming the Bible as their infallible guide, declared that subjects had a clear injunction "not to meddle with those who are given to change," and to be duly obedient to the divinely established secular powers.[50]

With little modesty one of Connecticut's Tories described the colony's Loyalists as its best people, "Steady, Sober, Discret, Religious, and understanding men."[51] Some Tories undoubtedly were, for these were virtues that abounded in Connecticut. Even Samuel

Holden Parsons admitted in one of his less partisan moments that a Tory could be a gentleman, except, of course, "in his political creed."[52] But if the Tories were not all ignorant scoundrels, as some Whigs preferred to believe, neither were they all gentlemen by eighteenth-century standards.

Generally speaking, the Tories included a cross-section of all levels of Connecticut's social and economic classes. Some were able to claim descent from "Ancient and reputable" families.[53] Colonel Eleazer Fitch, who had been Governor Trumbull's business partner and was one of those rare persons, a Windham Tory, traced his ancestry back to the colony's founding fathers, and numbered the famous Major John Mason among his forbears.[54] Even after hostilities had broken out, Tories filled political and military posts, especially in the governments and trainbands of the western towns. And as late as 1775 and 1776 the Assembly had to "purge" the militia of inimical officers, while in several communities, chiefly in Fairfield County, many of the local officials continued to be open British sympathizers.[55] So were those who held the handful of royal jobs in the colony.[56] Some Tories were college graduates, mostly Anglican ministers with Yale degrees,[57] and a few were practising lawyers and physicians, both with and without the benefit of formal collegiate training.[58]

In an agricultural economy, where according to Silas Deane a man who had 250 fertile acres was considered rich, and neither great wealth nor abject poverty was common, it is not surprising to discover that most Tories seemed to have been moderately prosperous farmers.[59] Inventories of confiscated estates and Tories' claims for compensation indicate that a large percentage of Loyalists owned fair-sized improved farms and buildings in addition to varying amounts of personal property.[60] And a small number were artisans, such as hatters, weavers, cobblers, blacksmiths and glovers, most of whom later protested to British commissioners that they had been in "good circumstances" before the Revolution took them from their trades and destroyed their fortunes.[61]

There were not many in Connecticut who could have counted their wealth in the thousands of pounds, but among these few very rich were some Tory merchants, lawyers, and landholders.[62] At the other end of the economic scale, however, were to be found supporters of the mother country who confessed that they were "rather low in their circumstances."[63] All that some of these less fortunate persons had to show as their worldly possessions, before the patriots confiscated them, were tiny pieces of land and a few head of cattle.[64] And other Tories had no real estate at all, although they claimed that before the Revolution they had owned some small amounts of moveable and personal goods.[65]

How many Tories were there in Connecticut, and what percentage of the population did they constitute? These are important questions, but it is impossible to answer them with absolute certainty. More than fifty years ago Professor Tyler's pioneering article underscored the difficulties of attempting to arrive at even approximate conclusions concerning the numbers of American Tories.[66] Fortunately, however, rough estimates are not too difficult to make in the case of Connecticut.

At the outset, one can quickly dismiss the exaggerated figures openly stated or suggested by Connecticut's own Tories. Redding's Loyalist deputy, William Heron, claimed in 1780 that only one-tenth of the people of Connecticut favored independence,[67] implying that the other nine-tenths still retained some degree of sympathy for a united empire under the British throne. Consider Tiffany's guess was less extreme; but his statement that one-third of the colonial population could be counted as supporters of the King and Parliament has little evidence to substantiate it in his own province.[68]

Much closer to what was probably the truth was the estimate made over one hundred years ago by Hinman, and repeated by every writer who has since mentioned the subject, that about two thousand men were Tories.[69] Although this number may be somewhat of an underestimate, it is more reasonable than any other figure when examined in the light of all the scattered bits of circumstantial evidence.

In 1774 the conservative party's chief candidate, ex-Governor Thomas Fitch, received 2655 ballots for the Council. Most of the freemen who voted for Fitch in this election probably became Tories. William Samuel Johnson, who was still considered a Whig in 1774, got 4793 votes for assistant in that year.[70] But the following year, when Johnson had taken on the character of a Tory in the eyes of most freemen, his total fell to 2582 votes.[71] And in the last colonial election only 1272 freemen supported the moderate Tory lawyer.[72] Most, if not all, of these freemen were probably Loyalists. It is fair to add to their ranks at least an equal number of British partisans who either did not have the right to vote, or if they did, prudently refrained from taking any open stand in favor of unpopular candidates.

This estimate of between 2000-2500 male Tories is strengthened by other fragmentary testimony. According to Stiles, there were 2200 Anglican families in Connecticut in 1774.[73] The heads of these families were probably almost all pro-British. Two years later Stiles reported that approximately "a quarter of the pple west of Stratford River" were Tories.[74] Connecticut's last colonial census, taken quite fortuitously in 1774, shows that the towns in Fairfield County had a total of about six thousand males between the ages of twenty and seventy.[75] If Stiles' percentage is accepted as correct, Fairfield County alone had at least 1500 Tories.

Another 500-1,000 Loyalists were probably scattered in the other counties, especially in the New Haven and Litchfield towns. Between 1774 and 1776 the committees of inspection in these communities had occasion to investigate and proclaim many persons as unfriendly to the united colonies. Furthermore, one out of every seven families in New Haven County and one out of every twenty-two families in Litchfield County, according to Stiles, belonged to the Episcopal church and may therefore be suspected of having been in sympathy with the Loyalist cause.[76] And at the end of 1775

Derby's rector, the Rev. Richard Mansfield, believed that several thousand men in the three western counties, New Haven, Litchfield, and Fairfield, were prepared to join the British forces if an army could be sent to the colony.[77]

Over thirty-eight thousand men between the ages of twenty and seventy were counted in the colony in 1774.[78] About 6 per cent of them, therefore, can be considered to have been Tories.[79] The proportion is much smaller, of course, when the total white population of more than 190,000 is used as the basis of comparison; and it was even less in the radical eastern counties. But the proportion was much larger in the western part of the province, and, as one might expect, it was highest in Fairfield County.

It was in that county, where in 1774 every third person was a member of the English church, that one Tory described the people as having been most seriously "divided in Sentiment respecting the Justice and Expediency of the War."[80] In 1776 Stiles conservatively placed the percentage of Tories in Fairfield County at one-fourth of the population.[81] Most of the Tories who lost their property during the war resided in Fairfield County.[82] In 1777 Brigadier General Gold S. Silliman, whose command was then located in western Connecticut, reported that although about a thousand Fairfield County Loyalists had already gone over to the British, there were still "more fixed and inveterate Tories" in the towns of that county "than there is [*sic*] in the whole State beside."[83]

When the privileged, self-governing colony of Connecticut plunged into its revolutionary war for independence, it did so against the protests of a substantial minority of its people. This most conservative segment of the population had been formed and hardened during several decades of bitter controversy with the more numerous Whig party over local and imperial issues. When the last crisis confronted the colonies in 1774, that minority again could not agree with the patriots, as one Tory put it, "which was in the Right and which in the wrong."[84]

The war provided the answer. As in every other colony, the

Revolution in Connecticut was also a civil war. And its Tories suffered—as minority parties have always suffered in fratricidal conflicts—imprisonment, loss of property, and exile. Even families were tragically broken.[85] Shortly after Connecticut celebrated its first anniversary as an independent State, one of its Tories bitterly protested the sorry predicament of his fellow dissenters in these words: "Nabour was against Nabour, Father against the Son and the son against the Father, and he that would not thrust his one blaid through his brothers heart was cald an Infimous fillon."[86]

Notes
Bibliographical Essay
Index

⇶⇶⭅⭅

Notes

CHAPTER ONE

1. *Connecticut Courant,* March 1, 1774, p. 1; Charles M. Andrews, *Our Earliest Colonial Settlements* (New York, 1933), 113; Andrews, "On Some Early Aspects of Connecticut History," *New England Quarterly,* 17 (1944), 4. See also Nelson P. Mead, *Connecticut as a Corporate Colony* (Lancaster, 1906), 1-2; Lawrence H. Gipson, *The British Empire before the American Revolution* (Caldwell, Idaho, and New York, 1936-42), III, ch. 4.

2. Thomas Buckingham, *Moses and Aaron God's Favour to His Chosen People, in Leading Them by the Ministry of Civil and Ecclesiastical Rulers,* Election Sermon (New London, 1729), *passim;* Timothy Edwards, *All the Living must surely die and go to Judgment,* Election Sermon (New London, 1732), 30.

3. Timothy Cutler, *The Firm Union of a People Represented; and a Concern for it urged,* Election Sermon (New London, 1717), 61; Jared Eliot, *Give Caesar his Due, Or the Obligation that Subjects are under to their Civil Rulers,* Election Sermon (New London, 1738), 37.

4. Isaac Stiles, *A Prospect of the City of Jerusalem,* Election Sermon (New London, 1742), 31-33; Judah Champion, *A Brief View of the Distresses, Hardships and Dangers our Ancestors Encounter'd* (Hartford, 1770), 31.

5. Samuel Peters, *A General History of Connecticut* (New Haven, 1829), 208. Peters' notorious work must be used with great caution

despite his assertion that his history was "unbiassed by partiality or prejudice."

6. Joseph Fish, *Christ Jesus the Physician and his Blood the Balm, recommended for the Healing of a diseased People,* Election Sermon (New London, 1760), 52.

7. *Ibid.,* 5. See also Joseph Bellamy, n.t., Election Sermon, May 13, 1762 (New London, 1762), 26; Azariah Mather, *Good Rulers a Choice Blessing,* Election Sermon (New London, 1725), 19-20; Elnathan Whitman, *The Character and Qualifications of Good Rulers,* Election Sermon (New London, 1745), 40; Samuel Hall, *The Legislature's Right, Charge and Duty in respect of Religion,* Election Sermon (New London, 1746), 32; Ashbel Woodbridge, n.t., Election Sermon, May 14, 1752 (New London, 1753), 25, 43; Benjamin Throop, *Religion and Loyalty, the Duty and Glory of a People,* Election Sermon (New London, 1758), 19, 35-36.

8. Andrews, *Earliest Colonial Settlements,* 124-25.

9. *Acts and Laws of Connecticut* (New London, 1750), 240, hereafter cited as *Conn. Code* (1750).

10. Bellamy, Election Sermon, 26.

11. For a description of the numerous and varied functions performed by the many town officers see *Hartford Town Votes, 1635-1716,* Connecticut Historical Society, *Collections,* 6 (1897), 317-18; Elijah B. Huntington, *History of Stamford* (Stamford, 1868), 172-73; Bernard C. Steiner, *A History of . . . Guilford* (Baltimore, 1897), 140-45; Lawrence H. Gipson, *Jared Ingersoll, A Study of American Loyalism in Relation to British Colonial Government* (New Haven, 1920), 23-24.

12. *A Brief View,* 31.

13. Each town elected deputies in April and September to the Assembly, which met in at least two sessions a year, May and October. When the voters chose their representatives for the fall session they also voted by written ballot for twenty men. At the October session the twenty candidates who received the largest number of votes were declared nominated to run for the Council, and of these the twelve who received the highest number of votes in April made up the Council for the following year. *Conn. Code* (1750), 45-46; see also Gipson, *Ingersoll,* 19-20. In her visit to Connecticut in 1704 Madam Knight discovered that Connecticut's "Cheif Red Letter day is St. Election." Sarah K. Knight, *The Journal of Madam Knight* (New York, 1935), 44.

14. *Conn. Code* (1750), 28-29.

15. *The Public Records of the Colony of Connecticut 1636-1776* (Hartford, 1850-90), XI, 631, hereafter cited as *Conn. Col. Recs.;* Andrews, *Earliest Colonial Settlements,* 134-35; Royal R. Hinman, ed., *Letters from the English Kings and Queens . . . to the Governors of Connecticut, Together with the Answers Thereto from 1639-1749* (Hartford, 1836), 356-57, hereafter cited as Hinman, *Letters; Conn. Code* (1750), 30-31; *The Fitch Papers 1754-1766* (2 vols.), in Connecticut Historical Society, *Collections,* 18 (1920), 215, hereafter cited as *Fitch Papers,* II.

16. Peters, *History,* 105-6, 268; see also Gershom Bulkeley, *Will and Doom or The Miseries of Connecticut* (1692), in Conn. Hist. Soc., *Colls.,* 3 (1895), 90, 199, 243. It was Professor Andrews' judgment that "the Connecticut leaders wanted self-government, as the churches were self-governed, but not necessarily self-government based on any universal privilege, either political or religious." "On Some Early Aspects of Connecticut History," 10.

17. Charles M. Andrews, *The Colonial Period of American History* (New Haven, 1934-38), II, ch. 4, especially 104-12, 142-43*n;* Andrews, *Connecticut's Place in Colonial History* (New York, 1924), 31, 35; *The Wolcott Papers 1750-54,* in Conn. Hist. Soc., *Colls.,* 16 (1916), xxv.

18. John Bulkley, *The Necessity of Religion in Societies,* Election Sermon (New London, 1713), 40; Samuel Estabrook, *Peace and Quietness of a People,* Election Sermon (New London, 1718), 18-19; Peter Raynolds, *The Kingdom is the Lord's,* Election Sermon (New London, 1757), 18.

19. The Rev. Samuel Hall argued that the worst tyranny was better than no government, "because while the Government is never so Tyrannical that Tyranny can only express it self in the Enormities of a Few, the Multitude must in the mean time be kept within the bounds of Right and Reason." *The Legislature's Right, Charge and Duty,* 12-13.

20. Andrews, *Col. Per.,* II, 106. Strictly speaking, the law did not require admitted inhabitants to be members of a congregation, but practically speaking all who were admitted probably were. They certainly had to be religious and godly men. Perry Miller has analyzed the political and religious theories in the founding of Connecticut in "Thomas Hooker and the Democracy of Early Connecticut," *New Eng. Quar.,* 4 (1931), 663-712.

21. In one respect the differences were broadened. Under the charter of 1662 the right to vote for deputies was vested only in the freemen. See also *Conn. Col. Recs.,* I, 290, 293, 331, 351, 389, 417-18; II, 253.

22. *Conn. Code* (1750), 80-81, 99, 232. A freeman could be disfranchised on complaint that he had "walked Scandalously." For an early example of this see Ellen D. Larned, *History of Windham County* (Worcester, 1874-80), I, 273.

23. *Conn. Col. Recs.,* II, 66; III, 111-12; V, 21-22; VI, 146, 356.

24. *Hartford Town Votes 1635-1716,* 128.

25. Frances M. Caulkins, *History of Norwich* (Hartford, 1866), 102.

26. *Hartford Town Votes 1635-1716,* 132, 148, 171, 196; Samuel Orcutt, *The History of the Old Town of Derby* (Springfield, 1880), 74; *Diary of Joshua Hempstead 1711-1758,* in New London County Historical Society, *Collections,* 1 (1901), 41, 53, hereafter cited as Hempstead, *Diary; Conn. Col. Recs.,* V, 482-86.

27. *Conn. Code* (1750), 99.

28. Larned, *Windham County,* I, 234.

29. Gipson, *Ingersoll,* 22-23; see also Daniel M. Mead, *A History of the Town of Greenwich* (New York, 1857), 70.

30. Mead, *Conn. as a Corporate Colony,* 10 *n*2.

31. Larned, *Windham County,* I, 329; Henry Bronson, *History of Waterbury* (Waterbury, 1858), 248.

32. Bulkeley, *Will and Doom,* 129.

33. Gipson, *Ingersoll,* 19; Ezra Stiles to Benjamin Gale, Oct. 1, 1766, Ezra Stiles Papers, Yale University. See also Andrews, *Connecticut's Place,* 29-31; George C. Groce, *William Samuel Johnson* (New York, 1937), 54 *n*7. Lemuel A. Welles has argued—unconvincingly, it seems to me—that democracy did exist in seventeenth-century Connecticut. For his evidence see *Wyllys Papers,* in Conn. Hist. Soc., *Colls.,* 21 (1924), 191*n*.

34. William Burnham, *God's Providence in Placing Men in their Respective Stations and Conditions Asserted and Shewed,* Election Sermon (New London, 1722), 1-2, 6, 16, 17; Anthony Stoddard, n.t., Election Sermon, May 10, 1716 (New London, 1716), 4, 9-16, 28-29.

35. Woodbridge, Election Sermon, 24; see also Governor Law's speech to the Assembly, May 1742, *Wolcott Papers,* 456.

36. James Lockwood, *The Worth and Excellence of Civil Freedom*

and Liberty illustrated, Election Sermon (New London, 1759), 16, 24-25. Early in the Revolution Governor Trumbull explained some of the difficulties of governing New Englanders whose pulse "beats high for Liberty." "Indeed," he wrote to Washington, Dec. 7, 1775, "there is great difficulty to support liberty, to exercise Government, to maintain subordination, and at the same time to prevent the operation of licentious and levelling principles, which many very easily imbibe." Letter Book, Jonathan Trumbull Papers, XXIX, 231, Connecticut State Library.

37. The quotation is from the 1710 Massachusetts election sermon. Alice M. Baldwin, *The New England Clergy and the American Revolution* (Durham, 1928), 38, 41, 49. See also Nathaniel Hunn, *The Welfare of a Government Considered,* Election Sermon (New London, 1747), 14. According to Hunn liberty was not "the letting loose the golden Reins of Government to the licentious Humours and lusts of People. No, this would be the worst state of Slavery, a Slavery to the worst of Tyrants, unbridled Lust." In 1723 the Rev. Eleazar Williams criticized "Unsubduedness to Government." This licentious spirit which "would have all men alike," Williams declared, defied the divine decree to obey authority. *An Essay to Prove That when God once enters upon a Controversie . . . He will Manage and Issue it,* Election Sermon (New London, 1723), 16.

38. According to Roger Wolcott, however, the people acquired the faults of "too much censoriousness and detraction, and as they had much cyder many of them drank too much of it." Roger Wolcott, "A Memoir for the History of Connecticut," Conn. Hist. Soc., *Colls.,* 3 (1895), 332, hereafter cited as Wolcott, "Memoir."

39. *Wolcott Papers,* xxv-xxvi; Groce, *Johnson,* 54; Hinman, *Letters,* 10-12; Gideon H. Hollister, *History of Connecticut from the first Settlement of the Colony* (Hartford, 1857), I, 529.

40. Caulkins, *Norwich,* 84.

41. Hempstead, *Diary,* 178, 267, 361-62, 419.

42. George L. Walker, ed., *Diary of Rev. Daniel Wadsworth 1737-1747* (Hartford, 1894), 8, hereafter cited as Wadsworth, *Diary.* Hempstead, *Diary,* 83, 205; Benjamin Trumbull, *A Complete History of Connecticut . . . to the Close of the Indian Wars* (New Haven, 1818), I, 141, 227.

43. Andrews, *Connecticut's Place,* 32; see also 31, 35. In 1782 one citizen proudly noted that the freemen did not change their officers

"annually with the seasons." *Conn. Courant,* March 26, 1782, p. 2.

44. Jonathan Todd, *Civil Rulers the Ministers of God, for Good to Men,* Election Sermon (New London, 1749), 30-32, 51, and *passim.* See also Estabrook, *Peace and Quietness,* 22; Eliot, *Give Caesar His Due,* 16; Benjamin Lord, *Religion and Government subsisting together in Society,* Election Sermon (New London, 1752), 28-29; Noah Hobart, *Civil Government the Foundation of Social Happiness,* Election Sermon (New London, 1751), 50-51; James Lockwood, *Religion the Highest Interest of a civil Community,* Election Sermon (New London, 1754), 23; Hunn, *Welfare of a Government,* 9; Moses Dickinson, n.t., Election Sermon, May 8, 1755 (New London, 1755), 54.

45. Connecticut's first settlers, however, did not dissent from the religious principles of the Massachusetts churches. Andrews, *Col. Per.,* II, 82.

46. *Conn. Col. Recs.,* I, 21; see also Paul W. Coons, *The Achievement of Religious Liberty in Connecticut,* Connecticut Tercentenary Commission, *Publications,* 60 (1936), 1, 3, 9.

47. William Worthington, *The Duty of Rulers and Teachers in Unitedly Leading God's People,* Election Sermon (New London, 1744), 10, 17, 19; Hunn, *Welfare of a Government,* 6. Samuel Estabrook's admonition "And above all things let Religion be promoted" can be found in practically every eighteenth-century sermon. *Peace and Quietness,* 15.

48. Trumbull, *History,* I, 288.

49. *Conn. Col. Recs.,* I, 21.

50. *Ibid.,* 523-25. Benjamin Trumbull thought that the preface to the code of 1650 was sufficiently solemn to introduce "a body of sermons." See Trumbull, *History,* I, 322.

51. *Conn. Col. Recs.,* I, 283-84, 303, 311-12, 324, 523-25, 545; II, 102, 281, 290; III, 65, 202-3; IV, 199.

52. *Ibid.,* V, 51, 87; Herbert L. Osgood, *The American Colonies in the Eighteenth Century* (New York, 1924), III, 300-1. The clergy was supposed to have helped Saltonstall become governor in 1708 in return for his aid in getting the Saybrook Platform adopted. John G. Palfrey, *History of New England* (Boston, 1858-90), IV, 490.

53. Maria L. Greene, *The Development of Religious Liberty in Connecticut* (Boston, 1905), ch. 6; see also Trumbull, *History,* I, 282-84.

54. *Conn. Col. Recs.,* V, 323; *Conn. Code* (1750), 69, 139-42, 143, 195.

55. *Conn. Code* (1750), 196-97.

56. Trumbull, *History,* I, 474.

57. Thomas Clap, *The Religious Constitution of Colleges* (New London, 1754), 1, 7-8; *The Talcott Papers 1724-1741* (2 vols.), in Conn. Hist. Soc., *Colls.,* 4 (1892), 58, hereafter cited as *Talcott Papers,* I. Compare Franklin B. Dexter, "The Founding of Yale College," and Simeon E. Baldwin, "The Ecclesiastical Constitution of Yale College," in New Haven Colony Historical Society, *Papers,* 3 (1882), 1-31, 405-42.

58. "Orders and Appointments to Be Observed in the Collegiate School in Connecticut," quoted in Franklin B. Dexter, *Biographical Sketches of the Graduates of Yale College with Annals of the College History* (New York and New Haven, 1885-1912), I, 347.

59. *Ibid.,* I, 773. Of the 505 graduates between 1745-62, more than one-third became ministers. *Ibid.,* II, 786.

60. Stiles, *Prospect of Jerusalem, 34.*

61. *Conn. Col. Recs.,* III, 299.

62. Greene, *Religious Liberty in Conn.,* 158-59, 160-71; see also Ellen S. Brinton, "The Rogerenes of Connecticut," *New Eng. Quar.,* 16 (1943), 3-13.

63. The early development of the Anglican church can be followed in Francis L. Hawks and William S. Perry, comps., *Documentary History of the Protestant Episcopal Church* (New York, 1863-64), I, 9, 17, 19-20, 23, 37, and *passim,* hereafter cited as Hawks and Perry, *Doc. Hist.*

64. See, for example, the warning in Eliphalet Adams, n.t., Election Sermon, May 10, 1733 (New London, 1734), 67-68.

65. Hawks and Perry, *Doc. Hist.,* I, 9, 17, 30. Col. Caleb Heathcote, who was instrumental in establishing the Episcopal church in Connecticut, made this comment about the colony's Puritanism: "They have abundance of odd kind of laws, to prevent any dissenting from their Church, and endeavour to keep the people in as much blindness and unacquaintedness with any religion as possible." To the Secretary of the Society for the Propagation of the Gospel, Nov. 9, 1705, *ibid.,* 9.

66. *Conn. Col. Recs.,* V, 50-51; Greene, *Religious Liberty in Conn.,* 156-57, 187-88.

67. Hawks and Perry, *Doc. Hist.,* I, 9, 20, 23-24, 34, 39-44; Osgood, *Amer. Colonies in the 18th Cent.,* II, 43-44.

68. Samuel Johnson to the Secretary of the S.P.G., Jan. 1, 1725, Herbert and Carol Schneider, eds., *Samuel Johnson His Career and*

Writings (New York, 1929), III, 219; see also 217-18, 222-23, hereafter cited as Schneider, *Johnson.*

69. Hawks and Perry, *Doc. Hist.*, I, 53.

70. *Ibid.*, I, 45.

71. *Conn. Col. Recs.*, III, 301; VII, 584.

72. *Ibid.*, III, 296. Compare this description of Connecticut's soil with Trumbull, *History*, I, 29, and *Fitch Papers*, II, 211.

73. *Conn. Col. Recs.*, III, 297; VII, 583-84.

74. Charles H. S. Davis, *History of Wallingford* (Meriden, 1870), 422; Orcutt, *Derby*, 85; Larned, *Windham County*, I, 259.

75. The increase in the lists of Connecticut's towns between 1699 and 1730 may be followed in *Conn. Col. Recs.*, IV, 297, 329, 521-22; V, 170, 526-27; VI, 220, 570; VII, 304-5. The general description of the New England countryside later in the eighteenth century by the author of the essays on *American Husbandry* was probably true of Connecticut. Harry J. Carman, ed., *American Husbandry* (New York, 1939), 46. Gov. Wolcott's "Memoir" (1759), however, said of Connecticut at the opening of the eighteenth century: "Their buildings were good to what they had been, but mean to what they are now; their dress and diet mean and course to what it is now." "Memoir," 332.

76. *Conn. Col. Recs.*, III, 297; VII, 583-84; Trumbull, *History*, I, 453.

77. *Conn. Col. Recs.*, III, 296, 297, 299; VII, 582-84; Trumbull, *History*, I, 453.

78. In 1680 Connecticut listed the following reasons for the colony's small trade: the "want of men of estates to venture abroad, and of money at home for the management of trade, and labour being so deare with us." *Conn. Col. Recs.*, III, 299; see also 301.

79. *Ibid.*, 298, 299.

80. *Ibid.*, 308.

81. *Ibid.*, VII, 582-83.

82. *Ibid.*, VI, 95.

83. Richard J. Purcell, *Connecticut in Transition 1775-1818* (Washington, 1918), 210, 307-9; Alfred Andrews, *Memorial History of New Britain* (Chicago, 1857), 85; Andrews, *Connecticut's Place*, 31, 35. For examples of ministerial doctrine on the hierarchical order of society and the necessity of man's observing it, see Bulkley, *Necessity of Religion*, 23, 35; Stoddard, Election Sermon, 4, 5-7, 9, 14; Cutler, *Firm Union of a People*, 39-40; Stephen Hosmer, *A Peoples Living in Ap-*

pearance and Dying in Reality Considered, Election Sermon (New London, 1720), 33; Adams, Election Sermon, 52.

84. Rule of the Wethersfield church, March 12, 1706-1707, John W. Barber, *Connecticut Historical Collections* (New Haven, 1838), 121.

85. Trumbull, *History,* I, 308.

86. Wadsworth, *Diary,* 6; see also Knight, *Journal,* 63; Larned, *Windham County,* I, 331.

87. The colony's report to the Board of Trade, 1680, said that Connecticut had "few Servants . . . and less Slaves," and that it was seldom that any wanted relief. *Conn. Col. Recs.,* III, 298, 300. The Assembly made certain, however, that the town authorities took measures to have the estates of the idle and poor cared for. *Ibid.,* VI, 112-13. The numbers of slaves increased. In 1730 there were 700 in the colony and 1000 in 1749. Lorenzo J. Greene, *The Negro in Colonial New England 1620-1776* (New York, 1942), 90.

88. Knight, *Journal,* 37, 66-67; see also Carman, *Husbandry,* 46, 50.

89. Hempstead, *Diary,* 100; Henry R. Stiles, ed., *History . . . of Ancient Windsor* (Hartford, 1891), I, pt. 2, 562-63; Mead, *Greenwich,* 77-79; Davis, *Wallingford,* 429-30; Orcutt, *Derby,* 129-30; Orcutt, *History of Torrington* (Albany, 1878), 8-9. See also Huntington, *Stamford,* 174-76; Edwin Hall, comp., *The Ancient Historical Records of Norwalk* (Norwalk, 1847), 61, 83; Osgood, *Amer. Colonies in the 18th Cent.,* III, 275; Peters, *History,* 234-35.

90. Charles M. Andrews, *Connecticut and the British Government,* Conn. Tercentenary Commission, *Publs.,* I (1933), 2. In 1692 Gershom Bulkeley had charged that Connecticut's rulers "assume all authority in things spiritual and temporal, civil and military, both as to legislation and execution, and proceed in their methods, without any real respect to the laws of England." *Will and Doom,* 101 and *passim.*

91. Bulkley, *Necessity of Religion,* 68; Buckingham, *Moses and Aaron,* 41; Jonathan Marsh, *God's Fatherly Care of his Covenant Children,* Election Sermon (New London, 1737), 17.

92. *Fitch Papers,* I, xxvi; Andrews, *Earliest Colonial Settlements,* 122-23; Andrews, *Connecticut's Place,* 9; Andrews, *Col. Per.,* II, 138. See also Bulkeley, *Will and Doom,* 131, 238; Knight, *Journal,* 34.

93. Andrews, *Connecticut and the British Government,* 2-3, 20-21. For examples of the British effort to tighten their hold on the chartered colonies, see Andrews, *Col. Per.,* IV, 255, 377, 382-83, 386-87, 392-94, 406-7; Osgood, *The American Colonies in the Seventeenth Century*

(New York, 1907), III, 396-400, 423; Osgood, *Amer. Colonies in the 18th Cent.,* I, 101-2, 104-6, 403. Ministers frequently gave thanks to divine providence for saving the colony from "being stript and deprived" of its privileges. Adams, Election Sermon, 40-41; Nathaniel Chauncey, *The Faithful Ruler Described and Excited,* Election Sermon (New London, 1734), 33.

94. Upon learning that a writ of *quo warranto* had been issued, Connecticut's leaders petitioned King James II on "bended knees" to preserve the colony's "liberties and properties as formerly." Hinman, *Letters,* 169-71.

95. For example, the oath to support the acts of navigation and trade which Governor Leete took, May 1680. Trumbull, *History,* I, 356.

96. When it seemed in the Hallam case that a petition to the King might be allowed before all legal remedies had been exhausted in the colony, Connecticut's agent, Sir Henry Ashurst, pointedly protested (1700) that such a proceeding would be "extraordinary and extrajudiciall" and would violate the "fundamental priviledges of the colony." Hinman, *Letters,* 291. The decision of the Connecticut courts was upheld in this instance. For a description of the controls that the British government exercised over Connecticut in the colonial era see Andrews, *Connecticut's Place,* 15-17; Andrews, *Col. Per.,* IV, 401; Elmer B. Russell, *Review of American Colonial Legislation* (New York, 1915), 102 and *n*1, 103-4.

97. Connecticut's report to the Board of Trade in 1680 declared that it could not tell exactly how many "English, Scotts and Irish" entered the colony because "there are so few . . . Som yeares come none; sometimes a famaly or two, in a year." *Conn. Col. Recs.,* III, 298.

CHAPTER TWO

1. Samuel Whitman, *Practical Godliness the Way to Prosperity,* Election Sermon (New London, 1714), 25-29, 36; Williams, *An Essay,* 9-20, 49; William Russel, *The Decay of Love to God in Churches Offensive and Dangerous,* Election Sermon (New London, 1731), 22; Adams, Election Sermon, 43-45, 59; Chauncey, *The Faithful Ruler,* 49.

2. Wadsworth, *Diary,* 9.

3. Todd, *Civil Rulers,* 43.

4. *Connecticut Gazette,* New Haven, April 4, 1761, p. 4.

5. In 1727 collectors of the town taxes were allowed to assign to the Anglican ministers the money taken from Anglicans in their communities. Two years later both the Quakers and Baptists were exempted from the upkeep of the established church. *Conn. Col. Recs.,* VII, 106-7, 237, 257. For measures taken against the Rogerenes see *ibid.,* VI, 166.

6. Nathanael Chauncey, *Honouring God the True Way to Honour,* Election Sermon (New London, 1719), 47.

7. *Conn. Col. Recs.,* V, 436, 529-31.

8. Trumbull, *History,* II, 135, 136.

9. Samuel Woodbridge, *Obedience to the Divine Law Urged on All Orders of Men,* Election Sermon (New London, 1724), 21; see also Whitman, *Practical Godliness,* 25-27; Williams, *An Essay,* 49; Russel, *Decay of Love to God,* 20-21.

10. On the religious causes of the Awakening see Greene, *Religious Liberty in Conn.,* 222-23. See also Williston Walker, *A History of the Congregational Churches in the United States* (New York, 1894), 251-61. Perry Miller has discussed the Half-Way Covenant more sympathetically in "The Half-Way Covenant," *New Eng. Quar.,* 6 (1933), 676-715.

11. "Extracts of Letters to the Rev. Thomas Prince," in Conn. Hist. Soc., *Colls.,* 3 (1895), 294; Trumbull, *History,* II, 135-36.

12. Greene, *Religious Liberty in Conn.,* 227-29; Walker, *Congregational Churches,* 256-58; *The Records of the General Association of the Colony of Connecticut 1738-1799* (Hartford, 1888), 9, 11, hereafter cited as Gen. Assoc., *Recs.;* Jared Ingersoll, An Historical Account of Some Affairs Relating to the Church Especially in Connecticut, 1-2, MS, Library of Congress.

13. Rev. Joseph Fish to Sarah Osborn, Nov. 24, 1743, Silliman Papers, Yale University. Joseph Fish, *The Examiner Examined, Remarks on a Piece wrote by Mr. Isaac Backus* (New London, 1771), 12; Larned, *Windham County,* I, 473-74.

14. Resolves of the General Association, Nov. 24, 1741, Stiles Papers.

15. Punderson to the Bishop of London, Dec. 12, 1741, Hawks and Perry, *Doc. Hist.,* I, 174. See also Rev. Joseph Fish to Sarah Osborn, Nov. 24, 1743, Silliman Papers; Ingersoll, Historical Account, 3-4;

Trumbull, *History,* II, 155-56. There are good, if not always favorable, accounts by contemporaries in Hempstead, *Diary,* 377, 379, 380, 402, 406-7, and Samuel Johnson's letters in Schneider, *Johnson,* I, 102-3; III, 228, 230.

16. On the religious principles of the Awakening see reverse side of the letter written by N. Pike to Ezra Stiles, April 4, 1786, Stiles Papers; "The Doings and Records of the Chh with Respect to the Seperatists" (Suffield), Historical Papers, *ibid;* Ebenezer Devotion, *An Answer of the Pastor and Brethren of the Third Church in Windham* (New London, 1747); Connecticut Archives, Ecclesiastical Affairs, X, 29, 61a, 290a; XV, 225a-e, State Lib., hereafter cited as Conn. Arch., Eccles. Affairs; Joseph Tracy, *The Great Awakening* (Boston, 1842), 317-19; Greene, *Religious Liberty in Conn.,* 234-39; R. C. Learned, "Separate Churches in Connecticut," in *Contributions to the Ecclesiastical History of Connecticut* (New Haven, 1861), 253; Amos A. Browning, "The Preston Separate Church," New London Co. Hist. Soc., *Records and Papers,* 2, pt. 2 (1896), 156.

17. Stiles, *Prospect of Jerusalem,* 23; see also Trumbull, *History,* II, 162.

18. Trumbull, *History,* II, 160, 162; Wadsworth, *Diary,* 73. Compare Jonathan Parsons, *A Needful Caution in a Critical Day* (New London, 1742), 27-28.

19. Trumbull, *History,* II, 162; Worthington, *Duty of Rulers and Teachers,* 17, 36; Roger Wolcott to Gov. Law, Dec. 9, 1745, *The Law Papers* (3 vols.), in Conn. Hist. Soc., *Colls.,* 13 (1911), 139, hereafter cited as *Law Papers,* II; Wolcott, "Memoir," 332; *The Declaration of the Association of the County of New Haven . . . Concerning the Rev. Mr. George Whitefield* (Boston, 1745), 2-4; Gen. Assoc., *Recs.,* 11, 12; James H. Trumbull, "The Sons of Liberty in 1755," *New Englander,* 35 (1876), 300. Looking back upon the revival from the perspective of the 1770's, Samuel Avery of Norwich commented: "There was much of the Spirit of God in it, But with all there was a Great deal of Infatuation and Enthusiasm, allso the mind of the people was as actually Infatuated as a fly in October." "Anti Alarm," in Samuel Avery Papers, New York Public Library, hereafter cited as Avery Papers.

20. Ten years after the death of his father Isaac Stiles, a zealous Old Light, Ezra Stiles wrote (1770) in a confidential letter, "There is a sin unto death; that sin my father sinned in opposing 'New Light'; this is imputed to me and in this life it is never to be forgiven." Dexter,

Biog. Sketches, I, 266. See also Henry M. Stiles, ed., *The History of Ancient Wethersfield* (New York, 1904), II, 599-600; Trumbull, *History,* II, 233.

21. Trumbull, *History,* II, ch. 8; Franklin B. Dexter, ed., *Extracts from the Itineraries and other Miscellanies of Ezra Stiles . . . With a Selection from his Correspondence* (New Haven, 1916), 251-52, hereafter cited as Stiles, *Itin.;* Worthington, *Duty of Rulers and Teachers,* 38; Todd, *Civil Rulers,* 55; *Declaration . . . Concerning George Whitefield,* 5-6.

22. Wadsworth, *Diary,* 46, 55, 71, 72, 74, 75, 81.

23. Todd, *Civil Rulers,* 55; Whitman, *Character and Qualifications of Good Rulers,* 37-38.

24. *Conn. Col. Recs.,* VIII, 438-39; Resolves of the General Association, Nov. 24, 1741, Stiles Papers; see also *Law Papers,* I, 5-10; Ingersoll, Historical Account, 4-5.

25. Samuel Johnson to the Secretary of the S. P. G., March 25, 1742, Schneider, *Johnson,* III, 231.

26. Rev. Joseph Fish to Sarah Osborn, Nov. 24, 1743, Silliman Papers.

27. Rev. Mr. Seabury to the Secretary of the S. P. G., May 3, 1742, Hawks and Perry, *Doc. Hist.,* I, 180; see also 244.

28. In 1742 Isaac Stiles called upon the colonial government to end the "Schismatical Conventions" and the divisions that were destroying the "Peace of this our Jerusalem." Stiles, *Prospect of Jerusalem,* 46-48; see also Trumbull, *History,* II, 167.

29. *Conn. Col. Recs.,* VIII, 454-57, 482, 500-2, 500n, 521-22, 555-56; IX, 20, 28-30; Yale College, *The Judgment of the Rector and Tutor of Yale-College Concerning Two of the Students who were Expelled* (New London, 1745); Browning, "Preston Separate Church," 162; Greene, *Religious Liberty in Conn.,* 243-45, 255, 262-64, 299. For the Old Light justification of these measures see *Wolcott Papers,* 145; Todd, *Civil Rulers,* 67-68. According to Governor Talcott the preaching of the New Light minister James Davenport was dangerous "to all good orders in Church and State." He recommended, therefore, "that the Civill authority, the Ministers and people . . . use their Joynt Interest, by advice, Influence and authority, to Incourage what is vertuous and praiseworthy, and to Suppress every disorderly and Vile practice, and what so Ever tends to the hurt and Reproach of Religion." *Talcott Papers,* II, 373; see also 374.

30. *Wolcott Papers*, 145.

31. *Conn. Col. Recs.*, IX, 337, 380; X, 43, 219, 429, 570-71; XI, 27, 344, 415-17, 461-63, 517-18; XII, 153-54; Dexter, *Biog. Sketches*, I, 183-84; "History of the North Church," in *Contribs. . . . Eccles. Hist.*, 437-38; Greene, *Religious Liberty in Conn.*, 248-53, 261-63.

32. Stiles, *Itin.*, 582-83; see also I. Stiles to E. Stiles, March 22, 1758; letters of Jared Eliot and Chauncey Whittelsey to Stiles, Stiles Papers; Hawks and Perry, *Doc. Hist.*, II, 4-5; the advertisement by the Rev. Robert Ross of Stratfield of his forthcoming pamphlet against "Enthusiasm" and "false Religion," *Conn. Gaz.*, Nov. 28, 1761, p. 4.

33. *Conn. Col. Recs.*, IX, 203-204.

34. Leonard Bacon, *Thirteen Historical Discources* (New Haven, 1839), 232; Roger S. Boardman, *Roger Sherman* (Phila., 1938), 72-73; Trumbull, "Sons of Liberty," 303. Benjamin Gale charged that some became New Lights merely to advance their political ambitions. A. Z. [B. Gale], *A Reply to a Pamphlet Entitled the Answer of a Friend in the West* (New London, 1755), 27-28.

35. *Conn. Col. Recs.*, VIII, 512n; Trumbull, *History*, II, 174, 232; Ingersoll, Historical Narrative, 12.

36. See, for example, *Conn. Gaz.*, Sept. 24, 1757, p. 1; Oct. 15, 1757, p. 1. Roger Wolcott warned against party ambitions disguised "under the Paint of Religion." *Ibid.*, March 28, 1761, p. 1.

37. Greene, *Religious Liberty in Conn.*, 238; George C. Groce, "Benjamin Gale," *New Eng. Quar.*, 10 (1937), 701.

38. On President Clap, Yale, and the New Lights see Dexter, *Biog. Sketches*, II, 357; Trumbull, "Sons of Liberty," 305-6; Greene, *Religious Liberty in Conn.*, 280-82; Stiles, *Itin.*, 6. The political implications of the 1754 election are discussed in Trumbull, "Sons of Liberty," 309. See also Trumbull, *History*, II, 233, and "Jared Ingersoll Papers," in the New Haven Colony Hist. Soc., *Papers*, 9 (1918), 228, hereafter cited as "Ingersoll Papers."

39. Lyman had transferred from the First Church to the Separatist White Haven Church in April 1758. He represented New Haven in the Assembly, 1759-67. Dexter, *Biog. Sketches*, II, 48-49.

40. Lyman to Williams, Sept. 3, 1759, William Williams Papers, Conn. Hist. Soc. Chauncey Whittelsey thought that the New Haven and Wallingford "Male Contents" had hatched the plot. President Clap of Yale and some of the New Light clergy were also suspected of being "at the Bottom of the Scheme." According to Whittelsey "The

Gentlemen to be dropt out of the Administration" were Gov. Fitch and Councillors Newton, Silliman, Burr, Chester, Wolcott, Edwards, and Hamlin. "To effect the Scheme, Nominations were drawn up and Emissaries sent out with them from Dan to Beersheba to spread groundless Reports to the Prejudice of the Govr etc. and to stir up the Disaffected." Whittelsey to Ezra Stiles, Sept. 25, 1759, Stiles Papers.

41. On the Wallingford affair and the election of 1759 see Chauncey Whittelsey to Ezra Stiles, Sept. 25, 1759, Stiles Papers; Bacon, *Thirteen Historical Discourses,* 267-70, Davis, *Wallingford,* 198, and ch. 9; Gen. Assoc., *Recs.,* 43-44; 48-49, 50-51.

42. Johnson to the Archbishop of Canterbury, July 13, 1760, Hawks and Perry, *Doc. Hist.,* I, 310.

43. W.S. Johnson to J. Beach, Jan. 4, 1763, Schneider, *Johnson,* III, 266. Colonel Nathan Whiting inquired of Jared Ingersoll, Sept. 22, 1763, "do the Saints Govern, or do Some of you Men of the World, take upon you Worldly matters?" "Ingersoll Papers," 303.

44. Stiles, *Prospect of Jerusalem,* 56-58. In 1742 Governor Law warned the Assembly that "it has ever been of ill Consequences to a State wn different sentiments in matters of Religion have been permitted to break in upon and perplex the Civil State to the making Parties and Divisions in it. . . ." Connecticut Miscellaneous Papers 1637-1783, Force Transcripts, L.C.; printed in *Wolcott Papers,* 456.

45. Lockwood, *Civil Freedom,* 16, 18. See also the interesting pamphlet, *A Letter to the Clergy of . . . Connecticut From an Aged Layman* (New Haven, 1760). The author charged that the Wallingford controversy was being exploited by the leaders of the political New Lights, "a few artful and designing Men, with a View to promote some Party Scheme of their own." See 4, 9, 13, 20-22.

46. Fish, *Christ Jesus the Physician,* 13, 15-16, 35, 46, 51-52.

47. Stiles, *Itin.,* 299.

48. Tracy, *Great Awakening,* 133, 315, 324; Browning, "Preston Separate Church," 153; Trumbull, *History,* II, 160, 170-71, 192; Hawks and Perry, *Doc. Hist.,* I, 174, 180-81, 195-96, 201; Larned, *Windham County,* I, 393-485; Frances M. Caulkins, *History of New London* (New London, 1852), 452; "Historical Sketch of Fairfield East Association," *Contribs. . . . Eccles. Hist.,* 298.

49. Hawks and Perry, *Doc. Hist.,* I, 111. See also 112, 166-69, 172-73, 199-200 and *passim; Conn. Col. Recs.,* X, 132-33; *Talcott Papers,* II, 10; *Wolcott Papers,* 108-9, 118-19, 519.

50. Stiles, *Itin.,* 424, 586; S. Whittelsey to E. Stiles, May 30, 1764, Stiles Papers; Hawks and Perry, *Doc. Hist.,* I, 185, 190, 201, 211; II, 70. In the summer of 1760 the Rev. Samuel Johnson was able to boast that "The Church is generally in an increasing and flourishing condition, and much the more so, on account of the violent contentions of the Dissenters among themselves, which in effect drive people into the Church." To the Archbishop of Canterbury, July 13, 1760, Hawks and Perry, *Doc. Hist.,* I, 310.

51. H. Jones, "On the Rise, Growth and Comparative Relations of Other Evangelical Denominations in Connecticut to Congregationalism," in *Contribs. . . . Eccles. Hist.,* 267; Hawks and Perry, *Doc. Hist.,* I, 311; Stiles, *Itin.,* 110, 112-14.

52. Stiles, *Itin.,* 110, 112-14, 157; Hawks and Perry, *Doc. Hist.,* II, 29, 31; Groce, *Johnson,* 38 *n*18.

53. Johnson bluntly declared that Connecticut's charter was "the foundation of all their insolence. Happy would it be for the Church of England if it were taken away." Letter dated Sept. 26, 1726, Hawks and Perry, *Doc. Hist.,* I, 111.

54. To the Secretary of the S. P. G., April 14, 1751, *ibid.,* 278; see also 279.

55. Johnson to the Archbishop of Canterbury, July 13, 1760, Connecticut MSS, General Convention, Records of the Protestant Episcopal Church, Hawks Transcripts, 419-20, New York Historical Society, hereafter cited as Conn. MSS, Hawks Transcripts. At another time Johnson had described Connecticut's government as "much too popular" and its supposed liberty as "licentiousness, a Junto rule." Schneider, *Johnson,* I, 149.

56. Hawks and Perry, *Doc. Hist.,* I, 57, 94, 99, 110, 181. Samuel Johnson thought that the chief difficulty of Connecticut's Anglicans was "the want of a King's governor and a bishop." Johnson to General Nicholson, May 27, 1724. See Schneider, *Johnson,* III, 218, 221, 222, 280. Another Anglican minister, the Rev. Mr. Graves, prayed that God would quickly alter the charters of Massachusetts and Connecticut so that "true church governors and officers" could be placed over them. Graves to the Secretary of the S. P. G., April 20, 1765, Conn. MSS, Hawks Transcripts, 497.

57. See, for example, *Law Papers,* III, 341, 429-30.

58. Conn. MSS, Hawks Transcripts, 399.

59. Julian P. Boyd, ed., *The Susquehannah Company Papers*

(Wilkes-Barre, 1930-34). See also Edith A. Bailey, *Influences toward Radicalism in Connecticut 1754-1775,* in Smith College, *Studies,* 5, no. 4, 179-248. Another organization, the Delaware Company, was closely tied up with the history of the Susquehannah Company. Its affairs, however, are rather obscure. These two companies seem to have been considered together during the 1760's and 1770's.

60. Statistics on Connecticut's population may be found in Hinman, *Letters,* 355, 363; *Conn. Col. Recs.,* VII, 584; X, 617-18, and 618*n,* 623; XI, 575*n,* 630.

61. Albert L. Olson, *Agricultural Economy and the Population in Eighteenth Century Connecticut,* Conn. Tercentenary Commission, *Publs.,* 40 (1935), 13-16; Boyd, *Susquehannah Papers,* I, xlvi.

62. *Ibid.,* xlii-xlv; Dorothy Deming, *The Settlement of the Connecticut Towns,* Conn. Tercentenary Commission, *Publs.,* 6 (1933), 52-53.

63. Boyd, *Susquehannah Papers,* I, i; Ezra Stiles to C. D. Eberling, Feb. 20, 1795, Stiles Papers; Roger Wolcott to J. Hamilton, March 13, 1754, W. G. Lane Papers, Yale University, typescript of original in L. C.; Hollister, *History,* II, 18; *Conn. Col. Recs.,* VIII, 153; X, 88-89; XII, 441. An example of the great increase in the prices of unimproved land held for speculation is cited in Stiles, *Itin.,* 161.

64. Boyd, *Susquehannah Papers,* I, 25, 26.

65. *Ibid.,* I, lviii; *Conn. Col. Recs.,* VII, 582; see also XI, 629.

66. Boyd, *Susquehannah Papers,* I, 1-28.

67. Some of these men were Eliphalet Dyer, Jedidiah Elderkin, Samuel Gray, John Fitch, George Wyllys, Roger Wolcott Jr., Phineas Lyman, and Daniel Edwards. The proprietors of the Delaware Company also included men whose names were significant in the pre-revolutionary history of the colony. Among them were Hezekiah Huntington, Jabez Fitch, Isaac Tracy, Samuel Huntington, Zebulon Wallbridge, Benedict Arnold, and Silas Deane. *Ibid.,* I, lxxiv, lxxvi, lxxxvii, 197, 261-68.

68. *Ibid.,* I, 28.

69. *Ibid.,* I, lxxxi-lxxxiv, and 272; see also Stiles, *Itin.,* 183.

70. Boyd, *Susquehannah Papers,* I, 42, 185, 272-73.

71. *Ibid.,* I, 280.

72. *Ibid.,* I, 42-43, 51; II, 51.

73. *Ibid.,* I, 55-58. Johnson did not think very much of the people of Connecticut, whom he described as "Crafty Inhabitants of the N. Jerusalem." See pp. 83-84.

74. *Ibid.,* I, 50-51, 60-63, 180-81.

75. *Ibid.,* II, 3-4, 25, 33-34, 51-52, and *passim* on the Indian question. On Sir William Johnson's attitude, see *ibid.,* II, 64, 122-23.

76. On Dyer see George C. Groce, "Eliphalet Dyer: Connecticut Revolutionist," in Richard B. Morris, ed., *The Era of the American Revolution* (New York, 1939), 290-304.

77. On the Dyer mission see Samuel Gray to Jonathan Trumbull, Aug. 28, 1761; Joseph Trumbull to Jonathan Trumbull, Dec. 10, 1763, Jonathan Trumbull Papers, Personal and Private Correspondence, Conn. Hist. Soc., hereafter cited as Trumbull Papers, Personal. The Dyer mission is traced in Boyd, *Susquehannah Papers,* II, xxxvi-xli, 72-73, 80, 291-96.

78. *Ibid.,* 130-31.

79. *Conn. Gaz.,* June 19, 1762, p. 4; Boyd, *Susquehannah Papers,* II, 135, 145.

80. *Ibid.,* 147-49.

81. *Ibid.,* II, 193, 195.

82. *Ibid.,* 219. The Delaware companies took similar action. See pp. 233-34. The attitude of many of the Susquehannah Company's proprietors is described in letters written by Ezra Stiles and Sir William Johnson. See *ibid.,* II, 230-31, 218; Stiles, *Itin.,* 189.

83. John Armstrong reported to the Pennsylvania Council, March 20, 1754, that "some Principal Persons in the Government covertly encourage them, and have paid their Contributions." Boyd, *Susquehannah Papers,* I, 72; see also 133 *n2,* 186, 191, 195; II, 30, 166.

84. Stiles to P. Webster, May 21, 1763, Stiles Papers, also in Boyd, *Susquehannah Papers,* II, 231 *n*34. Stiles was a member of the company. In the same year Lewis Gordon, after investigating the situation in the Wyoming Valley, declared that "it is strongly affirmed that every individual Member of the upper House and chief part of the lower House of Assembly of Connecticut are interested and concerned in the said purchase." In 1762 Daniel Brodhead found the settlers believing that "they were abetted and encouraged . . . by all the Power of their Government of Connecticut." Boyd, *Susquehannah Papers,* II, 30, 166.

85. A company committee in 1762 included Jonathan Trumbull, Jedidiah Elderkin, Samuel Gray, and Eliphalet Dyer. *Conn. Gaz.,* July 10, 1762, p. 3. Stiles' view is in his letter to Webster cited in the preceding note. For a list of the men who were prominent in the affairs of the Delaware Company in 1763 see *Conn. Gaz.,* May 7, 1763, p. 2.

86. Roger Wolcott to James Hamilton, March 13, 1754, Lane Papers.

87. Boyd, *Susquehannah Papers,* I, 191.

88. *Ibid.,* III, 241. Joseph Chew was at least one conservative who joined the company with other motives. He explained that it was "out of a mere Banter" expecting "we should have some Little Deversion for our Money." "Ingersoll Papers," 282.

89. Chew told Eliphalet Dyer, June 9, 1763, that he had begun "to entertain a very poor opinion of the Success of the Susquehanna Company." Boyd, *Susquehannah Papers,* II, 252; see also 166.

90. Ezra Stiles to P. Webster, May 21, 1763, Stiles Papers, also in Boyd, *Susquehannah Papers,* II, 229. See also Joseph Chew to Jared Ingersoll, June 8, 1763, "Ingersoll Papers," 281. In the latter Chew congratulated Ingersoll for leaving the company. "Your Behaviour at Hartford," he wrote, "has answered my Expectations. . . . I wish all I know had the same noble Spirit; we should have Less Confussion then I think is Coming Fast upon us."

91. Ezra Stiles to P. Webster, May 21, 1763, Stiles Papers, also in Boyd, *Susquehannah Papers,* II, 230.

92. *Conn. Col. Recs.,* VI, 95. The year was 1718.

93. Hinman, *Letters,* 352, 354, 362-63; *Talcott Papers,* I, 263-64; *Wolcott Papers,* 182; *Conn. Col. Recs.,* X, 626; XI, 629; Isaac W. Stuart, *Life of Jonathan Trumbull* (Boston, 1859), 69-70.

94. *Talcott Papers,* I, 250. On the importance of the trade with the West Indies see *Wolcott Papers,* 98, 182.

95. *Connecticut Journal,* New Haven, Aug. 31, 1770, p. 4; *Conn. Gaz.,* Nov. 5, 1763, p. 2. In 1760 New Haven merchants alone were said to owe £20,000 to merchants in New York. Stiles, *Itin.,* 83.

96. *Conn. Col. Recs.,* III, 299.

97. *Ibid.,* VII, 494-95.

98. *Ibid.,* VII, 512-13.

99. *Ibid.,* VI, 84-87; Trumbull, *History,* II, 45.

100. *Fitch Papers,* I, 315; *Law Papers,* III, 427; *Wolcott Papers,* 74-75.

101. Gipson, *Ingersoll,* 89-91; *Conn. Col. Recs.,* VII, 479; *Fitch Papers,* II, 61, 69-71, 72-73; *The Pitkin Papers,* in Conn. Hist. Soc., *Colls.,* 19 (1921), 239, 242.

102. The report for 1756 is in *Conn. Col. Recs.,* X, 623. The 1749 report may be found in Hinman, *Letters,* 363, and the statement for

1730 in the *Talcott Papers,* I, 262-63, and *Conn. Col. Recs.,* VII, 584. Jared Eliot's sixth essay declared that Connecticut was "under such Difficulties to make Returns for Goods imported, that many have thought it would be best that we should make our own Clothes, and by this Means lessen our Importation, which, indeed, would be better than to run into an endless and irrecoverable Debt." *Essays Upon Field-Husbandry in New England* (Boston, 1760), 135.

103. Mead, *Conn. as a Corporate Colony,* 33.

104. *Conn. Col. Recs.,* VIII, 22; *Talcott Papers,* I, 262-63. Gov. Talcott asserted that Connecticut "should rejoice to have our British Commodities directly from Great Britain, without the additional cost of passing thro the neighbouring Provinces, if by any means we could make Returns." He also pointed out that "We in this Colony are so far from incumbring a trade directly to Great Britain, that we all lament the want of it. We are studying all ways possible to promote it, but the want of staple commodities wherewith to make our Returns has defeated our projects hitherto." See pp. 264, 272.

105. *Conn. Col. Recs.,* IX, 286.

106. *Ibid.,* 283-85.

107. *Ibid.,* 393.

108. *Ibid.,* 510-11. See also *Law Papers,* III, 388; *Pitkin Papers,* 244.

109. Joseph Trumbull to Richard Jackson, Jan. 24, 1764, Joseph Trumbull Papers, Conn. Hist. Soc.

110. See, for example, *Conn. Jour.,* Aug. 31, 1770, p. 4; and Knight, *Journal,* 41-42, 43.

111. The history of Connecticut's currency in the colonial period may be followed in Henry Bronson, "A Historical Account of Connecticut Currency, Continental Money, and the Finances of the Revolution," New Haven Colony Hist. Soc., *Papers,* 1 (1865), chs. 3-5.

112. Wolcott, "Memoir," 332.

113. *Talcott Papers,* II, 208-13.

114. The Rev. Jonathan Marsh complained in 1721, "We are said to be in the way to sink into Ruine for the want of a Medium of Trade." Jonathan Marsh, *An Essay to Prove the Thorough Reformation of a Sinning People is not to be Expected . . . Except the Heart of the People be Prepared for it,* Election Sermon (New London, 1721), 47. Compare this, however, with the later remarks in Woodbridge, *Obedience to the Divine Law,* 21-22; and Mather, *Good Rulers,* 34.

115. Mead, *Conn. as a Corporate Colony,* 50-51.

116. Connecticut Archives, Trade and Maritime Affairs 1668-1789, I, 161ff, State Lib.; see also *Conn. Col. Recs.,* VII, 390-92; *Talcott Papers,* I, 268*n.*

117. Caulkins, *New London,* 243; *Conn. Col. Recs.,* VII, 421-22; *Talcott Papers,* I, 268-70.

118. On the settlement of the Society's affairs see Conn. Arch., Trade and Maritime Affairs, I, 185-233; also *Conn. Col. Recs.,* VII, 449-56, 478, 502, 507-8, 560; VIII, 24, 69, 73-74, 234-35, 471-72; IX, 438-39, 445; *Pitkin Papers,* 220-29.

119. In a long letter to Governor Talcott, dated May 7, 1733, Capt. James Packer of Groton urged the immediate emission of a large sum of paper money. Packer thought it was an opportune time to "Ingross" the trade of Massachusetts and "thereby to Shift the immence burthen of Debts which lie upon our Shoulders on to theirs." *Talcott Papers,* I, 279-82. When, however, the colonial wars forced the provincial government to issue paper money in amounts which caused it to depreciate and to drive already scarce metals out of circulation, there was a loud clamor for stabilization. Worthington, *Duty of Rulers and Teachers,* 35; Hunn, *Welfare of a Government,* 12, 22; Todd, *Civil Rulers,* 58, 61; Wolcott, "Memoir," 332; *Law Papers,* III, 438-39; *Wolcott Papers,* 60-66, 102; Mead, *Conn. as a Corporate Colony,* 53 *n*3.

120. When the New London Society asked, May 1733, to be allowed to resume its activities under proper restrictions, the Assembly turned it down with the declaration that any "society of merchants whose undertakings are vastly beyond their own compass, and must depend on the government for their supplies of money, and must therefore depend on their influence on the government to obtain it, is not for the peace and health of the government." *Conn. Col. Recs.,* VII, 449.

121. See Connecticut's report to the Board of Trade, 1762, in *ibid.,* XI, 629-30.

122. *Conn. Col. Recs.,* VII, 583; X, 625-26; XI, 629; Edward E. Atwater, ed., *History of the City of New Haven to the Present Time* (New York, 1887), 31.

123. Stiles, *Itin.,* 28. See also *Wolcott Papers,* 98, 182; Stuart, *Trumbull,* 70; Royal R. Hinman, *A Historical Collection of the Part Sustained by Connecticut During the War of the Revolution* (Hartford, 1842), 15. On the importance of the New Haven trade with the West Indies see the lists of ships and their cargoes in Foreigners Outwards and Foreigners Inwards 1762-1801, District of New Haven Customs

Records, National Archives.

124. *Wolcott Papers,* 71.

125. *Ibid.,* 110-12.

126. Jonathan Trumbull Jr. to Joseph Trumbull, Oct. 3, 1763, Joseph Trumbull Papers. It is interesting to compare the younger Trumbull's attitude toward smuggling with the regular assertion of the Connecticut authorities during these decades that there was no smuggling in the colony. For the latter see *Talcott Papers,* I, 234, 250; Hinman, *Letters,* 363. Trumbull's brother Joseph reported, however, that the British looked upon the people of Connecticut as "a Lawless Crew who live entirely by Smuggling." In this letter he anticipated that the British would "send some of their own *Hangars On* to take the place and keep us honest." Joseph to Jonathan Trumbull Jr., Dec. 24, 1763, Trumbull Papers, Personal. Between 1735 and 1750 no duties were collected in Connecticut under the Molasses Act, and only £99 was taken in for prizes. Gipson, *Ingersoll,* 112-13 *n*3.

127. It is interesting to compare these developments with Massachusetts' contemporary experience. See John C. Miller, "Religion, Finance and Democracy in Massachusetts," *New Eng. Quar.,* 6 (1933), 29-58.

CHAPTER THREE

1. See above, ch. 1, *n*93.

2. *Conn. Col. Recs.,* VII, 570-79; *Talcott Papers,* I, 189, 218; II, 436, 446-47; Hempstead, *Diary,* 197.

3. *Conn. Col. Recs.,* VII, 254; *Talcott Papers,* I, 227-28 and *passim.* Connecticut's land laws were finally upheld in 1745 when the Privy Council dismissed a petition of Samuel Clark (Clark *v.* Tousey) which had contested the colony's intestacy law. *Conn. Col. Recs.,* IX, 587-93, and *Law Papers,* I, *passim.*

4. *Talcott Papers,* II, 166*n,* 257, 286-87; *Conn. Col. Recs.,* IX, 453; Andrews, *Col. Per.,* IV, 393-94.

5. Osgood, *Amer. Colonies in the 18th Cent.,* III, 284-85; *Talcott Papers, passim; Wolcott Papers,* 139; *Fitch Papers,* II, 313-14, 342.

6. *Fitch Papers,* I, 16, 34-36, 37-42. See also Professor Gipson's

analysis of the reasons advanced by the General Assembly against the plan. *British Empire,* V, 148-50.

7. *Fitch Papers,* II, 92. The General Association also congratulated the new monarch very warmly. Gen. Assoc., *Recs.,* 46.

8. James Lockwood, *A Sermon Preached at Wethersfield July 6, 1763* (New Haven, 1763), 7; Stephen White, *Civil Rulers Gods by Office and the Duties of such Considered and Enforced,* Election Sermon (New London, 1763), 26-27.

9. Noah Welles, *Patriotism Described and Recommended,* Election Sermon (New London, 1764), 26, 29. Lockwood had also complained that there was more "Sin in the Land" than there had been before the war. *Sermon Preached at Wethersfield,* 29-30.

10. *Fitch Papers,* II, 247-49.

11. Joseph Trumbull, however, then in England, wrote to his father's firm in Connecticut that he was "sorry the Duty on Molasses is so high, but hope it will not wholly destroy the Trade; the Duties on the other Articles are not so great as to make any considerable difference to the Consumer nor any to the Merchant." In a short time he was to think very differently on the matter. Trumbull to Trumbull and Fitch, April 19, 1764, Trumbull Papers, Personal.

12. *Fitch Papers,* II, 261-73, 275-76. See also the document "Remarks on the Trade of the Colony," *ibid.,* 277-79.

13. Ernest E. Rogers, ed., *Connecticut's Naval Office at New London . . . Including the Mercantile Letter Book of Nathaniel Shaw Jr.,* New London Co., Hist. Soc., *Colls.,* 2 (1933), 8, hereafter cited as Shaw, *Letter Book.*

14. Samuel Gray to Jonathan Trumbull, April 14, 1764, Trumbull Papers, Personal. Gray did not think that Dyer had "Sufficiantly vallued or [*sic*] precious priviledges till now." Dyer had informed Gray, Feb. 10, 1764, that the ministry was "vastly Jealous of the growing Power and Interest of the Colonies." British troops sent to America were to be used "as a Rod over the Colonies, to be a Check upon them." See also Dyer's letter dated March 10, 1764. Both in Connecticut Miscellaneous Papers 1740-1787, Stevens Transcripts, L.C.

15. *Conn. Col. Recs.,* XII, 240.

16. Ingersoll to T. Whately, July 6, 1764, "Ingersoll Papers," 296-97.

17. See the two articles taken from the *Public Ledger* and published in the *Conn. Courant,* May 6, 1765, p. 1, and July 22, 1765, p. 1.

18. Joseph Bellamy, Election Sermon, 28-29; Lockwood, *Sermon Preached at Wethersfield,* 31.

19. Jonathan Trumbull to Lane and Booth, Aug. 1, 1763, Jonathan Trumbull Papers, Mercantile Correspondence, Conn. Hist. Soc., hereafter cited as Trumbull Papers, Mercantile.

20. *Conn. Courant,* Dec. 3, 1764, p. 1; see also Jan. 2, 1765, p. 2.

21. Jonathan Trumbull to Lane and Booth, Jan. 9, 1764, Trumbull Papers, Mercantile.

22. Jonathan Trumbull to Joseph Trumbull, May 28, 1764, Joseph Trumbull Papers.

23. Joseph Trumbull to Thomas Collinson, Jan. 20, 1765; see also Jonathan Trumbull Jr. to Joseph Trumbull, May 27, 1764, *ibid.*

24. Ingersoll to T. Whately, July 6, 1764; Jared Ingersoll, *Mr. Ingersoll's Letters Relating to the Stamp Act* (New Haven, 1766), 7, hereafter cited as Ingersoll, *Letters.*

25. In East Haddam "good wild lands" sold for £3 an acre in 1762, whereas they had brought £4 only two or three years before. Stiles, *Itin.,* 50-51. In New Haven the value of estates reported for tax purposes showed a decline of £480 between 1760 and 1765. In the preceding five-year period land values had increased £10,251. Atwater, *New Haven,* 31.

26. J. Ledyard to Jonathan Trumbull, Nov. 6, 1764, Trumbull Papers, Personal.

27. Gipson, *Ingersoll,* 252-53. The Rev. Noah Welles referred in his election sermon for the year 1764 both to Connecticut's fame for its "litigious disposition" and the currently large number of lawsuits. *Patriotism Described,* 25.

28. Stiles, *Itin.,* 188. Samuel Gray wrote to Eliphalet Dyer, n.d. (*ca.* 1764), that "The Distress of our Coloney is very great on account of their private Debts." Conn. Misc. Papers, Stevens Transcripts.

29. *Conn. Col. Recs.,* XIII, *passim.*

30. Gipson, *Ingersoll,* 252. Professor Gipson has ably analyzed the complicated question of Connecticut's tax policy in this period in his study *Connecticut Taxation 1750-1775,* Conn. Tercentenary Commission, *Publs.,* 10 (1933).

31. *Fitch Papers,* II, 289, 292-93, 297-98. Some types of papers were omitted from the final draft of the act. *Ibid.,* 326. The Tory minister, the Rev. Samuel Peters, claimed that Connecticut's opposition to the Stamp Act was in part due to the fact that it affected the "judges, the lawyers, the ministers, and deacons, the sheriffs and constables." Peters, *History,* 221-22.

32. As early as Feb. 27, 1764 Jonathan Trumbull wrote to his son Joseph that the news of the British attitude and proposed British policies was ominous. A month later, March 14, 1764 Joseph Trumbull informed Edward Dixon that "America has been on the Anvil in the House of Commons." Should the Stamp Act pass Joseph pessimistically predicted "farewell Liberty in America." Jonathan Trumbull Jr. Papers, 108a, 119, State Lib. On the other hand, it is interesting to note that the Rev. Edward Dorr's election sermon, delivered on May 9, 1765, was entirely devoted to the theme of its title, *The Duty of Civil Rulers to be Nursing Fathers to the Church of Christ* (Hartford, 1765). Although Dorr referred to the Lockeian theory of the social contract—see, for example, p. 17—he ignored the Stamp Act completely.

33. Joseph Trumbull to Jonathan Trumbull, March 24, 1764; see also the letter dated Dec. 10, 1763, Trumbull Papers, Personal.

34. Jonathan Trumbull Jr. to Joseph Trumbull, May 27, 1764, Joseph Trumbull Papers.

35. Stiles to John Hubbard, June 12, 1764, Stiles Papers; Whittelsey to Stiles, April 16, 1765, Stiles, *Itin.,* 587.

36. Gray to Eliphalet Dyer, n.d., (*ca.* 1764), and Dyer to Gray, Feb. 10 and March 20, 1764, Conn. Misc. Papers, Stevens Transcripts. See also Dyer to Jared Ingersoll, April 14, 1764, Jared Ingersoll Papers, Force Transcripts, L.C.

37. *Conn. Col. Recs.,* XII, 256, 299. Stiles, *Itin.,* 202. Committees of the Massachusetts and Rhode Island legislatures had urged Connecticut in June and October to join a united opposition against the Sugar Act and proposed Stamp Act. *Fitch Papers,* II, 284-85, 291. It was in October that Governor Bernard proposed to Halifax, Secretary of State for the Southern Department, that "the two republics of Connecticut and Rhode Island be dissolved." Andrews, *Col. Per.,* IV, 394 *n2.*

38. "Reasons Why the British Colonies in America Should Not Be Charged With Internal Taxes . . . Humbly Offered For Consideration in Behalf of the Colony of Connecticut," *Conn. Col. Recs.,* XII, 653-71; Fitch to Richard Jackson, Dec. 7, 1764, *Fitch Papers,* II, 304; see also 296; Stiles, *Itin.,* 202; Jared Ingersoll to T. Whately, July 6, 1764, "Ingersoll Papers," 299.

39. Under the rules of the House of Commons petitions against money bills were inadmissable. Ingersoll to Gov. Fitch, March 6, 1765; Richard Jackson to Fitch, March 9, *Fitch Papers,* II, 334, 341.

40. Ingersoll to Gov. Fitch, Feb. 11, 1765, *ibid.,* 324-26.

41. *Ibid.,* 326.

42. Gov. Fitch to Richard Jackson, Feb. 23, 1765, William Samuel Johnson Papers, Conn. Hist. Soc., hereafter cited as Johnson Papers; *Pitkin Papers,* 273.

43. Jared Ingersoll to [?], Feb. 1, 1766, Emmet Collection no. 4897, N. Y. Pub. Lib.; see also Gipson, *Ingersoll,* 137-38. Ingersoll explained to William Livingston, Oct. 1, 1765, that he had gone to England the previous winter "with the strongest prejudices against the Parliamentary Authority in this Case; and came home, I don't have to say convinced, but confoundedly begad and beswompt, as we say in Connecticut." "Ingersoll Papers," 349.

44. Ingersoll to Connecticut General Assembly, Sept. 18, 1765, Connecticut Papers, Bancroft Transcripts, N. Y. Pub. Lib., hereafter cited as Conn. Papers. The letter also appears in the "Ingersoll Papers," 338. As early as July 6, 1764 Ingersoll admitted that his neighbors were suspicious of him because of his lack of Puritanism and his apparent sympathies for the "Court interest." To T. Whately, "Ingersoll Papers," 298, 299.

45. At the same time that William Samuel Johnson offered himself for the Stratford job he congratulated Ingersoll as follows: "Since we are doomed to Stamps and Slavery, and must submit, we hear with pleasure that your gentle hand will fit on our Chains and Shackles who I know will make them set easie as possible." Johnson to Ingersoll, June 3, 1765, "Ingersoll Papers," 324; see also 324-27.

46. *New London Gazette,* Sept. 13, 1765, p. 2; see also *Conn. Gaz.,* Aug. 9, 1765, p. 3; and *Conn. Courant,* Aug. 26, 1765, p. 2.

47. *Conn. Gaz.,* Aug. 9, 1765, p. 4.

48. See, for example, the files of the *Conn. Gaz.* for July-Sept. 1765.

49. The Rev. Stephen Johnson of Lyme was the "Freeman" who wrote the series of five articles ending Nov. 1, 1765 in the *New London Gaz.* "Cato" in the *Conn. Gaz.* was Yale's Professor Daggett. See *Conn. Gaz.,* Aug. 9, 1765, p. 3, in the Stiles Papers for Stiles' reference to Daggett and the copy of the *New London Gaz.,* Nov. 1, 1765, p. 4, in the Yale Library for Stiles' notation of Johnson's name next to the article by "Freeman." See also Hollister, *History,* II, 130-31.

50. *Conn. Gaz.,* Sept. 6, 1765, p. 3; *New London Gaz.,* Aug. 23, 1765, p. 2; *Conn. Courant,* Sept. 2, 1765, p. 2.

51. *Conn. Gaz.,* Sept. 6, 1765, p. 3.

52. [B. Church], *Liberty and Property vindicated and the St—pm-n burnt* (Boston, 1765), 8, 11.

53. *Conn. Gaz.,* Sept. 6, 1765, p. 3.

54. Compare "Civis" in *ibid.,* Aug. 30, 1765, p. 1, with "Cato" in *New London Gaz.,* Sept. 6, 1765, p. 1.

55. Quoted in Gipson, *Ingersoll,* 165 *n1.*

56. Joseph Chew had predicted in a letter to Ingersoll, June 9, 1763, that the "Religious junto or those who assume that carracter, will, thro this Colony into the greatest Confusion. You cannot imagine what pains this Party take and how their Disciples and Emissarys are dispersed throt the Government." "Ingersoll Papers," 283. Benjamin Gale, in a pamphlet published in 1769, expressed the opinion that the blocking of the Susquehannah Company's plans by the Crown and Governor Fitch had produced "resentments" in the eastern towns, and thus had "some influence to excite the *sons of liberty* in that quarter of the government, to distinguish themselves so eminently above their brethren, in other parts of this government." Boyd, *Susquehannah Papers,* III, 241-42.

57. Gale to Jared Ingersoll, Jan. 13, 1766, "Ingersoll Papers," 373.

58. Trumbull, "Sons of Liberty," 312.

59. Gipson, *Ingersoll,* 168 *n1,* and Wales to Ingersoll, Aug. 19, 1765, "Ingersoll Papers," 325-26.

60. *Conn. Gaz.,* Sept. 6, 1765, p. 2.

61. Miller to Jared Ingersoll, Sept. 10, 1765, "Ingersoll Papers," 331.

62. *Fitch Papers,* II, 355; see also *New London Gaz.,* Sept. 13, 1765, p. 3.

63. Articles by "Civis" and "A Friend to the Publick and No Enemy to Stamp Officers," *Conn. Gaz.,* Aug. 30, 1765, p. 1.

64. "A Friend to the Publick."

65. Gov. Fitch to William Pitkin, Sept. 12, 1765, *Fitch Papers,* II, 356. Town meetings were held to instruct the deputies. The Hartford and New Haven meetings are described in the *Conn. Courant,* Sept. 23, 1765, pp. 1, 2.

66. J. Miller to Ingersoll, Sept. 10, 1765, "Ingersoll Papers," 330.

67. *Conn. Gaz.,* Sept. 20, 1765, p. 3. See also Ingersoll's account, *ibid.,* Sept. 27, 1765, pp. 1-2. David Humphreys later described those who forced Ingersoll to resign as the "*yeomanry,*" "*multitude,*" or "*people,*" but not "*mob,*" which generally signifies a disorderly concurrence of the rabble." *The Life and Heroic Exploits of Israel Putnam* (New York, 1834), 67. According to Hollister, Colonel Putnam was one of the principal instigators of the affair, but he was unable to participate in it. *History,* II, 139.

68. *Conn. Gaz.,* Sept. 27, 1765, p. 1; *Conn. Courant,* Sept. 23, 1765, p. 2.

69. *Conn. Gaz.,* Sept. 27, 1765, pp. 1-2. Ingersoll later described his thoughts on being "attended by such a retinue." He declared that it made him understand better "than ever . . . before that passage in the Revelation which describes *death on a pale horse, and hell following him.*" Ingersoll mounted a white horse during the incident. Humphreys, *Putnam,* 67-68.

70. "Ingersoll Papers," 340; the original manuscript is in the General Assembly Papers, Box 1, Conn. Hist. Soc.

71. *Conn. Col. Recs.,* XII, 410. The Assembly, ever careful about the colony's independence, warned the delegates "to form no such junction with the other Commissioners as will subject you to the major vote of the commissioners present." They were also instructed to report all their doings to the governor and especially to the Assembly for "acceptance and approbation." One of two other clauses of instructions that apparently were not approved by the Assembly told the delegates to give "proper attention" to all hints and arguments that Gov. Fitch might give them. "Instructions to Connecticut Commissioners," Sept. 19 or 20, 1765, William Samuel Johnson Papers, L.C.

72. *Conn. Courant,* Sept. 23, 1765, p. 2.

73. This had prompted a conservative observer to wonder why a special meeting was necessary at all. *Conn. Gaz.,* Sept. 20, 1765, p. 3.

74. *Ibid.,* Sept. 27, 1765, p. 3.

75. *Ibid.,* Oct. 11, 1765, p. 1; see also *New London Gaz.* Sept. 27, 1765, p. 1.

76. *Conn. Gaz.,* Oct. 4, 1765, p. 4; Moses C. Tyler, *The Literary History of the American Revolution* (New York, 1897), I, 99-100.

77. Tyler, *Literary History,* I, 100. See also the draft copy of an article against the Stamp Act that William Williams probably sent to a newspaper late in 1765, Williams Papers.

78. "Addison" in the *New London Gaz.,* Sept. 6, 1765.

79. Stiles to B. Ellery, Oct. 23, 1765, Stiles Papers.

80. Ingersoll to Whately, Nov. 2, 1765, and to Jackson, Nov. 3, 1765, Ingersoll, *Letters,* 40, 45. John Hubbard, a prominent New Haven freeman, wrote to Stiles, Sept. 21, 1765, "It is said our Lower House is much changed whether for the better I don't hear." Stiles, *Itin.,* 511.

81. Franklin B. Dexter, ed., *The Literary Diary of Ezra Stiles* (New Haven, 1901), I, 55, 133, hereafter cited as Stiles, *Diary.*

82. Connecticut Archives, 1st Revolutionary Series, I, 29, State Lib., hereafter cited as Conn. Arch., Rev. Ser.; *Conn. Col. Recs.,* XII, 420.

83. *Conn. Col. Recs.,* XII, 422.

84. Stiles to B. Ellery, Oct. 23, 1765, Stiles Papers.

85. *Conn. Col. Recs.,* XII, 421-22; *Fitch Papers,* II, 367.

86. Ingersoll to Richard Jackson, Nov. 3, 1765, Ingersoll, *Letters,* 42.

87. Stiles, *Itin.,* 221-22. Thirty-nine deputies did not vote. See also *Conn. Gaz.,* Oct. 25, 1765, p. 2. According to the Conn. Arch., Rev. Ser., I, 32, the resolutions were adopted in the lower house "with great Unanimity." The five deputies who voted against the resolutions were Norwalk's two representatives, Joseph Platt and Thomas Fitch Jr.; one of Newtown's deputies, Capt. Henry Glover; Seth Wetmore of Middletown; and Benjamin Gale of Killingworth. Stiles, *Itin.,* 221-22, and *Conn. Col. Recs.,* XII, 412-13.

88. Ingersoll to T. Whately, Nov. 2, 1765, Ingersoll, *Letters,* 45.

89. *A New Collection of Verses applied to the First of November AD 1765 Including a Prediction that the Stamp Act shall not take place in North America* (New Haven, 1765), broadside in N. Y. Pub. Lib.

90. Dexter, *Biog. Sketches,* I, 248.

91. Stiles Papers, Bancroft Transcripts, N. Y. Pub. Lib.

92. [Thomas Fitch], *An Explanation of Say-Brook Platform . . . by One That Heartily Desires the Order, Peace, and Purity of These Churches* (Hartford, 1765), 39. There is also some possibility that Fitch may have been influenced by Anglican teaching. *Fitch Papers,* I, xxxvii.

93. Stiles Papers, Bancroft Transcripts. Stiles thought that this was "the first thing that really lost him with the people."

94. Connecticut Executive, "Some General Hints for the Connecticut Commissioners to be used or not as they Shall be tho't best by them," William Samuel Johnson Papers, L.C.

95. Stiles Papers, Bancroft Transcripts.

96. H. Conway to the Governor of Connecticut, Oct. 24, 1765, *Fitch Papers,* II, 362.

97. Jonathan Trumbull, speaking for towns in eastern Connecticut, had previously informed the governor rather dryly of the people's confidence in Fitch's desire "to do Ev-thing for the Security of our Liberties and welfare so we hope." *Ibid.,* 355.

98. Eliphalet Dyer to W. S. Johnson, Dec. 15, 1765, Johnson Papers.

Stiles wrote to B. Ellery on Oct. 23, 1765, that he believed the governor would take the oath. Stiles Papers.

99. L. Hubbard to E. Stiles, Nov. 6, 1765, Stiles Papers; see also Stiles, *Itin.,* 512. Dyer later claimed that he had been the only one in the Council who had stood up to speak against taking the oath. Dyer to W. S. Johnson, Dec. 8, 1765, Johnson Papers. The juring Councillors' home towns were: Ebenezer Silliman, Fairfield; John Chester, Wethersfield; Benjamin Hall, Wallingford; Jabez Hamlin, Middletown.

100. Fitch to Richard Jackson, Nov. 13, 1765, *Fitch Papers,* II, 372.

101. Thomas Fitch, *Some Reasons that Influenced the Governor to Take and the Councillors to Administer the Oath* (Hartford, 1766), 7.

102. *Ibid.,* 7-8.

103. *Ibid.,* 11-12.

104. Fitch to C. Lowndes, Dec. 24, 1765, *Fitch Papers,* II, 381.

105. Fitch, *Some Reasons that Influenced the Governor,* 14.

106. *Ibid.;* Ingersoll to T. Whately, Nov. 2, 1765, "Ingersoll Papers," 352.

107. Dyer to W. S. Johnson, Dec. 8, 1765, Johnson Papers.

108. The reference to Connecticut's liberty is in Jonathan Lee, *But Godliness with Contentment is Great Gain,* Election Sermon (New London, 1766), 18.

109. *Conn. Courant,* March 11, 1765, p. 1. See also the issue of April 1, 1765, p. 1, and the petition of the Fairfield County merchants, May 1765, in *Fitch Papers,* II, 345-47.

110. J. Huntington to his father, May 27, 1765, Jedidiah Huntington Papers, Conn. Hist. Soc.; *Conn. Courant,* May 20, 1765, p. 1. The issue for July 8, p. 3, also reported "the greatest scarcity of bread corn in the back towns for this few weeks past."

111. Ingersoll to Richard Jackson, Nov. 3, 1765, "Ingersoll Papers," 359.

112. *Fitch Papers,* II, 379; Margaret E. Martin, *Merchants and Trade in the Connecticut River Valley 1750-1820,* in Smith College, *Studies,* 24, nos. 1-4, p. 30. William Samuel Johnson, who had a large number of clients in all parts of the colony, reported that the people of western Connecticut were "excessively in debt to the neighboring Govts." Johnson to Dyer, Dec. 31, 1765, Letter Book, 165, Johnson Papers.

113. Ingersoll to Richard Jackson, Nov. 3, 1765, "Ingersoll Papers," 357.

114. *A New Collection of Verses,* N. Y. Pub. Lib.

115. *Conn. Gaz.,* Nov. 15, 1765, p. 2.

116. L. Hubbard to E. Stiles, Nov. 6, 1765, Stiles Papers; see also Stiles, *Itin.,* 513.

117. *Ibid.*

118. Ingersoll to the Commissioners of Stamps, Dec. 2, 1765, Ingersoll, *Letters,* 55.

119. "Ingersoll Papers," 368; *Fitch Papers,* II, 380.

120. Stewart to J. Temple, Dec. 19, 1765, *Pitkin Papers,* 276-77. See also *Conn. Gaz.,* Jan. 17, 1766, p.2. A group of the colony's most prominent merchants had petitioned for some relief for the "declining Trade" and measures to prevent "Total Stagnation." *Fitch Papers,* II, 364.

121. *Conn. Gaz.,* Jan. 24, 1766, p. 2.

122. Stiles, *Itin.,* 513; *Conn. Gaz.,* Jan. 31, 1766, p. 2; Feb. 7, p. 1; Feb. 14, pp. 2-3; Feb. 21, p. 2; Feb. 28, pp. 1-2.

123. Stiles to B. Ellery, Oct. 23, 1765, Stiles Papers.

124. *Ibid.*

125. See Ingersoll's account in the *Conn. Gaz.,* Sept. 27, 1765, p. 1.

126. *Ibid.,* p. 2.

127. *Ibid.,* p. 1. See also Ingersoll to Richard Jackson, Nov. 23, 1765, Ingersoll, *Letters,* 44.

128. *Conn. Col. Recs.,* XII, 411.

129. *Conn. Courant,* Sept. 23, 1765, p. 1.

130. Ingersoll to T. Whately, Nov. 2, 1765, "Ingersoll Papers," 352.

131. *New London Gaz.,* Nov. 15, 1765, p. 2; see also *Conn. Gaz.,* Dec. 6, 1765, p. 1.

132. Dyer to W. S. Johnson, Dec. 8, 1765, Johnson Papers.

133. *Conn. Courant,* Dec. 30, 1765, p. 4; see also p. 3.

134. C. Whittelsey to E. Stiles, Dec. 24, 1765, Stiles, *Itin.,* 588.

135. Humphreys, *Putnam,* 68.

136. *Conn. Gaz.,* Jan. 24, 1766, p. 2.

137. *Ibid.,* pp. 1-2.

138. Dyer to Johnson, Dec. 15, 1765, Johnson Papers. Johnson condemned the violence of the mob and attributed the western clamors to men of the "same little scoundrel turn of Mind." Johnson to Dyer, Dec. 31, 1765, Letter Book, 164-65, *ibid.*

139. *Conn. Gaz.,* Nov. 22, 1765, p. 2; Feb. 14, 1766, p. 4. At the same time, however, they admitted that Parliament had the power "in some special Cases" to make laws extending to the colonists "where the Power

of the Colonies is inadequate." The anticipated objections to this qualification were raised in the Feb. 28th issue of the *Conn. Gaz.*, p. 2.

140. *Ibid.*, March 15, 1766, pp. 1-2.

141. *Ibid.*, April 5, 1766, p. 3. For meetings of the Sons of Liberty of Litchfield County and other towns see *Conn. Courant,* Feb. 10, 1766, p. 3, Feb. 24, p. 1, and March 24, p. 4.

142. *Conn. Gaz.*, Dec. 27, 1765, p. 2; Jan. 10, 1766, p. 2. See also Dyer to W. S. Johnson, Dec. 15, 1765, Johnson Papers; Ingersoll, *Letters,* i-ii.

143. Ingersoll to W. S. Johnson, Dec. 2, 1765, "Ingersoll Papers," 362.

144. Quoted in James T. Adams, *Revolutionary New England 1691-1776* (Boston, 1923), 326.

145. Chew to Ingersoll, Feb. 5, 1766, "Ingersoll Papers," 377.

146. Hutchinson to [?], Dec. 27, 1765, Hutchinson Correspondence, Bancroft Transcripts, N. Y. Pub. Lib.

147. Hutchinson to [?], Jan. 2, 1766, *ibid.*

148. Gray to W. S. Johnson, Dec. 9, 1765, Schneider, *Johnson,* I, 360.

149. *Conn. Courant,* Feb. 10, 1766, p. 4; March 24, p. 4.

150. *Conn. Gaz.,* April 5, 1766, p. 2.

151. Arnold was at this time in the West Indies trade. His defense was an open attack upon the British laws regulating colonial commerce and a justification of smuggling. *Ibid.*, Feb. 12, 1766, p. 4. See also *Conn. Courant,* Feb. 10, 1766, p. 3, and Boardman, *Sherman,* 92-93.

152. *Conn. Gaz.,* Feb. 7, 1766, p. 1.

153. Joseph Trumbull to Jonathan Trumbull, Dec. 22, 1765, Trumbull Papers, Mercantile.

154. Whittelsey to E. Stiles, Dec. 27, 1765, Stiles, *Itin.,* 588.

155. Quotation taken from the circular sent by Henry Conway to Connecticut, Oct. 24, 1765, *Fitch Papers,* II, 362.

156. Ingersoll to T. Whately, Nov. 2, 1765, "Ingersoll Papers," 353.

157. Ingersoll, *Letters,* 48n.

158 *Conn. Gaz.,* Feb. 14, 1766, p. 4.

159. Ingersoll to [?], Feb. 1, 1766, Emmet Collection no. 4897.

160. Welles, *Patriotism Described,* 14-15.

161. Abel Stiles to Ezra Stiles, April 18, 1766, Stiles Papers. Abel declared that he was "far from friendly to violence unless when self defence warrants it yet I . . . rejoyce in the general opposition made . . . and I really think there have been as few things exceptionable in the Conduct of the pple during this alarming Season as Could be expected."

162. *Conn. Gaz.,* Aug. 16, 1765, pp. 1, 2; Aug. 30, p. 1; Sept. 13, p. 2;

Oct. 25, p. 2. Samuel Avery claimed that in 1765 it was sufficient for "some of those hot Spirits but to point at a person or House and say Liberty property and no stamps, and the Infatuated people would be ready to fall on and mob or even murder the man, or pull down the House." "Anti Alarm," Avery Papers.

163. *Conn. Gaz.,* Feb. 21, 1766, p. 2; March 29, pp. 1-2.

164. Stiles to John Hubbard, June 12, 1764, Stiles Papers.

165. "It is much beyond me," Stiles wrote, "to see how Violence can be vindicated in opposing the Stamp Act, or any other Act of Parliament, whether unconstitutional or not, till every other method has been used." Stiles also sympathized with the Massachusetts Tory's violent treatment at the hands of Boston's radicals, and commented "How detestable is Oclocracy." Stiles to Hutchinson, Oct. 5, 1765, *ibid.* It seems that this letter was not actually sent. Those excerpts which have been quoted in the text were included in another letter dated Dec. 28, 1765 that Stiles also addressed to Hutchinson. See note on the copy of the October letter in the Conn. Misc. Papers, Stevens Transcripts. In another passage of the October letter Stiles asserted that he had "hoped never to have seen the day when the Colonies should resist the Parent State: nor will I ever take Part in such Resistance."

166. Stiles to [?], Oct. 23, 1765, Stiles Papers. This letter read in part: "For several years there has been Talk of the Revocation of the Charters—and tho' I have often expressed a high sense of the value of charter Lib[erties] etc. yet I often said years ago if . . . parlt should dissolve them I would be still a loyal Subject and submit to a change of Govt."

167. *Ibid.*

168. Stiles to B. Ellery, Oct. 23, 1765, *ibid.*

169. Stiles to B. Franklin, Nov. 6, 1765, *ibid.*

170. Stiles to the Lords of the Treasury, Nov. 6, 1765, *ibid.* "I beg Leave to recognize my Allegiance to his Majesty," Stiles wrote in this letter, "and to declare that as I ever have so I shall continue to make it as a part of my pastoral Labor to [?] and perpetuate that Allegiance and Obedience to the King."

171. J. Hubbard to E. Stiles, Jan. 2, 1766, *ibid;* Stiles, *Itin.,* 509. Joseph Chew did not favor the Stamp Act, but he could not countenance "Violences and invasions of private Property." Chew to Ingersoll, Feb. 15, 1766, "Ingersoll Papers," 378-79.

172. Joseph Trumbull to Jonathan Trumbull, Dec. 22, 1765, Trum-

bull Papers, Mercantile. In the same letter Joseph asked his father if he knew who was organizing the people and setting them on. Joseph thought that the leaders of the mobs, Ledlie, Durkee, and Park were merely fronts for "somebody of more Consequence and Craft" and named Dyer as the head of the ringleaders. There is another letter elsewhere in the Trumbull Papers which points to the conclusion that Jonathan Senior himself was closely associated with the organizing activities of the radicals. On Dec. 25, 1765 Moses Park and Hugh Ledlie wrote to the elder Trumbull explaining that they would have reported to him in person what they had done, but that bad weather had made it impossible to be in Pomfret at the "Time assigned." Trumbull Papers, Personal.

173. Lewis H. Boutell, *The Life of Roger Sherman* (Chicago, 1896), 52-54; Boardman, *Sherman*, 91-92.

174. Gray to W. S. Johnson, Dec. 9, 1765, Schneider, *Johnson*, I, 360.

175. Pomeroy to E. Stiles, Jan. 27, 1766, Stiles Papers.

176. Lee, *Godliness with Contentment*, 15, 27.

177. *Conn. Gaz.*, Jan. 10, 1766, p. 2.

178. *Conn. Courant*, Jan. 13, 1766, p. 4.

179. See, for example, the report of the New Haven meeting, Sept. 5, 1765, *Conn. Gaz.*, Sept. 13, 1765, p. 2; the Norwalk town meeting of Nov. 12, 1765, in Hall, *Norwalk Historical Records*, 126; and the New Haven meeting of Feb. 3, 1766, in *Conn. Gaz.*, Feb. 14, 1766, p. 4. Even the Milford Sons of Liberty felt it necessary to denounce the popular custom of insulting the regular civil authorities. *Conn. Gaz.*, April 5, 1766, p. 3.

180. As late as 1763 the Anglican ministers had complained of a "malignant spirit of opposition to the church," and of "indecent reflections . . . most flagrant misrepresentations . . . and the most false and abusive personal invectives" against the S. P. G., the English establishment and its clergymen. See, for example, the letters sent to the S. P. G. by the Rev. Mr. Winslow, July 1, 1763, and by the Rev. Mr. Dibblee, Sept. 29, 1763, Hawks and Perry, *Doc. Hist.*, II, 48, 52. Nevertheless the Episcopal church continued to grow. See Chauncey Whittelsey's worried comments on this in his letter to Ezra Stiles, March 9, 1765, Stiles, *Itin.*, 586.

181. Lee, *Godliness with Contentment*, 18.

182. The younger Johnson thought the subject was too "delicate not to say dangerous." William S. Johnson to the Rev. Mr. Palmer, Dec. 19, 1765, Johnson Papers.

183. Conn. MSS, Hawks Transcripts, 502; Hawks and Perry, *Doc. Hist.*, II, 87. In September 1765 the clergy reported to the S. P. G. that "altho' the commotions and disaffection in this country is [*sic*] very great at present relative to what they call the imposition of stamp duties; yet . . . the people of the Chh of Engld in general in this colony . . . and . . . those in particular under our respective charges are of a contrary temper and conduct." Conn. MSS, Hawks Transcripts, 500-1; see also Hawks and Perry, *Doc. Hist.*, II, 92, 104-7. It must be remembered, of course, that the missionaries would emphasize these solid contributions of their labors.

184. Conn. MSS, Hawks Transcripts, 501.

185. *Ibid.*, 502.

186. *Ibid.*, 508-9.

187. *Ibid.*, 507-8; also 503, 506, 514; Hawks and Perry, *Doc. Hist.*, II, 83, 85-87, 89-90.

188. Hubbard to E. Stiles, Jan. 2, 1766, Stiles Papers; Stiles, *Itin.*, 509-10.

189. See Gale's description of the factions within the Sons of Liberty in his letter to Ingersoll, Jan. 13, 1766, "Ingersoll Papers," 373.

190. *Conn. Gaz.*, Aug. 30, 1765, p. 1; Oct. 25, p. 2.

191. Ingersoll to T. Whately, Nov. 2, 1765, "Ingersoll Papers," 352.

192. J. Hubbard to E. Stiles, Jan. 2, 1766, Stiles Papers; Stiles, *Itin.*, 509.

193. *Conn. Gaz.*, Jan. 10, 1766, p. 2.

194. *Conn. Courant*, Jan. 13, 1766, p. 4.

195. C. Whittelsey to E. Stiles, Dec. 24, 1765, Stiles Papers; Stiles, *Itin.*, 588.

196. A. Z. [B. Gale], *The Present State of the Colony of Connecticut Considered* (New London, 1755), 19.

197. Johnson to E. Dyer, Dec. 31, 1765, Letter Book, 165, Johnson Papers.

198. *Conn. Courant*, Jan. 27, 1766, p. 3.

199. Gale to J. Ingersoll, Jan. 13, Feb. 8, 1766, "Ingersoll Papers," 372-74. Gale raged, "A more wicked Sceem never was on foot in this Colony to destroy us." He predicted, probably hopefully, that "such proceedings will meet with Rubbers in the *Head* if not the *Tail*."

200. *Conn. Courant*, Feb. 24, 1766, p. 1.

201. *Ibid.*, March 31, 1766, p. 3.

202. Abel Stiles to E. Stiles, April 18, 1766, Stiles Papers.

203. *Conn. Courant*, March 31, 1766, p. 3.

204. Abel Stiles to E. Stiles, April 18, 1766, Stiles Papers.

205. Lee, *Godliness with Contentment,* 23.

206. *Conn. Col. Recs.,* XII, 342, 451, 453-54. Silliman and Hall, who had been Judges of the Superior Court for years, were not re-appointed in May 1766. The new court was now composed of firm Whigs. Jonathan Trumbull was the Chief Judge; the others were Robert Walker, Matthew Griswold, Eliphalet Dyer, and Roger Sherman. *Ibid.,* 4, 123, 244, 343, 454-55.

207. Dyer to W. S. Johnson, Dec. 8, 1765, Johnson Papers.

208. Stiles later explained the election as follows: "The Episco render themselves important thus. Dr. Johnson a Lawyer become a Son of Liby was sent to the Congress. They struck a Bargain with the Sons of Liby was sent to the Congress. They struck a Bargain with the Sons take Johnson into the Council. By this Strategem he got 2000 Votes, which added to 1000 Episco Votes and the Western Votes, bro't him in." Stiles, *Itin.,* 64. Gale also believed that the "*N. Light Faction,* now *Calld Sons of Liberty*" had originally brought about Johnson's election. Gale to W. S. Johnson, June 10, 1767, June 30, 1768, Johnson Papers.

209. Stiles, *Itin.,* 63-64. Stiles made this comment about the election of 1767. It was probably equally true in 1766.

210. Moses Dickinson, *A Sermon Delivered at the Funeral of . . . Thomas Fitch* (New Haven, 1774), 22.

211. Stiles' comments about the 1767 election are again appropriate for the 1766 election. Stiles pointed out that the western part of the colony, which had been "more awed by the Anti american Measures," had backed Fitch and that Silliman, Hall, Chester, and Hamlin "had few or no Votes on East Side except the Chh." *Itin.,* 63-64. The men who were defeated in 1766 were those whom the New Lights had tried to turn out of office in 1759 and 1760. See C. Whittelsey to E. Stiles, Sept. 25, 1759, Stiles Papers; Stiles, *Itin.,* 581-82; S. Johnson to the Archbishop of Canterbury, July 12, 1760, Schneider, *Johnson,* I, 294.

212. Silliman referred to these people as supporting Ingersoll, in which case they undoubtedly voted for Fitch. G. S. Silliman to J. Ingersoll, March 1, 1766, "Ingersoll Papers," 380. J. Davenport wrote from Saybrook to Stiles, May 10, 1766, that Fitch and the four Assistants had been "droped, to my great Sorrow. . . .we had the pleasure in this Parish of being all peaceable and unanimous in these Tumults and voted as usual all [40?] Men for Fitch and the 4 assistants." Stiles Papers.

213. *Conn. Gaz.,* June 14, 1766, p. 1.

214. *Conn. Courant,* May 12, 1766, p. 1.

215. *Conn. Gaz.,* June 7, 1766, p. 2; *Conn. Courant,* June 2, 1766, p. 3.

216. The news reached New Haven from Boston on May 19th. Connecticut Broadsides, III, no. 19, L.C. See also Conway to Fitch, *Fitch Papers,* II, 397-99.

217. *Conn. Col. Recs.,* XII, 467 and *n; Conn. Courant,* May 26, 1766, p. 4.

218. *Conn. Gaz.,* May 24, 1766, p. 2; *New London Gaz.,* May 23, 1766, p. 3.

219. E. Stiles to C. Whittelsey, June [?], 1766, bound in *College Pamphlets,* V, no. 6, between 10-11, Yale University; Stiles to S. Langdon, May 24, 1766 and to F. Alison, Sept. 5, 1766, Stiles Papers. In these letters Stiles reveals himself as an ardent Whig who believed that the successful enforcement of the Stamp Act would have meant the death of "civil and religious Liby."

220. *Conn. Gaz.,* May 24, 1766, p. 2; *New London Gaz.,* May 23, 1766, p. 3.

221. Jonathan Trumbull Jr. to Joseph Trumbull, May 27, 1764, Joseph Trumbull Papers.

222. E. Stiles to S. Langdon, May 24, 1766, Stiles Papers.

223. A Connecticut Tory later described this period as follows: "Yea the Vulgar Sort of People, by being Irritated by Their own leaders, Grew outragious, and acted more like Apes, Than humane Creaters, by Committing Repeated Riots and abusing the Persons of many Sober, prudent and loyal Subjects." Consider Tiffany, The American Colonies and the Revolution, bk. 4, p. 6, typescript, L.C.

224. *New London Gaz.,* Oct. 4, 1765, pp. 1-2; [Ebenezer Devotion], *The Examiner Examined in a Letter from a Gentleman in Connecticut to His Friend in London* (New London, 1766), 14; [Benjamin Throop], *A Thanksgiving Sermon upon the Occasion of the . . . Repeal of the Stamp Act* (New London, 1766), 12; Church, *Liberty and Property,* 10.

225. Benjamin Gale to E. Stiles, Oct. 15, 1767, Stiles Papers.

⇥⟫⟫-⟫⟫-⟫⟫-⟫⟫-⟫⟫-⟫⟫-⟫⟫-⟫⟫-⟫⟫-⟫⟫-⟫⟫-⟫⟫-✕-⟨⟨⟨-⟨⟨⟨-⟨⟨⟨-⟨⟨⟨-⟨⟨⟨-⟨⟨⟨-⟨⟨⟨-⟨⟨⟨-⟨⟨⟨-⟨⟨⟨-⟨⟨⟨-⟨⟨⟨

CHAPTER FOUR

⇥⟫⟫-⟫⟫-⟫⟫-⟫⟫-⟫⟫-⟫⟫-⟫⟫-⟫⟫-⟫⟫-⟫⟫-⟫⟫-⟫⟫-✕-⟨⟨⟨-⟨⟨⟨-⟨⟨⟨-⟨⟨⟨-⟨⟨⟨-⟨⟨⟨-⟨⟨⟨-⟨⟨⟨-⟨⟨⟨-⟨⟨⟨-⟨⟨⟨-⟨⟨⟨

1. *Conn. Courant,* June 23, 1766, p. 2; June 30, p. 3; *Conn. Gaz.,* June 28, p. 2; Gipson, *Ingersoll,* 237-38. At the end of the same year a crowd of Lebanon men were found guilty of rioting and fined at the Windham County Court. *Conn. Col. Recs.,* XIII, 216-17.

2. *New London Gaz.,* Oct. 31, 1766, p. 1; *Conn. Courant,* Nov. 10, 1766, p. 3.

3. *Pitkin Papers,* 18, 20-22. In July 1766 Yale prudently disciplined Joseph Lyman, a member of the junior class, for a speech that he had delivered in the College chapel the previous December. Lyman was charged with having cast some "unjustifiable Reflections on that August Body the British Parliament." Dexter, *Biog. Sketches,* III, 170.

4. *New London Gaz.,* Oct. 3, 1766, p. 4. In reviewing these events about a decade later, Samuel Avery pointed out that the radicalism of the Stamp-Act days had been perpetuated even after the act had been repealed. "But happy would it have been," Avery wrote, "if this [civil enthusiasm] had Stoped . . . when the Offensive act was Repealed. But those Choice Spirits would not be Easy with haveing gained their will, in the Repeal of the Stamp Act, but must keep continually writing and wrangling on the Subject, boasting themselves of what great things they had done in Obtaining the Repeal, as tho: the parliment was Obliged to Repeal the Act." Fragment in the Avery Papers.

5. *Conn. Gaz.,* May 17, 1766, p. 1.

6. Rev. Mr. Newton to the Secretary of the S. P. G., Dec. 10, 1766, Hawks and Perry, *Doc. Hist.,* II, 104; Conn. MSS, Hawks Transcripts, 523.

7. *Pitkin Papers,* 11-14, 45, 47; *Conn. Col. Recs.,* XII, 501. These lands had been in dispute since early in the century. See above, ch. 3, *n*5. Johnson's letters to the governors of the colony during his agency abroad (1766-71) constitute a mine of information on the attitudes of the leading British politicians toward America. These letters, which also include some replies from Govs. Pitkin and Trumbull, are in the Jonathan Trumbull Papers, State Lib., hereafter cited as Trumbull Papers, State Lib. Practically all of them were copied to make up the William Samuel Johnson Papers, Bancroft Transcripts, N. Y. Pub. Lib.

They were also printed in the *Trumbull Papers,* Massachusetts Historical Society, *Collections* (4 vols.), 5th ser., 9 (1885), 211-490, hereafter cited as *Trumbull Papers,* I.

8. See, for example, Richard Jackson to Jonathan Trumbull, Nov. 8, 1766, Trumbull Papers, State Lib., II, 121.

9. Gage to Shelburne, Feb. 20, 1767, in Clarence E. Carter, ed., *The Correspondence of General Thomas Gage with the Secretaries of State 1763-1775* (New Haven, 1931-33), I, 120, 121, hereafter cited as Carter, *Gage Corres.; Conn. Col. Recs.,* XII, 541-42; J. Devotion to E. Stiles, Feb. 6, 1767, Stiles, *Itin.,* 460. Gov. Pitkin took the opportunity to compare Connecticut's behavior in this incident with Boston and New York, and asked Johnson to emphasize "the loyalty" of the colony. Pitkin to Johnson, June 17, 1767, William Samuel Johnson Papers, Bancroft Transcripts.

10. Johnson to Gov. Pitkin, May 16, July 13, 1767, Feb. 13, 1768, William Samuel Johnson Papers, Bancroft Transcripts.

11. Johnson to E. Silliman, Dec. 8, 1767, and to B. Gale, Sept. 29, 1768. Correspondence of Samuel and William Samuel Johnson, Bancroft Transcripts, N. Y. Pub. Lib., hereafter cited as Johnson Corres., Bancroft Transcripts.

12. Pitkin to W. S. Johnson, Nov. 17, 1767, Conn. Papers.

13. Gipson, *Connecticut Taxation 1750-1775.* See also *Pitkin Papers,* 86, 153; W. S. Johnson to Joseph Trumbull, April 15, 1769; Joseph Trumbull to Johnson, Jan. 7, 1769; Jonathan Trumbull to Johnson, July 4, 1768; Johnson to Jonathan Trumbull, Sept. 29, 1768, Johnson Papers.

14. Gipson, *Connecticut Taxation 1750-1775, passim.*

15. Devotion to E. Stiles, April 22, 1767, Stiles, *Itin.,* 462.

16. Governor Pitkin to Richard Jackson, Feb. 14, 1767, *Pitkin Papers,* 75; letter from Jedidiah Huntington, May 16, 1768, Jedidiah Huntington Papers; see also *Conn. Courant,* Dec. 22, 1766, p. 3; Aug. 17, 1767, pp. 1, 4.

17. Samuel to W. S. Johnson, June 8, Oct. 5, 1767, Schneider, *Johnson,* I, 404, 421.

18. *Conn. Col. Recs.,* XIII, 16-18, 24, and *passim;* Joseph Chew complained to William Samuel Johnson, July 6, 1767, that trade was in a "very Languishing" condition. Johnson Papers. See also Jonathan Trumbull's correspondence with Lane and Booth for the years 1766-69, Trumbull Papers, Mercantile; Gipson, *Ingersoll,* 253-54.

19. Jonathan Trumbull to W. S. Johnson, Dec. 8, 1766, June 23, 1767, Johnson Papers; see also draft letters of Trumbull, June 15, 22, 1767, Trumbull Papers, Mercantile.

20. Trumbull to Lane and Booth, June 15, 22, 1767, Trumbull Papers, Mercantile; see also Trumbull's numerous letters to his other British and American creditors for the years 1765-70, *ibid.*

21. The same writer declared that "Our papers are almost entirely fill'd with Advertisements of Insolvencies." *Conn. Courant,* June 22, 1767, p. 4; see also Aug. 17, p. 4.

22. Gipson, *Ingersoll,* 254.

23. Gov. Pitkin to the Board of Trade, Dec. 5, 1766, *Pitkin Papers,* 55-56.

24. Gale to W. S. Johnson, Feb. 20, 1767, Johnson Papers.

25. *Pitkin Papers,* 99-103; Trumbull Papers, Personal, letters dated April 25 and July 1, 1768. In the first letter Trumbull wrote, "Unhappy for us Boston and New York are the importers of British Manufactures for us." In the second he hoped "that in some future Time the Trade of our Colony will become direct to our Mother Country, which is a point of the utmost Importance both to the Colony and the Individuals concerned in its Trade." In the year 1769, 7790 gross tons of shipping entered Connecticut ports from the British and foreign West Indies, while 9971 tons of shipping came in from other American ports, the Bahamas, etc. Only 150 tons of shipping came from Great Britain and Ireland. During the same period 580 tons of shipping were cleared from Connecticut to Great Britain and Ireland, while 9201 tons were cleared for the British and foreign West Indies and 7985 for the American continent, the Bahamas, etc. Martin, *Merchants and Trade in the Conn. River Valley,* 21.

26. Pitkin to H. Conway, Aug. 4, 1766; see also Pitkin to Jackson, Feb. 14, 1767, and to Johnson, Nov. 17, 1767, Trumbull Papers, State Lib., II, pt. 1, 105b, pt. 2, 140a, 158a; *Pitkin Papers,* 19, 74. Pitkin's letter to Conway complained that "The Regulations upon the Importation of Forreign Molasses Sugars etc. are particularly grievous to this Colony, whose Trade consists chiefly of Articles fit only for the West India Market. Those Regulations have in fact been a principle Means of our Poverty and Inability to Discharge our Debts with the American Trader and the British Merchant; have really in a Manner stagnated all Business amongst us."

27. Gipson, *Ingersoll,* 112-13 *n3.*

28. Capt. Durell, Commander of the "Cygnet," bitterly complained to the Commissioners of the Customs, Aug. 14, 1766, that the New London merchants did not pay "ready Obedience and Deference" to the British laws and put obstacles in the way of the Collector. *Pitkin Papers,* 40-42; see also 182, 197. The arrival of a Surveyor at New London caused the town newspaper to report that the creation of the office "had given great dissatisfaction to the merchants here." Several weeks later the paper declared that the Board of Commissioners were "destroying our commerce." *New London Gaz.,* Sept. 8, 1769, p. 4; Sept. 15, p. 2; Sept. 22, p. 1. Even the politically conservative merchant Joseph Chew hoped that some day he would be "Fix'd upon a Farm out of the way of Custom House Officers Courts of Admiralty etc." Chew to W. S. Johnson, Dec. 9, 1769, Johnson Papers; see also Chew to Sir William Johnson, July 13, 1768, Boyd, *Susquehannah Papers,* III, 22; Caulkins, *New London,* 483.

29. Shaw to P. Vandervoort, Feb. 13, 1767; see also Shaw to J. Stoddard, May 15, 1769, Shaw, *Letter Book,* 190, 205. In his letter to Vandervoort Shaw strongly cautioned the New York merchant to "take Care to have them landed in the most Secret Manner for we have not clear'd them att the Custom House."

30. D. Stewart to T. Bradshaw, June 7, 1769, *Pitkin Papers,* 182. For the small yields of the customs duties at New Haven and New London, see *ibid.,* 97-98, 147, 158.

31. On the writs of assistance see *Pitkin Papers,* 40, 184-86; Roger Sherman and E. Silliman to W. S. Johnson, June 25, Nov. 10, 1768, Johnson Papers; Jonathan Trumbull to W. S. Johnson, July 14, 1769, Jonathan Trumbull Papers, Political and Official Correspondence, Conn. Hist. Soc., hereafter cited as Trumbull Papers, Political. J. Chew to Sir William Johnson, May 29, 1769, Boyd, *Susquehannah Papers,* III, 130.

32. D. Stewart to T. Bradshaw, June 7, 1769, *Pitkin Papers,* 182, 186; see also 197, 201-3; *Conn. Gaz.,* July 25, 1767, p. 4; *Conn. Courant,* July 31, 1769, p. 3; J. Chew to W. S. Johnson, July 6, 1767, Johnson Papers. See the Trumbull Papers, State Lib., II, pt. 2, 219a-d, 221ab, 223ab, for an example of violence in Rhode Island against the anti-smuggling laws. Nathaniel Shaw Jr. of New London was the owner of the ships involved in this incident in which the King's sloop "Liberty" was burned. When the "Liberty," which Shaw called "Our Cruseing Pyrate," left New London for Newport, Shaw had heaved a sigh of

relief and had prayed she would never return. Shaw to J. Stoddard and
P. Vandervoort, May 15, 1769, Shaw, *Letter Book,* 205-6.

33. See the documents in the *Pitkin Papers,* 194-96.

34. *Conn. Courant,* Sept. 25, 1769, p. 1; see also p. 3; *Conn. Jour.,*
Sept. 22, 1769, p. 3; Jonathan Trumbull to W. S. Johnson, March 3, 1770,
Trumbull Papers, I, 420.

35. John Devotion described the new duties as a "Snare." Devotion to E. Stiles, Feb. 8, 1768, Stiles, *Itin.,* 471.

36. Gale to E. Stiles, Oct. 15, 1767, *ibid.,* 493.

37. Trumbull to Phineas Lyman, July [?], 1768, Trumbull Papers,
Personal.

38. Jared Ingersoll heard no "grumbling . . . as yet" in July 1767,
which was shortly after the colony had been informed by William
Samuel Johnson of the new taxes. Ingersoll to Johnson, July 23, 1767,
Johnson Papers. Dickinson's *Letters* awakened the Rev. John Devotion to the danger of the taxes. Devotion to Stiles, Feb. 8, 1768, Stiles,
Itin., 471. Eastern Connecticut was especially appreciative of Dickinson's work in this regard. *Conn. Courant,* May 9, 1768, p. 1. Connecticut received the circular letter of the Massachusetts House of
Representatives against the Townshend duties in February 1768, but
did not answer it until June. *Pitkin Papers,* 108-12; *Conn. Jour.,* July
8, 1768, p. 3.

39. Johnson had advised Connecticut's magistrates to be cautious.
Johnson to Trumbull and to Pitkin, March 14, May 16, 1767, *Trumbull
Papers,* I, 234, 488. In May both houses of the legislature set up committees to consider possible measures. Conn. Arch., Rev. Ser., I, 43.

40. *Conn. Col. Recs.,* XIII, 87-88; see also Gov. Pitkin's letter to the
Earl of Hillsborough, *ibid.,* 84-86. A manuscript copy of Pitkin's letter
is in the Trumbull Papers, State Lib., II, pt. 2, 179a-d. The petition was
addressed to the King and not to Parliament in order to avoid the
assumption that the latter had the legal right to tax the colonies. E.
Silliman to W. S. Johnson, Nov. 10, 1768, Johnson Papers. It was
inevitable that the petition would be rejected for tending "to deny and
draw into question the supreme Authority of the Legislature of Great
Britain." Hillsborough to Pitkin, Nov. 15, 1768, *Pitkin Papers,* 153-54.

41. Hart to E. Stiles, March 14, 1769, Stiles Papers; Stiles, *Itin.,*
498. At an earlier time, Hart, referring to the double danger of the
Anglican and anti-American interests to the colony, wrote to Stiles,
"We ought ever to be loyal, but not too meek and passive. . . . The

spirit of manly and vigorous resentment of wrongs is the guardian of the peace and liberties and rights of the world." March [4?], 1767, Stiles Papers.

42. *Conn. Col. Recs.*, XIII, 86, 89.

43. Letter dated June 10, 1768, William S. Johnson Papers, Bancroft Transcripts.

44. Letter dated June 6, 1768, *ibid.*

45. Sherman to Johnson, June 25, 1768; Trumbull to Johnson, June 23, 1767, July 4, 1768; Williams to Johnson, July 5, 1768, Johnson Papers. See also Jonathan Trumbull to Phineas Lyman, July [?], 1768, Trumbull Papers, Personal. Trumbull's statesmanlike views, expressed in the 1767 letter to Johnson, deserve to be quoted more fully. He wrote: "Great Britain and her Colonies Interests are Mutual and Inseparable; so long as the Colonies want protection, and supplies of necessary Manufactures from the Mother Country, it can't be their Interest to Separate, and it is always the Interest of the Mother Country to keep them dependent and employed, in such Productions, in such Industry, in raising such Commodities, or in performing such services as will return most Benefit to its Native Country. But if Violence or methods tending to Violence be taken to maintain this Dependence, it tends to hasten a Separation. If mutual Jealousies are Sown, it will require all their Address to keep the Colonies dependant and employed so as not at least to prejudice the Mother Country, and it is certainly more easily and effectually done by gentle and Insensible methods, than by power or force."

46. Williams to Johnson, July 5, 1768, Johnson Papers.

47. J. Devotion to E. Stiles, Feb. 8, 1768, Stiles, *Itin.*, 471; *Conn. Jour.*, Dec. 11, 1767, p. 3; Dec. 25, p. 1; Feb. 15, 1768, p. 3.

48. For examples of the newspaper campaign see *Conn. Jour.*, Dec. 18, 1767, p. 3; Jan. 6, 1769, pp. 3-4; Jan. 20, p. 2; articles of "Philo Patriae," April 1768, and articles late in 1768 and in early 1769, *New London Gaz.*

49. Reports of town meetings are in *Conn. Jour.*, Dec. 25, 1767, p. 3; *New London Gaz.*, Dec. 25, 1767, p. 1; Jan. 1, 1768, p. 3; Supplement, Jan. 22; March 18, p. 1; April 1, p. 4; April 29, p. 2; *Conn. Courant,* May 9, 1768, p. 1.

50. *Conn. Col. Recs.*, XIII, 72-74.

51. *Pitkin Papers,* 189-90, 193-94; *Conn. Jour.*, July 28, 1769, p. 1; Arthur M. Schlesinger, *The Colonial Merchants and the American*

Revolution 1763-1776 (New York, 1918), 150-51; *Conn. Col. Recs.,* XIII, 236*n; Conn. Courant,* Nov. 6, 1769, p. 3.

52. *Conn. Courant,* Jan. 15, 1770, p. 2; Jan. 29, pp. 2-3; Feb. 5, pp. 2-3; Feb. 26, p. 3; *Conn. Jour.,* Supplement, March 2; March 9, p. 2; J. Chew to W. S. Johnson, Feb. 24, 1770, Johnson Papers; William Williams to S. Gray, Jan. 29, 1770, Williams Papers.

53. J. Chew to W. S. Johnson, Feb. 24, 1770, Johnson Papers. On the position of some farmers, however, see Gipson, *Ingersoll,* 281, and the arguments of "X," *Conn. Jour.,* Feb. 2, 1770, p. 4.

54. G. Chapman to W. S. Johnson, July 20, 1769; Williams to Johnson, July 24, 1769, Johnson Papers; Dexter, *Biog. Sketches,* III, 303.

55. Pitkin to Johnson, June 1, 1769, Johnson Papers; Trumbull to Johnson, March 3, 1770, William S. Johnson Papers, Bancroft Transcripts. For statistics on the sharp decline of commerce in the years 1768 and 1769 see Virginia D. Harrington, *The New York Merchant on the Eve of the Revolution* (New York, 1935), 358-60.

56. The Anglican rector, the Rev. E. Kneeland, wrote unsympathetically to William S. Johnson, Feb. 23, 1770: "The people are mightily reformed; they use but few British goods and the reason is they have neither money or credit to procure them." Johnson Corres., Bancroft Transcripts.

57. See, for example, *Conn. Courant,* Nov. 13, 1769, p. 3; Jan. 1, 1770, p. 3; June 18, p. 3; *New London Gaz.,* Feb. 9, 1770, p. 1; April 20, p. 4; June 15, p. 4; July 6, p. 1. See also the records of Windham's town meetings, Jan. 12, June 27, Sept. 13, Oct. 24, 1768, Conn. Misc. Papers 1637-1783, Force Transcripts.

58. Chapman to William S. Johnson, July 20, 1769, Johnson Papers.

59. Williams to W. S. Johnson, July 24, 1769, *ibid.* See also Williams to N. Wales and S. Gray, Jan. 29, 1770, Williams Papers.

60. *Conn. Courant,* June 18, 1770, p. 3; *New London Gaz.,* June 15, 1770, p. 4; July 6, p. 1.

61. Williams to N. Wales and S. Gray, Jan. 29, 1770, Williams Papers.

62. *Conn. Jour.,* July 27, 1770, p. 1; Aug. 17, p. 1; *Conn. Courant,* July 23, pp. 1-2; July 30, pp. 1-2; Aug. 6, p. 3; Aug. 27, p. 3; Sept. 3, p. 3; *New London Gaz.,* Aug. 10, p. 3; Aug. 24, p. 3; Sept. 7, pp. 1-2; Sept. 28, p. 3. See also MSS Hartford Town Votes, II, 233, Town Clerk's Office, Hartford; New Haven merchants to Wethersfield and Hartford merchants, July 26, 1770, Emmet Collection no. 357, N. Y. Pub. Lib.;

Stiles, *Diary,* I, 69. There was a similarly hostile reaction in June towards the Rhode Island merchants: *Conn. Courant,* June 11, 1770, p. 4; *Conn. Jour.,* June 15, p. 4.

63. *Conn. Jour.,* Aug. 3, 1770, p. 1; Aug. 10, p. 1; Aug. 31, p. 4; *New London Gaz.,* Oct. 26, 1770, p. 1; Nov. 2, pp. 1-2.

64. Law and Dyer to W. S. Johnson, Dec. 15, 18, 1770, Johnson Papers.

65. Chapman to Johnson, Dec. 11, 1770, *ibid.* Chapman went on to say, "When you come whome and are at Leisure, we shall have many a laughter at this and many other things." See also *New London Gaz.,* Dec. 28, 1770, p. 3; *Conn. Courant,* Jan. 15, 1771, p. 2.

66. *Conn. Courant,* Jan. 25, 1771, p. 2. Between Jan. 1768-Jan. 1769 only 70 tons of shipping were cleared from New York to Connecticut ports while 618 tons were cleared from Boston. The totals for the next year jumped to 4471 and 3181 tons respectively. There was a similar increase in the tonnage of ships leaving Connecticut ports for New York and Boston. Harrington, *New York Merchant,* 359-62.

67. *Conn. Jour.,* Oct. 5, 1770, p. 3. Another law, however, encouraging the whale and cod fisheries was passed in October 1770. See *Conn. Col. Recs.,* XIII, 365. For the story of the 5 per cent duty see *Trumbull Papers,* I, 387, 392-93, 419-20; *Conn. Col. Recs.,* XIII, 72-74, 299.

68. Jonathan Trumbull to W. S. Johnson, Jan. 29, 1770, draft copy in the Trumbull Papers, State Lib., XX, pt. 1, 6b; also in the Johnson Papers, and printed in the *Trumbull Papers,* I, 400-1, 403. This letter also described Trumbull's views on Britain's commercial policies. Instead of restricting the colonial economy, Trumbull argued, the mother country should "encourage our raising such growth, and making such Manufactures as will not prejudice their own in any degree equal to the advantage they bring—when any such commodities are raised or made, they ought to be taken off our hands, or the best markets pointed out to us, and the people ought not to be forced to find out other markets by Stealth; nor the Trade loaded with Duties, and encumbered with officers to suck our Vital blood." Later in the year Trumbull again protested to Johnson that "a Civil List to be established here, our property given and granted, Duties for raising a revenue imposed, without a single Voyce from us, a Board of Commissioners, new formed Courts of Admiralty, pensioners etc—are new and extreamly disagreeable to people not Used and unwilling to See such Modes of proceeding." Trumbull Papers, State Lib., XX, pt. 1, 15a.

69. Gale to Stiles, Oct. 15, 1767; Hart to Stiles, Aug. 12, 1768, in Stiles, *Itin.,* 493-94, 496.

70. E. Stiles to John Hubbard, March 9, 1770, Stiles Papers.

71. Trumbull to Phineas Lyman, July 28, 1769, Trumbull Papers, Political. Half a year later Trumbull informed W. S. Johnson that "The people of all the Colonies except officers and their dependants are firmly United, to maintain and support their rights and priviledges." Letter dated Jan. 29, 1770, Trumbull Papers, State Lib., XX, pt. 1, 6b. The governor had emphasized the same points in earlier letters to Johnson and Richard Jackson. See the draft copies to Johnson dated Jan. 24, July 14, 1769, Trumbull Papers, Political; and to Jackson, July 17, 1769, Trumbull Papers, Personal. Johnson also recognized that British policy was antagonizing not only the lower classes in the colonies, but the "calm sedate sober People." Johnson to Robert Temple, May 13, 1769, Johnson Papers.

72. The committees set up by the towns during the non-importation movement were dominated by radicals, many of whom were merchants. This was especially true in the eastern towns. The membership of some of these committees are noted in the following sources: *Conn. Jour.,* Dec. 25, 1767, p. 3; July 27, 1770, p. 1; New Haven merchants to Wethersfield and Hartford merchants, July 26, 1770, Emmet Collection no. 357. On the other hand it is interesting to note the similarity in the hostile reactions of the politically radical merchant, Nathaniel Shaw Jr., and the conservative merchant, Joseph Chew, to the British commercial program. Compare Shaw's letters for these years in Shaw, *Letter Book,* and the letters of Chew to W. S. Johnson in the Johnson Papers.

73. For complaints about Connecticut's slowness in opposing the Townshend acts see the *Conn. Jour.,* Dec. 25, 1767, p. 1; Feb. 5, 1768, p. 3.

74. "A Farmer," *ibid.,* Feb. 22, 1771, pp. 2-3.

75. Rev. E. Kneeland to W. S. Johnson, Feb. 23, 1770, Johnson Corres., Bancroft Transcripts. The arrival of troops in Boston late in 1768 helped, at least temporarily, to quiet the radicals in the Connecticut Assembly. This led Ebenezer Silliman to comment happily that after the troops came "no Liberty schemes as they were called were so much as proposed." Some conservative wit called the soldiers "Peace Makers." Silliman to Thomas Hutchinson, Dec. 8, 1768, Hutchinson Corres., I, Bancroft Transcripts. Joseph Trumbull condemned

the "Wild Vegearies" of the people of Lebanon and thought the town had been "Stupid" to have acted the way it did when the British troops entered Boston. On the other hand he applauded Boston's "prudent Conduct." Trumbull to W. S. Johnson, Jan. 7, 1769, Johnson Papers.

76. B. Gale to W. S. Johnson, June 30, 1768, Johnson Papers. Johnson immediately told Gale that "The Doctrine which you say has been advanced there . . . would sound very harsh here and will be Considered as a Treasonable Position." Letter dated Sept. 29, 1768, *ibid.*

77. Silliman to Johnson, Nov. 10, 1768, *ibid.*

78. Williams to W. S. Johnson, Jan. 24, 1769, *ibid.* In an earlier letter to Johnson, July 5, 1768, Williams had called England America's "Step mother country."

79. Chew to Johnson, July 14, 1768, Jan. 14, 1769, Feb. 24, 1770, *ibid.* Samuel Avery of Norwich also was critical of the "Imprudent conduct of the Colonies." He thought they were too quick to complain "scold [?] Resolve Agree Combine etc etc etc." He excused Parliament's slowness in repealing the obnoxious duties as the result of the colonies' "Imprudence," which made the British feel that their prestige would again be injured as it had been during the Stamp Act controversy. As Avery put it, "All this the Colony lay to A Corrupt Ministry when in fact it is owing in a great measure to their own Lunacy." "Anti Alarm," Avery Papers.

80. Devotion to E. Stiles, Feb. 8, 1768, Stiles, *Itin.,* 471. Devotion, however, favored "acting vigorously." He was sorry to see "Boston and other Places vapour so much about their *posse.* Should be more pleased if they and all others would be content with *Agendo* and Reflection upon it—privately, or without Noise increase our own Manufactures."

81. Hubbard to E. Stiles, March 28, 1768, Stiles Papers. This principle might have been the consideration that prompted the "few wise heads" in the Assembly to dissuade the "infatuated" radicals from attempting to place a 5 per cent duty on all English imports in 1770. According to George Chapman, the more conservative deputies had thus prevented the radicals from showing their folly. Chapman to W. S. Johnson, Dec. 11, 1770, Johnson Papers.

82. Gale to W. S. Johnson, June 30, 1768; Jan. 30, 1769, Johnson Papers. See also Gale's letter to Johnson, June 10, 1768.

83. *Christ, the Foundation of the Salvation of Sinners, and of Civil and Ecclesiastical Government* (Hartford, 1767). For political ideas in the sermon, see pp. 15, 16, 24.

84. Richard Salter, n.t., Election Sermon, May 12, 1768 (New London, 1768); Eliphalet Williams, n.t., Election Sermon, May 11, 1769 (Hartford, 1769); Stephen Johnson, *Integrity and Piety the best Principles of a good Administration of Government,* Election Sermon (New London, 1770); Champion, *A Brief View.*

85. Williams, Election Sermon, 20; see also Johnson, *Integrity and Piety,* 5-6. During the Revolution Gov. Trumbull, depressed by numerous evidences of the subordination of patriotism to selfish interests, wrote to Samuel Huntington: "Our political systems have been too long form'd upon the hypothesis, 'that the people are virtuous,' whereas all exertions of government ought to be founded on this axiom, 'that mankind are vicious,' and influenc'd only by this one first principle of their nature, love of their own good. The art of government, therefore, is to render individual and public good inseparable, and to *lead* men thro' their own interest to advance the interest of their own country." Dec. 13, 1779, *Trumbull Papers,* Mass. Hist. Soc., *Colls.,* 7th ser., 2 (1902), 460, hereafter cited as *Trumbull Papers,* III.

86. Williams, Election Sermon, 30; see also Eells, *Christ, the Foundation of the Salvation of Sinners,* 15, 16; Eliphalet Huntington, *The Freeman's Directory; or, Well Accomplished, and Faithful Rulers Discribed* (Hartford, 1768), 21-22.

87. Salter, Election Sermon, 8-9; Williams, Election Sermon, 26-29, 30; Johnson, *Integrity and Piety,* 9, 13-14, 19, 29; see also Champion, *A Brief View,* 29.

88. Rev. Mr. Dibblee to the Secretary of the S. P. G., Oct. 28, 1765, Conn. MSS, Hawks Transcripts, 500.

89. Rev. Mr. Beach to the Secretary of the S. P. G., April 14, 1768, *ibid.,* 554.

90. Rev. Mr. Peters to the Secretary of the S. P. G., June 25, 1768, Dec. 26, 1770, *ibid.,* 559-60, 609. Peters made it very clear that he would never "trim between Charles and Oliver." He feared, however, that if his political views were to become known to the people "the fanatic Mob will judge my Life too cheap a Victim to pacify their belching Stomachs."

91. Malbone to J. Robinson, April 8, 1770, Hawks and Perry, *Doc. Hist.,* II, 155-56.

92. Johnson's political philosophy is excellently summarized in Evarts B. Greene's "William Samuel Johnson and the American Revolution," *Columbia University Quarterly,* 22 (1930), 157-78.

93. Groce, *Johnson*, 75.

94. Johnson to Williams, Sept. 27, 1768, Johnson Papers. See also Johnson's letters to Pitkin and Trumbull in *Trumbull Papers*, I, *passim*. When his agency was over Johnson claimed that "I might have obtained very good things by deserting the Interests" of America or "by abusing and misrepresenting it, or by licking the dust of the feet of Ministers. . . . I have been an enthusiast in American affairs." Johnson to E. Dyer, March 30, 1771, Johnson Papers.

95. N. Rogers to Johnson, Feb. 20, 1769, Johnson Papers.

96. Samuel Johnson to the Archbishop of Canterbury, Sept. 25, 1767, Johnson Corres., Bancroft Transcripts.

97. W. S. Johnson to N. Rogers, Nov. 15, 1769, Johnson Papers.

98. Johnson to Pitkin, March 19, July 13, 1767; to Jonathan Trumbull, Oct. 16, 1769, *Trumbull Papers*, I, 220, 239-40, 374-75. See also Johnson to R. Sherman, Sept. 28, 1768; to B. Gale, Sept. 29, 1768, Johnson Papers.

99. Johnson to R. Sherman, Sept. 28, 1768; to B. Gale, Sept. 29, 1768; to N. Rogers, Jan. 4, 1769, Johnson Papers. Compare Jonathan Trumbull to Johnson, Jan. 24, 1769, Trumbull Papers, Political.

100. See Johnson to Jared Ingersoll, Jan. 2, 1768, and March 8, 1769, "Ingersoll Papers," 420, 424-25. In the latter Johnson wrote pessimistically: "I fear yet farther provocations on both sides, severities on this and reluctance and Opposition on that. Perhaps we must both *feel* more effectually the folly of Quarreling before we shall have the Wisdom to be reconciled, tho' the longer it is delay'd the more the wound festers and rankles, and the Cure becomes every day more doubtful and difficult. However, I will still hope and pray God that some proper Remedy may be found before it becomes totally incurable."

101. See, for example, Johnson's letters to Pitkin and Trumbull, *Trumbull Papers*, I, 234, 294, 318, 488.

102. Letters to Pitkin and Joseph Trumbull, *ibid.*, 310, 319, 321, 333, 348-49. See also Johnson to George Chapman, to Benjamin Gale, July 29, 1767, Sept. 29, 1768, Johnson Papers.

103. For Johnson's thoughts on these matters see his letters to Col. Walker, March 31, 1767; to T. Burr, July 28, 1768; to B. Gale and Jonathan Trumbull, Sept. 29, 1768; to R. Temple, Feb. 4, 1769; to E. Dyer, Jan. 22, 1768, Johnson Papers. On Putnam see Joseph Chew to Sir William Johnson, July 13, 1768, in Boyd, *Susquehannah Papers,*

III, 22; on Parsons see Samuel H. Parsons to Samuel Adams, Nov. 30, 1768, Samuel Adams Papers, N. Y. Pub. Lib.; on Dyer see Dyer to W. S. Johnson, March 10, 1769, Johnson Papers.

104. Johnson to E. Silliman, Dec. 8, 1767; to B. Gale, Sept. 29, 1768, Johnson Papers. An undated letter, probably written by Joseph Trumbull to his father, states that it was Johnson's opinion that "the least handle would be gladly Seised to deprive us of our Charter, for which Reason, we ought to be a little Cautious, how we appear first and foremost in any Scheme of Opposition." Trumbull Papers, Personal. See also Johnson to Gov. Trumbull, Nov. 15, 1770, *Trumbull Papers,* I, 467.

105. Jonathan Trumbull to Johnson, Nov. 19, 1770, Trumbull Papers, State Lib., XX, 15ab.

106. Johnson to R. Temple, Feb. 4, 1769; to N. Rogers, April 22, 1769, Johnson Papers.

107. Johnson to R. Temple, May 13, 1769, *ibid*. In a letter to Benjamin Gale, April 10, 1769, Johnson fully explained his views on American independence. He thought it "pretty probable that we shall go on contending and fretting each other till . . . we become separate and Independent Empires. That . . . event is hastening with rapid progress. . . . Whether we shou'd wish it or end[eavo]r to prevent it depends upon the course we should take after such a separation should take place. If we were wise and could form some System of free Govern't upon just Principles we might be very happy without any Connection with this Country. But should we ever agree upon any thing of this Nature, should we not more probably fall into Factions and Parties amongst ourselves, destroy one another and become at length the easy prey Probably of the first Invaders." Johnson therefore concluded that it would be more desirable to remain a part of the British empire. "It is our true Interest to settle the Controversy as soon as possible upon reasonable Principles. This obviously shou'd be the object of our deliberations and endeavors at present at least, since plainly it is not yet time to think of an immediate separation. What shall be done hereafter when we can no longer keep together belongs to our Posterity and will be better judged of when the Event must take place than at this distance." Johnson Papers.

108. Johnson to N. Rogers, Jan. 4, April 22, 1769, *ibid*.

109. Trumbull to W. S. Johnson, July 4, 1768, *ibid*. In August 1768 a rumor in Boston had it that the Connecticut "Grumbletonians" were

called Tories supposedly "from their paucity and insignificancy." *New London Gaz.,* Aug. 19, 1768, p. 2. For later uses of these epithets see the issue of March 9, 1770, p. 1; *Conn. Courant,* March 19, 1770, p. 3; Sept. 10, p. 2.

-->>>->>>->>>->>>->>>->>>->>>->>>->>>->>>->>>->>>->>>->>>-><-(((-(((-(((-(((-(((-(((-(((-(((-(((-(((-(((-(((-(((-(((-

CHAPTER FIVE

-->>>->>>->>>->>>->>>->>>->>>->>>->>>->>>->>>->>>->>>->><-(((-(((-(((-(((-(((-(((-(((-(((-(((-(((-(((-(((-(((-(((-

1. *Conn. Courant,* June 26, 1769, p. 3. See also Gen. Assoc., *Recs.,* 66. Dr. Cross has emphasized the error of the colonial assumption that British policy had ecclesiastical as well as political objectives. At the same time he has also recognized that the colonists' fears in this regard, while "a pure figment of the imagination," were instrumental in turning them against the mother country. Arthur L. Cross, *The Anglican Episcopate and The American Colonies* (Cambridge, 1924), ch. 8.

2. Stiles, *Itin.,* 269. Stiles put the total number of families in the colony at 30,000. See also in this connection the exaggerated claims later made by Samuel Peters about the growth of the Anglican church during these years. Samuel Peters Papers, I, 96, N. Y. Hist. Soc., hereafter cited as Peters Papers.

3. Rev. Mr. Beach to the Secretary of the S. P. G., April 13, 1767, Conn. MSS, Hawks Transcripts, 530. Beach also claimed that this was "the first instance of this kind in this colony, if not in all N. England." See also Hawks and Perry, *Doc. Hist.,* II, 125. Samuel Whittelsey had written to Stiles, May 30, 1764, informing him that it was in western Connecticut that "the Church of England is now making her strongest Efforts." Stiles Papers.

4. J. Devotion to E. Stiles, April 25, 1768, Stiles, *Itin.,* 474; see also 471-72.

5. Rev. Mr. Viets to the Secretary of the S. P. G., Nov. 22, 1766, Conn. MSS, Hawks Transcripts, 522; Viets to S. P. G., June 26, 1768, Hawks and Perry, *Doc. Hist.,* II, 124.

6. Letter dated Nov. 10, 1766, Schneider, *Johnson,* I, 378. See also Conn. MSS, Hawks Transcripts, 507, 523, 554.

7. Letter dated March 25, 1767, Hawks and Perry, *Doc. Hist.,* II, 107-8. In 1769 Peters and the Rev. Mr. Graves were accused of violating

the governor's proclamation for a fast and favoring an American episcopate. Peters' reply was not couched in soft language. *Conn. Courant,* May 15, 1769, p. 2; May 29, p. 2.

8. Kneeland to W. S. Johnson, Feb. 23, 1770, Johnson Corres., Bancroft Transcripts.

9. Stiles to Dr. Chauncy, Oct. 24, 1766, Stiles Papers; see also Stiles to Dr. Alison, Sept. 5, 1766, *ibid.*

10. Stiles to [?], Nov. 17, 1766; see also N. Welles to Stiles, Nov. 21, 1766; W. Hart to Stiles, March [4?], 1767. Stiles had faith, however, that "excepting incidental Collisions and temporary Conflicts, LIBERTY and CONGREGATIONALISM will be co-triumphant Sisters in America." Stiles to Dr. Chauncy, March 3, 1768, Stiles Papers.

11. Stiles, *Diary,* I, 16, entry for July 8, 1769. See also the letters written by C. Whittelsey and W. Hart to Stiles in the Stiles Papers.

12. Stiles to N. Welles, Nov. 22, 1766, Stiles Papers.

13. Rev. Mr. Beach to the S. P. G., April 14, 1768, Conn. MSS, Hawks Transcripts, 554; see also letters from Andrews, June 25, 1766; Scovil, July 8; Johnson, July 15; the Connecticut and New York clergy, Oct. 8; Beach, April 13, 1767; Dibblee, Oct. 1, Hawks and Perry, *Doc. Hist.,* II, 90, 92, 94, 100-2, 108-9, 111.

14. To the Secretary of the S. P. G., May 10, 1768, Conn. MSS, Hawks Transcripts, 556. The Rev. Mr. Graves complained, Nov. 20, 1767: "Alas! that . . . his Majesty's religion [is] daily subject to Independent and Congregational iniquity and depredation." Hawks and Perry, *Doc. Hist.,* II, 119.

15. June 10, 1768, *Trumbull Papers,* I, 288.

16. Sherman's letter is in Boutell, *Sherman,* 64-68; Trumbull to R. Jackson, Dec. 15, 1769, Trumbull Papers, State Lib., XX, 3. See also Trumbull to W. S. Johnson, Dec. 12, 1769, *Trumbull Papers,* I, 390.

17. To the Secretary of the S. P. G., May 14, 1768, Conn. MSS, Hawks Transcripts, 554-55.

18. To W. S. Johnson, April 22, 1768, Schneider, *Johnson,* I, 439. On the pamphlet debate over episcopal and presbyterian ordination see, for example, *ibid.,* 500; Noah Welles, *A Vindication of the Validity and Divine Right of Presbyterian Ordination* (New Haven, 1767). Connecticut's General Association gave its thanks to Dr. Chauncy "for the good service he has done to the cause of religion, liberty, and truth in his judicious answer to the appeal for an american episcopate, and

in his defence of the New-england churches and colonies." Gen. Assoc., *Recs.*, 63.

19. To the Secretary of the S. P. G., Oct. 1, 1767, Conn. MSS, Hawks Transcripts, 540.

20. *Pitkin Papers,* 207-11.

21. Stiles, *Itin.,* 269.

22. See above, ch. 2, *n*5. What the Separatists had to contend with may be seen in the advice given by the Rev. Noah Welles to the General Assembly in 1764. The minister reminded the deputies that while "sober dissenters" might be tolerated "we justly expect the continuance of your more peculiar and distinguishing regard to the constituted churches of this colony, as established by law." Welles, *Patriotism Described,* 26.

23. Stiles, *Itin.,* 286-90, 295-98, 511, 591; *Conn. Col. Recs.,* XIII, 108, 259, 269-70, 341, 345, 393, 406, 492. See also the correspondence of John Whiting, John Devotion, and Chauncey Whittelsey with Ezra Stiles for these years in the Stiles Papers.

24. Devotion to Stiles, April 25, 1768, Stiles, *Itin.,* 474.

25. Dibblee to the Secretary of the S. P. G., Oct. 8, 1770, Hawks and Perry, *Doc. Hist.,* II, 159.

26. *Conn. Courant,* March 30, 1767, p. 1. A petition from Separatists in eight towns declared in 1767: "The Cry had gone through this North America like lightning, (as it ware) Liberty and Property, the Attention Labour and Measures that this Colony and North America has ben at and taken to Secure their Natural and Civil Rights, Argues Strongly in our favour." Conn. Arch., Eccles. Affairs, XV, 225e; see also 232e.

27. "Jack New Li[ght]," *Conn. Courant,* Dec. 5, 1768, p. 1.

28. *Conn. Jour.,* Jan. 27, 1769, pp. 1-2; for other arguments presented in favor of the established church see *New London Gaz.,* Oct. 7, 1768, pp. 1-2; Dec. 23, p. 4; *Conn. Jour.,* Feb. 17, 1769, pp. 1-3; March 17, pp. 1-2; *Conn. Courant,* Sept. 12, 1768, p. 3; April 17, 1769, pp. 1-2. See also Williams, Election Sermon, 38-40, for criticism of the "protestant dissenters." On the other hand Stratford's pastor, the Rev. Izrahiah Wetmore, boldly declared himself for the separation of church and state in 1773. See his Election Sermon, n.t., May 13, 1773 (New London, 1773), 29, and the special appendix, 31-39.

29. For arguments supporting the Separatists see *New London Gaz.,* Aug. 26, 1768, pp. 1-2; Sept. 2, p. 4; Nov. 11, pp. 1-2; *Conn. Jour.,*

Jan. 20, 1769, pp. 2-3; Feb. 3, pp. 2-3; March 3, p. 1; March 31, pp. 1-2.

30. *Conn. Col. Recs.,* XIII, 360. See also William Williams, Journal at New Haven, entries under dates Oct. 22, Nov. 1, 1770, Conn. Hist. Soc.

31. *Connecticut Acts and Laws, May 1777* (New London, 1777), 464-65.

32. For the democratic trends in Separatist thought see the *Conn. Courant,* March 7, 1768, p. 4; Dec. 5, p. 1; and Conn. Arch., Eccles. Affairs, X, 290ab; XV, 225e, 232e.

33. Theophilus Chamberlain in the *Conn. Jour.,* Feb. 10, 1769, p. 1; also comment by "Eleutheros," Feb. 17, p. 3.

34. A. McEwen, "Congregationalists in Their Relation to Other Religious Sects Characterized by Error, Fanaticism, or Disorder," in *Contribs. . . . Eccles. Hist.,* 284-85. The Anglican rector, the Rev. Mr. Beach labelled Sandemanism "new fashioned Antinomianism." Beach to the Secretary of the S. P. G., Oct. 6, 1766, Hawks and Perry, *Doc. Hist.,* II, 99-100. See also Williston Walker, "The Sandemanians of New England," in American Historical Association, *Annual Report for 1901,* 1 (1902), 136-49. Seth Pomeroy Jr. described the characteristics of this sect in an interesting letter to Ezra Stiles, Jan. 27, 1766. "You may have heard of the new religious Sect lately sprung up in Danbury, properly called *Glassites,* tho by some styled *Kissites,* from their *holy kissing.* . . . Their peculiars seem to be kissing, frequent singing, celebrating the Lords Supper every Sabbath . . . they are frequent and liberal in contributions, and talk of a *Community of estates.* . . . They go near to deny the *Humanity* of our Savior or are very backward in speaking of it." Stiles, *Itin.,* 551.

35. "Historical Sketch of Fairfield East Association," in *Contribs. . . . Eccles. Hist.,* 298-99. The two ministers were Ebenezer White and James Taylor. The disciplining of White was considered by some as too severe and gave "Occasion . . . to call in Question the Authority of Councils; yea they dare to assert that all Ecclesiastical Councils are but advisory." S. Whittelsey to E. Stiles, May 30, 1764, Stiles Papers; see also J. Devotion to Stiles, Nov. 1, 1766, *ibid.*

36. Rev. Mr. Beach to the S. P. G., Oct. 6, 1766, Hawks and Perry, *Doc. Hist.,* II, 99-100. John Devotion informed Stiles, April 25, 1768, that "Sandemanism relishes better in the West than in the East of this Colony." Stiles, *Itin.,* 475.

37. *Conn. Col. Recs.,* XII, 367.

38. McEwen, "Congregationalists," 285.

39. See above, ch. 2, 33.

40. See above, ch. 3, 52 and *n*56. Compare, however, Boyd's discussion in the *Susquehannah Papers,* II, xlii.

41. See above, ch. 2, 34-35.

42. Boyd, *Susquehannah Papers,* III, 43. The Delaware companies followed the example of the more prominent company in meetings held Jan. 3, 1769, *ibid.,* 50, 52. See also Joseph Trumbull to W. S. Johnson, Jan. 7, 1769, Johnson Papers.

43. Connecticut Archives, Susquehanna Settlers, I, 11a-d, 17a-d, 18, 19ab, State Lib., hereafter cited as Conn. Arch., Susq. See also in Boyd, *Susquehannah Papers,* III, 53-56, 60-63, 191-92, 194-95; and on the lobbying activities of Eliphalet Dyer and Christopher Avery, see 189-90, 193.

44. Conn. Arch., Susq., I, 20; also in Boyd, *Susquehannah Papers,* III, 191-92.

45. Boyd, *Susquehannah Papers,* III, 155, 170-73.

46. *Ibid.,* 176-77, 179.

47. *Ibid.,* IV, p. xi.

48. Letter dated Dec. 29, 1769, "Ingersoll Papers," 429.

49. Benjamin Gale, *Doct. Gale's Letter to J. W. Esquire* (Hartford, 1769), to which Dyer responded with *Remarks on Dr. Gale's Letter to J. W. Esq.* (Hartford, 1769). Gale then answered Dyer with *Observations on a Pamphlet entitled Remarks on Dr. Gale's Letter to J. W. Esq. Signed E. D.* (Hartford, 1769). These have been collected and printed in Boyd, *Susquehannah Papers,* III, 224-46, 247-68, 268-92. Samuel Avery of Norwich also drew up a reply to the anti-Susquehannah charges. The latter, he said, were being made by the "enemies to the Colony." Avery's purpose was to make "those things . . . appear as they truly are—cleansed of all the Smoak and dirt that has been th[r]own upon it [Susquehannah Company]." Draft copy of an article on the company in the Avery Papers. Avery became a member of the company in 1761. After the Revolution he was a prominent speculator in Vermont, Pennsylvania and New York lands. He remained interested in the Susquehannah Company's project, however, and became involved in litigation over it in the 1790's. In 1803 he published a stout pamphlet, *The Susquehannah Controversy Examined* (Wilkes-Barre, 1803). Weary of the long drawn out dispute, Avery wrote in the preface to this book, "This controversy has cost the lives of hun-

dreds, and has been the ruin of thousands, and has injured the state millions, and has worn out one generation—time has swept them away, I am left alone to tell thee; and the second generation is fast advancing on their way. It is time it was settled." See p. v. There is a short sketch of Avery and his speculations in E. M. Avery and C. H. Avery, *The Groton Avery Clan* (Cleveland, 1912), I, 226-28.

50. See, for example, the charges made against the company and the answers in Boyd, *Susquehannah Papers,* IV, 8-10; also Gale's first pamphlet, *ibid.,* III, 237, and Dyer's reply, 256. On the other hand Samuel Avery did not think it necessary to defend the company's alleged association with the "Paxton Boys." According to Avery the "Paxton Boys" were justified in their conflict with the proprietary government. Fragment in the Avery Papers.

51. Boyd, *Susquehannah Papers,* III, 236-38, 240, 270-73. See also the arguments in *The State of the Lands said to be once within the Bounds of the Charter of . . . Connecticut . . . Considered By the Publick's Humble Servant,* in *ibid.,* IV, 345-55, 358-59; *Conn. Courant,* Oct. 20, 1769, pp. 1-2.

52. Boyd, *Susquehannah Papers,* III, 238-39. Daniel Edwards, a member of the company, admitted in 1754 that a successful settlement would draw off "very large Numbers of our Substantial Inhabitants" and would therefore "be at least at present a great Detriment to this Colony." *Ibid.,* I, 184.

53. *Ibid.,* III, 233.

54. *Ibid.,* IV, 356-57. As early as 1754 John Armstrong wrote to the Governor of Pennsylvania that "Several Gentlemen" thought that one of the company's plans was "to put such men at the Head of Government . . . as would Confirm their Indian Title." *Ibid.,* I, 192. See also *Conn. Jour.,* Dec. 29, 1769, p. 4.

55. Boyd, *Susquehannah Papers,* III, 288; IV, 358-59. "Philo Coloniae" asked "Will not the opulent and interested PENN level his complaints to the throne against the assembly . . . and must not the assembly be put to the expence and hazard of defending the title of the adventurers?" *Conn. Jour.,* Oct. 20, 1769, pp. 1-2; see also Dec. 29, 1769, p. 4; *Conn. Courant,* May 21, 1770, pp. 1-2. A biblically minded critic referred to the Susquehannah advocates as "Workers of Iniquity," who "whet their Tongues like a Sword, and bend their Bows to Shoot their Arrows, ever utter Words; that they may shoot them in Secret at the Perfect; they commune of laying Snares privily." Quoted in Boyd, *Susquehannah Papers,* II, 332-33.

56. Samuel Avery charged that it was the opponents of the Susque-hannah project who were really planning to "confound and overrun this Govt. and involve them in Ruine and the loss of their charter." Fragment in the Avery Papers. Avery admitted, however, that there were "many Judicious Honest men who are men of Integrity and friends to the Interest of the Colony who for want of acquaintance in the matter have been misled in this affair." Reverse side of letter dated Norwich, Nov. 1770, *ibid.*

57. See Dyer's pamphlet in Boyd, *Susquehannah Papers,* III, 247-68.   ,

58. *Ibid.,* 261. Dyer claimed that only ten men owned more than 1000 acres in Connecticut, only a few had farms over 200 acres and "thousands have no lands." See p. 259. Samuel Avery's conclusions were similar to Dyer's. He asked whether any "person of common sense can think that the Inhabitants of this Govt will be held here as Slaves to work at day wages and farm hand when there is such a universal open-ing in the Country around us for a great many Hundd miles where they may go out and get Inheritances for their Children." If these farmers did not get their lands from Connecticut, Avery argued, they would look for them elsewhere. The result would be a drain upon the popula-tion of the colony. But "if these same people were incouraged to Settle within this Govt to the westward, it would have a tendency to increase the popularity of the Colony, Instead of depopulating it as is Suggested; indeed I humbly conceive there is nothing will keep up the consequence and popularity of this Colony but only their spreading themselves over them western parts of the Govt." Fragment in the Avery Papers.

59. Williams to Johnson, July 24, 1769, Johnson Papers.

60. Johnson was the pastor of the North Society in Groton from 1749-72. After 1772 he devoted much of his energies to the Susque-hannah project. In 1773 he became the minister to the company's settlers. With his family he fled from the Wyoming Valley after the 1778 mas-sacre, but returned in 1781. He died in Wilkes-Barre in 1797. See Dexter, *Biog. Sketches,* I, 649-51.

61. Quoted in Boyd, *Susquehannah Papers,* III, x.

62. *New London Gaz.,* Sept. 22, 1769, p. 1. On the same day, Sept. 12, a meeting was held to consider whether the town's inhabitants would apply to the Assembly "for a Grant of 20 miles Square of the Colony Lands west of and adjoyning to the Susquehannah purchas." Samuel Huntington was appointed agent and it was resolved that he should ask the legislature to grant that land "to the Inhabitants of Said

Norwich with ample Right for them to purchas the Native Right of Said Lands." Miscellaneous MSS, Yale University.

63. *Conn. Courant,* May 15, 1769, p. 3; Boyd, *Susquehannah Papers,* III, 240.

64. J. Chew to Sir William Johnson, May 29, 1769, in Boyd, *Susquehannah Papers,* III, 129. Compare J. Trumbull to R. Sherman, March 30, 1770, Trumbull Papers, State Lib., XX, pt. 1, 7ab.

65. Johnson to J. Trumbull, Feb. 26, 1770, Trumbull Papers, State Lib., XXX, 274-77. Johnson, however, had "a very good Opinion of the legal Right of the Colony to those Lands." *Ibid.,* 273. See also Johnson to Dyer, Feb. 27, 1770, Johnson Papers.

66. Dyer to Johnson, Dec. 15, 1770, Johnson Papers. See also the governor's cool letter to Johnson, Nov. 19, 1770, Trumbull Papers, State Lib., XX, pt. 1, 15a. Johnson's sentiments noticeably strained the relationship between him and some of his "Eastern Friends" who according to George Chapman began to spread the rumor that Johnson was "a pensioner to the Penns." Chapman to Johnson, Dec. 11, 1770, Johnson Corres., Bancroft Transcripts.

67. Jackson to Trumbull, Feb. [?], 1770 and May 7, 1770, Trumbull Papers, State Lib., III, 10b; XXX, 309b.

68. Boyd, *Susquehannah Papers,* IV, xvii-xviii, xxxv *n*91; III, 189-90, 193; J. Chew to Sir William Johnson, May 29, 1769, *ibid.,* III, 129; W. S. Johnson to R. Jackson, Aug. 31, 1770, Johnson Papers.

69. W. S. Johnson to R. Jackson, Aug. 31, 1770, Johnson Papers.

70. Johnson to Dyer, Sept. 12, 1767, *ibid.* It is interesting to note that at this time Johnson did not agree with the "very many" who thought that the Susquehannah Company's project was "prejudicial to the Colony." But Benjamin Gale was certain that "the body of the Freeman hate and fear the consequences of the Susquehannah affairs." Gale to Ingersoll, Dec. 29, 1769, Boyd, *Susequehannah Papers,* III, 219.

71. Chew to Sir William Johnson, Aug. 15, 1768, Boyd, *Susquehannah Papers,* III, 24. Chew also commented sarcastically about the ties between Connecticut's Puritanism and the Susquehannah Company's more worldly ambitions. He wrote to the same correspondent, April 18, 1769, of a company meeting that had undoubtedly been "Opened by a Prayer that the Lord would be with and assist his saints and Elect people and send the proprietors and inhabitants of Pennsylvania from the lands they have set their hearts upon." *Ibid.,* 100.

72. These were William Williams' comments on the anti-Susquehannah majority in the lower house of the legislature in 1769. Williams to W. S. Johnson, July 24, 1769, Johnson Papers.

73. J. Chew to Sir William Johnson, May 29, 1769, in Boyd, *Susquehannah Papers,* III, 129.

74. Dyer to W. S. Johnson, Nov. 10, 1769, Johnson Papers.

75. Dyer to W. S. Johnson, Aug. 8, 1769, and Johnson to Jackson, Aug. 31, 1770, *ibid.* Col. Israel Putnam, however, one of the colony's popular Whig leaders was bitterly attacked by Dyer for holding the Susquehannah Company to be a "foolish wild goose scheme." Putnam seems to have had other speculative land interests. See J. Chew to Sir William Johnson, May 29, Oct. 30, Nov. 29, 1769, in Boyd, *Susquehannah Papers,* III, 130, 190, 205-6. Boyd believes that former Governor Fitch himself may have been the author of a pamphlet upholding Connecticut's claims to the disputed western lands; see in this connection, *ibid.,* 292*n,* and the pamphlet printed on 292-330. Even if this were the case the political elements that supported Fitch obviously did not support the company.

CHAPTER SIX

1. *Conn. Jour.,* March 24, 1769, p. 2. See also *Conn. Courant,* March 20, 1769, pp. 2-3.

2. "Observations on the several commanders of the Ship Connecticut, Oct. 10, 1769, by an old decrepid Seaman who laments the Ship's misfortune," quoted in Jonathan Trumbull, *Jonathan Trumbull* (Boston, 1919), 88-89. A copy of this is also in Conn. Misc. Papers 1740-87, Stevens Transcripts.

3. All four former councillors had in the meantime been elected to represent their respective towns at the October 1766 session of the Assembly. *Conn. Col. Recs.,* XII, 493-94.

4. "Plaind Facts" appeared in the *Conn. Courant,* Jan. 12, 1767, p. 1. See also "Justice," *ibid.,* March 9, 1767, p. 2. "Constant Customer" attributed the article by "Plaind Facts" to Gale: *ibid.* For further circumstantial evidence pointing to Gale's authorship of "Plaind Facts" see

the correspondence between Ezra Stiles and Gale for 1767 in the Stiles Papers.

5. Silliman resided in Fairfield, Hall in Wallingford, Hamlin in Middletown, and Chester in Wethersfield.

6. "Constant Customer," *Conn. Courant,* March 9, 1767, p. 2; "F. Q.," *New London Gaz.,* Feb. 20, 1767, p. 1.

7. "Senex," *Conn. Courant,* March 9, 1767, p. 1.

8. "Plain Truth," *ibid.,* Feb. 23, 1767, p. 2; "A. Z.," March 2, 1767, pp. 1-2, and *Conn. Gaz.,* March 14, 1767, p. 1. See also "H. L." in *Conn. Courant,* March 30, 1767, p. 1, and "Titus Moderate," April 6, 1767, Supplement.

9. *Conn. Gaz.,* March 14, 1767, p. 2; "Justice," *Conn. Courant,* March 9, 1767, pp. 1-2.

10. Conservative arguments may be found in "Justice," *Conn. Courant,* March 9, 1767, pp. 1-2; "Freeman," March 16, p. 1; March 23, p. 1; "Pacificus," April 6, pp. 2-3. The latter observed with "much Anxiety and Concern, that Factions have been gradually gaining ground in this Colony for more than thirty Years."

11. "Senex," *Conn. Courant,* April 16, 1767, Supplement. This contributor noted that the disputes over the New London Society, paper money, and other issues, including the Stamp Act, had centered in the eastern towns. He admitted that another possible reason was their proximity to Rhode Island which was "noted for Contentions."

12. *Conn. Courant,* April 6, 1767, p. 3; *Conn. Gaz.,* March 28, 1767, p. 1.

13. "General Plan," *Conn. Gaz.,* March 28, 1767, p. 2; also in *Conn. Courant,* April 6, 1767, pp. 1-2. See also *Conn. Gaz.,* April 11, 1767, p. 2. The Rev. John Devotion believed that only the election of Fitch and the "Old Senators" would revitalize Connecticut's fast expiring political orthodoxy, and Benjamin Gale predicted dolefully that if the political New Lights remained in office "the peace and happiness of this Govt is at an end." Devotion to Stiles, Feb. 6, 1767; Gale to Stiles, April 17, 1767, Stiles Papers; Stiles, *Itin.,* 461-62, 492. See also *Conn. Courant,* March 16, 1767, quoted in Boyd, *Susquehannah Papers,* II, 332-33; "Plain Facts," *Conn. Gaz.,* April 11, 1767, p. 1.

14. J. Hubbard Jr. to E. Stiles, March 21, 1767, Stiles Papers.

15. Devotion to Stiles, June 6, 1767, *ibid.* Samuel Johnson thought that there never had been, nor would there ever be, political struggles

equal in bitterness to the campaign of 1767. Johnson to W. S. Johnson, April 24, 1767, Schneider, *Johnson,* I, 400.

16. H. Silliman to E. Stiles, April 17, 1767, Stiles Papers.

17. Examples of appeals for moderation from both radical and conservative pens may be found in articles by "Peace Good Agreement, No Party," and "Bellander," *Conn. Courant,* April 6, 1767, pp. 1, 2; "Candor," March 23, 1767, pp. 1-2; and "H.L.," March 30, 1767, p. 1.

18. *Conn. Gaz.,* Sept. 27, 1767, March 14, 1767.

19. H. Silliman to E. Stiles, April 17, 1767, Stiles Papers; T. Hosmer to J. Ingersoll, April 14, 1767, "Ingersoll Papers," 404. To Silliman and to Hosmer it seemed "as tho the Affairs of the Election wd take a Different turn this Spring from what it Did Last."

20. Johnson to W. S. Johnson, March 12, April 24, 1767, Schneider, *Johnson,* 394, 400.

21. Devotion to Stiles, April 22, 1767, Stiles Papers; also in Stiles, *Itin.,* 462; Gale to Stiles, April 17, 1767, Stiles Papers.

22. Gale to Stiles, April 17, 1767, Stiles Papers.

23. Two lists of returns, substantially the same, have been found. One is in Gale's letter to W. S. Johnson, June 10, 1767, Johnson Papers. The other is on a slip of paper dated "June 8 or thereabouts," preceding the letter from J. Davenport to E. Stiles, May 10, 1766, Stiles Papers. The figures published in Stiles, *Itin.,* 63-64, were taken from those given on this slip of paper. On Silliman see also J. Devotion to Stiles, June 6, 1767, Stiles Papers; Stiles, *Itin.,* 465.

24. Gale to W. S. Johnson, June 10, 1767, Johnson Papers.

25. Stiles, *Itin.,* 63-64.

26. Ingersoll to Johnson, July 23, 1767, Johnson Papers; Johnson to Ingersoll, Nov. 12, 1767, "Ingersoll Papers," 416. See also Gale to Johnson, June 10, 1766, Johnson Papers.

27. Gale to Stiles, April 17, 1767, Stiles Papers; Stiles, *Itin.,* 492-93.

28. J. Devotion to Stiles, June 6, 1767, Stiles Papers; Stiles, *Itin.,* 465. According to Devotion, Gale "had the Offer of acquiting himself, but Refused to Confess or acquit."

29. Gale to Johnson, June 10, 1767, Johnson Papers.

30. Gale to Johnson, Dec. 1, 1767, *ibid.*

31. Hubbard to Stiles, June 1, 1767, Stiles Papers.

32. Devotion to Stiles, April 22, 1767, *ibid.* Gale agreed with Devotion. Commenting upon the 1767 election he wrote to Johnson, "I think

we are in a fine way and Riding Post Haste into the Rhode Island Method of Faction." Letter dated June 10, 1767, Johnson Papers.

33. Huntington to Johnson, July 1, 1767, Johnson Papers. See also Joseph Trumbull to Jonathan Trumbull, May 19, 1767, Trumbull Papers, Personal.

34. Johnson to Ingersoll, June 9, 1767, "Ingersoll Papers," 409. See also "A.Z.," *Conn. Courant,* June 1, 1767, p. 1.

35. Stiles to [Gale], May 2, 1767, Stiles Papers.

36. *Ibid.;* see also letter dated April 30, 1767. The former deserves to be quoted at some length. "I should be sorry," Stiles wrote, "that the Old Lights should joyn the Episcopalians and Antiamericans in talking believing and almost hoping the loss of charter . . . depend upon it they [Anglicans] foresee that if they can separate you [Old Lights] from them [New Lights], and joyn you themselves and push the Partization vigorously—that in the first place this will consolidate the N. Lights on both sides the River and take the N. L. from the West and joyn to the body of the East united under the Title Sons of Liberty, there will not remain a Majority and prove the overthrow of the O. Lights—and in the second place, that you will be irritated and joyn the chh in petitioning for Change of Government. And this will most exactly suit all your Enemies. Whereas if all unite as Sons of Liberty and forget and lose the Names of O and N [Light] very much in this of Liberty, you will prevent any great Accumulation of Interest under the N. L[ight] Banner." The Newport Tories, according to Stiles, "Laugh at the Effect wc the Junction of the Chh and O. Lights will have with you." Stiles declared in his letter of April 30, "I freely say I had rather see the political Administration in the hands of . . . New Lights in Connecticutt, than to see a Loss of Charters. Power surrendered can never be resumed. Besides the Haughtiness of certain —is more intolerable than the constitutional Sin of Enthusiasm; and besides the New Lights have approved themselves Sons of Liberty whose Excesses . . . were . . . in a good Cause, that of Liberty."

37. Stiles to [Gale], April 30, 1767, *ibid.*

38. Gale to Stiles, Oct. 15, 1767, *ibid.*

39. Stiles to Gale, May 1, 1767, *ibid.* In a letter dated the previous day, Stiles had expressed the hope that the distinctions between Old and New Light, "Armin[ianism] and Calv[inism]" would soon be ended and that both sides of the river would assume the "heaven born name of 'Sons of Liberty.'" Stiles again questioned whether it

was "more desirable to be under the Gov [ernment] of Episco [palians] who most thoroly hate and dispise us than under the others [New Lights], who are fellow Dissenters and who hate us but half so much, and from Enemies may in the next Generation be made Friends." *Ibid*.

40. Gale to Stiles, Oct. 15, 1767, *ibid*.

41. Gale to W. S. Johnson, June 10, 1767, Johnson Papers. The "purge" was criticized in *Conn. Gaz.,* July 25, 1767, p. 3; *Conn. Courant,* July 20, p. 1; and defended in *Conn. Gaz.,* Aug. 22, p. 1.

42. J. Devotion to E. Stiles, June 6, Oct. 15, 1767, Stiles Papers; Stiles, *Itin.,* 465, 470. Silliman had been elected to represent Fairfield in the lower house in October 1766 and May 1767, but he was defeated in October 1767. See *Conn. Col. Recs.,* XII, 494, 546, 606.

43. "Phileleutheros," *Conn. Jour.,* Jan. 8, 1768, p. 2. "Bellander" replied for the conservatives by repeating the old charge that the "oriental" towns had long been the colony's chief troublemakers. *Ibid.,* Jan. 29, 1768, p. 2.

44. See the articles in *New London Gaz.,* April 8, 1768, p. 3; resolutions adopted at a Norwich meeting, *Conn. Courant,* July 4, 1768, p. 3.

45. See articles by Gale, *Conn. Courant,* May 15, 1769, pp. 2-3; *Conn. Jour.,* May 19, p. 1, in reply to the charges made by Thaddeus Burr, a Fairfield Whig, *Conn. Jour.,* May 12, 1769, p. 1. See also "Tom Lanyard's" letter to the freemen, *Conn. Courant,* June 5, 1769, p. 3. Gale published his first pamphlet on the Susquehannah Company in October and his second in February 1770. As the year came to a close another conservative accused the company of exploiting party differences to "secure to themselves and friends every place of public trust in the government." *Conn. Jour.,* Dec. 29, 1769, p. 4. In the same month Gale predicted that the company would find the new governor very helpful since Trumbull would "not dare to Disoblige his Eastern Friends, as he has not many Western ones." Nor did Gale anticipate that the new Deputy-Governor, Matthew Griswold, would defy the "Mobile Vulgus." Gale to Jared Ingersoll, Dec. [?], 1769, Boyd, *Susquehannah Papers,* III, 221.

46. See the warnings against political strife in Salter, Election Sermon, 36-37, and Huntington, *Freeman's Directory,* 23. See also "Tom Lanyard's" complaint about the bitter divisions between the colony's "*Starboard Men* and *Larboard Men*." *Conn. Courant,* March 20, 1769, p. 2; *Conn. Jour.,* March 24, 1769, p. 3.

47. *Conn. Courant,* May 16, 1768, p. 3; B. Gale to W. S. Johnson, June 30, 1768, Johnson Papers. Most of the deputies turned against Fitch because they were uncertain as to how he would counter the demand of the customs officers for search warrants. *New London Gaz.,* Nov. 4, 1768, p. 1; *Conn. Courant,* Dec. 12, 1768, p. 4.

48. The votes are cited by Gale in his first pamphlet on the Susquehannah Company. Boyd, *Susquehannah Papers,* III, 226.

49. William Williams to W. S. Johnson, July 24, 1769, Johnson Papers; Samuel Johnson to W. S. Johnson, May 25, 1769, Schneider, *Johnson,* I, 455.

50. E. Dyer to W. S. Johnson, Nov. 10, 1769, Johnson Papers.

51. *Ibid.;* see also the fragment on the election in the MS Votes for Governor and Assistants, Conn. Hist. Soc., and *Conn. Col. Recs.,* XIII, 236.

52. Fragment on the election in the MS Votes for Governor and Assistants; see also J. Chew and E. Dyer to W. S. Johnson, Dec. 9, 1769, Nov. 10, 1769, Johnson Papers. Dyer, who had hoped to become the new deputy-governor, blamed William Williams, at least in part, for his defeat. See Williams to Dyer, Nov. 26, 1773, Miscellaneous MSS, Williams, N. Y. Hist. Soc.

53. Fragment on the election in MS Votes for Governor and Assistants; see also William S. Johnson's comments in letters to Jared Ingersoll, Jan. 18, 1770; to J. Chew, Feb. 13, 1770; and to E. Dyer, Feb. 27, 1770, Johnson Papers.

54. "The old party keeps up," Dyer wrote to Johnson, "they seem not quite discouraged, they seem determined to make some struggle at least every year to regain their seats but hitherto in Vain." Letter dated Aug. 8, 1769, Johnson Papers. Jedidiah Huntington, however, was very pleased by the "Steadiness and Prudence of the major Part of the Colony." To Jabez Huntington, May 12, 1769, Jedidiah Huntington Papers.

55. *Conn. Courant,* July 4, 1768, p. 3; Dec. 12, p. 4; Oct. 24, p. 2; *New London Gaz.,* Aug. 19, 1768, p. 2; Sept. 9, pp. 1-2; Oct. 14, p. 1; Nov. 18, p. 1.

56. Gale to Stiles, Aug. 23, 1766, Stiles Papers. Stiles added the following as a note to the copy of his letter to Gale, Oct. 1, 1766: "This is in answer to Dr. Gales Letter [concrg ?] a plan proposing to construe Connecticut Charter as investing the House of Deputies with the exclusive Election of Govr, D. Govr and Assistants—and proposing

to introduce that practice: Because the Struggles about the Stamp Act had divided the colony into two parties." *Ibid.*

57. Stiles to Gale, Oct. 1, 1766, *ibid.* But Titus Hosmer, a rising Middletown lawyer, and some of his friends approved the plan as a means of releasing the colony "from the Danger of Faction and Intestine Divisions." Hosmer to Gale, July 30, 1766, Benjamin Gale Papers, Yale University.

58. See article by "Ignoramus," *Conn. Jour.,* Jan. 13, 1769, pp. 2-3; *Conn. Courant,* Jan. 23, 1769, pp. 2-3. Compare Gale's comments in his second pamphlet on the Susquehannah Company, Boyd, *Susquehannah Papers,* III, 282.

59. Gale to W. S. Johnson, Jan. 30, 1769, Johnson Papers.

60. Williams to W. S. Johnson, July 24, 1769, *ibid.*

61. J. Chew to W. S. Johnson, Dec. 9, 1769, and E. Dyer to Johnson, Nov. 10, 1769, *ibid.* See also Gale's remarkable prediction in his second pamphlet on the Susquehannah Company. Boyd, *Susquehannah Papers,* III, 281. That the race would be close was also indicated by the October nominations, in which Trumbull got 2671 votes and Fitch 2242. Fragment in the MS Votes for Governor and Assistants.

62. Trumbull's commercial ventures had deeply involved him in debt. His financial difficulties were so serious that he had to plead with his creditors for leniency. He maintained that he would be better able to meet his obligations if he continued in office than if he were defeated. An undated manuscript in the Trumbull Papers, Mercantile, declares that Trumbull's position in the government "is such as makes it difficult for me to Transact therein [debts] at present, as the further Divulging the Knowledge of my Circumstances may Occasion an Alteration in our next Election—my Continuance in the Station in which I am now placed will better enable me to do what will be for the Interest of Mr. Lane."

63. "Observations on the several commanders of the Ship Connecticut . . . by an old decrepid Seaman who laments the Ship's misfortune," quoted in Trumbull, *Trumbull,* 88-89. A copy of this ballad is in the Conn. Misc. Papers 1740-87, Stevens Transcripts. Joseph Chew referred to the verses in a letter to W. S. Johnson, Dec. 9, 1769, Johnson Papers. Chew promised Johnson that upon the latter's return to Connecticut he would have Fitch sing the song to them to the tune of the "Vicar of Bray."

64. *New London Gaz.,* March 23, 1770, p. 3; March 30, p. 1. Some

radicals were quite nervous. When an old "Grumbletonian" expressed
the hope at the general meeting of the merchants at Middletown, Feb.
20, 1770, that the objectives of the convention had no "politics in it,"
they roundly denounced him for maliciously insinuating that it would
be desirable to oust the incumbent administration. *Ibid.,* March 9, 1770,
p. 1; March 30, p. 2. See also *Conn. Courant,* Feb. 19, 1770, p. 3; March
19, p. 3.

65. *Conn. Courant,* March 26, 1770, p. 4; *New London Gaz.,*
March 30, 1770, p. 1. The Rev. Judah Champion bemoaned the terrible
"divisions in church and state." What made him even sadder was that
"Some wou'd subject themselves to that yoke which neither we nor
our fathers were able to bear." *A Brief View,* 43.

66. *Conn. Courant,* April 2, 1770, pp. 1-2.

67. "Observator," *ibid.,* 1.

68. *Ibid.*

69. Fragment in the MS Votes for Governor and Assistants; *Conn.
Col. Recs.,* XIII, 285; *Conn. Courant,* May 14, 1770, p. 3. The complaint
that Hubbard had made about the totals of the 1767 election is equally
applicable to the 1770 election. The largest vote given to a councillor in
1770 was 4967. But a total of 9771 votes was cast for governor. The
question naturally arises: Why was the largest vote for assistant only
one-half as much as the vote for governor?

70. This elaborate breakdown of the October 1770 nominations
is to be found in a fragment preserved in the MS Votes for Governor and
Assistants. The final totals received by some of the candidates, especially the radicals, may have been 130-40 more than the figures listed
above in the text. Since these extra votes were not broken down by
counties, however, and since it is not likely that they fundamentally altered the general distribution, they were not included in the above
discussion. These additions are on another fragment in the hand
of William Williams in the same collection.

71. W. S. Johnson to William Williams, Nov. 1, 1769; see also
Johnson to J. Miller, Feb. 12, 1770, Johnson Papers. In the middle of
the heated campaign of 1770 Nathan Whiting, a prominent New Haven
moderate, confessed to Johnson that "we have in the different Colonies
so much party Politicks mixt in with the professions of Patriotism that
I sometimes much fear the consequence." Whiting to Johnson, March
10, 1770, *ibid.*

72. Fitch was being considered for some important post as early

as 1767. Richard Jackson to Jared Ingersoll, Feb. 20, 1767, "Ingersoll Papers," 403. See also W. S. Johnson to Ingersoll, May 16, Nov. 12, 1767, and Jackson to Ingersoll, March 12, 1768, *ibid.,* 407, 415, 422. Speaking for the conservatives, Silliman wrote to Massachusetts' conservative Lieut.-Gov., Thomas Hutchinson, Dec. 8, 1768: "there are Some of them at Least Left to the only Consolation of a Consciousness of haveing done that which they Sincerely thot in the time of it not only their indispensable Duty but for the greatest Safety for their Country. Your Humble Servant counts himself one of this Sort being not of Sufficient Note as to recommend him to the Notice Smiles and approbation of the King or his Ministers, and so unhappy as to offend so many among whom he dwells as that he is not now Serviceable or useful among them in the Stations he before Sustained." *Pitkin Papers,* 156. In the summer of 1770 Silliman indicated to Hutchinson that he would not mind getting the post of Collector at New Haven. In describing the politics of his colony the former councillor expressed his loss of faith in Connecticut's political system. He wrote to Hutchinson, Aug. 11, 1770, "the whole Government here is in the Hands of the People so that they are subject to no Controul and Consequently every one that holds any Considerable Post in this Government the Continuance of his Employ is very Precarious and if his Judgmt be not great Enough to foretell what will please the people let his Abilities and Integrity be what it will he stands a miserable chance so that the Study of mankind seems to be of the greatest Importance in our policy." Transcript in Silliman Papers, Yale University.

CHAPTER SEVEN

1. Revs. Hubbard and Tyler to the Secretary of the S. P. G., April 4, May 5, 1772, Hawks and Perry, *Doc. Hist.,* II, 181-83. Tyler, however, explained that "what little toleration" the Anglicans enjoyed was "solely occasioned, by some degree of fear which our rulers still entertain of the British Government and of losing their invaluable charter as they term it." Tyler to the Secretary of the S. P. G., Oct. 9, 1771, *ibid.,* II, 171.

2. *Conn. Courant,* May 19, 1772, p. 1.

3. *Conn. Col. Recs.,* XIV, 5.

4. W. S. Johnson to R. Jackson, Oct. 21, 1771; T. Fitch to Johnson, Oct. 18, 1773, Johnson Papers.

5. Chester's obituary, *Conn. Courant,* Sept. 24, 1771, p. 3. For Hall, see Wetmore, Election Sermon, 27*n.*

6. *Conn. Courant,* May 14, 1771, p. 1.

7. Trumbull to W. S. Johnson, Jan. 15, 1771, Johnson Papers.

8. Johnson to Gov. Trumbull, Jan. 2, 1771, *Trumbull Papers,* I, 470; to A. Wedderburn, Oct. 25, 1771, Oct. 5, 1772; to R. Jackson, May 30, 1772, Johnson Papers. It is interesting to compare Johnson's views with those of the more conservative Gov. Hutchinson of Massachusetts. See Hutchinson to J. Harrison, May 11, 1772, Hutchinson Corres., III, Bancroft Transcripts.

9. Trumbull Papers, State Lib., XX, pt. 1, 60. See also his speeches to the Assembly, Oct. 1771, and May 1772, *ibid.,* 31, 35ab, 49ab, 50a.

10. J. Fish to E. Stiles, Dec. 15, 1771, Stiles Papers.

11. On the Baptists see Greene, *Religious Liberty in Conn.,* 329. Compare *Conn. Col. Recs.,* XIII, 463; see also Trumbull Papers, State Lib., III, pt. 1, 41, 44ab, 48a-c; XX, pt. 1, 19ab. On the Anglicans see the letters written by Godfrey Malbone to W. S. Johnson during the years 1771 and 1772 in the Johnson Papers; *Conn. Courant,* May 28, 1771, p. 1; Conn. MSS, Hawks Transcripts, 606, 616-19, 637-40. Compare *Conn. Col. Recs.,* XIII, 548, 549-50.

12. Connecticut clergy to the Bishop of London, May 29, 1771, Hawks and Perry, *Doc. Hist.,* II, 176-77. The clergy emphasized the point that "There never were so few rebels, there never were in proportion, so many loyal subjects bred in any Church, as has been in the Church of England."

13. Johnson to the Bishop of Oxford, Jan. 15, 1774, Johnson Papers; Rev. Dr. Berkeley to Johnson, Oct. 19, 1772; Johnson to Myles Cooper, June 18, 1773; Johnson to Mr. Stuyvesant, May 18, 1773, Johnson Corres., Bancroft Transcripts.

14. Stiles, *Diary,* I, 244, 283, 284, 287, 359-60, 393. See the letter written by the Rev. Mr. Beach to the Secretary of the S. P. G., Oct. 20, 1773, Hawks and Perry, *Doc. Hist.,* II, 192, in which the claim was made that in Beach's two parishes at Newtown and Redding the Anglican congregations were larger than those of the established church.

15. Chauncy to E. Stiles, June 14, 1771, Stiles, *Itin.,* 451.

16. John Ledyard had predicted that the resumption of large scale importations of British goods through New York into Connecticut would be "mischievous." To W. S. Johnson, Dec. 12, 1770, Johnson Papers.

17. Trumbull Papers, State Lib., III, pt. 2, 96, 113, 114; XX, pt. 1, 46, 49, 53.

18. The history of the merchants' society may be followed in the *Conn. Jour.,* June 8, 1770, p. 1; May 12, 1772, p. 2; April 2, 1773, p. 1; *Conn. Courant,* June 4, 1770, p. 1; Feb. 4, 1772, p. 3; Oct. 13, p. 4; *New London Gaz.,* April 3, 1772, p. 1; June 12, p. 3.

19. Richard Jackson to Gov. Trumbull, March 25, 1772, Trumbull Papers, State Lib., XXI, 23.

20. For a description of Connecticut's imports from the British and foreign West Indies through New London and New Haven, Jan. 1771-Jan. 1772, see the tables between pp. 266-95 in Stella H. Sutherland, *Population Distribution in Colonial America* (New York, 1936). Connecticut's exports to Britain for the same period are listed in tables between 296-317. The colony's last report to the Board of Trade early in 1774 described its direct imports from Britain as "few," but estimated the annual value of its imports purchased from Boston and New York at about £200,000. Only £10,000 worth of Connecticut's commodities were sold directly to the British Isles. In comparison, it is important to note that the exports through New London alone to the neighboring colonies totalled £20,000 annually, while the value of the port's foreign trade, which was chiefly with the West Indies, was placed at £50,000 a year. New Haven directly imported only £4000 worth of British manufactures and "India goods" from the mother country, but its merchants took £40,000 worth of the same products from Boston and New York annually. *Conn. Col. Recs.,* XIV, 344-45, 498. Stiles estimated the annual value of the British goods taken by Connecticut through New York alone at £100,000 sterling, *Diary,* I, 516.

21. Joseph Chew petitioned the Assembly, Oct. 1771, for relief, explaining that he owed debts of £15,406 but that his assets were only a few pounds in cash and £5000 in paper of very doubtful value. He complained that because of "many misfortunes in years past sustained in the course of his trade and business he is now from prosperous circumstances reduced to poverty and want. . . ." *Conn. Col. Recs.,* XIII, 527-28. For other examples see *ibid.,* XIV, 14-18, 25-26, 28-30, 31, 33-34, 98-99, 115, 177, and *passim.* Complaints about the evil consequences of so many of Connecticut's farmers and merchants being in

debt to New York merchants were voiced in *Conn. Jour.,* Oct. 11, 1771, p. 1; May 8, 1772, p. 1; *Conn. Courant,* Feb. 18, 1771, p. 1; May 19, 1772, pp. 1-2. There was also a rising protest against Connecticut's laws imposing imprisonment for debt. See "Justinian," *A Letter to the Legislative Authority of Connecticut Wherein is shewn, that the Law, and Practice of the Colony, in Regard to Debt and Gaol is not According to the Foundation of Civil Law which is compiled for public Good* (Hartford, 1770). Among the points emphasized by the author was the fact that the colony's economy inevitably involved many in debt. See pp. 7-9.

22. *Conn. Col. Recs.,* XIV, 345.

23. *Ibid.,* 344, 345, 498.

24. See Shaw's letters to Thomas and Isaac Wharton, May 17, June 12, Aug. 14, 1771, Shaw, *Letter Book,* 224, 226, 228. See also Shaw to P. Vandervoort, Jan. 1, 1772, *ibid.,* 234, and P. Desmoulins to Shaw, Jan. [?], 1771, Shaw MSS, New London Co. Hist. Soc.

25. *Conn. Col. Recs.,* XIV, 344, 345, 498.

26. *New London Gaz.,* April 2, 1773, p. 3; Stewart and Moffat to Trumbull, Feb. 16, March 18, 26, 1773, Trumbull Papers, State Lib., III, pt. 2, 136-37, 142-43; Trumbull to Stewart and Moffat, March 19, 22, 1773, *ibid.,* XX, pt. 1, 63, 64, 65. The governor was careful, however, to make it clear that he did not favor smuggling. "I wish," he wrote in the letter of March 22, "some Method might be fal'n upon to prevent the like in future, so detrimental to the fair Trader, and manifestly tending to disquiet the People, and to encourage such as are disposed to transgress the Laws of Trade, especially when they find it may be done with impunity."

27. "Americanus," *New London Gaz.,* Feb. 5, 1773, p. 1; Feb. 26, p. 1; "A Freeman," *ibid.,* March 5, pp. 1-2; March 12, pp. 1-2; see also "Freeman," *Conn. Courant,* Feb. 23, 1773, p. 3; March 9, p. 1; "Regulus," April 6, p. 2.

28. Johnson to R. Jackson, Feb. 26, 1773, Johnson Papers. The people, Johnson reported, "threaten destruction to the Judges who shall give their opinion in favor" of the writs. On the action of the Superior Court see the *Conn. Courant,* March 23, 1773, p. 3. Silas Deane suggested that the colony's newly-created Committee of Correspondence write to the other provincial committees for their support. Deane to Joseph Trumbull, July 20, 1773, Joseph Trumbull Papers.

29. *Conn. Courant,* June 8, 1773, p. 1; June 15, 1773, p. 1.

30. Unfortunately, the results of the elections for these years are incomplete. The following is sufficient, however, to show the relative strength of the two parties. In the October 1771 nominations Trumbull received 2868 and Fitch 1824 votes. In the elections the following spring Trumbull got 3879 votes while 2503 ballots were scattered among several candidates. Fitch had only 1471 votes for the Council; Ebenezer Silliman received 1189 and Jabez Hamlin 1662 ballots. Robert Walker, who got the smallest number of votes of the successful candidates for the upper house, received 2482 ballots. In the eastern town of Lebanon the fall nominations in 1772 yielded Fitch and Silliman the grand total of 3 votes each. Trumbull received 90. The totals for the 1772 nominations showed Trumbull with 2937 and Fitch with 1581 votes. Fragments in the MS Votes for Governor and Assistants.

31. *Conn. Courant,* April 2, 1771, p. 1.

32. In May 1773, however, Jabez Hamlin, one of the juring former councillors, was again elected an assistant. *Conn. Col. Recs.,* XIV, 74. This cannot be considered a victory for the conservative party since Hamlin does not seem to have been as closely associated with that group as Fitch and the other former councillors were. Hamlin's votes in the nominations show a regular increase whereas the ballots of the others do not. MS Votes for Governor and Assistants. By 1773 Hamlin had apparently succeeded in rehabilitating his political standing among the freemen. Thereafter he continued to play an active part in the political affairs of the colony and state. See index, Hamlin, Jabez in *Conn. Col. Recs.,* XIV, XV; *The Public Records of the State of Connecticut* (Hartford, 1894-1922), I, hereafter cited as *State Records.*

33. *Conn. Courant,* Sept. 3, 1771, p. 2.

34. *Ibid.,* Oct. 1, 1771, p. 4.

35. *Ibid.,* April 16, 1771, p. 2.

36. *Conn. Jour.,* Sept. 13, 1771, p. 3.

37. *New London Gaz.,* Jan. 24, 1772, p. 4.

38. *Ibid.,* Oct. 23, 1772, p. 1.

39. The election sermon of 1772 noted that "Lately our country was shocked as with an earthquake:—The shocks were repeated—was all in trembling for her liberties . . . What a shining contrast do our eyes now behold. . . . The world rejoiceth, but will not charity tremble? the arrows are still pointed to the heart of our liberties." Mark Leavenworth, *Charity illustrated and Recommended to all Orders of Men* (New London, 1772), 51.

40. *Ibid.* Leavenworth's sermon was devoted almost exclusively to moral and religious themes. The few political references were, of course, Whig in character. See 22-23, 25, 41-42.

41. W. S. Johnson to T. Pownall, April 25, 1772, Johnson Papers.

42. Leavenworth used the phrase in his sermon, *Charity illustrated,* 45. He pointed out that "licentious liberty . . . taking occasion from some late occurrences, has been for some years struggling for the ascendant in church and state."

43. Johnson to E. Dyer, March 30, 1771, Johnson Papers. "I might have obtained very good things," Johnson claimed, "by deserting the interests of the country that gave me my birth, by abusing and misreprepresenting it, or by licking the dust of the feet of ministers or of the slaves of ministers . . . I have been an enthusiast in American affairs. . . . I fondly thought myself a humble laborer engaged . . . in erecting the glorious temple of American Liberty . . . I preferred being engaged in this work to every other pursuit." See also Johnson to R. Law, March 27, 1771, *ibid.*

44. Johnson to A. Wedderburn, Oct. 25, 1771, *ibid.* Johnson was at the time seeking the chief justiceship of New York, and he took pains to underscore his loyalty to the Crown. "No Man," he maintained, "I am sure has a more entire affection and veneration for his Majesty or a heart more devoted to his serv[ic]e than I have and it would make me very happy to be in a situation to give him the most effectual proofs of it in a Country where it is certain he extremely needs faithful servants." On Johnson's search for preferment see his letter to Wedderburn, Oct. 5, 1772, *ibid.* Johnson told John Temple, however, that he would not take any position "that may not be enjoyed with peace, reputation and the good of those with whom I live." Letter dated April 30, 1772, *Bowdoin and Temple Papers,* Mass. Hist. Soc., *Colls.,* 6th ser., 9 (1897), 291.

45. Johnson to the Rev. Dr. Berkeley, Feb. 23, 1773, Johnson Corres., Bancroft Transcripts.

46. *Conn. Jour.,* Feb. 12, 1773, p. 1. Tyler assigns this to John Trumbull, *Literary History,* I, 430.

47. Referring to the last phases of the non-importation movement in Connecticut, this writer declared it was "curious to recollect how we met together in various towns, how we made speeches, how we threatened, how we drew up resolutions, how we printed them in the papers, and wrote essays on liberty, and railed against importers and

burnt effigies, and drank toasts. After this, things returned into the old channel, and we heard no more about Liberty." *Conn. Jour.,* April 2, 1773, p. 1.

48. This radical claimed that "not one in twenty" was bothering to discover what the "Writ of Assistants [*sic*]" meant to them. *Ibid.*

49. Johnson to the Rev. Dr. Berkeley, Feb. 23, 1773, Johnson Corres., Bancroft Transcripts; to R. Jackson, Feb. 26, 1773; to John Pownall, Feb. 27, 1773, Johnson Papers.

50. Stiles to the Rev. Mr. Spencer, Feb. 16, 1773, Stiles Papers, Bancroft Transcripts. In the same letter Stiles reaffirmed his "perfect confidence that the future Millions of America will emancipate themselves from all foreign oppression."

51. Stiles, *Diary,* I, 344, entry of Feb. 19, 1773.

52. Stiles' comments on the "Prerogative people" are in *ibid.,* I, 381, entry of June 10, 1773.

53. Parsons to Adams, March 3, 1773, Adams Papers.

54. Benjamin Trumbull, *A Discourse Delivered at the Anniversary Meeting of the Freemen of the Town of New Haven, April 12, 1773* (New Haven, 1773), 5.

55. See, for example, *ibid.,* 27.

56. *Ibid.,* 30-33. It was a fundamental political axiom with Trumbull that "Every free state . . . should maintain a most vigilant care and guard against foreign, or independent rulers, and against all such measures as are calculated to introduce them."

57. *Conn. Jour.,* April 2, 1773, p. 1.

58. Conn. Arch., Rev. Ser., I, 53bc; *Conn. Col. Recs.,* XIV, 156; *New London Gaz.,* June 4, 1773, p. 3. See also Silas Deane to Joseph Trumbull, July 20, 1773, Joseph Trumbull Papers.

59. Erastus Wolcott, Nathaniel Wales Jr., Samuel H. Parsons, and Joseph Trumbull to John Hancock, June 16, 1773, Emmet Collection no. 641, N. Y. Pub. Lib.; see also Charles S. Hall, *Life and Letters of Samuel Holden Parsons* (Binghampton, 1905), 21-22; communication to the Virginia committee, Aug. 10, 1773, Emmet Collection no. 259.

60. George M. Curtis, "Meriden and Wallingford in Colonial and Revolutionary Days," New Haven Colony Hist. Soc., *Papers,* 7 (1908), 307.

61. *Conn. Courant,* Oct. 12, 1773, p. 4. Parson's name is written next to the article, signed "Observation," in the issue possessed by the Conn. Hist. Soc.

CHAPTER EIGHT

1. For examples of the opposition to the company see the long article in the *Conn. Courant,* May 21, 1770, pp. 1-2; and William Williams' description of the reaction of some deputies to Johnson's letter against the colony assuming the company's claim, William Williams Journal at New Haven, entry for Oct. 31, 1770. On the frontier conflicts see Boyd, *Susquehannah Papers,* IV, 67, 69, 71-78, 81-82, 153-57, 170, 230.

2. See the following interesting documents illustrating Trumbull's efforts on behalf of the company in one incident early in 1771, Boyd, *Susquehannah Papers,* IV, 175-76, 182-83, 183-98, and the notes on the latter pages.

3. Olson, *Agricultural Economy and the Population in Eighteenth Century Connecticut,* 8.

4. Olson cites an example in Colebrook in 1780 of the non-resident proprietors holding 14,681 acres to the 3716 held by the actual inhabitants of the town. *Ibid.,* 25. Of the 10,000 acres in the society of Torrington in 1768, 7000 belonged to non-resident owners. *Conn. Col. Recs.,* XIII, 111. See also Mead, *Conn. as a Corporate Colony,* 69-73, 79, on the growth of absentee proprietorship, especially in western Connecticut.

5. W. S. Johnson to R. Jackson, May 30, 1772, Johnson Papers.

6. On the growth of Connecticut's population see *Conn. Col. Recs.,* XIV, 499. On the eve of the Revolution Connecticut had 39 inhabitants to the square mile. Only Rhode Island's proportion was higher. Sutherland, *Population Distribution,* 37. Connecticut was "so full of Inhabitants," Silas Deane maintained, "that there is not more than Twelve Acres to a person." Deane to Patrick Henry, Jan. 2, 1775, *The Deane Papers* (5 vols.), N. Y. Hist. Soc., *Colls.,* 19 (1887), 36, hereafter cited as *Deane Papers,* I.

7. Stiles, *Diary,* I, 439. One of the reasons advanced by some Stamford Baptists for their emigration was the "fully settled" condition of the country. "As population increases, the surplusage must go abroad for settlements." Quoted in Greene, *Religious Liberty in Conn.,* 329.

8. Deane to P. Henry, Jan. 2, 1775, *Deane Papers,* I, 35.

9. W. S. Johnson to R. Jackson, May 30, 1772, Johnson Papers.

Deane claimed that "a Connecticut Farmer with Two Hundred and Fifty Acres of good Land, is a rich man." Deane to P. Henry, Jan. 2, 1775, *Deane Papers,* I, 36.

10. The Susquehannah Company's settlers were "so wretchedly poor," according to Silas Deane, "that the place [the Wyoming lands] was an asylum from the gaol, or an assignment in service to most of them." Deane to Samuel H. Parsons, April 13, 1774, *Correspondence of Silas Deane 1774-1776,* Conn. Hist. Soc., *Colls.,* 2 (1870), 131-32, hereafter cited as *Deane Corres.*

11. Boyd, *Susquehannah Papers,* IV, 95.

12. *Ibid.,* 212-13.

13. *Conn. Col. Recs.,* XIII, 427-28; Conn. Arch., Susq., I, 21. The previous March a petition claiming 3026 subscribers from several towns asked the Assembly to extend its jurisdiction over the western lands *all the way to the Mississippi.* Trumbull Papers, State Lib., III, pt. 1, 53ab.

14. Gov. Trumbull to R. Jackson, Jan. [?], 1772, *ibid.,* XX, pt. 1, 38; Jackson's not so optimistic reply, March 25, 1772, XXI, 23. On Sept. 18, 1771 Deputy Gov. Griswold had suggested to Trumbull that Connecticut's case be transmitted to England as quickly as possible because delay might be prejudicial "and Disappoint the People of the Colony." *Ibid.,* III, pt. 1, 71; see also 73ab. In his October 1771 speech Trumbull asked the Assembly to consider the Susquehannah matter. *Ibid.,* XX, pt. 1, 31.

15. Conn. Arch., Susq., I, 26a-c; Boyd, *Susquehannah Papers,* IV, 314.

16. O. Gore to Z. Butler, May 27, 1772, Boyd, *Susquehannah Papers,* IV, 328.

17. *Conn. Courant,* Sept. 29, 1772, pp. 2-3; Oct. 13, p. 3.

18. The questions asked of the English lawyers, and their opinions, are in a document dated May 5, 1773, Johnson Papers; see also Trumbull, *History,* II, 472-73. Gov. Trumbull's speech to the Assembly, May 1773, informed the deputies that the Mohegan case had been finally settled, but that the opinion of the English lawyers on Connecticut's western claims had not yet been received. Trumbull Papers, State Lib., XX, pt. 1, 67. On the final disposition of the Mohegan case, see Thomas Life to Gov. Trumbull, March 3, 1773, *ibid.,* III, pt. 2, 139.

19. *Ibid.,* XX, pt. 1, 72cd. Samuel Avery had composed a similar argument in 1770: Connecticut "ranks prity well up with many of the

other Govts, and is thought of some consequence nay is something popular, but where will it be . . . when the other Govts have extended themselves over two, three, four, five and even to ten times the land they now have under Improvemt—let me answer here this Govt must then be Ranked with that little Turbulent Govt Rhode Island, and when it losses its popularity I have the utmost Reason to fear it will cease to be a Govt at all." Fragment in the Avery Papers.

20. *Conn. Col. Recs.,* XIV, 161; MS in Conn. Arch., Susq., I, 34.

21. On the composition of the committee and its mission see *Conn. Col. Recs.,* XIV, 161-62, 217-18; Trumbull, *History,* II, 474; Williams to Dyer, Nov. 26, 1773, Misc. MSS, Williams, N. Y. Hist. Soc.; Trumbull Papers, State Lib., III, pt. 2, 160, 161, 162; IV, pt. 1, 47.

22. When Pelatiah Webster learned that Connecticut had asserted its claim to the western lands he suggested to William Samuel Johnson that the colony join with those southern colonies that had sea-to-sea charters to push their claims together. "If these things could be Suggested to those Colonies, and they Shod See the Advantage and Catch the flame, (as I doubt not they wod) the matter would become so Interesting that opposing it wd (in the present Ticklish State of the Colonies) become dangerous and Impolitic in the Court of Great Britain." Webster went on to say that Massachusetts "grown of late pretty formidable to the British Ministry may on a Proper hint find means to Extend their Claim to the S. Sea also." Webster to Johnson, Jan. 3, 1774, Johnson Papers. Johnson thought that Webster's ideas were "too elevated to be immediately adopted by our prudent Assembly who are you know rather remarkable for circumspection and Caution than for any great and bold designs." This is a most surprising comment, coming from one of Connecticut's most moderate and cautious politicians. However, it is interesting to note that Johnson felt that Webster's ideas were more likely to succeed than any of the Connecticut Assembly. Johnson passed on Webster's suggestions to Dyer and mentioned them to others in the colony. See Johnson to Webster, Jan. 22, 1774, Johnson Papers.

23. *Conn. Col. Recs.,* XIV, 217; MS in Conn. Arch., Susq., I, 42.

24. *Conn. Col. Recs.,* XIV, 218-19, and *n; Conn. Courant,* Feb. 15, 1774, p. 2.

25. Stiles quotes this price as having been offered to him on Jan. 21, 1774, *Diary,* I, 434. Jonathan Trumbull had paid only $9 for a share in 1761. In 1772 the value of a share varied between $40 and $60. See Boyd, *Susquehannah Papers,* IV, xxiv. Joseph Trumbull probably an-

ticipated a rise in the values of the company's shares and advised
Thomas Wharton, Nov. 23, 1773, to buy into the company. Joseph
Trumbull Papers.

26. Gipson, *Ingersoll,* 323-24.

27. Smith to Johnson, Jan. 18, Feb. 17, 1774, Johnson Papers.
"Your Colony," Smith wrote in the letter dated Feb. 17, "have now
sufficiently declared themselves, and must stand or fall by the Issue;
in which much weightier matters than the Pennsylvania Lands are
involved—For we are under no apprehensions about any Thing within
our Charter Limits." Again on April 25, Smith told Johnson that no
reasonable man could expect the Crown to sanction Connecticut's
claims to all the land up to the very Pacific. "Why then," he asked,
"risque your own Constitution and disturb us."

28. Johnson to T. Life, Nov. 23, 1773, and to R. Jackson, Nov. 5,
1773. See also Jackson's reply, April 5, 1774. As early as 1770 Johnson's
lukewarm attitude toward the Susquehannah Company's scheme had
prompted some eastern radicals to denounce him as a "penshoner to
the Penns." Johnson seems to have come close to being similarly denounced in 1774. George Chapman to Johnson, Dec. 11, 1770; Johnson
to Dr. Smith, April 25, 1774. Johnson asked Smith and Rittenhouse
to forgive "us this claim upon [parts?] of yr Country." On the 29th
of April Johnson thanked Smith for sending him a copy of his anti-
Susquehannah pamphlet. Johnson thought the arguments were good
and put those who were against Connecticut's title "in a very advantageous point of light." Compare, however, Johnson's opinion on
the general question of colonial expansion in his letter to John Sargent,
Oct. 31, 1772, Johnson Papers.

29. Deane envisioned the expansion of Connecticut to the Mississippi. See his elaborate plans for the creation of a company and settling
the West in the following documents: Deane to W. S. Johnson, Feb. 7,
1774, Johnson Papers; Deane to Samuel Holden Parsons, April 13, 1774;
"Rules for Admission of Associates," enclosed in a letter from E. Hazard to Deane, June 1, 1774, *Deane Corres.,* 131-32, 134; and Deane to
P. Henry, Jan. 2, 1775, *Deane Papers,* I, 35. As a merchant Deane knew
the problems of his class. It is most important, therefore, to note that he
did not believe that manufacturing or trade could flourish in the colony
until all the back lands had been colonized. He was convinced that
"whenever a People can have Land on easy Terms, and that must be
the Case with Us," trade would languish. Not "untill the Lands are
taken up, farr in Land, so farr that people disposed to emigrate can't

bear the expence of their removal there," would manufacturing or trade have a chance to prosper. Deane to Johnson, Feb. 7, 1774, Johnson Papers.

30. *Ibid.* On the other hand it must be noted that at least one of Connecticut's Tories later thought that the claim of the Susquehannah Company was "within The limits of Connecticut Charter." Tiffany, American Colonies, bk. 6, p. 27.

31. Trumbull, *History,* II, 474.

32. Advertisement of a pamphlet, *Conn. Courant,* Jan. 18, 1774, p. 3; "An Old Friend to Connecticut," April 5, p. 1; "Many," Feb. 22, p. 2; "Son of Liberty," *Conn. Jour.,* March 11, 1774, p. 1; see also Dec. 3, 1773, p. 2.

33. Jared Ingersoll to Jonathan Ingersoll, March 12, 1774. The people of Pennsylvania, the former wrote, regarded the Connecticut settlers as "Goths and Vandals," and to protect themselves "they will naturally Court the friendship of the Mother Country." "Ingersoll Papers," 446.

34. Gipson, *Ingersoll,* 324-25. Ingersoll learned from Johnson that the people of Connecticut were out of temper with him for his activities against the western claim. Johnson to Ingersoll, Jan. 29, 1774, Johnson Papers.

35. Ingersoll's letter was written to the *Conn. Jour.,* March 7, published March 18, and reprinted in the *Courant,* March 22, 1774, p. 2. See "Ingersoll Papers," 444-45. As early as Nov. 22, 1773, Ingersoll had commented in a letter to Jonathan Ingersoll, "if things are come to that pass, that some folks maynt say what they please about those they don't like, I think its very hard indeed." "Ingersoll Papers," 438.

36. A suggested resolution against the western claim listed the following objections: "Wherefore as this controversy will bring this colony under a heavy load of expence (which at present we are not able to bear) without the most distant prospect of success; and if obtained would be of no real advantage to this Colony, as it would drain us of our inhabitants; lessen the present value of our lands; and involve us in inextricable difficulties, with regard to the exercise of our present form of government, which cannot be exercised in so extensive a territory." *Conn. Jour.,* Dec. 3, 1773, p. 2.

37. *Conn. Courant,* Feb. 22, 1774, p. 2.

38. See Roger Sherman's article in *Conn. Jour.,* April 8, 1774, pp. 1-2, and Stiles' "To the Candid Public," *Conn. Courant,* Supplement, March 1, 1774.

39. *Conn. Jour.,* April 15, 1774, p. 3; see also issue of April 22, p. 1, and *Conn. Courant,* March 1, 1774, pp. 1-2.

40. Benjamin Trumbull, *A Plea in Vindication of the Connecticut Title to the Contested Lands* (New Haven, 1774), 96. "There is not one," Trumbull argued, "who has not an interest in the controversy, and who will not be affected by the decision of it." *Ibid.,* 3. On April 8, 1774, Benjamin Trumbull had informed the governor that a pamphlet from his pen would soon be forthcoming to answer Smith and Ingersoll. Trumbull Papers, State Lib., III, pt. 2, 191a.

41. *Conn. Jour.,* April 8, 1774, pp. 1-2; Boutell, *Sherman,* 78.

42. Anon., *Civil Prudence Recommended to the Thirteen United Colonies of North-America* (Norwich, 1776), 10. "It seems to be a grief to some of better fortune," the author of this pamphlet caustically observed, "that these [poor farmers] cannot be detained and shut in among them for slaves, to improve their land, etc. for it is the multitude of inhabitants that makes rents high, and the produce of the land valuable." See also Benjamin Trumbull's defense in the *Conn. Courant,* April 19, 1774, p. 3; April 26, pp. 3-4.

43. *Conn. Courant,* April 26, 1774, pp. 3-4. In explanation of his proposed plan that Connecticut expand to the Mississippi, Silas Deane declared "that Seven, or Eight hundred Miles Extent of the finest Country and happiest climate on the Globe is really worth their having, even if it should cost a few Thousands in the pursuit." Deane to W. S. Johnson, Feb. 7, 1774, Johnson Papers.

44. "Connecticutensis," *Conn. Courant,* March 8, 1774, p. 1; "To the Candid Public," Supplement, March 1, 1774. Silas Deane denounced the anti-expansionist party as "ignorant partisans and incendiaries." Deane to Gov. Trumbull, April 11, 1774, Trumbull Papers, State Lib., III, pt. 2, 192ab.

45. *Conn. Courant,* March 15, 1774, p. 1.

46. *Ibid.,* April 5, 1774, p. 4.

47. *Ibid.,* March 29, 1774, p. 1.

48. *Ibid.,* April 5, 1774, p. 4. See also "Join or Die," *New London Gaz.,* April 8, 1774, p. 3.

49. Trumbull, *History,* II, 479. According to Trumbull "the malcontents were for turning out the gentlemen of the upper house and forming a new assembly." See also Benjamin Trumbull to Gov. Trumbull, April 8, 1774, Trumbull Papers, State Lib., III, pt. 2, 191a.

50. *Conn. Courant,* March 8, 1774, p. 1; *New London Gaz.,* March 11, 1774, p. 2.

51. *Conn. Courant,* March 8, 1774, p. 3; March 22, p. 3; see also Fairfield Revolutionary Records, 1; Stamford Rev. Recs., 1; Redding Rev. Recs., 1, transcripts, State Lib.

52. New Haven Inhabitants, *To the Select-Men. . . ,* broadside, March 11, 1774, N. Y. Pub. Lib.; *Conn. Courant,* March 15, 1774, p. 2. Professor Daggett of Yale expressed his dismay to Gov. Trumbull at New Haven's going along with the "Cabal." Daggett to Trumbull, March 14, 1774, Trumbull Papers, State Lib., III, pt. 2, 187ab. Joseph Trumbull was equally upset at New Haven's "very extraordinary" position. Joseph to Jonathan Trumbull, March 19, 1774, Trumbull Papers, Personal.

53. *Conn. Courant,* March 8, 1774, p. 3; March 22, p. 3.

54. Silas Deane to Gov. Trumbull, March 21, April 11, 1774, Trumbull Papers, State Lib., III, pt. 2, 186ab, 192ab.

55. Deane to Joseph Trumbull, April 11, 1774, Joseph Trumbull Papers.

56. Deane to Gov. Trumbull, April 11, 1774, Trumbull Papers, State Lib., III, pt. 2, 186ab.

57. "Many" announced on March 22 that the convention would be postponed for one week in order to allow more time for additional towns to choose delegates: *Conn. Courant,* March 22, 1774, p. 3. "The Alarm" said that the 23 towns sent a total of 45 delegates. *Ibid.,* April 5, p. 4.

58. The italics are mine. Trumbull, *History,* II, 474-78.

59. "The Alarm," *Conn. Courant,* April 5, 1774, p. 4.

60. *Ibid.*

61. Julian P. Boyd, *The Susquehannah Company: Connecticut's Experiment in Expansion,* Conn. Tercentenary Commission, *Publs.,* 34 (1935), 38. Litchfield, Woodbury, and Derby, however, turned down the remonstrance although they had sent delegates to Middletown. Samuel Gray to Gov. Trumbull, April 30, 1774, Trumbull Papers, State Lib., III, pt. 2, 199a.

62. Redding Rev. Recs., 2, transcripts, State Lib.

63. Fairfield Rev. Recs., 1-2; Stamford Rev. Recs., 2; see also Goshen Rev. Recs. (Litchfield Co.), 1, transcripts, State Lib.

64. *Conn. Jour.,* April 15, 1774, p. 3; April 22, p. 3; April 29, p. 4. The conservative writer in the issue of April 22 attacked the local clergy for the prominent part they had taken against the remonstrance. The ministers "were so very modest," he charged, "as to crowd them-

selves into the meeting and scratch against the Remonstrance." He hoped that "the people of this town are not as yet so horribly priest ridden, as to tamely sacrifice their interest, rights, and privileges to gratify the views and designs of an interested set of men."

65. *Conn. Courant,* April 5, 1774, p. 1; *Conn. Jour.,* April 8, 1774, p. 2.

66. *Conn. Courant,* April 26, 1774, p. 4.

67. Proprietors Records, Susquehannah Company, 93, Conn. Hist. Soc.

68. The entire incident may be traced in the following letters: Silas Deane to Joseph Trumbull, April 11, 1774; E. Dyer to Trumbull, April 19, 1774; Timothy Greene to Trumbull, April 21, 1774, Joseph Trumbull Papers.

69. April 25, 1774, Johnson Papers.

70. Johnson to Dr. Smith, *ibid*.

71. "Colonist," *New London Gaz.,* April 22, 1774, p. 1; reprinted in the *Conn. Courant,* May 3, 1774, p. 1. The latter date was but one week before the Assembly was scheduled to meet.

72. Trumbull, *History,* II, 479.

73. E. Dyer to Joseph Trumbull, April 19, 1774, Joseph Trumbull Papers.

74. Joseph Trumbull to Jonathan Trumbull, April 17, 1774, Trumbull Papers, State Lib., III, pt. 2, 196ab. On the other hand, Saybrook returned "as usual more than half" its votes to former Governor Fitch.

75. Five hundred men were present at the election and Trumbull and Dyer "had every vote." Samuel Gray to Jonathan Trumbull, April 30, 1774, *ibid.,* III, pt. 2, 199a. See also Boyd, *Susquehannah Company,* 38-39.

76. E. Dyer to Joseph Trumbull, April 19, 1774, Joseph Trumbull Papers; MS William Williams Diary, Jan.-April 1774, entry for Monday, April 11, L.C.

77. Silas Deane to Joseph Trumbull, April 11, 1774, Joseph Trumbull Papers.

78. Hartford Votes, II, 247, 248.

79. Fragment dated May 13, 1774, MS Votes for Governor and Assistants. Surprisingly enough, Gov. Trumbull's speech of thanks upon his re-election gives no hint of the political battle just concluded. Trumbull Papers, State Lib., XX, pt. 1, 82a, 84ab.

80. *Conn. Courant,* May 31, 1774, p. 4.

81. Conn. Arch., Susq., I, 55; *Conn. Col. Recs.,* XIV, 261-62.

82. Johnson thought that the passage of the Quebec Act destroyed the Susquehannah claims by "annexing the Country in dispute to the Prove. of Canada." Johnson to R. Jackson, Aug. 30, 1774, Johnson Papers. Pennsylvania's proprietors, however, continued to push their petition against Connecticut's claim in the Privy Council. On that and Connecticut's reaction see Gov. Trumbull to W. S. Johnson, Dec. 17, 1774, *ibid;* Johnson to Gov. Trumbull, Aug. 30, 1774, and Trumbull to T. Life, March 24, 1775, Trumbull Papers, Political.

83. Johnson to R. Jackson, Aug. 30, 1774, Johnson Papers. For the later history of Connecticut's western claims see Groce, *Johnson,* 113-17, 123-27.

CHAPTER NINE

1. Shaw to P. Vandervoort, Oct. 22, 1773, Shaw, *Letter Book,* 251; W. S. Johnson to R. Jackson, Nov. 5, 1773, Johnson Papers. Samuel Avery blamed the merchants for getting "some choice Spirits to stir up those Lunatick Infatuated people which are ready to believe all that is said to them." "Anti Alarm," Avery Papers.

2. See *Conn. Courant* and *New London Gaz.* for Nov., Dec., 1773, Jan. 1774.

3. *Conn. Courant,* Dec. 14, 1773, p. 3.

4. *Ibid.,* Dec. 21, 1773, p. 1.

5. *Ibid.,* Dec. 28, 1773, p. 4.

6. Johnson to the Bishop of Oxford, Jan. 15, 1774, Johnson Papers.

7. *God Brings About His Holy and Wise Purpose or Decree* (Hartford, 1774), 23.

8. Hempstead, *Diary,* 711.

9. *Conn. Courant,* Feb. 15, 1774, p. 3; Feb. 22, p. 2.

10. *New London Gaz.,* Feb. 18, 1774, p. 1.

11. *Ibid.,* March 11, 1774, p. 2.

12. [?] to Talcott, March [29?], Conn. Papers.

13. *New London Gaz.*, March 18, 1774, p. 3 and comment in *Conn. Courant,* March 29, 1774, p. 3.

14. Samuel Lockwood, *Civil Rulers an Ordinance of God for Good to Mankind* (New London, 1774), 8.

15. *Ibid.,* 10-11, 16-22.

16. *Ibid.,* 39.

17. Nicholas Ray to Johnson, April 4, 1774, Johnson Papers.

18. Several months later the Rev. Ebenezer Baldwin pointed out to the people of western Connecticut that charters "are now taken away without so much as a pretence of law; without so much as a trial, or hearing of the party concerned, by the almost omnipotent power claimed by the British parliament. . . . If charters," he asked, "if the solemn promises of kings are to be thus trifled with, what security can we have in any thing?" "An Appendix Stating the Grievances the Colonies labour under from several late Acts of the British Parliament," 48, 65, in Samuel Sherwood, *A Sermon Containing Scriptural Instructions to Civil Rulers, and all Free-born Subjects* (New Haven, 1774).

19. Deane to Samuel H. Parsons, April 13, 1774, *Deane Corres.,* 130-31.

20. *Conn. Courant,* May 24, 1774, p. 3; June 7, p. 1; June 14, p. 3; *New London Gaz.,* June 24, 1774, p. 1. Under the pen-name of "Cato Americanus," William Williams prepared an article for the newspapers praising Boston's radicals and promising universal support to the town. See draft copy, To the Inhabitants of Boston, dated June 1774, Williams Papers.

21. Samuel Adams to S. Deane, May 18, 1774, in Harry A. Cushing, *The Writings of Samuel Adams* (New York, 1904-8), III, 116-17.

22. Deane to Adams, May 26, 1774, Adams Papers; Deane to E. Silliman, June 13, 1774, in Worthington C. Ford, ed., *Correspondence and Journals of S. B. Webb* (New York, 1893-94), I, 29; see also 27-28.

23. The resolutions of Connecticut's towns were extensively reported in the press: see *Conn. Courant, New London Gaz., Conn. Jour.,* for May, June, July and August. Extracts from the town records may also be found in the transcripts in the Connecticut State Library: see, for example, Killingly Rev. Recs., 1-3; Preston Rev. Recs., 1-2; Norwich Rev. Recs., 1-2.

24. *Conn. Courant,* May 24, 1774, p. 3; *Norwich Packet,* June 2,

1774, p. 3; Peter Force, ed., *American Archives,* 4th ser. (Washington, 1837-46), I, 336.

25. Gen. Assoc., *Recs.,* 75-77; Force, *Amer. Arch.,* 4th ser., I, 442-43.

26. Stiles, *Diary,* I, 441, entry of May 26, 1774.

27. *Conn. Col. Recs.,* XIV, 347-49; see also *Conn. Courant,* June 21, 1774, p. 1.

28. Conn. Arch., Rev. Ser., I, 46a-d; *Conn. Col. Recs.,* XIV, 349-50.

29. Conn. Arch., Rev. Ser., I, 56ab; *Conn. Col. Recs.,* XIV, 324 and *n.* See also *Conn. Courant,* July 19, 1774, p. 3; Aug. 2, p. 3; Aug. 9, p. 3.

30. A letter from Silas Deane to W. S. Johnson described the events at the meeting that chose Sherman and Trumbull. Eight men, "schemers too," were present. As soon as an eastern man was nominated it was urged that a western man be designated to balance the representation. When Sherman was first nominated four committeemen favored him and an equal number opposed him. Finally Sherman and Trumbull were chosen. Deane asked Johnson to do what he could to keep Sherman from attending the Congress. See Deane to Johnson, Aug. 4, 1774, Johnson Papers.

31. William Williams had his doubts about Deane's Whiggism. He warned Samuel Adams that Deane was "not genuine," and that he was likely to place his private interests ahead of his patriotism. Williams to Adams, July 30, 1774, Adams Papers.

32. Johnson to N. Rogers, Jan. 4, 1769, Johnson Papers.

33. Johnson to R. Jackson, Aug. 30, 1774, *ibid.*

34. Johnson to R. Jackson, Aug. 30, 1774; to B. Latrobe, July 25, 1774, *ibid.*

35. Johnson to R. Jackson, Aug. 30, 1774, *ibid.* Jackson had written to Johnson urging him and "other discreet persons earnestly to dissuade" the colony "from taking any part in the outrages." April 5, 1774, *ibid.*

36. Beach to Johnson, Sept. 8, 1774; Deane to Johnson, Aug. 1, 1774, *ibid.* On the reaction of the eastern sections of the colony to Johnson's declination see Thomas Mumford's letter to Silas Deane, Sept. 3, 1774, *Deane Corres.,* 147.

37. Suffield's Separatist minister, Israel Holly, had predicted that the "calamity" precipitated by the Boston tea party would be made worse by "divided sentiments among us concerning what is right and best for us to do, while some take one side the question and some the other." *God Brings about his Holy and Wise Purpose or Decree,* 23.

38. *New London Gaz.,* Feb. 25, 1774, p. 1; July 29, p. 2; *Conn. Jour.,* June 17, 1774, p. 4; June 24, p. 4; *Conn. Courant,* June 21, 1774, p. 2; July 12, p. 4.

39. See, for example, the resolutions of the following towns: Farmington, *Conn. Courant,* May 24, 1774, p. 3; Norwich, *ibid.,* June 14, p. 3; Windham, *New London Gaz.,* July 1, p. 3; Lebanon, *Conn. Courant,* June 7, p. 3; and *New London Gaz.,* July 29, p. 1. Gov. Trumbull's town, Lebanon, expressed its wish for continued "constitutional Dependance" and declared that "nothing but a perservering Design . . . to deprive us of the Freedom which we have earned . . . can ever render us willing to become . . . independant." After the town meeting on June 21 the Whigs of Canaan, Litchfield County, retired to the local tavern where they drank several "loyal and constitutional Toasts." But they indicated in other ways that "Liberty and Property were the darling Objects for which, in Concurrence with all America, they would chearfully sacrifice both their Lives and Fortunes." *Conn. Courant,* July 12, 1774, p. 3.

40. *Conn. Courant,* Aug. 23, 1774, p. 1; Stiles, *Windsor,* I, pt. 2, 628.

41. Charles H. Levermore, *The Republic of New Haven* (Baltimore, 1886), 209; *Conn. Courant,* May 31, 1774, p. 4.

42. *Conn. Courant,* May 31, 1774, p. 4; Gipson, *Ingersoll,* 328-29. The Tory Abiathar Camp later claimed that New Haven's Loyalists "opposed the choosing of committees." Transcripts of the Books and Papers of the Commission of Enquiry into the Losses and Services of the American Loyalists . . . preserved amongst the Audit Office Records in the Public Record Office of England 1783-1790, XII, 29, N. Y. Pub. Lib., hereafter cited as Loyalist Transcripts.

43. *Norwich Packet,* July 14, 1774, p. 3.

44. Ingersoll boasted that Chandler's success was due, in part, to the fact that Chandler had "so openly" kept "my Company last Summer." Jared to Jonathan Ingersoll, Oct. 24, 1774, "Ingersoll Papers," 448. Chandler won despite "John Hampden's" appeal to the freemen to elect only those who were "warmly engaged to preserve our civil and religious principles." *Conn. Courant,* Sept. 19, 1774, p. 3.

45. *Conn. Courant,* June 28, 1774, p. 3. Mosely's description of his efforts is in the Loyalist Transcripts, XII, 672.

46. *Conn. Jour.,* Sept. 9, 1774, p. 3. Silas Deane also complained that there were too many preachers of prudence and caution in the

colony. See the draft of an article by Deane under the pseudonym "Cassius," Ford, *Webb Corres.,* I, 30-32.

47. Morgan to Joseph Trumbull, Sept. 3, 1774, Joseph Trumbull Papers.

48. Fitch died on July 18 at the age of 74. His passing was ignored by the colonial government. The radical *New London Gazette* merely announced the fact with no obituary in the issue of July 22, 1774, p. 3. The *Conn. Journal* had a fuller and more complimentary account, July 22, 1774, p. 3. See also Moses Dickinson, *A Sermon Delivered at the Funeral of . . . Thomas Fitch.* Dickinson declared that Fitch "bore his dismission with great patience, and resignation. I never heard him complain of the ingratitude, or injustice of the people, in their conduct toward him. After this he lived a retired life, and employed his time chiefly in reading." See p. 22. As late as April 5, 1774, however, Richard Jackson wrote W. S. Johnson that Fitch's chances of getting at least one of two jobs in the imperial service were good. Johnson Papers.

49. *New London Gaz.,* July 29, 1774, pp. 1-2; Sept. 30, p. 4; *Conn. Courant,* Sept. 12, 1774, p. 3.

50. Sherwood, *Sermon Containing Scriptural Instructions.* Sherwood was a Congregational pastor in Fairfield. The Rev. Ebenezer Baldwin of Danbury wrote another pamphlet that was printed as an appendix to Sherwood's sermon. *Ibid.,* 43-81.

CHAPTER TEN

1. *Norwich Packet,* July 14, 1774, p. 3.

2. Windham Rev. Recs., 5-6; Preston Rev. Recs., 6-8, transcripts, State Lib.

3. *New London Gaz.,* July 8, 1774, p. 2; Sept. 30, p. 3.

4. *Conn. Courant,* Aug. 23, 1774, p. 1; Sept. 26, p. 4.

5. *New London Gaz.,* Nov. 11, 1774, p. 3; Mansfield Rev. Recs., 5, transcripts, State Lib.

6. E. Le Roy Pond, *The Tories of Chippeny Hill, Connecticut* (New York, 1909), 47.

7. *New London Gaz.,* Sept. 30, 1774, p. 3.

8. *Ibid.,* Sept. 23, 1774, p. 3.

9. *Ibid.,* Sept. 9, 1774, p. 3.

10. Trumbull Papers, State Lib., IV, pt. 1, 23; *ibid.,* doc. 12; see also Ingersoll's letter to Jonathan Ingersoll, Oct. 24, 1774, in which he blamed "Parson [Benjamin] Trumbull" for sending "my Treasonable principles and Conduct to the good people of the East." "Ingersoll Papers," 449; Gipson, *Ingersoll,* 329-31. See also T. Morgan to Joseph Trumbull, Sept. 3, 1774, Joseph Trumbull Papers.

11. *New London Gaz.,* July 8, 1774, p. 3; see also the affidavit of Caleb Scott and Green's deposition, Trumbull Papers, State Lib., IV, pt. 1, 13, 14. According to the affidavit, when Green left Norwich the crowd "beat the drum . . . shouted and huzza'd and following Mr. Green they pelted him for a considerable distance thro the town with much rage and violence." The fact that Green was engaged in a debt-collecting trip did not dispose the radicals to be more lenient with him.

12. Gage to Trumbull, July 22, 1774, Trumbull Papers, State Lib., IV, pt. 1, 15.

13. Hezekiah Bissell, Benjamin Lothrop, Ebenezer Backus, and Timothy Larrabee to Gov. Trumbull, Aug. 5, 1774, *ibid.,* 16a-d. These Whig leaders maintained that the whole affair was a private matter and as such "does not concern Government any more than any other private Quarrel."

14. Trumbull to Gage, Aug. 10, 1774, *ibid.,* 17.

15. *Conn. Jour.,* Supplement, Aug. 19, 1774; Larned, *Windham County,* II, 129-30; Larned, "A Revolutionary Boycott," *Connecticut Quarterly,* 1 (1895), 153-54.

16. *Norwich Packet,* July 21, 1774, p. 3; July 28, p. 3.

17. *New London Gaz.,* Aug. 12, 1774, p. 2. See also *Norwich Packet,* Aug. 11, 1774, p. 2; Aug. 18, pp. 1, 4; Aug. 25, pp. 3, 4.

18. *Conn. Courant,* Oct. 17, 1774, pp. 1-2.

19. *Ibid.,* Sept. 19, 1774, p. 2. For a Tory version see Peters Papers, I, 42.

20. See Peters, A Narrative, Peters Papers, I, 3. When the rumor reached Hebron on Sept. 4, 1774, that violence had broken out in Boston, Peters urged the people to stay calm, denounced the reports as lies, and stated that even if they were true "you must not take up arms . . . it is high Treason . . . therefore if you die—die like Subjects at Home, and not go to Boston to be Hanged for Rebels—the church

People were Quieted—the Puritans (alias) Sons of Liberty took up Arms, Set off for Boston." Peters was notoriously loose with the facts and his writings must therefore be used with the utmost caution.

21. Peters Papers, I, 3; Force, *Amer. Arch.,* 4th ser., I, 711-12.

22. There are several contemporary accounts of this incident. See Stiles, *Diary,* I, 466-67, entry of Oct. 27, 1774; *Norwich Packet,* Sept. 8, 1774, p. 3; *New London Gaz.,* Sept. 16, 1774, p. 1; Trumbull Papers, State Lib., IV, pt. 1, 39a-c. Peters' versions are in the Peters Papers, I, 3, 72, 96; II, 73; VIII, 22, 39. Peters accused the governor of being behind the mob, and of saying that he was the servant of the people "and could not make the People obey him." The Tory rector also claimed that he had vainly sought the aid of the Superior Court at Hartford, the King's attorney, and the New Haven magistrates. A fantastic atrocity story about the incident was written by a refugee Connecticut Loyalist who fled to Canada after the war. William Bates, *Kingston and the Loyalists of 1783* (St. John, N.B., 1889), 6. Trumbull gave his own account of what took place in a letter to the Fairfield Whig, Thaddeus Burr, Oct. 24, 1774. The governor claimed that Peters had admitted to him "That the Committee treated him with Decency and Respect—that it was not his Intention to complain of any injury they have done him." Trumbull Papers, State Lib., XX., pt. 1, 95a. Burr had warned Trumbull, Oct. 13, that Peters' story might harm the colony if it got to England. *Ibid.,* IV, pt. 1, 29ab. Trumbull therefore sent a copy of his version of the affair to Connecticut's agent, Thomas Life, Jan. 9, 1775. *Ibid.,* XX, 98. See also *ibid.,* IV, 46a-d; Trumbull to Silas Deane, Nov. 14, 1774, Trumbull Papers, Political. Deane had been involved in the first affray with Peters.

23. Peters Papers, I, 2.

24. Tyler to Peters, Oct. 5, 1774, *ibid.,* I, 4; see also [?] to Peters, n. d., *ibid.,* I, 2.

25. Tyler to Peters, Oct. 5, 1774, *ibid.,* I, 4. Although Peters failed to burn Tyler's letter he recognized the prudence of destroying dangerous documents. See Peters' letter to his mother, Sept. 28, 1774, copy in the hand of E. Moseley, Lane Papers. The trouble that befell Peters was an object lesson to Jared Ingersoll on why not to include politics in his own letters. Jared to Jonathan Ingersoll, Oct. 24, 1774, "Ingersoll Papers," 448.

26. Jonathan to Samuel Peters, Dec. 26, 1774, Peters Papers, I, 10. These incidents did not improve the position of the Episcopal church

in the colony. Once within the safety of the British lines, Peters, in letters to his mother and Dr. Auchmuty in New York, described in lurid and exaggerated detail the violence that the Whigs had wreaked upon him and his church. Predicting "Hanging Work" as soon as additional British troops got to America, he requested that the other Anglican ministers in Connecticut collect every bit of information "touching Mobs and Insults offered the Clergy of our Churches or her Members." These letters of the refugee Tory were intercepted and published in the Connecticut press. The Whigs were, of course, infuriated. Six Anglican ministers, Richard Mansfield, James Scovil, Samuel Andrews, Bela Hubbard, Abraham Jarvis, and Ebenezer Kneeland felt it necessary to dissociate themselves from Peters. They therefore denied that they shared his views and rejected all responsibility for his actions. Their disavowal was supported by several politically prominent Whigs who stated that they believed the Episcopal ministers were entitled to the personal security and safety that "every other good subject" and "friend to his country" deserved. See *Norwich Packet,* Oct. 13, 1774, p. 3; copies of letters from Peters to his mother, Sept. 28, 1774, and to Dr. Auchmuty, Oct. 1, 1774, both in the hand of Ebenezer Moseley; Moseley to Gov. Trumbull, Oct. 8, 1774, Lane Papers. Abraham Jarvis disavowed Peters' views in the *Conn. Jour.,* Oct. 21, 1774, p. 4. The other five clergymen joined Jarvis in repudiating Peters in the next issue, Oct. 28, 1774, p. 1. See also W. S. Johnson to T. Burr, Oct. 28, 1774, Johnson Papers. After the war Tyler and Hubbard explained to Peters why the ministers had taken these measures. See Tyler to Peters, Jan. 9, 1784; Hubbard to same, Nov. 28, 1784, Peters Papers, II, 2, 22.

27. Fairfield County Court Records 1773-79, pp. 166, 243; Superior Court Records, XVIII, Fairfield Nov. 1774 session, n.p., State Lib.; see also *Conn. Jour.,* Oct. 10, 1774, p. 2.

28. Jared to Jonathan Ingersoll, Oct. 25, 1774, "Ingersoll Papers," 449; see also Peters Papers, I, 3.

29. Trumbull to J. Phelps, Sept. 8, 1774; to J. Spencer, Sept. 22, 1774, Trumbull Papers, State Lib., XX, pt. 1, 89d, 90; Deputy-Gov. Griswold to Gov. Trumbull, Aug. 20, 1774, *ibid.,* IV, pt. 1, 20a; J. Spencer to Trumbull, Sept. 14, 1774, *ibid.,* IV, 24.

30. Webb to Silas Deane, Oct. 10, 1774, Ford, *Webb Corres.,* I, 41-42; T. Hosmer to Deane, Sept. 4, 1774, and Simon Deane to Silas Deane, Oct. 15, 1774, *Deane Corres.,* 156, 191.

31. Spencer to Gov. Trumbull, Sept. 14, 1774, Trumbull Papers, State Lib., IV, 24.

32. New Milford Rev. Recs., 7, transcripts, State Lib.; *New London Gaz.,* Oct. 28, 1774, p. 2; Oct. 21, 1774, p. 1.

33. Peters Papers, VIII, 3, 24; see also docs. 46, 52, and Peters to Dr. Auchmuty, Oct. 1, 1774, Lane Papers.

34. *Conn. Jour.,* Supplement, Aug. 19, 1774; Aug. 25, p. 4; Nov. 18, p. 3; *New London Gaz.,* Aug. 5, 1774, p. 1; Aug. 26, p. 2; Oct. 7, p. 4; Oct. 14, p. 2; *Norwich Packet,* Aug. 25, 1774, p. 4; Nov. 24, p. 4.

35. Simon Deane had written to Silas Deane, Oct. 15, 1774, "the People seem to be in high spirits." *Deane Corres.,* 191.

36. *New London Gaz.,* Aug. 19, 1774, p. 1; *Norwich Packet,* Aug. 18, 1774, pp. 1, 4.

37. *New London Gaz.,* Nov. 11, 1774, p. 1; see also the piece by the radical "One who pities the Tories," *ibid.,* Aug. 12, 1774, p. 1.

38. *Norwich Packet,* Aug. 25, 1774, p. 3; *New London Gaz.,* Aug. 12, 1774, p. 2.

39. *New London Gaz.,* July 8, 1774, p. 1.

40. *Ibid.,* Sept. 30, 1774, p. 4.

41. Williams to Samuel Adams, July 30, 1774, Adams Papers.

42. Leffingwell to Silas Deane, Aug. 22, 1774, *Deane Corres.,* 140.

43. Hosmer to Deane, Sept. 4, 1774, *ibid.,* 155. For the resolutions of Connecticut's town meetings in the late summer see, for example, Coventry Rev. Recs., 1-5; Stafford Rev. Recs., 2-5; Ashford Rev. Recs., 1-3; Windham Rev. Recs., 8, transcripts, State Lib.

44. Stiles, *Diary,* I, 456; *Conn. Jour.,* Sept. 9, 1774, p. 3.

45. Gage to Dartmouth, Aug. 27, 1774, in Carter, *Gage Corres.,* I, 366-68.

46. Gage to Dartmouth, Sept. 2, 1774, *ibid.,* 370.

47. *New London Gaz.,* Sept. 16, 1774, p. 3; *Deane Corres.,* 161-62; *Huntington Papers,* Conn. Hist. Soc., *Colls.,* 20 (1923), 215-17.

48. Gage to Dartmouth, Sept. 12, 1774, in Carter, *Gage Corres.,* I, 374. Examples of the extra military precautions that towns took in the fall months may be seen in Wethersfield Rev. Recs., 2; Colchester Rev. Recs., 3; Lyme Rev. Recs., 3; Preston Rev. Recs., 3, transcripts, State Lib.

49. Gage to Dartmouth, Sept. 25, 1774, in Carter, *Gage Corres.,* I, 377. One of Connecticut's Tories later laughed at the colony's panicky reaction to the rumor. He found that "The Inhabitants of all the Towns That were Thus alarmed, were filled with Dreadfull Supprise; some

Vomiting out Imprecations; Some marched off, without any arms, Some Skulking, To avoid Danger, others Running This, and That way; Some praying, others laughing; Some Crying, others Curssing; and for Some hours a Continued Confusion Took place." Tiffany, American Colonies, bk. 4, p. 21. Peters' description of the event was filled with the customary amount of venom. According to him the Connecticut "Puritans (alias) Sons of Liberty took up Arms, Set off for Boston—cursing General Gage, King George 3rd—Lord North, Lord Bishops and their damnable Curates who teach nonresistance and many more such words." Peters Papers, I, 3.

50. Hosmer to Silas Deane, Sept. 4, 1774, *Deane Corres.*, 154.

51. Williams to Samuel Adams, July 30, 1774, Adams Papers; also in Boston Committee of Correspondence, Bancroft Transcripts, N. Y. Pub. Lib. See also *Norwich Packet*, Sept. 15, 1774, p. 4.

52. *Deane Corres.*, 157-61.

53. G. Saltonstall to S. Deane, Sept. 5, 1774, *ibid.*, 151-52; *Conn. Courant*, Aug. 23, 1774, p. 3; Sept. 19, p. 2. Israel Putnam, Pomfret's leading patriot, believed that non-consumption agreements were absolutely necessary. Putnam to Gov. Trumbull, Sept. 11, 1774, Trumbull Papers, State Lib., XX, pt. 1, 88a.

54. *Norwich Packet,* Sept. 22, 1774, p. 1. At the New Milford town meeting, Sept. 20, 1774, the inhabitants declared their "harts full of Loyalty and duty to our rightful Sovereign," but at the same time expressed their "warmest desire to hold Injoy and transmit inviolable to the Latest Posterity our Sacred and Inestimable Charter rights and privileges." New Milford Rev. Recs., 5-7; see also Mansfield Rev. Recs., 4-5, transcripts, State Lib.

55. Trumbull Papers, State Lib., XX, pt. 1, 94a-c.

56. *Conn. Col. Recs.*, XIV, 327-28.

57. *Ibid.*, 343, 346.

58. Webb to Silas Deane, Oct. 10, 1774, *Deane Corres.*, 188.

59. Deane to Samuel Adams, Nov. 13, 1774, Adams Papers.

60. Woodbury Rev. Recs., 23-24; Derby Rev. Recs., 1; Wallingford Rev. Recs., 1; Guilford Rev. Recs., 1-2; Branford Rev. Recs., 1, transcripts, State Lib.; see also Hartford Town Votes, II, 250; *Conn. Jour.*, Nov. 18, 1774, p. 3.

61. Stiles, *Diary*, I, 509; *Conn. Courant*, Jan. 30, 1775, p. 1; *New London Gaz.*, Feb. 3, 1775, p. 3; Feb. 17, p. 3; March 3, p. 3; *Conn. Jour.*, Jan. 4, 1775, p. 3; Feb. 8, p. 2; March 1, p. 2.

62. Stamford Rev. Recs., 2-4, transcripts, State Lib.; Force, *Amer. Arch.,* 4th ser., I, 827-28.

63. *Conn. Jour.,* Nov. 4, 1774, p. 3; Dec. 21, p. 1; Feb. 2, 1775, p. 3; Stratford Rev. Recs., 1-2; Norwalk Rev. Recs., 1, transcripts, State Lib. See also Hall, *Norwalk Historical Records,* 127; Force, *Amer. Arch.,* 4th ser., I, 1038-39, 1075; Fairfield Rev. Recs., 4-5. Fairfield had voted to aid Boston as early as September 20; see p. 2 of the Fairfield records.

64. Force, *Amer. Arch.,* 4th ser., I, 1038-39; *Conn. Jour.,* Dec. 21, 1774, p. 1.

65. Webb to Silas Deane, Oct. 10, 1774, in Ford, *Webb Corres.,* I, 41; Williams to Adams, Jan. 10, 1775, Williams Papers.

66. Stiles, *Diary,* I, 484, entry of Nov. 17, 1774.

67. According to the census of 1774 there were 335 males between the ages of 20-70 in the town. *Conn. Col. Recs.,* XIV, 488.

68. Ridgefield Rev. Recs., 1-3, transcripts, State Lib. Jared Ingersoll was not surprised to find the Ridgefield townsmen "speak their mind plainly and not in parables." Jared to Jonathan Ingersoll, Feb. 11, 1775, "Ingersoll Papers," 452.

69. For the proceedings of the Fairfield and Litchfield County conventions see *New London Gaz.,* March 3, 1775, p. 3; Trumbull Papers, State Lib., IV, pt. 1, 63; *Conn. Jour.,* March 1, 1775, p. 2.

70. Tories in Newtown, Danbury, Redding, New Milford, and Litchfield participated in these meetings. See the following: complaint of the Newtown Grand Jurors, Aug. 1776, in Fairfield Superior Court Papers 1770-79, State Lib.; *Conn. Jour.,* March 8, 1775, p. 1; *New London Gaz.,* March 3, 1775, p. 3; Force, *Amer. Arch.,* 4th ser., I, 1215-16, 1258-60, 1270.

71. R. Sterry to J. Huntington, Dec. 17, 1774, Lane Papers; *Conn. Courant,* Jan. 30, 1775, p. 4; April 3, p. 3; *New London Gaz.,* Feb. 10, 1775, p. 3; April 21, p. 3; Farmington Rev. Recs., 5-6, transcripts, State Lib.

72. Atwater, *New Haven,* 42.

73. *Conn. Courant,* March 6, 1775, p. 3; Jared to Jonathan Ingersoll, March 10, 1775, "Ingersoll Papers," 453. See also Ebenezer to Joshua Huntington, March 31, 1775, Lane Papers.

74. *Conn. Courant,* Feb. 20, 1775, p. 3; Force, *Amer. Arch.,* 4th ser., I, 1236. After the war Joseph Lyon, a Fairfield Tory, claimed that because of his opposition to Congress he was "much persecuted" by the mob and that he had been "obliged to hide in the Woods." See A.

Fraser, archivist, *Second Report of the Bureau of Archives for the Province of Ontario for 1904,* 225-26, hereafter cited as Ontario Bur. Arch., *Report for 1904.*

75. Force, *Amer. Arch.,* 4th ser., I, 1238-39.

76. Ridgefield Rev. Recs., 3, transcripts, State Lib.

77. Wales to William Williams, Feb. 4, 1775, Williams Papers. See also Williams' article signed "Americanus," addressed to Gage, April 7, 1775, *ibid.*

78. *Conn. Courant,* Jan. 23, 1775, p. 3.

79. Samuel H. Parsons to Silas Deane, Feb. 28, 1775, *Deane Corres.,* 204; see also Dexter, *Biog. Sketches,* III, 545.

80. See Wales' letter to Williams, Feb. 4, 1775, Williams Papers, for the maneuvering that preceded the calling of the Assembly. The special session adjourned on March 10. *Conn. Col. Recs.,* XIV, 388. See also Gage to Dartmouth, Feb. 20, 1775, Carter, *Gage Corres.,* I, 393.

81. Trumbull Papers, State Lib., XX, pt. 1, 101a-c. As late as Dec. 17, 1774, Trumbull had hoped that a special session would not be needed, but he admitted that an emergency might make it necessary. Trumbull to W. S. Johnson, Dec. 17, 1774, Johnson Papers.

82. *Conn. Col. Recs.,* XIV, 391-92.

83. Conn. Arch., Rev. Ser., I, 394; *Conn. Col. Recs.,* XIV, 392-93. Ebenezer Hazard applauded this step. "They deserve punishment," he wrote to Silas Deane, April 7, 1775, "for their daring opposition to Government." *Deane Corres.,* 213.

84. Shaw to P. Vandervoort, April 8, 1775, Shaw, *Letter Book,* 270.

CHAPTER ELEVEN

1. Towns continued to increase their stock of munitions. See, for example, Bolton Rev. Recs., 9 (Jan. 16, 1775); Waterbury Rev. Recs., 3 (Dec. 22, 1774); New London Rev. Recs., 10 (Jan. 27, 1775), transcripts, State Lib.

2. Trumbull to the Earl of Dartmouth, March 1775, *Conn. Col. Recs.,* XIV, 410-11; MS copies in Trumbull Papers, State Lib., IV,

61a-d; XX, pt. 1, 102a-c. Trumbull sent a similar letter to Thomas Life, March 24, 1775, *ibid.,* XX, pt. 1, 100a-d. Wethersfield's volunteer company, in drawing up a code of regulations, April 3, 1775, also disavowed "every thought of Rebellion to his Majesty . . . or opposition to Legal Authority." *Deane Corres.,* 216-17.

3. This Tory charged that the "old leaven the Republicans" had attempted to get the Assembly to raise an army immediately. A committee composed "of the most inflammatory and the truest malignant men, who openly declared for independence" favored the plan, but the more moderate members blocked it. Force, *Amer. Arch.,* 4th ser., II, 110-11.

4. *New London Gaz.,* March 17, 1775, p. 3; see also Force, *Amer. Arch.,* 4th ser., II, 111-14. There is an undated draft of this article in the Williams Papers.

5. Conn. Misc. Papers 1740-87, n.p., Stevens Transcripts.

6. Gideon Welles to George Bancroft, Jan. 16, 1843, Conn. Papers.

7. Stiles, *Diary,* I, 540.

8. Gipson, *Ingersoll,* 337; Boardman, *Sherman,* 127-28.

9. Connecticut Committee of Correspondence to Hancock, April 21, 1775, Force, *Amer. Arch.,* 4th ser., II, 372-73.

10. The caption appeared for the last time in the issue of April 24, 1775. It had first appeared in the 493rd issue, June 7, 1774.

11. Shaw to P. Vandervoort, April 25, 1775, Shaw, *Letter Book,* 271.

12. Trumbull told the Assembly that he had not intended to call an extraordinary session, but that the events at Lexington had now made it necessary. Trumbull Papers, State Lib., XX, pt. 1, 104a. In a letter to some unknown correspondent dated April 12, 1775, the governor wrote that it had been decided not to call a special meeting of the Assembly. Trumbull Papers, Political.

13. Trumbull recommended firmness, steadiness, deliberation, and unanimity "in the most important Affair that ever came under Consideration within these Walls." Trumbull Papers, State Lib., XX, pt. 1, 104a.

14. Jonathan Trumbull Jr. to Joseph Trumbull, April 28, 1775, Gov. Joseph Trumbull Papers, IV, 452a, State Lib., hereafter cited as Joseph Trumbull Papers, State Lib.

15. *Conn. Col. Recs.,* XIV, 415-16, 417, 419.

16. *Ibid.,* 95, 346-47, 432.

17. "An Act to exempt, for a limited Time, the Persons of Debtors, from being imprisoned for Debt," *ibid.,* 435-36.

18. *Ibid.,* 434-35.

19. *Ibid.,* 439; see also 435.

20. Warren's letters are in the *Trumbull Papers,* Mass. Hist. Soc., *Colls.,* 5th ser., 10 (1888), 284-88, hereafter cited as *Trumbull Papers,* II. See also Connecticut Committee of Correspondence to John Hancock, April 21, 1775, Force, *Amer. Arch.,* 4th ser., II, 372-73; Massachusetts Provincial Congress to Gov. Trumbull, April 23, 1775, Conn. Papers.

21. *Conn. Col. Recs.,* XIV, 416.

22. Trumbull Papers, State Lib., IV, pt. 1, 76a-c; also *Conn. Col. Recs.,* IV, 441.

23. After the engagements on the 19th Gage had sent a "Circumstantial Account" of the events to Trumbull. Trumbull Papers, State Lib., IV, pt. 1, 77; see also Joseph Trumbull Papers, State Lib., V, 580a-d. On the 21st Connecticut's Committee of Correspondence recommended to Massachusetts' leaders that the American version of the fighting be sent to England immediately in order "to prevent harsh measures, and strengthen the hands of our friends in Britain." Force, *Amer. Arch.,* 4th ser., II, 372-73. See also Conn. Arch., Rev. Ser., I, 121 for evidence that the lower house favored setting up a committee to draw up an account of the battle to be sent to England.

24. Connecticut House of Representatives to the Massachusetts Committee of Safety, quoted in Stuart, *Trumbull,* 177.

25. Jonathan Trumbull Jr. to Joseph Trumbull, May 4, 1775, Joseph Trumbull Papers, State Lib., IV, 453c.

26. Jonathan Trumbull Jr. to Joseph Trumbull, May 6, 1775, *ibid.,* 452a, 454a.

27. Mansfield's deputy, Colonel Experience Storrs, entered the following note in his diary for April 27, 1775: "Bad weather for Tories in the House—yet we have some." Quoted in George A. Gilbert, "The Connecticut Loyalists," *American Historical Review,* 4 (1899), 281 *n2.*

28. "Candidus," *Norwich Packet,* April 27, 1775, p. 1.

29. The Rev. Mr. Latrobe informed Johnson that Hillsborough and several members of the Board of Trade believed that "if all thought as Dr. Johnson, we should soon be in peace and harmony." Latrobe to Johnson, March 1, 1775, Johnson Papers.

30. Johnson's comments are written on a copy of Connecticut's letter to Gage, April 28, 1775, *ibid.*

31. Jedidiah to Jabez Huntington, May 2, 1775. Huntington reported from Roxbury that the mission had "altered the Countenances of the friends of this Country, they stand amazed. . . . the Negotiation with which Doct. Johnson and Col. Wolcott is charged has thrown a Chagrin upon the leading Men here which they do not know how to throw off." Jedidiah Huntington Papers, *Huntington Papers,* 219-20. See also Joseph Warren to the Governor and Legislature of Connecticut, May 2, 1775, *Trumbull Papers,* II, 296, and Warren's letter of May 5, 1775, *ibid.,* 302.

32. Trumbull to Warren, May 4, 1775, *Trumbull Papers,* II, 301.

33. *Conn. Col. Recs.,* XIV, 416*n.* Jedidiah Huntington to Joseph Trumbull, May 23, 1775, Joseph Trumbull Papers, State Lib., II, 151a. On the day the Assembly adjourned Jonathan Trumbull Jr. wrote to Joseph Trumbull that the legislature was now sorry that it had authorized the mission. He also reassured his brother that it was impossible for Johnson or Wolcott to influence anyone in the Assembly. Letter dated May 6, 1775, Joseph Trumbull Papers, State Lib., IV, 454a. Gage's reply to Trumbull was dated May 3, 1775, *Trumbull Papers,* II, 297-301. On the 13th Gage wrote Dartmouth about the mission that had come to him. "Whether the Assembly of Connecticut," Gage said, "wishes for Conciliatory Measures time alone must evince." By September, however, Gage had reached the conclusion that the embassy had been nothing more than an example of "Treachery and Deceit." Even before Dartmouth received Gage's last letter he had denounced Connecticut's maneuver as "an instance of . . . consummate duplicity." Gage to Dartmouth, May 13, Sept. 20, 1775, and Dartmouth to Gage, July 1, 1775, Carter, *Gage Corres.,* I, 398, 416; II, 200.

34. *Conn. Courant,* March 27, 1775, p. 4.

35. Gale to Silas Deane, Feb. 27, 1775, *Deane Corres.,* 202.

36. Samuel Gray to Joseph Trumbull, May 15, 1775, Joseph Trumbull Papers.

37. Jonathan Trumbull to E. Dyer, R. Sherman, and S. Deane, May 15, 1775, Trumbull Papers, Political.

38. Williams to [?], May 6, 1775, quoted in Groce, *Johnson,* 104.

39. Groce, *Johnson,* 104; Gale to W. S. Johnson, April 12, 1775, Johnson Papers.

40. Jonathan to Joseph Trumbull, May 15, 1775, Joseph Trumbull Papers, State Lib., IV, 457c; T. Mumford to S. Deane, May 14, 1775, *Deane Corres.,* 231. Johnson's margin was 200 votes. Erastus Wolcott

got 2399 votes. A list of the returns is in Samuel Gray's letter to Joseph Trumbull, May 15, 1775, Joseph Trumbull Papers.

41. *Conn. Col. Recs.,* XV, 5; Trumbull Papers, State Lib., XX, pt. 1, 105ab.

42. Trumbull Papers, State Lib., XX, pt. 1, 109.

43. Joseph Perry, n.t., Election Sermon, May 11, 1775 (Hartford, 1775), 7, 8-9, 16, 23. See also the nature of the argument in [Moses Mather ?], *America's Appeal to the Impartial World* (Hartford, 1775). The Anglican minister Richard Mansfield, who was a Tory, described the manner in which New England's Congregational pastors and political leaders exploited religious fears at this time. "A great Deal of . . . Rancour and Bitterness," he wrote to Samuel Peters, Jan. 12, 1776, "which is fixed in the minds of the New England People against British Government is manifestly owing to the great Pains which their Teachers have taken to inflame them. The main Drift of their Prayers, their Sermons, and Harangues at Town Meetings for Twelve Months past, hath been to make People believe that his Majesty, his Ministry, and the Majority in the two Houses of Parliament have a fixed Design against the Protestant Religion and English Liberties, and to introduce Popery and Slavery." Peters Papers, I, 21.

44. *Conn. Col. Recs.,* XV, 14-15, 18-31. Connecticut's constitutional position was elaborately defined in the preamble to the articles of war. See 18-21. Towns supplemented these measures with their own military preparations. On May 1, for example, Milford voted to have the "great Guns" mounted. Milford Rev. Recs., 3, 4; Branford Rev. Recs., 2; Stafford Rev. Recs., 7, transcripts, State Lib.

45. *Conn. Col. Recs.,* XV, 39; see also *Deane Corres.,* 235, 239, 243.

46. *Conn. Col. Recs.,* XV, 54.

47. *Ibid.,* XIV, 439; XV, 51-52; *New London Gaz.,* May 26, 1775, p. 2.

48. Trumbull Papers, State Lib., XX, pt. 1, 108a.

49. J. Huntington to Joseph Trumbull, May 23, 1775; Jonathan Trumbull Jr. to Joseph Trumbull, June 3, 1775, Joseph Trumbull Papers, State Lib., II, 151a; IV, 461b.

50. Jonathan Trumbull Jr. to Joseph Trumbull, June 3, 1775, *ibid.,* IV, 461b. See also T. Mumford to Silas Deane, May 14, May 22, 1775, *Deane Corres.,* 231, 235-36.

51. Gage to Dartmouth, May 25, 1775, Carter, *Gage Corres.,* I, 401.

52. The first meeting of the Governor and Council of Safety was

held on June 7, 1775. At that meeting the Council voted to send powder to the troops at Boston and Colonel Parson's regiment was ordered to march to the town's relief. News of Bunker Hill reached Lebanon about 10 o'clock on the 19th. *Conn. Col. Recs.,* XV, 84-85, 87. For the proceedings of this first session of the Governor and Council of Safety, see 84-90. A special session of the General Assembly was convened on July 1. About 40 new members, "chiefly warm Sons of Liberty," were present. In addition to raising two new regiments and providing for their equipment the legislature busied itself with other matters pertaining to the war. T. Mumford to S. Deane, July 2, 1775, *Deane Corres.,* 277; *Conn. Col. Recs.,* XV, 92-93, 97-98; see also Gov. Trumbull's correspondence in the Trumbull Papers, Political.

53. Church to Major Cane, July 22, 1775, Nathaniel Shaw MSS 1775-82, Force Transcripts, L. C.

54. Item dated July 11, 1775, Stiles Papers, Bancroft Transcripts. Nathaniel Shaw Jr. thought that it was no longer necessary to pay duties on imports. As he put it, "Its time to lay that Matter Aside for the Present." Shaw to Wharton, July 12, 1775, Shaw, *Letter Book,* 274.

CHAPTER TWELVE

1. Even radical Windham had a few Tories. See T. Larrabee's letter to Joseph Trumbull, June 3, 1775, Joseph Trumbull Papers. Timothy Dwight claimed at a later time that in July 1775 several of his intimate friends, "gentlemen of great respectability" and "firm whigs," were "hostile and contemptuous" towards the idea of independence. Dwight, *Travels in New-England and New-York* (London, 1823), I, 130-31. Compare R. Sherman to Joseph Trumbull, July 6, 1775, Joseph Trumbull Papers, State Lib., III, 243.

2. Windham's few Tories, according to Timothy Larrabee, seemed to be "Possesd with a Doumb Devil with Vengence Setled in their Brow." He did not think they would ever "be able to Belch out there [*sic*] foam untill there mouths are filled with Gravil." To Joseph Trumbull, June 3, 1775, Joseph Trumbull Papers.

3. Perry, Election Sermon, 12.

4. *Ibid.,* 12, 22, 23.

5. *Ibid.,* 16-17.

6. *Conn. Courant,* May 29, 1775, p. 3.

7. *New London Gaz.,* Sept. 29, 1775, p. 3.

8. *Ibid.*

9. Samuel Peters to Mr. Trout, April 14, 1775, Peters Papers, I, 14.

10. Later in the Revolution a Litchfield Tory claimed that when the war began "the Populace rose so high that I then thought it best to get out of the way of them I being afraid of my Life." Conn. Arch., Rev. Ser., XIII, 306a.

11. In a letter to Samuel Peters, March 20, 1778, the Rev. Mr. Inglis referred to Connecticut's patriots as the "mobs of trumbull . . . Sons of Oliver . . . trumpeters of rebellion." Peters Papers, I, 31.

12. After the war Timothy Hierlihy explained that at first "he could not openly declare his Sentiments for fear of immediate Imprisonment." Loyalist Transcripts, XII, 51. The reference to the "searching espionage" of the committees of inspection is in Richard H. Phelps, *A History of Newgate* (Albany, 1860), 30.

13. Ashbel Humphrey of Goshen confessed to the General Assembly in 1780 that when the Revolution started he had doubted the "Equity and Propriety" of the American cause. Nor had he cared to "conceal or disguise his Sentiments." In fact, he had spoken "too freely upon those Subjects among his Neighbors and acquaintance." This boldness, of course, quickly aroused the anger of those who "were zealous in the Cause of the Country, which flung him into the Hands of the *Comtees* of those times." The consequences were not pleasant for Humphrey. The community was forbidden "from all Trade and deal with him." So effective was this boycott that it "allmost brot him to the borders of despair." His property suffered "by the hands of Secret violence . . . and all merely for holding an Opinion or Sentiment differing in some Instances with the generality of the Country." Finally, he had felt himself so "insecure both in his Person and property, he was obliged to betake himself to the woods and for a long time to live the Life of a Fugitive." Humphrey fled to the British lines in September 1780. Conn. Arch., Rev. Ser., XXIII, 302. John Cable of Glastonbury claimed that he had been "again and again harrased by Committees and his Life endangered by inraged Mobs." Munson Jarvis of Stamford protested that he had been "frequently insulted and abused by the Mobs and advertized by the Committee of Safety

as an Enemy and Traitor to the cause of Liberty." Loyalist Transcripts, XII, 593-94, 637; see also 387-88, 423, 451. Thomas Dare, weigher, gauger, and tide-surveyor in New London, claimed that he had been "mobb'd and was obliged to go out of Town in the night for several Nights." Hugh E. Egerton, ed., *Royal Commission on the Losses . . . of the American Loyalists* (Oxford, 1915), 91.

14. After condemning two men for buying tea, New London's committee of inspection arranged to burn an equal number of barrels containing it. The ceremony was duly performed before a large crowd which was entertained by music as well as the bonfire. Three "huzzas" concluded the affair which was described as having been "conducted with due Order and Decorum and to the general Satisfaction of all the Well Wishers to their Country." *New London Gaz.,* Aug. 25, 1775, p. 3. See also *Norwich Packet,* April 27, 1775, p. 3; *Conn. Jour.,* Aug. 30, 1775, p. 2.

15. *Conn. Jour.,* Sept. 6, 1775, p. 3; *Conn. Courant,* Aug. 28, 1775, p. 3; Sept. 4, p. 4.

16. *Norwich Packet,* April 27, 1775, p. 3; *Conn. Jour.,* Aug. 30, 1775, p. 2.

17. *Conn. Jour.,* June 14, 1775, p. 3.

18. *Ibid.,* June 7, 1775, p. 4. Abiathar Camp, a student at Yale, was investigated by a committee of his class. Camp refused to appear before the committee, whereupon the young patriots wrote to the Tory student. Camp defiantly replied, June 13, 1775, "May it please your honors, ham-ham-ham- Finis cum sistula popularum gig, A man without a head has no need of a wig." The committee found the answer insulting and referred the entire matter to a committee of the several classes at the college. This committee condemned Camp for calling the Whigs rebels, declaring he would kill some of them in battle, and promising to treat any order of the student committees with ridicule. The young Tory was finally advertised as an enemy. *Conn. Jour.,* Aug. 30, 1775, p. 4. Camp's father had his own difficulties with the town committee of inspection. *Ibid.,* Oct. 4, 1775, p. 3.

19. *Conn. Courant,* May 13, 1775, p. 3; June 5, p. 1; Aug. 14, p. 3; *New London Gaz.,* May 19, 1775, p. 3.

20. *Conn. Courant,* June 19, 1775, p. 3; *Conn. Jour.,* Aug. 16, 1775, p. 3. The unfortunate New Milford Tory who got the tar and feathers first had to walk 20 miles to Litchfield carrying one of his own geese all

the way. The feathers from that bird were mixed with the tar and applied to him as "the new fashion discipline." After it was all over the Tory was forced "to kneel down, and thank them for their lenity."

21. *Conn. Courant,* May 8, 1775, p. 4; June 12, p. 3; July 3, p. 3; Aug. 21, p. 3; see also Loyalist Transcripts, Calendar of Original Memorials, IV, 48, N. Y. Pub. Lib.

22. Stiles got the rumor of the so-called insurrection from Benjamin Gale and the Rev. Mr. Ross of Fairfield. Stiles, *Diary,* I, 598, entry of Aug. 4, 1775. For the treatment of Waterbury's Tories by the local committee of inspection see *Conn. Courant,* July 17, 1775, p. 3; Aug. 14, p. 3; *Conn. Jour.,* Oct. 18, 1775, p. 4.

23. Derby, *Conn. Jour.,* Oct. 18, 1775, p. 4; Woodbury, Conn. Arch., 2d Rev. Ser., V, 123a, State Lib.; William Cothren, *History of Ancient Woodbury* (Waterbury, 1871-72), I, 188; *Conn. Jour.,* Aug. 30, 1775, p. 2; Wallingford, *Conn. Jour.,* July 26, 1775, p. 3; Sept. 6, p. 2.

24. *Conn. Jour.,* July 26, 1775, p. 3. Andrews subsequently denied that he had committed any wrong. *Ibid.,* Sept. 6, 1775, p. 2. His sermon was printed: *A Discourse Shewing the Necessity of Joining Internal Repentance with the External Profession of it . . . July 20, 1775* (New Haven, 1775), *passim.*

25. *Conn. Jour.,* Nov. 22, 1775, p. 4.

26. For proceedings in the towns of Windsor, Farmington, New Fairfield, Sharon, Willington, Suffield, Hartford, Goshen, Litchfield, and Woodbury, see *Conn. Courant,* Sept. 18, 1775, pp. 1-2; Oct. 16, p. 3; Dec. 4, p. 3; Dec. 11, p. 3; *Conn. Jour.,* Dec. 27, 1775, p. 3.

27. Mansfield to Peters, Jan. 12, 1776, Peters Papers, I, 21.

28. Mansfield had been forced to flee to Long Island leaving "my Parishes, my Family, and Friends . . . in order to escape violence and Imprisonment, if not immediate Death." *Ibid.*

29. Force, *Amer. Arch.,* 4th ser., II, 920; Huntington, *Stamford,* 251-52.

30. Force, *Amer. Arch.,* 4th ser., III, 718; Huntington, *Stamford,* 253-54.

31. Force, *Amer. Arch.,* 4th ser., III, 955; IV, 212-13.

32. *Conn. Jour.,* Sept. 20, 1775, p. 4; Oct. 18, p. 4; Nov. 29, p. 2.

33. Force, *Amer. Arch.,* 4th ser., III, 141-42. According to the census of 1774 Fairfield had 969 men between the ages of 20-70. *Conn. Col. Recs.,* XIV, 488.

34. Force, *Amer. Arch.,* 4th ser., III, 852. The disarming was

described by a Whig as follows: "Our people made them rise about three o'clock in the morning, when there was the greatest confusion imaginable. Some were taking an everlasting leave of their families, whilst others were crying ready to kill themselves, for they all expected to be hung immediately on coming down." Greenwich's committee of inspection disarmed a rather violent Tory in October. *Ibid.*, 941. Benjamin Jarvis of Norwalk had to surrender his firearms to his Whig neighbors in November. Loyalist Transcripts, XII, 7.

35. Force, *Amer. Arch.*, 4th ser., III, 641-42.

36. *Ibid.*, 1376.

37. Mumford to Silas Deane, June 12, 1775, *Deane Corres.*, 262. See also Jedidiah Huntington to Joseph Trumbull, Joseph Trumbull Papers, State Lib., II, 156.

38. *Conn. Courant,* Aug. 21, 1775, p. 3.

39. *Conn. Jour.*, Sept. 20, 1775, p. 2; *Conn. Courant*, Sept. 25, 1775, p. 3.

40. Mansfield Rev. Recs., 8, transcripts, State Lib.; *New London Gaz.*, Nov. 10, 1775, p. 3.

41. Gipson, *Ingersoll*, 340-41; Hinman, *Historical Collection*, 588-89.

42. Boardman, *Sherman*, 142.

43. *Conn. Col. Recs.*, XV, 108. On Connecticut's military effort during this period see *ibid.*, 106-32; *Trumbull Papers*, II, 1-9; *Deane Corres.*, 252; Edmund C. Burnett, ed., *Letters of Members of the Continental Congress* (Washington, 1921-36), I, 123, 143, hereafter cited as Burnett, *Letters*. By the middle of October it was obvious to Jedidiah Huntington that it was impossible to reconcile the colonies and Great Britain, "commonly though erroneously called the Mother Country." Huntington to Gov. Trumbull, Oct. 19, 1775, *Trumbull Papers,* I, 508.

44. *Conn. Col. Recs.*, XV, 123.

45. Trumbull Papers, State Lib., XX, pt. 1, 116ab; a slightly different draft, doc. 117ab.

46. Conn. Arch., Rev. Ser., I, 295ab.

47. D. Woodbridge to Joseph Trumbull, April 9, 1775, Joseph Trumbull Papers; Norwich Rev. Recs., 4-5, transcripts, State Lib. At the end of May 100 Boston Tories were still in the town. Jedidiah Huntington to Joseph Trumbull, May 23, 1775, Joseph Trumbull Papers, State Lib., II, 151b.

48. *Journals of the Continental Congress* (Washington, 1904-37), III, 280; Conn. Arch., Rev. Ser., I, 411ab.

49. *Conn. Col. Recs., XV,* 157.

50. *Ibid.,* 157-58, 158-59. Benjamin Stiles was charged with having said that Connecticut's delegates to the Congress were "three mean or good for nothing Dogs that they were no more fit for our Representatives than his Negro Jeff"; also that "if some part of the Ministers and some part of the Congress were Beheaded both Countries would be at Peace." Conn. Arch., Rev. Ser., V, 374. Stiles was later acquitted by both houses of the legislature. *Ibid.,* doc. 375a.

51. "Son of Liberty," *Conn. Courant,* Nov. 27, 1775, p. 3.

52. Conn. Arch., Rev. Ser., XIII, 232a. Information about Lewis may be found in *Conn. Col. Recs., XV,* 42, 134. Newtown does not seem to have been represented at the October 1775 session of the Assembly. *Ibid.,* XV, 134.

53. Conn. Arch., Rev. Ser., XIII, 232a.

54. Mansfield to the Secretary of the S. P. G., Dec. 29, 1775, Conn. MSS, Hawks Transcripts, 655-56.

55. *Conn. Courant,* Nov. 27, 1775, p. 3. On Dec. 13 the town voted to recompense Colonel Lewis for his efforts. Redding Rev. Recs., 5, transcripts, State Lib.

56. *Conn. Courant,* Dec. 4, 1775, p. 3.

57. Ridgefield Rev. Recs., 3-4, transcripts, State Lib.; Mansfield to the Secretary of the S. P. G., Dec. 29, 1775, Conn. MSS, Hawks Transcripts, 656.

58. "The same People in our Colony," Mansfield wrote to Peters on Jan. 12, 1776, "which at the Beginning of the present Disputes were loyal and averse to take up arms against the King, do, generally, and I believe I may say universally, retain their loyalty and Duty still: those Methods which the other party hath made Use of to gain them over to their side such a[s] Minute Men and Mobs, dragging them before ignorant dirty, domineering Committees of Inspection, imprisoning some and Tarring and feathering others, and the like, had no other Effect, than to confirm them the more as well in their Attachment to the British Government as in their Abhorrence of the Tyranny of their new made Masters." As for himself, Mansfield claimed that he could return to Connecticut, to his family and parishes, if he were willing to sacrifice his principles. But he asserted this was "too great a Price for the Purchase only of temporary Tranquility." Peters Papers, I, 21.

59. *Conn. Col. Recs.,* XV, 185.

60. Washington to Gov. Trumbull, Nov. 15, 1775, Trumbull Papers, State Lib., XXIX (Letter Book IV), 228.

61. *Ibid.,* XX, pt. 1, 119a.

62. Jonathan to Joseph Trumbull, Dec. 22, 1775, Joseph Trumbull Papers, State Lib., IV, 396.

63. Trumbull to John Hancock, Trumbull Papers, State Lib., XXIX (Letter Book IV), 37.

64. *Conn. Col. Recs.,* XV, 192-93. The procedure in seizing Tory estates is outlined on pp. 194-95.

65. *Ibid.,* 193.

66. *Ibid.,* 193-94.

67. The resolutions of the Congress on those days recommended that the Tories be disarmed. *Jour. Cont. Congress,* IV, 18-20, 205. See also the comments by Richard Smith and John Adams on the latter resolutions in Burnett, *Letters,* I, 388 and *n*4.

68. Gov. Trumbull informed Washington of Connecticut's measures against the Tories on Jan. 1, 1776. Washington was "happy" to get the news. Trumbull Papers, State Lib., XXIX (Letter Book IV), 238-39, 241. Schuyler was also very pleased to learn about "the effectual Steps your respectable Government has taken." He hoped New York would "follow so fair an example." *Ibid.,* XXVI (Letter Book I), 48.

69. Shaw to Samuel Wintworth, Jan. 16, 1776, Shaw, *Letter Book,* 278.

70. *Conn. Col. Recs.,* 203-4.

71. Superior Court Records, XVIII, Litchfield Feb. 1776 term, n.p.; Fairfield June 1776 term, n.p. See also the case of Oliver Welton in the New Haven Superior Court Records 1774-84, case dated May 30, 1776, State Lib.

72. Fairfield Superior Court Papers, Aug. 1776, in bundle dated 1770-79, State Lib. The Tories were accused of "Scandalous Walking and committing Scandalous offences." "Scandalous Walking" was an offense for which, upon conviction, the Superior Court could deprive freemen of their privileges. See *Conn. Code* (1750), 81.

73. For the proceedings and recommendations of the Fairfield County conventions see *Conn. Jour.,* Feb. 7, 1776, p. 2; Force, *Amer. Arch.,* 4th ser., IV, 765.

74. See, for example, *Conn. Courant,* Feb. 26, 1776, p. 3; April 8, p. 1; April 15, p. 4; *Conn. Jour.,* Feb. 21, 1776, p. 4; March 27, p. 3;

April 10, p. 2; April 24, p. 3; May 15, p. 3; June 5, p. 3; *New London Gaz.*, April 12, 1776, p. 3; Huntington, *Stamford*, 252-53. Derby's Anglican rector was one of the Tories who admitted his wrongs before the local committee of inspection. His resolution never to do so apparently had weakened. See *Conn. Jour.*, April 17, 1776, p. 4; Mansfield to S. Peters, Jan. 12, 1776, Peters Papers, I, 21.

75. *Conn. Courant*, April 1, 1776, pp. 3, 4. See also *Conn. Jour.*, Sept. 11, 1776, p. 4; proceedings of the Farmington Committee of Inspection, July-Aug. 1776, Transcript of the Journal of the Connecticut House of Representatives, Oct.-Nov. 1776, Conn. Hist. Soc.

76. Loyalist Transcripts, XII, 193, 388; Ontario Bur. Arch., *Report for 1904*, 909-10.

77. Conn. Arch., Rev. Ser., V, 405c; Conn. Arch., 3d Rev. Ser., I, 118b; Joseph Trumbull Papers, State Lib., I, 27a. In order to control the rapid spread of vigilante justice throughout America the Continental Congress on June 18 officially recorded its opposition to illegal assaults upon Tories and their property. *Jour. Cont. Congress,* V, 464.

78. Tory Newtown, however, apparently had no representatives at this session. *Conn. Col. Recs.,* XV, 269-71.

79. Appeals for unity, criticism of party and factional strife, and warnings against Tories and turncoats may be found in the following sources respectively: *Conn. Courant,* April 1, 1776, p. 3; Enoch Huntington, *The Happy Effects of Union and the Fatal Tendency of Divisions* (Hartford, 1776), sermon delivered at the freemen's meeting, Middletown, April 8, 1776, 15, 19-20, 27; Allyn Mather, *The Character of a Well Accomplished Ruler Describ'd* (New Haven, 1776), sermon delivered at the freemen's meeting, New Haven, April 8, 1776, 11-12, 15-16.

80. "Lucius" argued that the people's suspicions were groundless. He correctly predicted that a man of Johnson's character would not "remain unnoticed on the pages of future history," and therefore appealed to the voters to "conduct so towards him, that it may not there be recorded that you treated him unworthily." *Conn. Jour.*, March 13, 1776, p. 1; *Conn. Courant,* April 1, 1776, p. 4. Johnson got only 1272 votes in the spring elections, almost 300 more than he received in the nominations of the preceding fall, 991 votes. Governor Trumbull received 4144 nominating votes. *Conn. Col. Recs.,* XV, 173n. The May 1776 figures are enclosed in a letter from Gov. Trumbull to Joseph Trumbull, May 13, 1776, Joseph Trumbull Papers, State Lib., IV, 413.

81. E. Dyer to Joseph Trumbull, May 10, 1776, Joseph Trumbull Papers; and Dyer to Samuel Adams, May 10, 1776, Adams Papers. There was an interesting factional struggle within the patriot ranks. The old feud between Dyer and Deane on the one side and another faction led by William Williams had reached a climax in October 1775. The Assembly had then refused to re-appoint Dyer and Deane as the colony's delegates to the Continental Congress. Sherman, however, was re-elected. *Conn. Col. Recs.,* XV, 136-37. John Trumbull and Benjamin Gale had interesting explanations and comments on this: Trumbull to Deane, Oct. 20, 1775, *Deane Papers,* I, 86-87; Gale to Deane, Nov. 22, 1775, *Deane Corres.,* 323. Deane attacked the "rascally junto," "those party people . . . agitated and stirred on by that little malevolent prig in buckram [Williams ?]," who were responsible for having defeated Dyer and Deane. Thomas Mumford had kept Deane informed "of the intrigues of a certain party in the Assembly, of the class or Club at Munson's." The latter, it will be remembered, was New Haven's organization of radical Whigs. Deane had very little respect for Roger Sherman, whose Jesuitical practices, Deane scornfully declared, were common among Connecticut's "modern New Light Saints": Deane to Mrs. Deane, Jan. 13, Jan. 21, 1776, *Deane Corres.,* 347-51. Deane had originally opposed Sherman's appointment as a delegate to the Continental Congress: Deane to W. S. Johnson, Aug. 4, 1774, Johnson Papers. Dyer quite correctly described Deane as being "Confoundedly Chagrined at his recall": Dyer to Joseph Trumbull, Jan. 1, 1776, Joseph Trumbull Papers. The other side of the case is told, in part, in a letter from E. Ledyard to Williams, Feb. 9, 1776, Williams Papers.

82. Judah Champion, *Christian and Civil Liberty and Freedom Considered and Recommended,* Election Sermon (Hartford, 1776), 9, 10, 31.

83. Conn. Arch., Rev. Ser., IV, 73a, 74; *Conn. Col. Recs.,* XV, 283-84; see also 281-83.

84. *Conn. Col. Recs.,* XV, 281.

85. Jonathan to Joseph Trumbull, April 13, 1776, Joseph Trumbull Papers, State Lib., IV, 409.

86. Conn. Arch., Rev. Ser., V, 411.

87. John Davis to Gov. Trumbull, June 3, 1776; Jonathan to Joseph Trumbull, May 17, 1776, Joseph Trumbull Papers, State Lib., I, 27ab; IV, 414. The Tory merchants were Isaac Tomlinson and Azariah Pritchard. On Tomlinson see Egerton, *Royal Commission,* 377-78.

88. J. Chandler to Col. Joseph Cook, May 15, 1776, Conn. Arch., Rev. Ser., V, 405c; Captain Seth Harding to Gov. Trumbull, May 20, 1776, Trumbull Papers, State Lib., IV, pt. 1, 92a.

89. Trumbull to Harding, May 18, 1776, Trumbull Papers, State Lib., V, pt. 1, 32a.

90. *Conn. Courant,* May 20, 1776, p. 3.

91. *Conn. Col. Recs.,* XV, 398-99.

92. Several of Connecticut's patriots had anticipated separation months before the colonies declared their independence. See, for example, the letters of Oliver Wolcott to Samuel Lyman, Feb. 3, Feb. 19, April 17, 1776, Oliver Wolcott Papers, Conn. Hist. Soc.; Huntington, *Happy Effects of Union,* 20.

93. Conn. Arch., Rev. Ser., IV, pt. 2, 309, 338b; printed in *Conn. Col. Recs.,* 414-16.

94. *Conn. Col. Recs.,* XV, 411; see also 412-13.

95. Hancock to Trumbull, June 24, 1776; Trumbull to Hancock, July 6, 1776, Trumbull Papers, State Lib., XXIX (Letter Book IV), 62, 67.

96. Benjamin Rush, Diary, April 8, 1777, quoted in Burnett, *Letters,* II, 320.

97. Jonathan to Joseph Trumbull, April 13, 1776, Joseph Trumbull Papers, State Lib., IV, 409.

98. *Conn. Col. Recs.,* XV, 475; Jonathan to Joseph Trumbull, April 13, 1776, Joseph Trumbull Papers, State Lib., IV, 409.

99. *Conn. Courant,* June 17, 1776, p. 2.

100. *Ibid.,* July 15, 1776, p. 3. The committee dismissed the suspect after finding that there was no reasonable foundation for the charges against him.

101. *New London Gaz.,* June 7, 1776, p. 2.

102. David to Jonathan Trumbull Jr., July 2, 1776, David Trumbull Papers, Conn. Hist. Soc.

103. *Conn. Col. Recs.,* XV, 479-80.

104. *Conn. Jour.,* July 17, 1776, p. 1.

105. Jesse Root to Gov. Trumbull, July 1, 1776, Trumbull Papers, Political.

106. *Conn. Col. Recs.,* XV, 486-87. A pass testifying to Elkanah Tisdale's character and permitting him to travel is in the Trumbull Papers, State Lib., XX, pt. 1, 130a.

107. *New London Gaz.,* Aug. 30, 1776, p. 2.

108. *Conn. Courant,* Sept. 23, 1776, p. 1.

109. *Conn. Col. Recs.,* XV, 526-27. The petition, which was referred to the Assembly, is printed in Hinman, *Historical Collection,* 566-67.

110. Stiles, *Diary,* II, 62.

111. *State Records,* I, 1; see also 52.

112. Newtown was not listed among the towns represented in the May session. See *Conn. Col. Recs.,* XV, 269-71.

113. MS fragment, Journal of the House of Representatives, Oct. 1776, Conn. Hist. Soc. No deputies were listed for Newtown at this session. *State Records,* I, 2.

114. *State Records,* I, 3. The "Declaration of Independency" had been received by the Council of Safety on July 11th. On the following day the Council discussed the "matter and manner" of publishing it, but did not reach any decision. The question was again considered on the 18th, but it was finally agreed to leave the matter to the Assembly. *Conn. Col. Recs.,* XV, 475, 477, 486.

115. *State Records,* I, 3-4.

116. *Ibid.,* 4.

117. *Ibid.,* 4-5. See also Conn. Arch., Rev. Ser., IV, 341b.

118. *State Records,* I, 7-8; see also 34-35.

119. *Ibid.* The Council made three significant changes in the original draft drawn up by the deputies. These changes were incorporated in the final copy of the law. Two of them tended to soften the original provisions; the third had a contrary effect. Compare Conn. Arch., Rev. Ser., V, 420, and *State Records,* I, 4.

120. *State Records,* I, 27-28. On the 25th of October Norwalk's committee of inspection, the selectmen, and the justices of the peace petitioned the Assembly for assistance. They reported that the local patriots had become too impatient to deal with the Tories according to the regular legal procedure. On the previous day the patriots had seized a large number of Tories, and even as the petition was written they rounded up others. The petitioners wanted the suspects to "have a Day in Court to make their Defence." But the people were opposed to regular trials, claiming that under the existing law the Tories would merely be disarmed. The memorialists alleged that the town was "now . . . in the greatest need of the speedy Interposition" of the Assembly to guarantee "that Justice and Equity may be done." Conn. Arch., Rev. Ser., V, 416.

121. Jedidiah Huntington, however, tempered his optimism with some typical Puritan references to the heroic age of the first settlers: letter to Gov. Trumbull, Oct. 19, 1775, *Trumbull Papers*, I, 508.

122. Bulkeley had also maintained that "No man in the world [was] so sovereign as usurping subjects: they are as absolute and arbitrary as the great Turk, so far as they dare to go." Conn. Hist. Soc., *Colls.*, 3, p. 258. Bulkeley's *Will and Doom* was written in 1692. Some 80 years later Robert Traill, Portsmouth's Customs Collector, denounced the patriots as "a Rabble who carries destruction in one hand and no mercy in the other." Traill to Samuel Peters, n.d., [1775 ?], Peters Papers, VIII, 46.

123. Bulkeley, *Will and Doom,* 81-82; see also 226.

CHAPTER THIRTEEN

1. Connecticut was not entirely free of demands for democratic changes of the charter government. One would-be reformer admitted, March 21, 1776, that alterations of the government would not have to be as extensive in Connecticut as in the other colonies. His proposals for reform, however, were not minor. They would have ended the practice of the governor and Assembly filling all the "lucrative posts, offices and commissions," and given the freemen the power to elect the sheriffs, county judges, Superior Court judges, militia officers, and justices of the peace. This reformer's political motto was "No business that can be done by the people themselves should be trusted to their Delegates." At least one town went on record favoring the election of Connecticut's delegates to the Congress. However, there does not seem to have been any significant attempt to push these proposals. Force, *Amer. Arch.,* 4th ser., V, 450-51; 5th ser., II, 113-14.

2. This point is either expressed or implied in the following: Zephaniah Swift, *A System of the Laws of the State of Connecticut* (Windham, 1795-96), I, 58; Leonard Bacon, *The Early Constitutional History of Connecticut* (Hartford, 1843), 24; Gilbert, "Connecticut Loyalists," 274; Purcell, *Connecticut in Transition*, 2.

3. Petition of Nathaniel Guyer, July 1776, Fairfield Superior Court Papers, bundle dated 1770-79.

4. Tiffany, American Colonies, bk. 1, 42, 43; Samuel Peters to the Loyalist Commissioners, Peters Papers, I, 96. See also Peters, *History,* 245, 268. It is interesting to compare these views with Gershom Bulkeley's attacks on Connecticut in the late seventeenth century: *Will and Doom,* 90.

5. Trumbull to Washington, July 25, 1777, *Trumbull Papers,* II, 88. Trumbull's letter was inspired by Washington's difficulties in dealing with Connecticut's troops.

6. Boardman, *Sherman,* 340.

7. E. Stiles, *The United States Elevated to Glory and Honour,* Election Sermon (Worcester, 1785), 32-34.

8. In the 1790's the Rev. Samuel Peters made the startling claim that there had really been little difference between Connecticut's Old Lights and the Anglicans. He sharply distinguished the former from the "Calvinistic Puritans there called New Lights the open Enemies of Episcopacy and Monarchy and Forms of Prayers." See Verdmont Ideas, Peters Papers, VIII, 55. Stiles would have been horrified at Peters' description of Connecticut's Old Lights.

9. The pre-Revolutionary sectional split within Connecticut made a deep impression on the colony's former English agent. In a letter written to W. S. Johnson after the war Jackson referred to the recently published history of Connecticut written by the Tory refugee Samuel Peters. He correctly criticized the book as being full of errors. He thought it would be quite appropriate, therefore, to give a copy of the book to one of Gov. Trumbull's sons, then in England, "as he belongs to the Eastern side of the Colony [*sic*]." Jackson to Johnson, Nov. 30, 1784, Johnson Corres., Bancroft Transcripts.

10. Samuel Peters attributed the Revolution to "the merchants, lawyers, and clergy, who yet are not inimical to the aristocratic branch of government, provided they are admitted to share in it according to their merit." *History,* 273-74; see also 294. On the role of the New Light ministers see Alice M. Baldwin, *The Clergy of Connecticut in Revolutionary Days,* Conn. Tercentenary Commission, *Publs.,* 56 (1936), 7-8. When officers of the Groton fort were chosen in 1776, Thomas Mumford "quick nominated" Park Avery, aged preacher of the local Separatists. According to Ebenezer Ledyard this was "look'd upon by many good people of this place as a Party Plan." Ledyard to Jabez

Huntington, Feb. 9, 1776, *Huntington Papers,* 31. Only one New Light pastor, the Rev. John Smalley of New Britain, was a Tory: *Conn. Courant,* Oct. 17, 1774, pp. 1-2; Stiles, *Diary,* I, 490.

11. On Durkee see Amos A. Browning, "A Forgotten Son of Liberty," in New London County Historical Society, *Records and Papers,* 3, pt. 2 (1912), 257-79. Durkee joined the Susquehannah Company the same year that Jonathan Trumbull did. Three years later, in 1764, Durkee's commercial firm was dissolved. Soon after his partner died in 1767 Durkee was forced to mortgage his house and real estate as well as some other property to his New York creditor-merchants. It was at this time that Deputy-Gov. Trumbull was enmeshed in serious financial difficulties.

Dr. Edith A. Bailey concentrated her attention almost exclusively on the part played by the Susquehannah Company in contributing to the development of radicalism in Connecticut. In so doing she seriously underestimated the influence of the merchants and their grievances in the growth of anti-British sentiment. See Bailey, *Influences Toward Radicalism in Connecticut,* especially 180, 181, 247. Moreover, she failed to note that it was this merchant class that gave the Susquehannah Company most of its leaders. Land speculation quite naturally attracted merchants who not only were restricted in business by the mother country, but came out second best in competition with New York and Boston traders. Silas Deane, merchant, ardent expansionist, and a prominent organizer of the Whig party in the years immediately before the Revolution, thought of a thousand ways to improve Connecticut's commerce and industry. His final conclusion was that Connecticut's trade would languish until all the western lands were taken up. Only when the people who were "disposed to emigrate can't bear the expense of their removal" did Deane think that Connecticut's industry and trade would prosper. Deane was an enthusiastic supporter of the Susquehannah Company's western claims. See Deane to W. S. Johnson, Feb. 7, 1774, Johnson Papers. The anonymous author of *Civil Prudence Recommended* argued for the company and at the same time urged the colonial government to encourage trade. He believed "it would be best for any civil state to be mainly influenced and governed by commercial interest." See 9-10, 13.

12. Dyer to W. S. Johnson, Nov. 10, 1769, Johnson Papers.

13. Gale to Silas Deane, Feb. 27, 1775, *Deane Corres.,* 202-3; see also Franklin B. Dexter's comments on Abraham Davenport, prominent

Stamford politician, councillor, and judge of the county court, "Notes on Some of the New Haven Loyalists," in *A Selection From the Miscellaneous Papers of Fifty Years* (New Haven, 1918), 337. Gale said that he only wanted "to be esteemed a Friend of my Country, and a Lover of all honest, good and upright men, and an Enemy to all sorts of Tyranny, civil, military, and ecclesiastical." Gale to Deane, Feb. 27, 1775, *Deane Corres.,* 203. It is extremely doubtful, however, that Gale was really converted. Upon Gale's death, on May 6, 1790, Stiles wrote in his diary that Gale had always been "against the American Revolution." *Diary,* III, 393. According to Stiles, Gale, true to character, continued to express rather heterodox opinions after 1783. An example of those opinions may be found in a letter from Gale to his old friend William Samuel Johnson, May 16, 1786. "For my own part," Gale wrote, "I am a friend to the Civil, Natural and Religious Rights of mankind, but I fear before we get settled down to any fixed form of Government, in these American States, we shall be exposed either to the most absolute tyranny and despotism of an Aristocracy or the lawless and confused troubles of an Octocracy or the rabble of an uncontrollable Democracy. Our Independence was founded upon the last and what the end will be God only knows." Johnson Corres., Bancroft Transcripts. Stiles' final comment about Gale was most appropriate: "A singular character!" *Diary,* III, 393.

14. Samuel Gray to Joseph Trumbull, May 15, 1775; E. Dyer to Joseph Trumbull, May 10, 1776, Joseph Trumbull Papers.

15. Undated and unsigned manuscript in the Jeremiah Wadsworth Papers, box dated 1767-76, Conn. Hist. Soc.

16. See the petition of Titus Butler in the Conn. Arch., Rev. Ser., XIV, 363ab.

17. *Ibid.,* V, 376.

18. Trumbull to John Owen, March 26, 1779, Trumbull Papers, State Lib., XX, pt. 1, 188a.

19. Williams to Gov. Trumbull, Aug. 26, 1777, *Trumbull Papers,* III, 134.

20. Claude H. Van Tyne, *The Loyalists in the American Revolution* (New York, 1929), 192.

21. See the letter written by the Rev. Richard Mansfield to Samuel Peters, Jan. 12, 1776, Peters Papers, I, 21.

22. See the comment by the Rev. Mr. Mansfield, Conn. MSS, Hawks Transcripts, 655.

23. Bulkeley, *Will and Doom,* 93-97, 136.

24. Gershom Bulkeley, *The People's Right to Election or Altera-tion of Government in Connecticott Argued in a Letter* (1689), Conn. Hist. Soc., *Colls.,* 1 (1860), 71; Conn. Arch., Rev. Ser., XIII, 285ab; XXIII, 338; XXVII, 247; XXVIII, 244b.

25. Tiffany, American Colonies, bk. 4, pp. 1-2, 5-6. The colonies, according to Tiffany, had been "uneasy, Tho a free people, and were Indulged in Liberty; had priviledges Even Greater Than our Mother Country Injoyed Themselves." Bk. 9, pp. 21-22. See also Peters, *History,* 293.

26. Petition of Oliver Lyman, Jan. 1777, Nat. Arch.

27. Tiffany, American Colonies, bk. 6, p. 1; Loyalist Transcripts, XII, 247; Conn. Arch., Rev. Ser., XXIII, 302; Eleazer Fitch to [?], Oct. 15, 1776, Windham Superior Court Papers, Sept. 1778, State Lib.

28. Stephen Gorham was the complainant. Fragment in the Fair-field Superior Court Papers, bundle dated 1770-79.

29. Samuel to Hannah Peters, n.d., Peters Papers, VIII, 24. Stiles denounced the Anglican minister as an "infamous Paricide . . . full of Malice and Venom against his country and especially the Presby-terians." *Diary,* I, 467. Peters definitely knew no moderation in his hatred of Connecticut's Whigs. See also Bates, *Kingston and the Loyalists of 1783,* 6.

30. Samuel Peters to Deputy-Gov. Samuel Huntington, Dec. 6, 1784, Peters Papers, II, 24; see also I, 3; Peters to Dr. Auchmuty, Oct. 1, 1774, copy in the hand of E. Moseley, Lane Papers; Tiffany, Ameri-can Colonies, bk. 4, pp. 10, 11, 15; Thomas Moffat, Diary 1775-77, 1, L. C. For other examples of extreme Tory opinion see Conn. Arch., Rev. Ser., V, 374a; *Conn. Jour.,* Aug. 30, 1775, p. 2; Oct. 18, p. 4; Nov. 22, p. 4; *Conn. Courant,* Oct. 14, 1776, p. 3; case of Benjamin Butler, Superior Court Records, XVIII, March 1777 session, State Lib.; peti-tions in Loyalist Transcripts, XII, *passim.*

31. Trumbull Papers, State Lib., XI, pt. 1, 55a; case of Benjamin Kilborn, Superior Court Records, XVIII, Litchfield Feb. 1776 session.

32. The pardon act of May 1779 described several of those factors. *State Records,* II, 279-80. See also Benjamin Franklin and R. Morris to Silas Deane, Oct. 1, 1776, *Deane Papers,* I, 298; J. Eardley-Wilmot, *Historical View of the Commission for Enquiring into the Losses . . . of the American Loyalists* (London, 1815), 4.

33. *Conn. Courant,* March 27, 1775, p. 3.

34. Conn. Arch., Rev. Ser., XIII, 195a; XIV, 368ab, 370a; *State*

Records, I, 499, 503-04, 508; Abigail Silliman to G. S. Silliman, Feb. [11 ?], 1778, Silliman Papers.

35. Conn. Arch., Rev. Ser., XIII, 233a; XIV, 352a; XXIX, 251. One Tory thought that "the Ministerial troops were in the right," but he also heard that "if they conquered those that Joind them would have, some 100 some said 200 acres of Land." Case of Nathaniel Guyer, in Fairfield Superior Court Papers, bundle dated 1770-79.

36. Conn. Arch., Rev. Ser., XIV, 353a.

37. *Ibid.,* XIII, 242a, 272; XIV, 345b, 391; XXIII, 343, 350a, 362, 366, 368-69, 399-400, 408b; XXVI, 276a; XXVIII, 254a; XXIX, 344-45; Conn. Arch., 3d Rev. Ser., II, 126a. Similar petitions are scattered through the printed *State Records,* II-IV.

38. Petition of Samuel Roberts, Conn. Arch., Rev. Ser., XXIII, 300a.

39. Early in 1775 a Hartford conservative pessimistically pointed out that Connecticut's military preparations caused "all *prudent* Inhabitants [to] fear that our Parchment will soon totter." *Conn. Courant,* Jan. 23, 1775, p. 3. John Davis Jr. of Litchfield protested that he had been "branded and stigmatized for a Tory because I violently opposed Mobs and Riots." Conn. Arch., Rev. Ser., XIII, 306a. See also Conn. Arch., 3d Rev. Ser., I, 118ab; petition of Thompson Lyman, Jan. 1777, Nat. Arch.

40. When William Samuel Johnson returned from his mission to Gage to find the Assembly rapidly preparing for war he decided, as he later wrote, "to set myself down quietly to my studies convinced that I could not join in a war against England and much less could I join in a war against my own country." Mema of Doctr Wm Saml Johnson, Johnson Papers. A typewritten copy of this document was made available to me through the courtesy of Dr. George C. Groce, Johnson's biographer.

41. Jared Ingersoll expressed this point of view in a letter to Jonathan Ingersoll, Feb. 20, 1776. Describing Secretary Wyllys' and his own attitude, Ingersoll wrote, "Civil wars but ill agree with his natural turn or mine—our Characteristick prayer being 'Lord give Us peace in our day.'" "Ingersoll Papers," 460.

42. Thaddeus Burr, a Fairfield Whig, described one of these cautious Tories in a letter to Gov. Trumbull, Oct. 12, 1779. "He is of a weakly constitution," Burr wrote, "and naturally of a very timid make. Has either through fear, or from the influence of some of his Connections ever appeared rather unfriendly . . . he supposed it would

have been better for us to have setled the dispute without a seperation. In short He is what we call a moderate Man, carefully avoiding to do anything that would expose him to the Law." Trumbull Papers, State Lib., X, pt. 2, 181a. The Tory in question admitted that "he had his doubts and fears respecting the Expediency of the War, but not being able to Serve in the army he lived quietly upon his own Estate without medling with the Controversy either on the one side or the other." Conn. Arch., Rev. Ser., XX, 101a. See also *ibid.*, XXVI, 279a; XXXVI, 329b; Loyalist Transcripts, 151.

43. Dexter, "New Haven Loyalists," 336, 344; Dexter, *Biog. Sketches,* I, 400, 657; Stiles, *Diary,* III, 373; Gipson, *Ingersoll,* 374; Groce, *Johnson,* ch. 6.

44. Edmund B. O'Callaghan, ed., *Documents Relative to the Colonial History of the State of New York* (Albany, 1853-87), VIII, 807. Heron seems to have been the typical aristocrat in dress as well as sentiment. On one occasion he is supposed to have said of the people, "We must keep down the underbrush." Hall, *Life and Letters of Parsons,* 421.

45. Sherwood, *Sermon Containing Scriptural Instructions,* viii. An article in the *Conn. Courant,* Feb. 5, 1776, pp. 1-2, defended the Anglicans as good patriots, but the Whigs were not convinced.

46. The Rev. Jeremiah Leaming predicted that if the interests of the Anglican church in Connecticut were not properly cared for "America is totally ruined." The Anglicans, he warned, "will be the first Victims that will fall in this sad catastrophe." Leaming to the Secretary of the S. P. G., May 10, 1768, Conn. MSS, Hawks Transcripts, 556. After the Revolution the Rev. Ebenezer Dibblee of Stamford still believed that if an episcopate had been set up in America "many years before the late Revolution, it would have been their [British government's] best security against it." Dibblee to Samuel Peters, May 3, 1785, *Historical Magazine of the Protestant Episcopal Church,* I, no. 2 (1932), 64. In September 1774 the Rev. John Beach, Newtown's Tory rector, eagerly anticipated what he obviously hoped would "soon be a great alteration in the Governments of New England." Beach to W. S. Johnson, Sept. 8, 1774, Johnson Papers.

47. See the Rev. Richard Mansfield's elaborate comments on this in his letter to Samuel Peters, Jan. 12, 1776, Peters Papers, I, 21; see also doc. 46. Another Tory charged that the people had been incited by propaganda to the effect that the king was a Catholic, a tyrant, a

"Davil and what not." Case of Stephen Gorham, Fairfield Superior Court Papers, bundle dated 1770-79; see also Titus Hosmer to Silas Deane, Sept. 4, 1774, *Deane Corres.,* 155.

48. Rev. Richard Mansfield to the Secretary of the S. P. G., Dec. 29, 1775, Conn. MSS, Hawks Transcripts, 654. See also Mansfield to Peters, Jan. 12, 1776, Peters Papers, I, 21; Loyalist Transcripts, XII, 491; Hall, *Norwalk Historical Records,* 175-76.

49. After the Peters incidents late in 1774 six Anglican ministers publicly denied that they were in any way sympathetic to Peters' political views. At the same time Gov. Trumbull announced that the Episcopal clergy were in no danger of being prosecuted or of being expelled from the colony. *Conn. Jour.,* New Haven, Oct. 21, 1774, p. 4; Oct. 28, p. 1; Trumbull to T. Burr., Oct. 24, 1774, Trumbull Papers, State Lib., XX, pt. 1, 95. But during the next few years several Anglican ministers, including some of the very men who had repudiated Peters, became embroiled with the authorities for their Toryism. See, for example, Rev. Richard Mansfield to Samuel Peters, Jan. 12, 1776, Peters Papers, I, 21; *Conn. Jour.,* July 26, 1775, p. 3; Sept. 6, p. 2; Dec. 27, p. 3; March 27, 1776, p. 3; April 3, p. 3; April 17, p. 4; Conn. Arch., Rev. Ser., V, 448ab, 449, 451; *Conn. Col. Recs.,* XV, 158-59; Andrews, *Discourse Shewing the Necessity of Joining Internal Repentance with the External Profession of it.* In the summer of 1776 "Flavius" condemned the Anglican clergymen as being obviously disaffected. "While you pretend to neutrality," he charged, "we must necessarily consider you our most detestible enemies." *New London Gaz.,* Aug. 23, 1776, p. 1. Ezra Stiles and Samuel Peters agreed on one thing, the loyalty of the Episcopal clergy to the British. Stiles, *Diary,* I, 490-91; II, 45, 314-15; Peters, *History,* 297, 304. On the loyalty of the laity see Tiffany, American Colonies, bk. 4, p. 11; Mansfield to the Secretary of the S. P. G., Dec. 29, 1775, Conn. MSS, Hawks Transcripts, 654-55; Rev. Mr. Tyler to S. Peters, Oct. 5, 1774; Mansfield to Peters, Jan. 12, 1776, Peters Papers, I, 4, 21; Conn. Arch., Rev. Ser., XX, 103a; XXIX, 16.

50. Conn. Arch., Rev. Ser., VIII, 239a-c; Dexter, "New Haven Loyalists," 341-42. Boston's Sandemanians were also Tories. See Samuel Adams to S. Collins, Jan. 31, 1775, Cushing, *Writings of Samuel Adams,* III, 173.

51. Tiffany, American Colonies, bk. 4, p. 18. On the other hand the Tories took great pleasure in referring to the patriots as low

riff-raff and their leaders as bankrupts. See Peters' characteristically unreliable comments in Conn. Arch., 2d Rev. Ser., V, 3d. Compare Joseph Galloway's general description of the Loyalist and Whig parties as quoted in Burnett, *Letters,* I, 54-55.

52. Parsons to the Judges of the Superior Court, Nov. 22, 1782, Trumbull Papers, State Lib., XVII, pt. 2, 172a.

53. Petition of Nathaniel Guyer, July 1776, Fairfield Superior Court Papers, bundle dated 1770-79.

54. Caulkins, *Norwich,* 312; Larned, "Revolutionary Boycott," 153; Hollister, *History,* I, 508.

55. Cases of Tory militia officers appear in the Conn. Arch., Rev. Ser., I, 420, 427; V, 397ab, 404a, 405a-c; *Conn. Col. Recs.,* XV, 51-52, 54, 203-4, 439, 442. One of the first jobs of the May 1775 session of the General Assembly "was to turn every known Tory out of the Commission of the Peace." Hosmer mentions nine men who "were omitted on this account." Hosmer to Silas Deane, May 22, 1775, *Deane Corres.,* 238. See also the complaint of the Windham radicals to the effect that the county sheriff was a Tory. Item dated Sept. 3, 1776, Trumbull Papers, State Lib., V, pt. 1, 169a-c, 170a-c. By this late date, however, only an insignificant fraction of the approximate total of 3000 public offices in the town, county, and state governments could have been occupied by British sympathizers.

56. Loyalist Transcripts, Calendar of Original Memorials, II, 316, 321-22; Ontario Bur. Arch., *Report for 1904,* 1156; Egerton, *Royal Commission,* 91, 172-73.

57. Less than 25 of the more than 1000 Yale graduates alive at the outbreak of the Revolution were outright Tories. Dexter, "New Haven Loyalists," 345.

58. Dexter, *Biog. Sketches,* I, 653; III, 9, 214-15; Loyalist Transcripts, XII, 400, 407-8; Loyalist Transcripts, Calendar of Original Memorials, II, 310; John T. Farrell, ed., *Superior Court Diary of William Samuel Johnson* (Washington, 1942), lviii; Dexter, "New Haven Loyalists," 336-37.

59. The reference to the 250 acres is in Silas Deane to P. Henry, Jan. 2, 1775, *Deane Papers,* I, 36. In the eighteenth century the farmers of Fairfield County, where loyalism was most common, were reputed to be the most prosperous in the entire colony. An article in the *Conn. Courant,* Oct. 17, 1768, p. 4, pointed out that the soil of the town of Fairfield was "remarkably fertile," and was owned "principally [by]

great farmers." Upon settling in the town of Danbury the Rev. Ebenezer Baldwin found its inhabitants to be "Plain, honest wealthy Farmers." Baldwin to Miss B. Baldwin, May 8, 1770, Simeon E. Baldwin Papers, Yale University. A Stamford Tory later claimed that the people of Norwalk and Stamford "were wealthy farmers" and, of course, Anglicans and Loyalists. Bates, *Kingston and the Loyalists of 1783*, 8. Several decades later Timothy Dwight reported that the soil of Fairfield County was "better than that of any other in the State, being generally rich, and producing everything which the climate will permit." *Travels*, III, 519.

60. See the Tories' descriptions of their property in the Loyalist Transcripts, XII, *passim*, and in the Ontario Bur. Arch., *Report for 1904, passim*. These may be compared with the final awards made by the British Government, Loyalist Transcripts, XI, XXVIII, *passim*, and the inventories of confiscated estates in the MSS Probate Papers, State Lib.

61. Loyalist Transcripts, XII, 349, 351, 355, 365, 369, 639-40, 648, 651; Ontario Bur. Arch., *Report for 1904*, 204-6, 838, 1155.

62. See, for example, New Haven Probate Papers, folder no. 2295; Conn. Arch., Rev. Ser., XXXVI, 324; Loyalist Transcripts, XI, 90, 112, 118, 168, 214, 218, 250, 294, 296; XXVIII, 7-8, 15, 23, and *passim*. Tory claims to the British commissioners were, of course, frequently exaggerated. Compare Samuel Peters' claim and the supporting evidence with the award that was finally made. Peters Papers, I, 96; II, 43, 73; Loyalist Transcripts, XI, 250. In examining the confiscated estates of the Tories the state officials often found large outstanding debts against them. See the case of Joshua Chandler, Loyalist Transcripts, XI, 112; Ontario Bur. Arch., *Report for 1904*, 286-87; New Haven Probate Papers, no. 2479.

63. Conn. Arch., Rev. Ser., VIII, 152a, 153.

64. Loyalist Transcripts, XII, 57, 231, 359, 429, 437, 623; Ontario Bur. Arch., *Report for 1904*, 716-17, 812.

65. Loyalist Transcripts, XII, 265, 299, 315, 318, 467; Ontario Bur. Arch., *Report for 1904*, 900, 1123.

66. Moses C. Tyler, "The Loyalists in the American Revolution," *Amer. Hist. Rev.*, 1 (1895), 27.

67. O'Callaghan, *Docs. Rel. to the Col. Hist. of N. Y.*, VIII, 807.

68. Tiffany, American Colonies, bk. 4, p. 18.

69. Hinman, *Historical Collection*, 12; Gilbert, "Connecticut Loyal-

ists," 278; Epaphroditus Peck, *The Loyalists of Connecticut,* Conn. Tercentenary Commission, *Publs.,* 31 (1934), 3.

70. Fragment dated May 12, 1774, MS Votes for Governor and Assistants.

71. Samuel Gray to Joseph Trumbull, May 15, 1775, Joseph Trumbull Papers.

72. Jonathan to Joseph Trumbull, May 13, 1776, Joseph Trumbull Papers, State Lib., IV, 413.

73. Undated item in the Stiles Papers, Historical. Stiles' figures were probably based upon the survey made by Durham's Congregational pastor, the Rev. Elizur Goodrich. See Purcell, *Connecticut in Transition,* 52. Samuel Peters exaggerated the strength of the Episcopal church. He later claimed that the Anglicans numbered about one-third of the colony's population, or about 60,000 people, and owned "near" one half of the land. Peters to Samuel Seabury, Aug. 30, 1783; to the Loyalist Commissioners, Dec. 6, 1783, Peters Papers, I, 75, 96.

74. Stiles, *Diary,* II, 62.

75. *Conn. Col. Recs.,* XIV, 491.

76. Undated item in the Stiles Papers, Historical. In 1779 Stiles claimed that about 42 per cent of the adult males in the town of New Haven were either Tories or "timid Whigs." *Diary,* II, 352-53. According to the census of 1774, there were 1864 men in the town between the ages of 20-70. *Conn. Col. Recs.,* XIV, 486. This would have meant that more than 750 men were either Loyalists or lukewarm patriots. On the strength of the conservative elements in New Haven on the eve of the Revolution see Gipson, *Ingersoll,* 328-29; Loyalist Transcripts, XII, 29; Atwater, *New Haven,* 482. Litchfield's historian writes, "The fact is not to be disguised that there had been from the first a formidable minority of the voters . . . who were bitter opponents of the 'Great Rebellion.' " Payne K. Kilbourne, *Sketches and Chronicles of the Town of Litchfield* (Hartford, 1859), 108.

77. Hawks and Perry, *Doc. Hist.,* II, 200-1.

78. *Conn. Col. Recs.,* XIV, 491.

79. Sabine was certain that the number of Connecticut's Tories was larger in proportion to the population than it was in any other New England colony. Lorenzo Sabine, *Biographical Sketches of Loyalists of the American Revolution* (Boston, 1864), I, 27. This guess has been repeated by others. See Tyler, "Loyalists in the American Revolution," 28; George E. Ellis, "The Loyalists and Their Fortunes," in

Justin Winsor, ed., *Narrative and Critical History of America* (Boston, 1884-89), VII, 189.

80. The proportion is taken from an undated manuscript in the Stiles Papers, Historical. See also the Rev. Mr. Beach to the Secretary of the S. P. G., Oct. 20, 1773, April 12, 1774, in Hawks and Perry, *Doc. Hist.,* II, 192, 195. The quotation is from the petition of a Fairfield County Tory suspect. Conn. Arch., Rev. Ser., XX, 101a.

81. Stiles, *Diary,* II, 62.

82. Conn. Arch., Rev. Ser., XXXIV, *passim.*

83. Brigadier Gen. Gold S. Silliman to the Rev. Joseph Fish, July 1, 1777, Silliman-Fish Papers, Yale University.

84. Conn. Arch., Rev. Ser., XX, 95a.

85. *Ibid.,* VIII, 146, 148, 174; XIII, 307ab; XXVIII, 58a; Loyalist Transcripts, XII, 414, 663.

86. Petition of Stephen Gorham, July 22, 1777, in Fairfield Superior Court Papers, bundle dated 1770-79.

Bibliographical Essay

STUDENTS of early America will find rich and relatively unexplored manuscript fields relating to Connecticut. Such sources are especially abundant for the pre-Revolutionary history of the province. Without the information and insights that these documents afford, no history of eighteenth-century Connecticut could be complete, and the writing of this book would have been impossible.

Most of the collections are concentrated in libraries in Hartford, where the major bodies of manuscripts are to be found in the Connecticut Historical Society and the State Library, and in New Haven, New York City, and Washington.

Among the several important collections in the Historical Society four are extremely significant: the papers of William Samuel Johnson, those of Jonathan Trumbull, Connecticut's Revolutionary governor, and of his son, Joseph, and the manuscripts of William Williams, Trumbull's son-in-law and an ardent Whig. Of these the Johnson papers are by far the most revealing and the bulkiest, consisting of four bound volumes and many boxes crammed with loose manuscripts, mostly letters. Johnson maintained an extensive correspondence with men of varied political and religious principles, Whigs, moderates, Anglicans, and Tories. Johnson's sentiments are clearly outlined in the copies of his own letters, and it is possible to find many different points of view in the letters that he received. Both economic and political developments stand out in the three boxes of Jonathan Trumbull's correspondence, Personal and Private, Political and Official, and Mercantile, and the same is true of the papers of Joseph Trumbull, who was for a time his father's business associate. The Joseph Trumbull papers comprise a huge collection; however, all except the first box, which covers the years 1761-1775, and several items in the second box, deal primarily with the war period. In contrast with the size of the collections already mentioned, the papers of William Williams require only one box, but they include some key documents, especially on the political events leading up to the Revolution. Other manuscripts that were helpful, although not so basic for this study as the four groups just described, were the papers of Jedidiah Huntington, Oliver Wolcott (both father and son), David Trumbull, some items in boxes I and III of the General Assembly papers, and the fragmentary but very interesting nomination and election totals in the box labelled "Votes for Governor and Assistants."

In the vaults and files of the State Library, there are several massive and important collections, among them the twenty-nine bound volumes, many of them in two parts, of the Jonathan Trumbull papers and the even larger body of manuscripts known as the Connecticut Archives. The former contains many letters sent to Trumbull, drafts of Trumbull's own letters and speeches, official documents, and miscellaneous items; these touch upon almost every phase of Connecticut history in the years immediately preceding and during the Revolution. Selections from the correspondence have been printed in the publications of the Massachusetts and Connecticut historical societies; however, there is much in this outstanding group that has never been completely exploited. The archives are arranged in several series. The series most important for the period under investigation was the Revolutionary War, First Series (36 vols.); other sections—Ecclesiastical Affairs, Susquehanna Settlers, and Trade and Maritime Affairs—were useful for the particular subjects defined by their titles.

Fortunately these archival documents have been indexed and are relatively easy to consult. It is more difficult to distill evidence from the records of the Probate, County, and Superior Courts, but he who is willing to sift the file papers will find his work rewarding. The probate papers, for example, helped to develop a clearer picture of the economic and social status of the Connecticut Tory, and the trial papers of the County and Superior Courts shed light on individual Tories and their political convictions. Also in the State Library are copies of the records of almost all of Connecticut's towns for the Revolutionary period. These transcripts, which begin in most cases with 1774-75 and cover the war years, are not so full as one might hope, but they show the reaction of Connecticut's sixty-odd "miniature republics" to the Revolutionary crisis. Other useful documents in the State Library are to be found in the five bound volumes of the Governor Joseph Trumbull papers, and there are a few items that relate to the Revolutionary era in the one-volume collection of Jonathan Trumbull, Jr., papers.

One of the most significant groups of manuscripts bearing on the history of eighteenth-century Connecticut, and indeed on all of New England, is the collection of Ezra Stiles papers at Yale University. Stiles' interests were encyclopedic and his voluminous writings touched upon every one of them. Although Stiles' ministry in the years before the war was in Newport, he maintained very close contact with his native colony, receiving and sending numerous letters to relatives and his many friends and associates in the church in Connecticut. The many letters that he preserved, including copies of his own letters, constitute a large and invaluable collection. Other manuscripts in the possession of Yale are the W. G. Lane Memorial Collection, containing letters of Matthew Griswold, Jonathan Trumbull, and Samuel Huntington; the Silliman papers, some of which relate to Connecticut history before and during the Revolution; the E. E. Chorley papers, many of them copies, which concentrate on the experiences of several Anglican ministers in Connecticut during the Revolutionary era; the Leffingwell family collection, which contains several items on the Norwich and Windham Committee of Inspection; the Silliman-Fish manuscripts, some of which describe conditions in the town of Fairfield during the war; and the Benjamin Gale manuscripts. Unfortunately, there is but one significant letter in the Gale papers, Titus Hosmer's reply to Gale's plan proposing to change the colony's system of elections. The other manuscripts are almost exclusively of a theological nature and were written by Gale after the Revolution. It is a pity that Gale's papers have not been preserved; if they were available, our knowledge of the political, economic, and religious history of Connecticut would probably be more complete, and certainly richer in dramatic incident.

Connecticut libraries hold the largest and most important bodies of manuscripts; valuable historical nuggets, however, are also to be found in unpublished sources in New York and Washington libraries. The Samuel Adams papers in the New York Public Library include some letters written by Connecticut Whigs; the Emmet collection holds a few interesting items, chiefly on Jared Ingersoll and the Stamp Act; and the fragments that comprise the Samuel Avery papers contain what I believe to be hitherto unused information on the Susquehannah Company and general political matters. The other pertinent manuscript material in this library falls under two major groups of transcripts. The first, in 70-odd volumes, is the Loyalist Transcripts, copied from the papers of the parliamentary commission that was set up after the Revolution to investigate the losses and services of the American Loyalists. Although the entire record of the commission was not copied, there is a tremendous fund of information in these large volumes. Testimony and other evidence relating to Connecticut Tories are to be found chiefly in volume XII; other scattered references to Connecticut are also in volumes XI and XXVIII, and volumes II and IV of the Calendar of Original Memorials. The second and even larger group of transcripts—over 200 volumes—was made by the indefatigable George Bancroft. This collection includes two volumes of the correspondence of Samuel and William Samuel Johnson, 1737-89; one volume of Connecticut Papers, letters written by Jonathan Trumbull, William Samuel Johnson, Jared Ingersoll, Roger Sherman and others, 1759-76; two volumes of the correspondence of William Samuel Johnson with Governors Pitkin and Trumbull, 1766-71; one volume of Ezra Stiles' papers, letters and miscellaneous material; three volumes of Thomas Hutchinson's correspondence, 1765-74; and one large folder on the Boston Committee of Correspondence, 1774. The originals of many of these were seen elsewhere, and some, such as Johnson's correspondence with Pitkin and Trumbull, have been published. Nevertheless these transcripts are extremely useful, especially for political developments; they are on the whole faithful copies of the originals, and in many cases are more legible.

While the William Samuel Johnson papers speak for the Anglican whose politics were moderately conservative, the Samuel Peters manuscripts (8 vols. in the New York Historical Society) represent the religious and political point of view of the extreme Anglican Tory. Many of the Peters papers have to do with this Anglican priest's post-Revolutionary career, but material in the first volume and scattered documents throughout the remainder of the collection relate to the period covered by this study. Another very useful body of papers in the New York Historical Society is the Connecticut volume of Hawks Transcripts of the records of the Protestant Episcopal Church, comprising letters sent by Anglican missionaries in Connecticut to the home office of the Society for the Propagation of the Gospel in Foreign Parts. Many of these letters were printed in Francis L. Hawks and William S. Perry, comps., *Documentary History of the Protestant Episcopal Church in the United States* (2 vols., New York, 1863-64); others, however, remain unpublished. In these papers one can trace the slow and difficult growth of the Anglican church from the time it was established in the Puritan colony up to the Revolution, and since religion in eighteenth-century Connecticut could not be separated from politics it is not surprising that the missionaries' letters frequently commented on provincial and imperial political questions. One other item in the New York Historical Society must be mentioned, the letter written by William Williams to Eliphalet Dyer, Nov. 26, 1773. This document, together with a few letters sent by Silas Deane to William Samuel Johnson (Johnson Papers, Connecticut Historical Society), brings to light an interesting factional quarrel that divided some of Connecticut's leading Whigs just before the Revolution.

Few manuscripts in the Library of Congress bear on the last few decades of Connecticut's colonial history. Jared Ingersoll's short Historical Account of Some Affairs Relating to the Church Especially in Connecticut briefly sketches some of the incidents and effects of the Great Awakening in the years 1740-43; the portfolio of William Samuel Johnson papers holds a few interesting items, especially on the Stamp Act Congress; William Williams' fragmentary diary for January-April 1774 has a sentence or two on the important election of 1774; and there are a few references each in the volume of Force Transcripts (Connecticut Miscellaneous Papers, 1637-1783) and the volume of Stevens Transcripts (Connecticut Miscellaneous Papers, 1740-87). Thomas Moffat, who spent some time in New London as a customs officer, tersely and bitterly comments on the Whigs and the Revolution in his diary for 1775-77. Consider Tiffany, an obscure Anglican Tory, explains the causes of the Revolution in a simple and rather crudely written history of the American colonies and the Revolution. This document, a typescript of the original discovered by Dr. Clarence E. Carter of the State Department, was placed in the library under restricted use; permission to examine and quote from it was kindly granted to me by Dr. Carter.

Two items concerned with economic developments remain to be mentioned. The first, in the National Archives, is a list of the ships that sailed from and entered the port of New Haven, 1762-1801, their destinations and ports of origin, and a summary of the chief commodities in their cargoes. The other is the Shaw manuscripts in the New London County Historical Society, some of which touch upon that port's coastal and West Indian trade before and after the Revolution.

Newspapers

Students of colonial America have long been aware of the importance of the provincial newspaper. Connecticut's papers in the colonial period were neither so numerous nor so polished, if that word may be used at all, as some of their contemporaries in the other colonies. The few that Connecticut had, however, were as much a mirror of provincial life as any other colonial newsletter, and of course they were invaluable for this study.

Connecticut's most important papers were Hartford's *Connecticut Courant,* the first number of which was probably published Nov. 26, 1764; the *Connecticut (New London) Gazette,* which appeared for the first time on November 18, 1763; another *Connecticut Gazette* published at New Haven from April 12, 1775, until it was discontinued on Feb. 19, 1768; and finally the *Connecticut Journal,* also of New Haven, which began publication on Oct. 23, 1767. The best files of the *New London Gazette* and the *Courant* are in the Connecticut Historical Society. The Society has also developed microfilm copies of the latter paper. These have been purchased by many libraries, and in New York City copies are available in the New York Historical Society, the New York Public Library, and the library of City College. The Yale University library has the most complete file of the *Connecticut Gazette* and the *Connecticut Journal.* Two other titles complete the list of provincial papers, the *New London Summary,* 1758-63, and the *Norwich Packet,* which apparently began Oct.

7, 1773, and continued beyond the period of this study. I consulted the file of the latter in the Connecticut State Library.

Printed Sources

The basic printed source is the 15 volumes of the *Public Records of the Colony of Connecticut 1636-1776,* I-III edited by James H. Trumbull, IV-XV by Charles J. Hoadly (Hartford, 1850-90). Behind the bare recital of laws, decisions, petitions, and appointments registered in these volumes is the dramatic story of the evolution of a few scattered, tiny communities into a self-governing colony and then into an independent state. The *Public Records of the State of Connecticut,* Charles J. Hoadly, ed. (3 vols., Hartford, 1894-1922) continues the official narrative through the better part of the Revolution. The periodic revisions of the provincial laws also present snapshots of the colony as it grew and matured. The code of 1750, *Acts and Laws of Connecticut* (New London, 1750), conveniently summarizes the statutes in effect at mid-century; not until after the Revolution did another code substantially modify the laws in the 1750 revision.

Town records afford another approach through official sources to the study of eighteenth-century Connecticut, but only few of these have been published. What local records neglect and time have not destroyed now generally lie stored away in the vaults and safes of the town halls. A survey of this material made more than forty years ago by Nelson P. Mead is "Public Archives of Connecticut," in American Historical Association, *Annual Report for 1906,* 2 (1908), 53-127. Certainly not all of it deserves the recognition of the printed page, but some of the records of the major towns might well be reproduced. What now appears in print for the eighteenth century are scattered extracts in local histories, and parts of the records of a few towns; a good example is the *Hartford Town Votes 1635-1716,* Connecticut Historical Society, *Collections,* 6 (1897).

The process of discovering what went on in the minds of Connecticut's magistrates as they wrote and rewrote laws, rendered decisions, settled disputes, argued, bargained, or pleaded with the royal government, or otherwise executed their official responsibilities, is not an easy task. Neither the journals of the lower house of the legislature nor those of the governor and council are known to exist for the years 1744-79, but it is sometimes possible to trace a point more fully in the manuscript archives and in the selections from the correspondence of Connecticut's governors during the middle years of the eighteenth century. The Connecticut Historical Society has published this correspondence, most of which is of an official character, in its *Collections*. Volumes 4 and 5 of that series (1892, 1896) reproduce the Talcott papers, edited by Mary K. Talcott, covering the years 1724-41. Volumes 11, 13, and 15 (1907, 1911, 1914) include correspondence and documents pertaining to the magistracy of Governor Law, 1741-50; Governor Wolcott's papers, 1750-54, are printed in volume 16 (1916); the papers of Governor Fitch, 1755-66, take up two volumes, 17 and 18 (1918, 1920), and those of Governor Pitkin, 1766-69, are printed in volume 19 (1921). These four collections were edited by Albert C. Bates.

Documents bearing on the delicate problem of the balance between Connecticut's privileges and the demands of the home government are of particular significance. An old but convenient compilation on the subject, covering the first century of Connecticut's history, is Royal R. Hinman, ed., *Letters from the English Kings and Queens . . . to the Governors of Connecticut, Together with the Answers Thereto from 1639-1749* (Hartford, 1836). Many references bearing on this point appear, of course, in the colonial records; and the printed correspondence of the governors cited above, which spans the period from 1724 to 1769, is largely taken up with the colonial-imperial relationship. Unfortunately, the papers covering Governor Trumbull's administration, which would embrace the years immediately before the outbreak of the Revolution, have not yet been published. The four volumes of Trumbull papers that were printed in the Massachusetts Historical Society, *Collections,* 5th series, 9 and 10 (1885, 1888) and 7th series, 2 and 3 (1902) concentrate upon the war itself, except for some early miscellaneous documents in volume 9 and that part of the same volume, pp. 213-490, which reproduces the extremely important correspondence between William Samuel Johnson and Governors Pitkin and Trumbull during Johnson's agency abroad, 1766-71. Other printed materials, including some correspondence, help to describe the repercussions of the mounting imperial crisis in Connecticut. The conservative's reaction is shown in the indispensable "Jared Ingersoll Papers," edited by Franklin B. Dexter, in the New Haven Colony Historical Society, *Papers,* 9 (1918), 201-472. On the Whig side was Silas Deane, whose correspondence for the years leading up to the Revolution is published in the Connecticut Historical Society, *Collections,* 2 (1870), 129-368, and in part in the New York Historical Society, *Collections for 1886* (1887) [edited by Charles B. Isham].

Additional useful references on the last days of the colony and the first years of statehood may be found in the following printed sources: *The Huntington Papers* [edited by Edward Gray and Albert C. Bates], Connecticut Historical Society, *Collections,* 20 (1923); Clarence E. Carter, ed., *The Correspondence of General Thomas Gage with the Secretaries of State 1763-1775* (2 vols., New Haven, 1931-33); Edmund C. Burnett, ed., *Letters of Members of the Continental Congress* (8 vols., Washington, 1921-36); Peter Force, ed., *American Archives,* 4th series (6 vols., Washington, 1837-46); and Royal R. Hinman, comp., *A Historical Collection . . . of the Part Sustained by Connecticut during the War of the Revolution* (Hartford, 1842).

Other printed materials supplement the official documents, not only on the political events preceding the Revolution, but on a variety of subjects and over a longer span of time. The four volumes of *The Susquehannah Company Papers,* excellently edited by Julian P. Boyd (Wilkes-Barre, 1930-34), bring together a tremendous store of information culled from many different sources on the speculative land ventures that embroiled Connecticut's relations with Pennsylvania after 1754 and ultimately became a major political issue within the colony. Unfortunately, the last volume does not go beyond 1772 and thus falls short of describing the events that reached a climax in the election of 1774. Although the collection does not carry the history of the company to its end, it nevertheless constitutes the fullest and best commentary on Connecticut's westward movement and organized land speculation in the colony in the eighteenth century. Another valuable economic source is the mercantile letter book of Nathaniel Shaw, Jr., in the New London County Historical Society, *Collections,* 2 (1933), 169-336. It is the most notable example in print of an extensive business correspondence of a major Connecticut merchant in the colonial period.

Two late seventeenth-century political tracts, reprinted in the Connecticut Historical Society, *Collections,* are of special interest because they practically anticipate the political philosophy of the Tory a century later: *The People's Right to Election or Alteration of Government in Connecticott Argued in a Letter,* 1 (1860), 60-81, and *Will and Doom or the Miseries of Connecticut by and under an Usurped and Arbitrary Power,* 3 (1895), 81-269. Written by Gershom Bulkeley, these were an aftermath of the abortive attempt of the royal government to destroy Connecticut's charter by absorbing the province into the Dominion of New England. As a supporter of royal prerogative, Bulkeley, like his eighteenth-century successors, had little love for Connecticut's cherished powers of self-government. After the Revolution a much less able but equally bitter Tory, William Bates of Stamford, enumerated with a good deal of exaggeration some of his experiences during the war and the trying days of the Tory emigration and settlement in Nova Scotia in *Kingston and the Loyalists of 1783* (St. John, N.B., 1889). Slender information on some Connecticut Tories who moved to Canada may also be found in A. Fraser, archivist,

Second Report of the Bureau of Archives for the Province of Ontario for 1904 (Toronto, 1905). One may read the protests of the many Anglican Tories who complained that they were hounded for their religious as well as their political convictions, and otherwise follow the development of the Anglican church in colonial Connecticut, in Francis L. Hawks and William S. Perry, comps., *Documentary History of the Protestant Episcopal Church in the United States . . . Containing Numerous Hitherto Unpublished Documents Concerning the Church in Connecticut* (2 vols., New York, 1863-64), and in the works of Connecticut's most important Anglican minister, Samuel Johnson, in Herbert and Carol Schneider, eds., *Samuel Johnson His Career and Writings* (4 vols., New York, 1929).

All but a few of the records of the established colonial church are unpublished, but a good deal of information about the religious and ecclesiastical history of eighteenth-century Connecticut may be drawn from the printed colonial records and the correspondence of the governors. The official *Records of the General Association of the Colony of Connecticut 1738-1799* (Hartford, 1888) do not contain much more than the bare decisions of that body, and personal records like diaries and letters are at times richer in their references to contemporary religious events. Comments on Connecticut's early religious history and on several other matters, including background material for the religious revival, are reported in the "Extracts of Letters to Rev. Thomas Prince," printed in the Connecticut Historical Society, *Collections,* 3 (1895), 275-320. The Rev. Daniel Wadsworth's *Diary* for the decade 1737-47, George L. Walker, ed. (Hartford, 1894), rather fully describes a conservative minister's reaction to the Great Awakening. The most notable examples of personal records that abound in comments on religious developments, and indeed upon almost everything else too, are the printed works of a more famous Puritan divine, Ezra Stiles. These include the *Literary Diary* (3 vols., New Haven, 1901) and a volume that was especially significant for this study, *Extracts from the Itineraries and other Miscellanies of Ezra Stiles . . . With a Selection from his Correspondence* (New Haven, 1916). Both of these works were very ably edited by Franklin B. Dexter.

Several other contemporary personal accounts are interesting and useful for their information on a range of topics, both local and colony-wide. Joshua Hempstead's bulky and yet tersely written *Diary,* printed in the New London County Historical Society, *Collections,* 1 (1901), outlines the routine of daily living in New London for almost fifty years, 1711-58; Sarah K. Knight includes comments on provincial Connecticut in 1704 in the *Journal of Madam Knight* (New York, 1935 edn.), describing her travels from Boston to New York; and Roger Wolcott's "A Memoir for the History of Connecticut," printed in the Connecticut Historical Society, *Collections,* 3 (1895), 325-36, sketchily describes some of the incidents in the early history of the province.

One type of printed source for the history of eighteenth-century Connecticut is particularly abundant, the contemporary pamphlet. Colonial writers recognized in the printing press a powerful ally in a dispute, no matter whether they were considering an abstruse religious point, the colony's political privileges, or some economic issue. Quite naturally, more was written on religious themes than on any other subject, but as secular interests grew in importance in the later years of the eighteenth century the economic and political tract appeared more frequently. It would serve no useful purpose to discuss every one of the many pamphlets that were consulted; moreover, practically complete lists of eighteenth-century Connecticut pamphlets can be conveniently found in James H. Trumbull, *List of Books Printed in Connecticut 1709-1800* (Hartford, 1904), and Albert C. Bates, *Supplementary List of Books Printed in Connecticut 1709-1800* (Hartford, 1938). Here it would be best to comment briefly on a few tracts that were typical or especially helpful.

Not many pamphlets were written upon exclusively economic

subjects, but among them are a few of outstanding merit. Jared Eliot's *Essays upon Field Husbandry in New England as It Is or May Be Ordered* (Boston, 1760) is of course the best contemporary discussion of agricultural conditions and of methods of improvement. There are also some references to Connecticut in the description of the New England countryside in the anonymous *American Husbandry,* Harry J. Carman, ed. (New York, 1939). Some of the conditions criticized by Eliot helped to create the discontent that spurred land-hungry Yankees to seek new farms and to support projects of land expansion. The Susquehannah Company affair gave rise to a number of interesting pamphlets, of which most of those published up to 1772 have been conveniently assembled in Boyd's *Susquehannah Company Papers.* One of these is a good example of this type of pamphlet and an effective statement of Connecticut's case in the critical year of 1774: *A Plea in Vindication of the Connecticut Title to the Contested Lands Lying West of the Province of New York Addressed to the Public* (New Haven, 1774), by the patriot minister Benjamin Trumbull.

No sharp distinction can be drawn between the economic and the political tract, or between the latter and the religious. Acrimonious political arguments take up many pages of the pamphlet literature on the Susquehannah Company, and in ostensibly religious works, especially after the Great Awakening, it is not unusual to find some political implications drawn from the discussion. The imperial crisis naturally provoked the publication of several political tracts. The two Connecticut conservatives who played leading roles in the Stamp Act drama explained and defended their positions to their skeptical neighbors: the former stampmaster, Jared Ingersoll, in his *Mr. Ingersoll's Letters Relating to the Stamp Act* (New Haven, 1766), and the governor, Thomas Fitch, in *Some Reasons that Influenced the Governor to Take and the Councillors to Administer the Oath Required ... by the Stamp Act* (Hartford, 1766). But those who sympathetically read the Whig pamphlets attributed to Ebenezer Devotion and to Benjamin

Church, *The Examiner Examined in a Letter from a Gentleman in Connecticut to his Friend in London* (New London, 1766) and *Liberty and Property Vindicated and the St—pm-n Burnt* (Boston, 1765), probably had little feeling for the stampmaster or the governor and their explanations.

Although secular interests expanded in eighteenth-century Connecticut, the religious tract continued to outnumber every other kind of pamphlet. Most were sermons, others theological debates or discussions of ecclesiastical systems. Few would be considered interesting reading today, but such pamphlets remain good revelations of the colonial mind and of various aspects of pre-Revolutionary life. The stubborn and bitter religious debates of New Light and Old Light divines during and after the Great Awakening were aired in a small flood of pamphlets, often repetitious and heavily weighted with theological abstractions. Again it is not necessary to cite more than a few as examples.

New Light principles were both stated and critized in *An Answer of the Pastor and Brethren of the Third Church in Windham to Twelve Articles Exhibited by Several of its Separating Members as Reasons of their Separation* (New London, 1747). Several years before, when the excesses of the Awakening had seemed to be getting out of hand, Lyme's moderate New Light minister Jonathan Parsons felt the need of urging *A Needful Caution in a Critical Day* (New London, 1742). Yale's authorities, however, were much more severe toward their own religious rebels, and after ousting two students explained and justified their disciplinary action in *The Judgment of the Rector and Tutors of Yale-College Concerning Two of the Students Who Were Expelled* (New London, 1745).

The debate went on, hot and acrimonious down the years. More than two decades after the revival began Robert Ross, who still hoped to convince the "enthusiasts" of their errors, appealed to them in *A Plain Address to the Quakers, Moravians, Separatists, Separate-Bapists, Rogerenes and other Enthusiasts...* (New Haven,

1762); and three years later a pamphlet supposedly written by Governor Fitch tried to soothe the troubled religious waters with *An Explanation of Saybrook Platform . . . by One That Heartily Desires the Order, Peace and Purity of These Churches* (Hartford, 1765). Much more belligerent was the Old Light divine, Joseph Fish, who attacked the Baptists and Separatists in *The Church of Christ a Firm and Durable House* (New London, 1767). But the Baptist minister Isaac Backus pithily retorted with *A Fish Caught in His Own Net* (Boston, 1768). This started a battle of words between Fish and Backus that continued to the eve of the Revolution. When the Rev. Ebenezer White was removed from his church in Danbury because of his Sandemanian leanings, the incident was fully discussed in *A Brief Narrative of the Proceedings of the Eastern Association . . . against Mr. White . . . since the Year 1762* (New Haven, 1764) and *A Vindication of the Proceedings of the Eastern Association in Fairfield County* (New Haven, 1764).

A more important dispute stemming from a minister's religious views was the so-called Wallingford controversy, which is especially interesting because it was exploited by the New Lights in an attempt to capture control of the provincial government. When Yale's Thomas Clap was accused of turning a political New Light because he advocated the establishment of a separate college congregation within the school—see his *The Religious Constitution of Colleges Especially of Yale College in New Haven* (New London, 1754)—an Old Light partisan (probably Benjamin Gale) writing under the initials "A. Z." had attacked Clap and his project by calling for an end of the colony's financial contribution to the college in *The Present State of the Colony of Connecticut Considered in a Letter from a Gentleman in the Eastern Part of Said Colony to His Friend in the Western Part of the Same* (New London, 1755). But this example of political counter-attack was more than matched by the New Light strategy which was the aftermath of the Wallingford controversy, as the conservative author,

"An Aged Layman," made clear in his worried appeal, *A Letter to the Clergy of the Colony of Connecticut* (New Haven, 1760). For a fuller treatment of the entire controversy see Franklin B. Dexter, "Thomas Clap and His Writings," New Haven Colony Historical Society, *Papers,* 6 (1894), 256-60, and George C. Groce, "Benjamin Gale," *New England Quarterly,* 10 (1937), 702 and *n*10.

Indeed, in the several decades before the Revolution it was unusual if the religious pamphlet did not strike some political note. This was particularly true of sermons. Thanksgiving sermons such as the Rev. James Lockwood's *Sermon Preached at Weathersfield, July 6, 1763 Being the Day Appointed by Authority for a Public Thanksgiving* (New Haven, 1763) might celebrate the preservation of cherished liberties from a foreign foe. Three years later ministers were expressing their thanks for the end of another kind of threat, this time from within the empire: [Benjamin Throop], *A Thanksgiving Sermon upon the Occasion of the Glorious News of the Repeal of the Stamp Act, Preached in New Concord, in Norwich June 26, 1766* (New London, 1766).

Fast days, town elections, and indeed, almost any convenient public celebration gave the ministers many opportunities to voice their political creed. Almost always they used the occasion to remind their audience of the greatness of the colony's political and religious heritage; and as the imperial crisis deepened, they more frequently exhorted their listeners and readers to preserve that heritage. Examples of such occasional sermons are Eliphalet Huntington, *The Freeman's Directory; or, Well Accomplished, and Faithful Rulers Discribed: A Discourse Delivered at the Freemen's Meeting in Killingworth April 11, 1768* (Hartford, 1768); James Dana, *A Century Discourse Delivered at the Anniversary Meeting of the Freemen of the Town of Wallingford April 9, 1770* (New Haven, 1770); Benjamin Trumbull, *A Discourse Delivered at the Anniversary Meeting of the Freemen of the Town of New Haven April 12, 1773* (New Haven, 1773); Allyn Mather, *The Character of a Well Accomplished Ruler Describ'd, A Dis-*

course Delivered at the Freemen's Meeting in New Haven, April 8, 1776 (New Haven, 1776); Judah Champion, *A Brief View of the Distresses, Hardships and Dangers Our Ancestors Encounter'd* (Hartford, 1770); Enoch Huntington, *Fast Sermon, Middletown, July 20, 1775* (Hartford, 1775).

Despite the visible gathering of the political storm-clouds after the enactment of the new tax on tea, Suffield's minister, the Rev. Israel Holly, remained confident that *God Brings About His Holy and Wise Purpose or Decree* (Hartford, 1774). Several months later, however, the Rev. Samuel Sherwood of Fairfield and the Rev. Ebenezer Baldwin of Danbury took special pains to advise their neighbors about the menace that threatened to overwhelm them. Sherwood delivered and published *A Sermon Containing Scriptural Instruction to Civil Rulers and All Free-Born Subjects. In Which the Principles of Sound Policy and Good Government Are Established and Indicated; and Some Doctrines Advanced and Zealously Propagated by New England Tories Are Considered and Refuted* (New Haven, 1774). Included in the volume were an "Address to the Freemen of the Colony," also prepared by Sherwood, and Baldwin's "Appendix Stating the Grievances the Colonies Labour Under from Several Late Acts of the British Parliament and Shewing What We Have Just Reason to Expect the Consequences of These Measures Will Be." But when the Anglican rector of St. Paul's Church in Wallingford, the Rev. Samuel Andrews, tried to use the occasion of the general fast in 1775 to profess his own political theories, which happened to be closer to the Tory version, in *A Discourse Shewing the Necessity of Joining Internal Repentance with the External Profession of It* (New Haven, 1775), he encountered serious trouble at the hands of the Whig authorities. By 1775, of course, the times demanded a complete unity of Whig convictions, as is demonstrated by the theme of the Rev. Enoch Huntington's sermon at the freemen's meeting in Middletown, April 8, 1776: *The Happy Effects of Union and the Fatal Tendency of Divisions* (Hartford, 1776).

A final type of contemporary source is the printed version of
the sermon delivered at the annual gathering of dignitaries in
May to learn the results of the colonial elections. Sixty such election sermons were consulted, extending from the opening years of
the eighteenth century through 1776, and most of them have been
referred to in the text or footnotes. Although much in them is
standard, in the regular definitions of Puritan morality, the exhortations to godliness, the discussions of the relationship between
church and state, and the descriptions of the good ruler and the
worthy subject, Connecticut's ministers were announcing not only
their own beliefs and prejudices but also those of most of the people in the province. These sermons, therefore, are valuable as
annual indices of current colonial opinion.

Secondary Works

The general setting of colonial and New England history is
described in several standard works, among which the following
were most useful: Herbert L. Osgood, *The American Colonies in
the Eighteenth Century* (4 vols., New York, 1924); Osgood, *The
American Colonies in the Seventeenth Century* (3 vols., New
York, 1907); Charles M. Andrews, *The Colonial Period of American History* (4 vols., New Haven, 1934-38); Andrews, *The
Colonial Background of the American Revolution* (New Haven,
1935); Lawrence H. Gipson, *The British Empire before the
American Revolution* (5 vols., Caldwell, Idaho, and New York,
1936-42); John G. Palfrey, *History of New England* (5 vols.,
Boston, 1858-90).

More specialized political, economic, and religious studies
also provided background material. James T. Adams, *Revolutionary New England 1691-1776* (Boston, 1923), devotes some attention to Connecticut, and Arthur M. Schlesinger, *The Colonial
Merchants and the American Revolution 1763-1776* (New York,
1918) includes brief accounts of the position taken by the Connecticut traders in the decade before the Revolution. Turning to

religious treatments, Williston Walker's *A History of the Congregational Churches in the United States* (New York, 1894) is a good survey of the legally established church in eighteenth-century Connecticut. *The Anglican Episcopate and the American Colonies* (Cambridge, 1924), by Arthur L. Cross, is a standard study of that important subject, but it gives no consideration to the issue in Connecticut. Alice M. Baldwin's *The New England Clergy and the American Revolution* (Durham, 1928) excellently summarizes the political philosophy and the patriotic activities of the Puritan minister, and draws upon many Connecticut sources. Finally, Joseph Tracy's *The Great Awakening* (Boston, 1842) is an old but worthy treatment of the religious revival.

The first two histories of Connecticut were written by eighteenth-century ministers, Benjamin Trumbull and Samuel Peters, both of whom participated in the events that led up to the Revolution. Trumbull was a moderate New Light and a Whig, Peters an Anglican and a Tory. Trumbull's work, *A Complete History of Connecticut . . . 1630 . . . to the Close of the Indian Wars* (2 vols., New Haven, 1818), heavily emphasizes religious and military history, and despite the author's prejudices is especially good on the former subject. Peters' *A General History of Connecticut* (New Haven, 1829) is not very much of a narrative history, and his partisan account is replete with inaccurate statements, and, at times, absurd exaggerations. Yet the book has some value, if only for its point of view.

Later general histories were not very helpful: Gideon H. Hollister, *The History of Connecticut from the First Settlement of the Colony to the Adoption of the Present Constitution* (2 vols., Hartford, 1857); W. H. Carpenter and T. S. Arthur, *The History of Connecticut* (Philadelphia, 1872); and G. L. Clark, *A History of Connecticut* (New York, 1914). But chapters in Nelson P. Mead's *Connecticut as a Corporate Colony* (Lancaster, 1906) and Richard J. Purcell's *Connecticut in Transition 1775-1818* (Washington, 1918) were useful. The best general commentary on colonial Connecticut, however, is to be found in Charles M. Andrews' works, of which an excellent example is the brief but brilliant essay on *Connecticut's Place in Colonial History* (New York, 1924).

Book-size studies of particular aspects of eighteenth-century Connecticut are not very numerous. Maria L. Greene's *The Development of Religious Liberty in Connecticut* (Boston and New York, 1905) is an excellent analysis of the breakdown of religious uniformity. Many years before the appearance of Greene's book, anniversaries had been the occasions for the publication of two useful works on the history of the Congregational church in Connecticut: Leonard Bacon, *Thirteen Historical Discourses, on the Completion of Two Hundred Years, from the Beginning of the First Church in New Haven* (New Haven, 1839), and *Contributions to the Ecclesiastical History of Connecticut Prepared under the Direction of the General Association to Commemorate the Completion of One Hundred and Fifty Years since Its First Annual Assembly* (New Haven, 1861). Two good examinations of economic phases of pre-Revolutionary Connecticut are Edith A. Bailey's pioneer study of the Susquehannah Company, *Influences toward Radicalism in Connecticut 1754-1775*, Smith College, *Studies in History*, 5, no. 4 (1920), and Margaret E. Martin's *Merchants and Trade in the Connecticut River Valley 1750-1820*, Smith College, *Studies*, 24, nos. 1-4 (1938-39). Another useful book on the economic history of Connecticut is Henry Bronson's old essay on Connecticut currency, "A Historical Account of Connecticut Currency, Continental Money and the Finances of the Revolution," in the New Haven County Historical Society, *Papers*, 1 (1865).

A few biographies merit mention. The best two happen to be portraits of conservative figures. Lawrence H. Gipson's *Jared Ingersoll, A Study of American Loyalism in Relation to British Colonial Government* (New Haven, 1920) is good biography and history, and George C. Groce's *William Samuel Johnson, A Maker of the*

Constitution (New York, 1937) is a new appraisal based upon the very large collection of Johnson manuscripts. Whig personalities have been less fortunate. Connecticut's Revolutionary governor, Jonathan Trumbull, has been the subject of two works: Isaac W. Stuart, *Life of Jonathan Trumbull* (Boston, 1859), and the more recent biography by a direct descendant and name-sake, Jonathan Trumbull, *Jonathan Trumbull* (Boston, 1919); but he deserves a third and superior study. The life of Roger Sherman has also been told twice, once by Lewis H. Boutell, *The Life of Roger Sherman* (Chicago, 1896) and more recently and engagingly by Roger S. Boardman, *Roger Sherman* (Philadelphia, 1938); the scarcity of material on the early part of Sherman's life, however, makes it difficult for any biographer to complete his portrait of the man. Two biographies emphasize the military contributions of two important Whigs during the Revolution but touch only incidentally on their political activities before 1775. One is David Humphreys' account of Connecticut's doughty patriot-warrior, Israel Putnam, *The Life and Heroic Exploits of Israel Putnam* (New York, 1834); the other is Charles S. Hall's defensive *Life and Letters of Samuel Holden Parsons* (Binghampton, 1905). William S. Johnson's biographer, George C. Groce, sketches the careers of two other Connecticut men who were central figures in the political events preceding the Revolution: "Eliphalet Dyer: Connecticut Revolutionist," in Richard B. Morris, ed., *The Era of the American Revolution: Studies Inscribed to Evarts Boutell Greene* (New York, 1939), 290-304, and "Benjamin Gale," in the *New England Quarterly,* 10 (1937), 697-716. The political principles of another conservative, William S. Johnson, are the subject of a fine article by Evarts B. Greene, "William S. Johnson and the American Revolution," *Columbia University Quarterly,* 22, no. 2 (1930), 157-78. Amos A. Browning points out that John Durkee was best known in his own day as an active leader of the Sons of Liberty in "A Forgotten Son Of Liberty," New London County Historical Society, *Records and Papers,* 3, pt. 2 (1912), 257-79. Finally, one must mention Franklin B. Dexter's useful series of volumes, *Biographical Sketches of the Graduates of Yale College With Annals of the College History* (6 vols., New York and New Haven, 1885-1912).

Town and county histories were generally disappointing. They are numerous enough; however, most of them are little more than worshipful genealogies or simple chronicles. Some reproduce extracts from the local records, and these are valuable. A few accounts, such as Frances M. Caulkins' *History of Norwich* (Hartford, 1866) and her *History of New London* (New London, 1852) are relatively superior. The other local histories that were useful are cited above in the text and footnotes.

A number of scholars have commented briefly upon different aspects of colonial Connecticut. The celebration of Connecticut's tercentenary was the occasion for the publication in New Haven, under the auspices of the Connecticut Tercentenary Commission, of 60 pamphlets re-evaluating various phases of the history of the colony and state. Among the more important of these publications were the pamphlets written by Charles M. Andrews, *Connecticut and the British Government,* no. 1 (1933); Dorothy Deming, *The Settlement of the Connecticut Towns,* no. 6 (1933); Lawrence H. Gipson, *Connecticut Taxation 1750-1775,* no. 10 (1933); M. H. Mitchell, *The Great Awakening and Other Revivals in the Religious Life of Connecticut,* no. 26 (1934); O. S. Seymour, *The Beginnings of the Episcopal Church in Connecticut,* no. 30 (1934); E. Peck, *The Loyalists of Connecticut,* no. 31 (1934); J. P. Boyd, *The Susquehannah Company: Connecticut's Experiment in Expansion,* no. 34 (1935); A. L. Olson, *Agricultural Economy and the Population in Eighteenth Century Connecticut,* no. 40 (1935); R. M. Hooker, *The Colonial Trade of Connecticut,* no. 50 (1936); and P. W. Coons, *The Achievement of Religious Liberty in Connecticut,* no. 60 (1936).

One of the chapters in Charles M. Andrews' *Our Earliest Colonial Settlements* (New York, 1933), 113-40, is an excellent essay on Connecticut; a final estimate of the province by the same author, "On Some Early Aspects of Connecticut History," appeared posthumously in the *New England Quarterly*, 17 (1944), 3-24. The *New England Quarterly* also published two interesting articles by Perry Miller that reconsider some religious and political aspects of provincial Connecticut, "Thomas Hooker and the Democracy of Early Connecticut," 4 (1931), 663-712, and "The Half-Way Covenant," 6 (1933), 676-715.

Turning to religious subjects, Amos A. Browning records interesting incidents relative to the Great Awakening in the town of Preston in "The Preston Separate Church," New London County Historical Society, *Records and Papers*, 2, pt. 2 (1896), 153-70; and a better church historian, Williston Walker, briefly considers the history and tenets of the Sandemanian sect in "The Sandemanians of New England," American Historical Association, *Annual Report for 1901*, 1 (1902), 133-62. James H. Trumbull claims to find in the political conflict between New and Old Light the origin of the Sons of Liberty and a political introduction to the events of 1765-66, "The Sons of Liberty in 1755," *New Englander*, 35 (1876), 299-313. A few articles touching upon the religious and educational history of Yale are Simeon E. Baldwin's "The Ecclesiastical Constitution of Yale College," New Haven County Historical Society, *Papers*, 3 (1882), 405-42, and two brief studies by Franklin B. Dexter, "The Founding of Yale College," and "Thomas Clap and His Writings," published respectively in the *Papers*, 3 (1882), 1-31, and 5 (1894), 247-71. Two papers by the same author discussing phases of New Haven history, "New Haven in 1784" and "Notes on Some of the New Haven Loyalists Including Those Graduated at Yale," also appeared in the *Papers* of the New Haven County Historical Society, 4 (1888), 117-38, and 9 (1918), 29-45. These four articles, together with twenty other short studies written by Dexter, many of which touch on subjects pertaining to the early history of Connecticut, were gathered and published in a convenient volume, *A Selection from the Miscellaneous Historical Papers of Fifty Years* (New Haven, 1918).

INDEX

Military measures, General Assembly votes, 180-81, 191, 196, 335-36 *n*52; of towns, 328 *n*48, 335 *n*44

Militia, Tory officers in, 186, 192

Miller, Jeremiah, quoted, 53

Mining, limited extent of, 36-37

Ministers, Congregational, on government, 8-9; on political stability, 9-10; on Connecticut's privileges, 17; complain of religious decline, 20; on Great Awakening, 22-23; on Stamp Act, 51, 68-69, 264 *n*49; on patriotism, 66; on British policy and Anglicanism, 96-98; on Separatists and religious liberty, 100-101; and Middletown remonstrance, 154; appeal to western towns, 169-70; Tory New Light, 174; Whig politics of, 140, 210-11, 230; and the Revolution, 195-96, 335 *n*43; on treatment of Tories, 199; on nature of liberty, 243 *n*37

Mobs, and Ingersoll resignation, 53-54; legislature condemns, 62; attack informer, 65; criticized, 65, 68, 269 *n*138, 275 *n*223; leaders of, 271-72 *n*172. *See also* Radicals, Tories

Moffat, Thomas, and New London smuggling, 133

Mohegan case, mentioned, 45; reopened, 79; settlement of, 313 *n*18

Molasses Act, revenue from, 82

Morgan, Theophilus, on conservatism of western towns, 168-69

Mosely, Isaac, Glastonbury Tory, 167-68

Mumford, Thomas, and Sugar Act, 46; on 1775 election, 195; on Tories, 203

New Britain, Tory minister in, 174

New Fairfield, Tories in, 209

New Hartford, measures against Tories in, 172

New Haven, voters in, 7, 8; and Stamp Act, 60-61, 65; merchants in debt, 81-82; and 1767 election, 117; and Susquehannah issue, 152, 154; supports Boston, 167; violence in, 176; popular feeling in, 178; bans Ridgefield and Newtown Tories, 184; divided town meeting in, 190; Tory militia officer in, 196; Tories in, 184, 201, 203-4, 215, 357 *n*76; decline in value of estates, 262 *n*25; nature of trade, 307 *n*20; ministers and Susquehannah Company, 318-19 *n*64

New Haven County, and 1770 nominations, 125-26; Anglicans in, 233; Tories in, 233-34

New Lights, principles, 22-23; measures against, 24; growth of, 24-25; in politics, 25-26, 252 *n*34, 265 *n*56; and 1766 election, 75; Stiles on politics of, 118-20, 300 *n*36, 300-301 *n*39; Gale on politics of, 119-20; enmity between Old Lights and, 250 *n*20

Wadsworth, Rev. Daniel, estate of, 16; on Great Awakening, 23

Wadsworth, Jeremiah, investigates Tories, 211-12; on excessive war suspicions, 225

Wales, Nathaniel, resigns stamp post, 52; quoted, 185

Wallingford, tax list, 14; wealth in, 16; "Wallingford controversy," 26, 252-53 *n*40, 253 *n*45; Sons of Liberty in, 63; debtor farmers in, 78; Tories in, 168, 201; patriotic feeling in, 178

Warren, Joseph, cited, 192

Washington, George, on Tories, 207, 208

Waterbury, freemen in, 8; Tory militia in, 192, 196, 205; rumor of Tory insurrection in, 201

Watson, Ebenezer, antagonizes Susquehannah Company, 154-55

Webb, Samuel B., condemns mob violence, 176; on war preparations, 181; on western towns, 182

Webster, Pelatiah, expansionist plans of, 314 *n*22

Welles, Lemuel A., cited, 242 *n*33

Welles, Rev. Noah, quoted, 45, 262 *n*27, 291 *n*22

West Indies, commerce with, 15; importance of to Connecticut economy, 36, 41, 82; restrictions on trade with foreign, 42, 46-47

Westminster Confession, and Saybrook Platform, 11

Westmoreland, created, 146; and 1774 election, 156

Wethersfield, and 1774 election, 156; town meeting described, 163; favors non-importation, 178; violence against Tories, 184-85; disavowal of rebellion in, 331-32 *n*2

Wetmore, Rev. Izrahiah, advocates separation of church and state, 291 *n*28

Whale fisheries, failure of, 87-88

Whigs, on imperial politics, 135-36; party of and Susquehannah issue, 150ff.; party of in 1774 election, 155-58; county meetings of, 179, 181; reaction to Gage mission, 193-94; party dominates colony, 194-95; in Ridgefield capture control of town government, 206-7; attitude towards Tories, 225-26

Whitefield, George, and Great Awakening, 22

Whitney, Sylvanus, punished for trading in tea, 202

Whittelsey, Rev. Chauncey, on Stamp Act, 48; criticizes mob violence, 65; on "Wallingford controversy," 252-53 *n*40

Whittelsey, Hezekiah, Toryism of, 172-73

Whittelsey, Samuel, quoted, 289 *n*3

Williams, Rev. Eleazer, quoted, 243 *n*37

Williams, William, in "Wallingford controversy" and election of 1759,